Actions for Gender Balance in Informatics Across Europe

Birgit Penzenstadler • Karima Boudaoud •
Antinisca Di Marco • Sonay Caner-Yıldırım
Editors

Actions for Gender Balance in Informatics Across Europe

Editors
Birgit Penzenstadler
Chalmers University of Technology
Göteborg, Sweden

University of Gothenburg
Göteborg, Sweden

Lappeenranta University of Technology
Lappeenranta, Finland

Antinisca Di Marco
University of L'Aquila
L'Aquila, Italy

Karima Boudaoud
Université Côte d'Azur
Nice, France

Sonay Caner-Yıldırım
Erzincan Binali Yıldırım University
Erzincan, Türkiye

ISBN 978-3-031-78431-6   ISBN 978-3-031-78432-3   (eBook)
https://doi.org/10.1007/978-3-031-78432-3

This work was supported by European Cooperation in Science and Technology EU COST ACTION CA19122

© The Editor(s) (if applicable) and The Author(s) 2025. This book is an open access publication.

Open Access This book is licensed under the terms of the Creative Commons Attribution 4.0 International License (http://creativecommons.org/licenses/by/4.0/), which permits use, sharing, adaptation, distribution and reproduction in any medium or format, as long as you give appropriate credit to the original author(s) and the source, provide a link to the Creative Commons license and indicate if changes were made.

The images or other third party material in this book are included in the book's Creative Commons license, unless indicated otherwise in a credit line to the material. If material is not included in the book's Creative Commons license and your intended use is not permitted by statutory regulation or exceeds the permitted use, you will need to obtain permission directly from the copyright holder.

The use of general descriptive names, registered names, trademarks, service marks, etc. in this publication does not imply, even in the absence of a specific statement, that such names are exempt from the relevant protective laws and regulations and therefore free for general use.

The publisher, the authors and the editors are safe to assume that the advice and information in this book are believed to be true and accurate at the date of publication. Neither the publisher nor the authors or the editors give a warranty, expressed or implied, with respect to the material contained herein or for any errors or omissions that may have been made. The publisher remains neutral with regard to jurisdictional claims in published maps and institutional affiliations.

This Springer imprint is published by the registered company Springer Nature Switzerland AG
The registered company address is: Gewerbestrasse 11, 6330 Cham, Switzerland

If disposing of this product, please recycle the paper.

This book is dedicated to the memory of Bara Buhnova, whose tireless efforts and unwavering dedication to promoting women and girls in the field of informatics have left an indelible mark. Bara's vision and mission will continue to inspire and guide us in our pursuit of a more inclusive and equitable future.

We also dedicate this work to all the women who came before us and who follow: our mothers, godmothers, grandmothers, and great-grandmothers, our ancestors, our sisters, and our daughters, the wisdom keepers, the ones who dare to stand up for themselves and others, and the ones who care for the community.

Your light shines on.

Acknowledgments

We extend our heartfelt gratitude to the COST (European Cooperation in Science and Technology) for funding and believing in this project, as well as for their unwavering commitment to fostering gender equity in all fields.

We also thank all members of the EUGAIN COST Action 19122 for their dedication, collaboration, and tireless efforts in advancing our shared mission.

Special gratitude also goes to our "fearless leader" Letizia Jaccheri for bringing this action together with loving enthusiasm, and to all working group leaders for pouring their hearts and souls into this initiative.

A special tribute goes to Bara Buhnova, whose unwavering dedication, vision, and grace have left an indelible mark on this initiative. Bara was not only a co-leader of this action but also a beacon of inspiration for promoting women and girls in the informatics field. Her passion, perseverance, and compassionate leadership profoundly shaped the EUGAIN project. While her untimely passing has left a deep void, her mission and legacy will live on through the work of this community and the many lives she touched.

Together, we have created a work that embodies hope, progress, and resilience.

EUGAIN features more than 160 members from over 45 countries, including 5 non-European ones. Its main aim is to improve gender balance in Informatics through the creation and strengthening of a truly multi-cultural European network of academics working at the forefront of the efforts in their countries, institutions and research communities. Learn more at eugain.eu

Informatics Europe, the initiator and Grant Holder institution of the EUGAIN COST Action, unites and empowers the Education and Research Informatics community across Europe. Connecting over 50,000 researchers from more than 200 member institutions in 30+ countries, Informatics Europe advocates for shared priorities and influences policy-making in Education, Research, and the Social Impact of Informatics. Learn more at informatics-europe.org

The book is based upon work from COST Action EUGAIN CA19122 (European Network For Gender Balance in Informatics), supported by COST (European Cooperation in Science and Technology).

COST (European Cooperation in Science and Technology) is a funding agency for research and innovation networks. Our Actions help connect research initiatives across Europe and enable scientists to grow their ideas by sharing them with their peers. This boosts their research, career and innovation.

www.cost.eu

Contents

Part I Introduction to EUGAIN

1 How to Read This Book: Personas Guiding Through EUGAIN Results 3
Birgit Penzenstadler, Monica Landoni, Alicia Julia Wilson Takaoka, Sonay Caner-Yıldırım, Karima Boudaoud, and Antinisca Di Marco
   1.1   Origin, Scope, Purpose and Plan 4
   1.2   Intended Audience and Their Personas 5
   1.3   Usage of the Personas Through the Book 11
   1.4   Gender-Forward Intersectionality 12
   1.5   Book Structure 13
   References 14

2 European Network For Gender Balance in Informatics (EUGAIN): Activities and Results 15
Letizia Jaccheri, Barbora Buhnova, Birgit Penzenstadler, Karima Boudaoud, and Valentina Lenarduzzi
   2.1   Introduction 15
   2.2   Background 16
   2.3   Successful Interventions 19
   2.4   The Aims of EUGAIN 21
   2.5   Implementation Through the Working Groups 21
   2.6   Results and Outputs 26
   2.7   Summary and Future Outlooks 27
   2.8   How You Use Our Results 27
   References 28

Part II From School to University: Intervention Methods

3 How Early Recruitment Helps Achieve Gender Diversity in Informatics 33
Rukiye Altin, Eliot Bytyçi, and Àngela Nebot
  3.1 Personas 33
  3.2 Introduction 34
  3.3 Recruitment Initiatives 36
  3.4 Challenges and Future Possibilities 46
  3.5 Reflections and Insights 46
  References 48

4 Students' Activities from Elementary to High School 53
Rukiye Altin, Ozge Mísírlí, Irene Zanardi, Claudia Maria Cutrupi, Sunny K. O. Miranda, Valentina Dagiene, and Monica Landoni
  4.1 Personas 53
  4.2 Introduction 54
  4.3 Draw a Software Engineer 55
  4.4 School-Based Activities 64
  4.5 After School Activities 70
  4.6 Open Questions 74
  References 74

5 Mentoring as a Tool for Better Gender Diversity in Informatics 79
Anna Szlavi, Serena Versino, Daniel Raffini, Tuva Cornelia Oppenhagen, and Letizia Jaccheri
  5.1 Introduction 79
  5.2 Background 80
  5.3 Methods 82
  5.4 Results 84
  5.5 Discussion 93
  5.6 Conclusion 98
  Appendix 98
  References 100

Part III From Bachelor/Master Studies to PhD

6 Voices of Female Informatics Students Across Universities 105
Özge Büyükdağlı, Miguel Goulão, Milena Vujošević Janičić, and Amal Mersni
  6.1 Introduction 105
  6.2 Methodology 108
  6.3 Perceptions of Female Respondents 112
  6.4 Insights from Current and Former PhD Students 129
  6.5 Conclusions 133
  References 134

7 WoCa Lunch: A Program for Female Students to Get Informed About PhD Studies 137
Milena Vujošević Janičić, Erika Ábrahám, Amal Mersni, Oleksandra Yeremenko, and Miguel Goulão
- 7.1 Introduction 137
- 7.2 Encouraging Initiatives 140
- 7.3 Women Career Lunch 144
- 7.4 Impact of WoCa Lunch 167
- 7.5 Possible Adaptions to Different Environments 169
- 7.6 Conclusions 170
- References 171

8 The Impact of Peers, Mentors and Role Models on Successful PhD Studies 175
Judith Knoblach, Ute Schmid, Miguel Goulão, Larissa Schmid, Milena Vujošević Janičić, and Karima Boudaoud
- 8.1 Introduction 175
- 8.2 What Are Peers, Mentors and Role Models? 177
- 8.3 Survey 178
- 8.4 The Role of Peers 179
- 8.5 Mentoring Programs 181
- 8.6 The Impact of Role Models on Career Choices 185
- 8.7 Who Can Benefit from This Chapter and How? 190
- 8.8 Conclusions 192
- References 193

Part IV From PhD to Professor

9 Good Practices for Promoting Gender Balance in Academia within Informatics: Evidence from Higher Education Institutions ... 199
Lili Nemec Zlatolas, Petroula Mavrikiou, Steve Kremer, Brenda Murphy, and Carla Teixeira Lopes
- 9.1 Introduction 200
- 9.2 Background 201
- 9.3 Methodology 203
- 9.4 Results 204
- 9.5 Discussion of Results 216
- 9.6 Conclusions 218
- Appendix: Questionnaire 218
- References 224

10 Good Practices for Improving Gender Balance and Diversity Throughout an Academic Career 227
Brenda Murphy, Carla Teixeira Lopes, Emanuela Merelli, Mara Gabriela Diaconu, Marie Gallais, Paloma Diaz, Paula Alexandra Silva, Petroula Mavrikiou, Silvia Ghilezan, and Steve Kremer
- 10.1 Introduction 228
- 10.2 Recruiting Women 229
- 10.3 Application Evaluation for Hiring and Promotion 231
- 10.4 Retaining Female Talent and Expertise 233
- 10.5 Promoting Women 235
- 10.6 Conclusion 239
- References 240

11 Breaking Barriers: Strategies for Achieving Equity in Academic Careers in ICT/Informatics/STEM 243
Paula Alexandra Silva, Brenda Murphy, Karima Echihabi, Katja Tuma, Paloma Diaz, Birgy Lorenz, and Marieke Huisman
- 11.1 Introduction 243
- 11.2 Towards an Inclusive and Diverse Environment in Academia 244
- 11.3 First Steps into Action 249
- 11.4 Conclusion 262
- References 263

Part V Cooperation with Industry and Society

12 Best Practices and Lessons from Academia-Industry Collaboration Initiatives 271
Alicia Julia Wilson Takaoka, Lenuta Alboaie, Claudia Maria Cutrupi, Andrea D'Angelo, Antinisca Di Marco, and Jane Hillston
- 12.1 Introduction 272
- 12.2 Background 274
- 12.3 Related Work: Shaping the Landscape of Best Practices in Cooperation with Industry 276
- 12.4 Methods 280
- 12.5 Results 282
- 12.6 Discussion 290
- 12.7 Conclusion 292
- 12.8 CRediT Taxonomy 293
- Appendix: Survey Questions 293
- References 294

13 Innovative Ways of Cooperating with Public Administration for Gender Equity in Informatics 299
Sonay Caner-Yıldırım, Miranda Harizaj, and Salome Shakarishvili
- 13.1 Introduction 299
- 13.2 Methods 300

	13.3	Results: Concrete Actions and Innovative Instruments to Promote Inclusion	309
	13.4	Discussion and Analysis of Best Practices	316
	13.5	Recommendations and Future Directions	319
	13.6	Conclusion	320
	13.7	How You Can Do This	321
	References		322

Part VI Strategy and Dissemination

14 Synergy Events: Design for Strong Impact 327
Simona Motogna, Karima Boudaoud, and Antinisca Di Marco
  14.1 EUGAIN Events 328
  14.2 Design and Planning of Events 330
  14.3 Assessment and Impact 334
  14.4 Challenges 337
  14.5 Recommendations 339

15 The EUGAIN Policy Recommendations: Strategic Dissemination Across the Media Jungle 343
Karima Boudaoud, Birgit Penzenstadler, Sonay Caner-Yıldırım, and Fanni Bobák
  15.1 Introduction: Why Policy Recommendations Matter 343
  15.2 The EUGAIN Policy Recommendations 345
  15.3 Creating Impact 364
  15.4 Dissemination Across Media Channels 368
  15.5 How You Can Do This 378
  15.6 What's Next? 379
  References 379

16 Policy Making as Extension of Disseminating Research Results: Policy Influence Plan Canvas 383
Birgit Penzenstadler, Simona Motogna, Patricia Lago, and Cristy Montes
  16.1 Why Policy Influence Plans Are Needed 383
  16.2 Background and Related Work 385
  16.3 The Policy Influence Plan Canvas 386
  16.4 Country-Specific Policy Influence Plans (PIPs): Implementation 390
  16.5 Following Through and Following Up 392
  16.6 How You Start Using the Canvas 395
  16.7 Conclusion 396
  References 396

Part I
Introduction to EUGAIN

Chapter 1
How to Read This Book: Personas Guiding Through EUGAIN Results

Birgit Penzenstadler ⓘ, Monica Landoni ⓘ, Alicia Julia Wilson Takaoka ⓘ, Sonay Caner-Yıldırım ⓘ, Karima Boudaoud ⓘ, and Antinisca Di Marco ⓘ

Welcome to the summary of the results of the EUGAIN project. Many researchers have poured their hearts into this COST Action project. A COST Action is a network building activity funded by the European Union. As such, the contributions in this book present a Euro-centric view from all corners of Europe—the Nordics (for example, Sweden and Norway), the South (for example, Italy and Albania), the East (for example, Turkey and Romania), and the West (for example, Portugal and France).

B. Penzenstadler (✉)
Chalmers University of Technology, Göteborg, Sweden

University of Gothenburg, Göteborg, Sweden

Lappeenranta University of Technology, Lappeenranta, Finland
e-mail: birgitp@chalmers.se

M. Landoni
Università della Svizzera italiana, Lugano, Switzerland
e-mail: monica.landoni@usi.ch

A. J. W. Takaoka
Rotterdam School of Management, Erasmus University Rotterdam, Rotterdam, The Netherlands
e-mail: takaoka@rsm.nl

S. Caner-Yıldırım
Computer Education and Instructional Technology, Erzincan Binali Yıldırım University, Erzincan, Turkey

K. Boudaoud
Laboratoire I3S, Université Côte d'Azur - CNRS - I3S, Sophia Antipolis, France
e-mail: karima.boudaoud@univ-cotedazur.fr

A. Di Marco
Dipartimento di Ingegneria e Scienze dell'Informazione e Matematica, University of L'Aquila, L'Aquila, Italy
e-mail: antinisca.dimarco@univaq.it

© The Author(s) 2025
B. Penzenstadler et al. (eds.), *Actions for Gender Balance in Informatics Across Europe*, https://doi.org/10.1007/978-3-031-78432-3_1

From the outset, we knew that women are underrepresented in Informatics at all levels, from undergraduate and graduate studies to participation and leadership in academia and industry. The main aim and objective of EUGAIN was to improve gender equity in Informatics at all levels through the creation of a European network of colleagues working at the forefront of the efforts for gender equity in Informatics in their countries and research communities.

In the last four years, we have created a community of researchers who care about equality, equity, inclusion, diversity, and accessibility. We present our findings and insights in this book.

1.1 Origin, Scope, Purpose and Plan

The primary purpose of this book is to serve as a comprehensive guide, translating research into best practices to promote gender inclusivity in Informatics, **spanning the entire educational and professional spectrum from early schooling to advanced career stages.** The handbook seeks to empower its readers by providing them with actionable recommendations to bridge the gender gap in Informatics. This initiative aims to have an immediate impact on the Informatics community by raising awareness and interest through its practical resources, and on society by encouraging more girls and women to pursue computer science and technological studies and follow related career paths. This book presents five years of research on gender equity and improving gender equity in Informatics across Europe. It translates current research on gender inclusivity into practical strategies and intervention methods, offering recommendations for the recruitment, retention, and promotion of women in computer science at different academic and industrial levels. Additionally, it provides insights into fostering mutually beneficial cooperation between universities and industries.

We have collected data from different target audiences and across various education and career levels to provide insights into why we have low participation rates among girls and women in the sciences, why we have a leaky pipeline in academia, and why women leave the industry.

We have analyzed this data and identified four target audiences for activities and policy influence. We provide recommendations for each of these groups on how to become active in advocacy and specific actions they can take in their daily environments to improve learning and work conditions, as well as retain women students and professionals.

We provide ample scenarios for how to apply our findings in practice and share materials both in the book and in free public access online documentation to disseminate this knowledge further.

The book serves as a joint European voice in Informatics to increase equity for women in the field. In particular:

- We provide six personas with which you, the reader, can identify, allowing you to select the most urgent actions based on your position and background.
- In each chapter, we present concrete options for applying the knowledge provided for the identified personas so that you, the reader, can put it into action immediately.
- We showcase data from many countries across Europe and thereby provide a platform for a diverse set of voices on gender equity in Informatics.

1.2 Intended Audience and Their Personas

We use personas [3] in this book to describe segments of the target audience such that the readers can identify themselves with one or several of them and get a better idea of how to use the book. Each of them has a triple-versioned name to represent different genders and cultural regions, as well as a role and a tagline:

- Kim/Kimmy/Kymi, the university professor—"Give me visuals and stories"
- Brandy/Bazyli/Bo, the industry manager—"With speed to excellence"
- Nicky/Nicole/Nicolas, the activist—"Same value deserves the same rights"
- Alex/Andrea/Anh, the school principal—"I raise the future generations"
- Des/Deniz/Derya, student about to graduate—"Life is an adventure"
- Jem/James/Jamila, school teacher—"Science rocks"

In the following, we introduce each of them:

Kim/Kimmy/Kymi, the university professor. "Give me visuals and stories"
Background:

- 44 years old, United Kingdom;
- PhD in Engineering, 3 kids;
- Runner, leadership mentor;

Work and skills:

- 12 years of teaching Computer Science;
- Lectures, assignments, exams;
- Loves service-based teaching;
- Collaborates with career office;

Needs:

- Wants to better help their students while teaching;
- Needs access to visualized data and guidelines;
- Stories to relay to the students as examples (Fig. 1.1);

Fig. 1.1 Kim/Kimmy/Kymi, the university professor

1 How to Read This Book: Personas Guiding Through EUGAIN Results

Brandy/Bazyli/Bo, the industry manager. "With speed to excellence"
Background:

- Grew up in the capital;
- Made first million at 29 years of age;
- Very ambitious team player;

Work and skills:

- Runs a team of 40 developers;
- Expert on collaborative communication style;
- Volunteer at a non-profit for pets;

Needs:

- "Overwhelmed" with the request for gender equity in his department;
- Wants to uplift their female team leads but no idea how;
- Quick solutions and easy implementation (Fig. 1.2);

Fig. 1.2 Brandy/Bazyli/Bo, the industry manager

Nicky/Nicole/Nicolas, the activist. "Same value deserves the same rights"
Background:

- Single and no kids;
- Social science background;
- Took care of younger siblings and doesn't want kids;

Work and skills:

- Organizes community gatherings;
- Works with equality office;
- Creates flyers and brochures;
- Gives talks at schools and companies;

Needs:

- Needs supportive data from research for their campaigns;
- Wants to influence communal and national politics;
- Needs Information on how others work on improving equity (Fig. 1.3);

Fig. 1.3 Nicky/Nicole/Nicolas, the activist

Alex/Andrea/Anh, the school principal. "I raise the future generations"

- 52 years old, divorced and 4 kids in patchwork family situation;
- Degree in education;
- Wanted to be a rock star;

Work and skills:

- Manages colleagues, students and their families all day long to keep peace;
- Consults with orientation officers and parents;
- Assigned advisor of local consortium on tech expertise;

Needs:

- Wants to better help their students while teaching;
- Needs visualized data and applicable guidelines;
- Wants stories to relay to the students as examples (Fig. 1.4);

Fig. 1.4 Alex/Andrea/Anh, the school principal

Des/Deniz/Derya, a student about to graduate. "Life is an adventure"
Background:

- Completing an MSc in Informatics;
- First in their family to graduate from a university;
- Excited about research and potentially about moving abroad for a while;

Work and skills:

- Research on MSc project;
- Active in student union;
- Job as a bartender at a juice bar;

Needs:

- Trying to decide between academia and industry;
- Orientation in the labor market as well as careers in research; knowing what to look for;
- Learn about opportunities for mobility grants to go abroad (Fig. 1.5);

Fig. 1.5 Des/Deniz/Derya, a student about to graduate

1 How to Read This Book: Personas Guiding Through EUGAIN Results

Fig. 1.6 Jem/James/Jamila, school teacher

Jem/James/Jamila, school teacher. "Science rocks"
Background:

- Sibling of five, parent of two;
- Inner city school;
- Avid urban gardener;

Work and skills:

- Teaches history and art, mostly in-class work;
- Experience with students from varying socio-economic and cultural backgrounds;
- Volunteers for after-school;

Needs:

- Excited about STEM and wants to support their students being open to that direction;
- Wants stories that counter exemplify cliches;
- Looks for in-class activities to inspire students (Fig. 1.6);

1.3 Usage of the Personas Through the Book

We use Personas in each chapter to explain how they (but really: You, the reader) can make use of the contents in the chapter. For example:

> **Alex, the school principal.** Looking at the resources in this chapter, Alex, the school principal, takes the recommendations to their next school board meeting. Some teachers are enthusiastic about developing role models in the classroom; others are a bit more skeptical. So Alex starts a group activity where the teachers pair up with a partner, interview each other on what role models they have in their lives, and create role model descriptions for each other.

1.4 Gender-Forward Intersectionality

Throughout this project and during our dissemination at conferences and in talks, we were often asked why we focus solely on women, since there are also other minorities that need support in achieving equity. This section aims to clarify that our approach extends beyond gender, recognizing that gender was historically the first focus in conversations about equity. We do strongly support **reaching equity for all minorities**.

Intersectionality is the recognition that characterizations create interconnected systems of disadvantage and oppression. It is a sociological analytical framework for understanding how groups' and individuals' social and political identities result in unique combinations of discrimination and privilege. The term was coined by Crenshaw [2] in the 1980s to point out the unique experiences that black women face, as their compound marginalization, traits as being both *black* and *a woman*, create impact. In looking to the future of informatics research and gender equity, we at EUGAIN recognize the need to acknowledge that gender is more than just a binary, and gender alone cannot capture one's experiences, both in informatics and beyond. Takaoka, Cutrupi, and Jaccheri [4] introduced the concept of *Gender-Forward Intersectionality* as a way for informatics researchers, particularly in empirical software engineering, to talk about diversity and inclusion in their work. Gender-forward intersectionality is defined as a perspective that uses gender as the starting point to identify and examine inequalities and discrimination, while also considering other intersecting traits.

In gender-forward intersectionality, gender is used as the starting point to explore how other traits and their unique intersections may also impact informatics experiences, both in design and use. In a previous study, Takaoka et al. [6] explore how women interact with tools designed for an inclusive transition to climate neutrality, as well as the accessibility features and limitations that people with visual and other impairments may need. Additionally, they discuss heuristics identified by women, during early prototyping, connecting them to gamification elements that can benefit a broad range of app users [5]. This same study also identifies that the omission of women in the design process can result in the exclusion of women from released products. Tuma et al. [7] present a study that evaluates risk analysis that begins with gender but also explores how traits like education, race, nationality, ethnicity, age, and seniority impact experiences in cybersecurity education.

However, gender-forward intersectionality has a broader reach than informatics. By using gender as a starting point to explore both individual and collective experiences, it is possible to identify the gaps in technology and software products when teams lack the richness and diversity of the users they serve. These gaps are visible as biases and ethical concerns, which are inherently social and cultural issues. These concerns highlight the need for the inclusion of diverse users and test cases, as well as the formation of more diverse teams throughout the design process, from school to professional working life. We are also witnessing the negative effects of technological dependence on public, physical, and mental health [1]. The continued embeddedness of technology in our modern world is only one aspect of how gender-forward intersectionality can be applied across disciplines. Even though gender-forward intersectionality was defined in an informatics context, the applicability and exploration of experiences and marginalization using gender as a starting point is inter- and transdisciplinary. We invite researchers in all schools to investigate marginalization, gender equity, and gender issues from using gender-forward intersectionality.

1.5 Book Structure

The book is composed of 16 chapters that are all based on research conducted within the last 5 years and are related to the EUGAIN Gender Balance in Informatics initiative. In the first part of the book, we focus on creating interest in STEM subjects and the related interventions, namely recruitment initiatives for the university, student activities inside and outside the classroom, and mentoring and career programs that can be provided by the school, after-school programs, or independent non-profit organizations. In the book's second part, we focus on the support during university studies and what we have learned about the status quo (female student voices across universities), research activities to support gender equity in students, and how to create community research projects for underrepresented minorities. In the book's third part, we target the currently very leaky faculty pipeline for female processors, specifically in best practices of what works and what doesn't for recruitment and retention of female candidates and continued collaboration between management and employees at the faculty. The fourth part zooms in on the cooperation with industry and society, both in terms of best practices for collaboration between academia and industry as well as innovative ways of cooperating with public administration.Finally, the part on strategy and dissemination gives an overview of the most crucial channels for voicing the importance of and influencing the gender equity in informatics. These channels include awards, policy making, and strategic dissemination of research results and role model examples in digital media.

Instead of providing detailed summaries for each of these chapters, we are providing a sample for the chapter "Female student voices across universities." In this chapter, we focus on the challenges and opportunities for female PhD students, as perceived by them. Using a mixed-methods approach, we draw on their personal experiences to extract valuable lessons learned on how to successfully navigate through the process of studying for a PhD. These include (1) a characterisation of the encouraging and discouraging factors on the decision to enroll in a PhD in Computer Science and how these differ by gender and other external factors, such as geographic location; (2) the factors that helped in successfully working towards a PhD, as well as the obstacles in the way, how to cope with them, and where to get help, when necessary. These first-person, relatable testimonies can help prospective and current female PhD students in Computer Science, as well as their supervisors and peers, to create more favorable conditions for these students to thrive in their PhD studies, mitigating the current lack of equity in PhD studies.

References

1. David Bakker, Nikolaos Kazantzis, Debra Rickwood, and Nikki Rickard. A randomized controlled trial of three smartphone apps for enhancing public mental health. *Behaviour Research and Therapy*, 109:75–83, 2018.
2. Kimberlé W Crenshaw. *On intersectionality: Essential writings*. The New Press, New York, NY, USA, 2017.
3. Lene Nielsen. *Personas-user focused design*, volume 15. Springer, 2013. https://link.springer.com/content/pdf/10.1007/978-1-4471-7427-1.pdf.
4. Alicia Julia Wilson Takaoka, Claudia Maria Cutrupi, and Letizia Jaccheri. Defining software engineering feminism as a field of software engineering, 2024.
5. Alicia Julia Wilson Takaoka and Letizia Jaccheri. Mapping gamification elements to heuristics and behavior change in early phase inclusive design: A case study. In *International Conference on Human-Computer Interaction*, pages 143–161. Springer, 2024.
6. Alicia JW Takaoka, Dirk Ahlers, Ferdinand Ward Ådlandsvik, Eivind Syrdalen Dovland, and Letizia Jaccheri. Towards understanding digital support contributing to climate neutral, inclusive, and beautiful cities: A systematic literature review. In *2023 IEEE/ACM 7th International Workshop on Green And Sustainable Software (GREENS)*, pages 30–37. IEEE, 2023.
7. Katja Tuma and Romy Van Der Lee. The role of diversity in cybersecurity risk analysis: An experimental plan. In *Proceedings of the Third Workshop on Gender Equality, Diversity, and Inclusion in Software Engineering*, pages 12–18, New York, NY, USA, 2022. Association for Computing Machinery.

Open Access This chapter is licensed under the terms of the Creative Commons Attribution 4.0 International License (http://creativecommons.org/licenses/by/4.0/), which permits use, sharing, adaptation, distribution and reproduction in any medium or format, as long as you give appropriate credit to the original author(s) and the source, provide a link to the Creative Commons license and indicate if changes were made.

The images or other third party material in this chapter are included in the chapter's Creative Commons license, unless indicated otherwise in a credit line to the material. If material is not included in the chapter's Creative Commons license and your intended use is not permitted by statutory regulation or exceeds the permitted use, you will need to obtain permission directly from the copyright holder.

Chapter 2
European Network For Gender Balance in Informatics (EUGAIN): Activities and Results

Letizia Jaccheri, Barbora Buhnova, Birgit Penzenstadler, Karima Boudaoud, and Valentina Lenarduzzi

2.1 Introduction

Women are disproportionately represented in fields such as Informatics (including Computer Science, Computer Engineering, Computing, ICT, Software Engineering) [26–28], spanning from undergraduate and graduate studies to leadership roles in academia and industry. Enhancing female participation in this domain presents a significant challenge for scholars, policymakers, and society as a whole as documented in several scientific studies [2, 6, 8, 9, 14, 26, 29]. Despite widespread recognition of the issue, progress has been sluggish, despite ongoing efforts for change throughout Europe. This motivated the emergence of the European Network

---

L. Jaccheri (✉)
Norwegian University of Science and Technology, Trondheim, Norway
e-mail: letizia.jaccheri@ntnu.no

B. Buhnova
Masaryk University, Brno, Czech Republic
e-mail: buhnova@fi.muni.cz

B. Penzenstadler
Chalmers University of Technology, Göteborg, Sweden

University of Gothenburg, Göteborg, Sweden

Lappeenranta University of Technology, Lappeenranta, Finland
e-mail: birgitp@chalmers.se

K. Boudaoud
Université de Nice Sophia Antipolis, Nice, France
e-mail: Karima.BOUDAOUD@univ-cotedazur.fr

V. Lenarduzzi
University of Oulu, Oulu, Finland
e-mail: Valentina.Lenarduzzi@oulu.fi

© The Author(s) 2025
B. Penzenstadler et al. (eds.), *Actions for Gender Balance in Informatics Across Europe*, https://doi.org/10.1007/978-3-031-78432-3_2

For Gender Balance in Informatics (EUGAIN COST Action) to join forces of 40 countries towards a change. The primary objective of this COST Action is to address the gender imbalance in Informatics by establishing and fortifying a diverse European network of academics actively advancing gender equality within their respective countries, institutions, and research communities. Leveraging their collective knowledge, experiences, challenges, successes, and failures, we aim to identify effective strategies that can be adapted and applied across various institutions and nations. Among its goals, the Action aims to provide the academic community, policymakers, industry stakeholders, and others with actionable recommendations and guidelines to tackle key challenges, including:

- Increasing female enrollment in Informatics programs and careers;
- Encouraging more female Ph.D. and postdoctoral researchers to pursue academic careers and apply for positions in Informatics departments;
- Offering support and mentorship to empower young women in their professional journeys and address barriers preventing them from reaching senior roles.

Chapter Structure Section 2.2 describes the background on gender gap in Informatics, Sect. 2.3 describes the successful interventions to address the gap, and Sect. 2.4 presents the aim of the EUGAIN project, introduced in this chapter. Section 2.5 describes the project implementation, Sect. 2.6 presents the obtained results, and Sect. 2.7 summarizes the entire chapter.

2.2 Background

When designing the European Network For Gender Balance in Informatics (EUGAIN), we started with a set of unstructured activities across Europe and knowledge derived from international research on the topic [19].

2.2.1 Gender GAP in STEM

The gender gap in STEM is widely discussed and recognized, but its relative size among various technology and engineering fields is less understood. Informatics (Computer Science, Computer Engineering, Computing, ICT) is one of the most heavily affected fields where the gender gap brings evident disparities. Areas such as Chemistry and Biology have significantly more balanced gender distribution (sometimes, the gender gap is even reversed, but only on lower career levels). However, gender imbalance is predominantly prevalent in Informatics, Engineering, and Technology, with not much progress observed in the past years, whether in Europe [10, 18] or the US [4]. A study published when EUGAIN was set in June 2019, based on a comprehensive and up-to-date analysis of Computer Science literature, has estimated that the gender gap in Computer Science research (parity between the number of male and female authors) will not close for at least 100 years [30].

2.2.2 Informatics Higher Education in Europe

Higher education statistics for European countries, collected over the past decade show that the strong female underrepresentation in Informatics higher education in Europe is a long-standing problem [19]. At the Bachelor level, in Austria, Belgium, Denmark, Finland, Germany, Ireland, Italy, Latvia, Lithuania, the Netherlands, Poland, Spain, Switzerland, and the UK, 80% or more of the students enrolling or graduating in Informatics Bachelor programs are male. In Bulgaria, Greece, Romania, and Estonia a slightly narrower gap exists, however, women do not represent more than 30% of the Bachelor students [17]. At the Master level participation of women increases in some countries, over 35% of the Master graduates in Bulgaria, Romania and Greece, and around 30% in the UK, Estonia, Ireland, and Latvia, but decreases in others, not surpassing 20% of the Master graduates in Austria, Belgium, Czech Republic, Germany, Italy, Lithuania, the Netherlands, Poland, Portugal, Spain, Switzerland [17]. At the Ph.D. level, except for Bulgaria, Romania, Estonia, Turkey, all other countries have less than 25% of women graduating from Informatics Ph.D. programs, corresponding in some cases to less than a handful of women, as the total number of Ph.D. graduates in many countries is quite small [10, 17]. A temporal analysis of the data shows that, on average, no significant progress in female participation in Informatics higher education has been observed over the past decade in Europe. The same is true for the US, as reported in [25]

Participation in Computer Science was examined by Sax [25], gathering data on college students for four decades and highlighting a persistent, sizable underrepresentation of women in Computer Science in the US. Moreover, only a few women graduating with a Ph.D. in Informatics pursue an academic career, and even fewer progress to the highest academic ranks of an associate or a full professor. Similarly to other STEM areas, in Informatics the pipeline is leaking and glass ceiling persists. In the whole of Europe across all STEM where women and men are balanced in tertiary education, women still take less than 26% of the full professor positions [10]. The very low number of women reaching senior academic positions results in a scarcity of successful female role models to influence the new generations. To be a distinct minority in academia also results in the overload of invitations and requests (committees, administrative department roles, etc.), which penalizes women's careers, impacting negatively their research productivity, their work-life balance, their personal life, and health.

2.2.3 Gender Gap in the IT Industry

The industry also inherits the male-dominated student population. Women are strongly underrepresented among ICT specialists in all EU Member States, which is in a striking contrast with total employment, where women and men are broadly balanced. Figures show that in 2021, an overwhelming majority (84.1%) of ICT specialists employed in the EU were men [12]. This was the case in every EU Member State, the highest shares of male ICT specialists were observed in the Czech Republic (92.6%), Slovenia (90.8%), France (89.7%), Belgium (89.2%), and Poland (89.1%), while Bulgaria (63.4%), Greece (70.6%), Denmark (72.0%) and Romania (70.8%) recorded the lowest [11]. The lack of women contributes to the extensive skills and talent gap between the number of graduates in higher education institutions and the number of job positions available in ICT in Europe. Currently, an average of 53% of European employers say they face difficulties in finding the right people with the right qualifications. The highest percentages were recorded in the Czech Republic (79%), Austria (78%), Malta (73%), Luxembourg (71%) the Netherlands (69%), Slovenia (65%), Germany (64%) and Denmark (61%) [11]. Hundreds of thousands of vacancies for ICT professionals in Europe remain unfilled, and this gap grows as our society moves to a pervasively digitalized world built on unprecedented technological developments. The talent gap in ICT is one of the most serious threats to the economic development of Europe.

The tech sector's dominantly male workforce intrinsically promotes the creation and development of systems prone to gender bias. From smartphone voice assistants (Android's Cortana, Apple's Siri, Microsoft's Alexa) that are all female with noticeable submissive personalities and ill-equipped to respond to user requests regarding crises that predominantly affect women (e.g., sexual assault) [31], to activity trackers that fail to measure steps in the, predominantly female activity of pushing a stroller. Transport networks that ignore the so-called "mobility of care" and AI recruiting technology developed trained predominantly on men's résumés are among the many examples, more are found on the EU Report of the Expert Group "Innovation through Gender" and the website of the international project on Gendered Innovations. Despite the clear negative impact and consequences of a strongly gender-unbalanced environment, unfortunately, the fight for gender balance and equality in Informatics is seen as a women's problem. Projects, programs, actions, and strategies are invariably led by highly motivated and achieving women who volunteer their time to establish a more equal environment and pave the way for the new generation of female scientists. Going beyond their daily work, they are responsible for the monumental effort, and comparatively more moderated funding, that has been spent on the efforts for gender equality in Informatics.

2.3 Successful Interventions

Despite some overall discouraging numbers [17], some remarkably successful examples at the university level are found in the US as well as in Europe. On a global level, we find work by UNESCO on closing gender divides in digital skills through education [31].

In the USA, the most famous examples are Harvey Mudd College and Carnegie Mellon where in the past decade gender parity has been achieved in Computer Science entrants and graduates [13]. Although inspiring, these efforts remain isolated and proved difficult to escalate to more institutions and to improve the national statistics.

Europe still lags behind the US in terms of funding, successful examples, and the level of organization of the community. Organizations and groups such as AnitaB.org[3], ACM-W [1], CRA Women [7], National Center for Women & Information Technology, IEEE Women in Computing Committee [16], Association for Women in Computing [5], and Girls Who Code in partnership with industry have established a thriving community empowered to inspire and encourage the new generations and to support the careers women in Computer Science. The most spectacular example of this community is the Grace Hopper Celebration, which in 2023 gathered over 30,000 attendees from over 80 countries, almost all women, at all stages in Computer Science studies and careers, providing an invaluable opportunity for women to find inspiration, networking, and strategies to thrive in their careers.

In Europe, we find examples of EU public-funded projects such as EQUAL-IST, Women4IT, and pan-European networks such as the Informatics Europe's Women in Informatics Research and Education Working Group and the ACM-WE Committee (both more oriented to women in the academic career); the CEPIS Women in ICT Task Force and the European Centre for Women and Technology (both more oriented to women in the ICT profession). Nevertheless, several commendable projects, internal policies, and strategies are found in many Universities, funded by national mechanisms, specifically to increase the number and retention of female students in Computer Science programs. Here are a few good examples:

- The Bamberg CS30 Strategy [21], Faculty of Information Systems and Applied Computer Sciences, University of Bamberg, Germany—Started in 2005 and aims at reaching a female/male ratio of at least 30% across all Computer Science programs. The number of women enrolling in first-year Computer Science studies has been increasing since 2013 and reached 37% in 2017, establishing a new record in Germany.
- The Girl Project Ada [20, 22], Faculty of Information Technology and Electrical Engineering, NTNU, Norway—Started in 1997 and aims at recruiting more girls to the ICT studies and prevent dropouts. The female share of entrants in ICT studies has, on average across different programs, almost doubled, going over 25% in the Computer Science program in 2017.

- CS4All initiative, School of Computer Science, TU Dublin, Ireland—Started in 2012 and aims at increasing the number of female students coming to Computer Science undergraduate programs and reduce the numbers failing to progress in the critical first year. The female share of enrolled students in a new Computer Science Bachelor Program, with a strong emphasis on Internationalisation and Globalisation (22%) is double the one of the standard Computer Science in the same period. Retention has been strongly improved, particularly for first-year students with an average 89% progression from year 1 to year 2 (the most critical), now the highest progression rate for Computer Science in Ireland.

Projects, internal policy, and strategy management for supporting the transition of female Ph.D. and Postdoctoral Researchers into Faculty positions and for developing the careers of female Faculty in Informatics Departments are also found across Europe, but the impact has been less significant, and the numbers of female researchers and professors, in general, remain discouragingly low.

Here are a few institutions that have implemented beneficial internal strategies and policies to increase the number of female researchers and faculty and support their careers:

- Faculty of Informatics TU Vienna, Austria
- School of Computer Science, TU Dublin, Ireland
- Department of Computer Science and Information Systems, University of Limerick, Ireland
- Institute for Computing and Information Sciences, Radboud University in Nijmegen, the Netherlands
- Faculty of Information Technology and Electrical Engineering, NTNU, Norway
- School of Electronics, Electrical Engineering & Computer Science, Queen's University Belfast, UK
- Department of Computer Science, University College of London, UK
- School of Informatics, University of Edinburgh, UK
- Department of Computer Science, University of Sheffield, UK
- Faculty of Mathematics and Computer Science, University of Bremen, Germany
- Department of Informatics, TU Munich, Germany
- Department of Informatics, University of Lille, France (initiative 1 and 2)
- Grenoble INP, University Grenoble Alpes, France

Many more Universities have individual projects or fellowships (involving directly or indirectly Informatics Departments) aiming at improving gender balance. A few bold examples, involving substantial funding, include the Irène Curie Fellowship at TU Eindhoven, the Gender Initiative for Excellence at Chalmers University of Technology, and the IDUN project at NTNU. Some National Informatics Associations and National Research Labs also have special interest groups, or Equal Opportunities offices with a focus on gender balance, to cite a few: Gesellschaft für Informatik in Germany, IPN (ICT Research Platform Netherlands), Société Informatique de France Inria, Max Planck Institute for Informatics.

Moreover, over the course of EUGAIN, we have supported the Minerva Awards within Informatics Europe. The Minerva award has been successfully presented for 9 years in a row, usually at the European Computer Science Summit (ECSS). The EUGAIN main event has been co-located with ECSS for three times and EUGAIN central persons have chaired and participated in the Minerva award committee. The Minerva award is sponsored by Google and represents a successful example of cooperation between academia and industry for the achievement of the goals. Examples of industry based interventions include the ODA Awards (Norway), the Europe's Top 50 Women In Tech, the Microsoft Power Women in Tech Award.

2.4 The Aims of EUGAIN

The overarching **challenge** of EUGAIN is to enhance the representation of women in the field of Informatics at various educational and professional levels. This involves strategies such as increasing the number of female students opting for Informatics in higher education, fostering an environment that ensures the retention and successful completion of studies by female students, and encouraging the participation of women in advanced academic roles, including Ph.D. and postdoctoral research positions. Additionally, the focus extends to supporting and inspiring young women in their careers, addressing key obstacles that hinder their progress toward senior positions within the field. To achieve these objectives, collaboration with network partners representing 40 countries is essential, leveraging their experiences to overcome challenges and implement effective measures across diverse institutions and countries, leading to sustained positive outcomes in the long run.

The main **research questions** investigate actions, policies, measurable results, geographical perspective, relation to industry, relation to school, intersectionality, and role of male colleagues. Table 2.1 provides research questions that were used when setting up investigations in this field of gender and computer science within EUGAIN.

The **objectives** of EUGAIN are divided into two main categories: Research Coordination Objectives (Table 2.2) and Capacity-building Objectives (Table 2.3).

2.5 Implementation Through the Working Groups

To ensure progress beyond the state of the art and encourage novel approaches and methods, three Working Groups (WGs) addressing the challenges of each transition: from School to University (WG1); from Bachelor/Master studies to Ph.D (WG2); from Ph.D./Postdoc to Professor (WG3) have been established, combining experts and perspectives from different institutions and COST countries. Two additional WGs, on Cooperation with Industry and Society (WG4), and Strategy and Dissemination (WG5) support and promote outreach of the activities and outcomes.

Table 2.1 Research questions used as starting point for investigations

Questions
How successful have the implemented actions and policies been? How can their impact be measured?
How much effort (people and time) and funding has been spent on projects that have had measurable and successful results?
How visible were these actions at the university, regional, national or international level?
How to replicate successful actions and policies in different institutions or countries?
How many countries have pre-established national networks with a focus on gender balance in Informatics/ICT? Have these networks had a positive impact on results and outcomes?
What is the proportion of Informatics Departments across Europe that have never implemented any measure or policy to improve gender balance?
Has the industry been involved in these efforts? Has this type of collaboration influenced positively the results? If not, how to foster more effective and successful partnerships?
Have male colleagues been leading or actively participating in the projects and actions, or does this remain primarily a women's problem? What has been different in cases with significant male engagement? Would the participation of more men (particularly in leading positions) have a positive impact on progress and results?
Why do some countries have better female participation in Informatics (studies or profession)? Why are they a minority? Are there cultural, historical, or economic reasons for this?
Are there Departments (or countries) that have policies for improving more general diversity and include other minorities?
Has the lack of Informatics as a foundational discipline in schools played an important role in the low numbers of female students in Informatics higher education?

Other dissemination and communication activities ensure reaching all interested stakeholders. Moreover, tangible deliverables will also promote the advancement of the state of the art (Table 2.4).

The main goals and activities of the different working groups are described below.

2.5.1 WG1: From School to University

The main objective of WG1 was to update and design a new set of measures on how to promote the education and participation of more female students in Informatics higher education. Moreover, it aimed to increase the number of applications and to ensure that students who started will thrive, make their voices heard, and complete their studies. In terms of tasks and activities, WG1 focused on collecting and evaluating current initiatives existing in the COST countries and institutions part of the Action, including targeted recruitment initiatives, activities for students (from primary to high school), mentoring and career programmes in academia and industry. It also collated examples of how female students voice can be encouraged across universities in generating information and ideas.

Table 2.2 Research coordination objectives

Research coordination objectives
Coordinate information gathering and collection of practices and initiatives for recruiting and retaining female students, researchers, and professors;
Support partners in assessing and evaluating existing practices and methodologies, facilitating the choice of what could be implemented according to the local situation (cultures, resources, etc.);
Coordinate data from across each WG to assist in the development of cross-validated instruments to help Informatics Departments set goals and priorities for female recruiting, integration, and promotion;
Collate collaboratively a handbook of interventions and web-based resources across all WGs for practical use by the academic community and stakeholders;
Deliver guidance and recommendations on how to overcome the challenges in a comprehensive policy document targeting policymakers and other relevant stakeholders at the national and the EU level;
Create visibility, both within the academic community and to other stakeholders, about the common issues and challenges facing the academic community, and local, national, and EU authorities in addressing gender balance in Informatics;
Create a communications strategy to spread information about the actions and results to the general public and stakeholders, using a website created for the project, social media channels, newsletters, and press releases;
Develop a common European understanding around the issues of female participation in Informatics, policy priorities, and areas of intervention; Involve industry stakeholders in the efforts to address the main challenges and create opportunities and synergies;
Develop and publish an Action website to become the reference point for addressing gender balance in Informatics, including an online repository of the evidence collected by the WGs, information about the networking activities organized, and channels for dissemination and communication.

2.5.2 WG2: From Bachelor/Master Studies to Ph.D

WG2 aimed to design a new set of measures on how to promote the participation of more female students in Ph.D. programs in Informatics and ensure that students who started will complete their Ph.D. studies. The main tasks of WG2 were to: (1) collect and assess cross-national action plans/guidelines (national or regional) to inform about research activities and role models in research and education; (2) collate current interventions/tools to inform about actions both in general terms and specifically regarding gender and diversity issues; (3) collate examples of how female Ph.D. student voices' can be encouraged across universities in generating innovative research projects and ideas and (4) gather evidence on their effectiveness across different groups and with regards to gender and age systematically reviewing completeness of the information, degree of usage, local evaluations carried out, and sustainability.

Table 2.3 Capacity building objectives

Capacity building objectives
Establish an efficient and lasting network of excellence to advance knowledge and methods to improve gender balance in Informatics;
Such a network shall encourage sustainable collaboration, and facilitate knowledge and experience sharing, with an emphasis on intervention best practices, through seminars, workshops, and short-term exchange visits, involving a comprehensive list of stakeholders;
Promote policy and intervention practices for recruiting and selection of female students, researchers, and professors, including guidelines for their monitoring and evaluation; disseminate the practices for further development by the wider academic community, fostering collaborative international projects;
Encourage publication (and support the drafting) of peer-reviewed papers, and presentations at important conferences and events, to create at an international level awareness of the gender gap in Informatics;
Increase awareness of the issues across disciplinary boundaries, both within and outside of academia, by promoting continued exchange and development of knowledge, practice, and policy guidance;
Cooperate with industry to foster career networks, creating mutually beneficial synergies, for students and early career researchers to find excellent career opportunities, and for the industry to tap into a pool of highly motivated talented individuals;
Act as a transnational platform facilitating multi-stakeholder engagement and co-creating processes and actions at local, national, European, and international levels.

Table 2.4 Deliverables

Main deliverables
A website (https://eugain.eu/);
a repository of initiatives and best practices;
booklets with practical recommendations (see Sect. 2.6.1);
a handbook with validated measures and guidelines helping university departments to recruit and retain female (students, PhD students, professors and researchers);
policy recommendation documents for local, national and international institutions;
publications, and presentations (see Sect. 2.6.2).

2.5.3 WG3: From Ph.D. to Professor

The main goal of WG3 was to identify successful practices to recruit more female professors in Informatics and to limit the dropout rate of women along the path to professorship and leader positions in academia. It aimed also to help to increase the proportion of women in international research projects. To reach this goal, WG3 focused on (1) collecting experiences from ongoing initiatives in COST countries universities and assess evidence [24]; (2) identifying HR policies and recruitment strategies aimed at increasing female recruitment and retention within Departments, Institutes/Faculties/Schools, Universities; (3) designing protocols for collaboration between the management and the employees at the faculty, with a focus on gender equality; (4) designing career development programme for Ph.D.

students and postdoctoral researchers; (5) developing a mentor scheme for women at the master's level to associate professor level; (6) creating international mentoring schemes between women in scientific positions at different levels and in different COST countries and (7) developing a strategy for recruiting women in externally funded projects, especially for EU funding.

2.5.4 WG4: Cooperation with Industry and Society

The main objective of WG4 aimed to assure that cooperation with stakeholders in industry and other sectors exists at a local, regional, national and EU level and that particular issues existing in each country are taken into consideration. It aimed also to analyse the existing practices put in place for university departments, institutes/faculties/schools to deal with external cooperation with a focus on gender issues and evaluate what assessment exists for these practices. The main tasks and activities of WG4 focused on: (1) collate evidence of successful industry-university collaboration across partners and countries [15, 23]; (2) gather and assess evidence of best practices on how collaboration with industry and other sectors have had positive impact on gender balance in Informatics/ICT; (3) collate action plans/guidelines on integration from national and regional authorities for policy evaluation and (4) engage with the IT/ICT sector to improve the integration of gender balance in their research portfolio and recruitment strategy.

2.5.5 WG5: Strategy and Dissemination

The objectives of WG5 were to: (1) raise awareness about the gender imbalance and bias in Informatics; (2) advocate and lobby for change; (3) disseminate the action results to all partners and national networks and (4) reach out to all external stakeholders. To reach these objectives, the main task of WG5 was to assure that the main activities, events, outcomes and deliverables of all WGs have the best visibility and reach the relevant stakeholders. This is done through the organization of an Annual European Workshop on gender balance in Informatics/ICT (during the project duration and on the longer term annually, after the end of the project) and face to face meetings with relevant policy officers at the EU level and national level (involving then the partner(s) in their country). Finally, WG5 is in charge of organizing an European Award for best practices in departments/institutes/schools/-faculties of European universities and research labs that encourage and support the careers of women in Informatics research and education (selected by a review panel of international experts).

2.6 Results and Outputs

In this section, we reported the main results we got during these four years as booklets and scientific outputs.

2.6.1 Booklets and Other Deliverables

We produced four booklets, available for free on our website https://eugain.eu:

1. *Booklet "From Ph.D. to Professor"*: includes the best practices for supporting the transition of Ph.D. and postdoctoral researchers into faculty positions.
2. *Booklet "From School to University":* includes the best practices and suggestions for recruiting and retaining women students.
3. *Booklet(s) "Future Informatics Students":* includes advice and advantages of studying and choosing Informatics as a career.
4. *Booklet "From Bachelor/Master Studies to Ph.D.":* includes the best practices and suggestions for retaining and supporting the transition of women students to Ph.D. positions.

Moreover, we produced a *Policy recommendation document* that includes a set of policy recommendations directed to policymakers, at the national and European level and an *Handbook of intervention methods* that provides an understanding of the factors that contribute to increasing the recruitment and retention of women computer scientists, methods, and intervention strategies.

2.6.2 Scientific Output

Based on the results obtained in this project, we published more than 50 papers both in International and National journals, conferences, and workshops. The complete list of publications is available online.[1] Conferences include the International Conference of Software Engineering (ICSE), IEEE International Conference on Software Analysis, ACM Conference on Innovation and Technology in Computer Science Education, IEEE/ACM International Conference on Software Engineering: Software Engineering Education and Training, ACM Women Encourage. Journals and magazines include prestigious ones like Education and Information Technologies journal, IEEE Software, and *Journal of Systems and Software*.

---

[1] https://eugain.eu/results/research-publications/.

2.7 Summary and Future Outlooks

By now we have understood the barriers and effective strategies towards improving gender balance in Informatics, summarized also within the booklets discussed in Sect. 2.6.1. EUGAIN has offered a platform for inspiration crossing cultural boundaries and for gathering insights on effective strategies towards addressing stereotypes, promoting role models, closing the confidence gap, growing a sense of belonging, and learning to give recognition and credit to all the talented women and other underrepresented talents in Informatics.

At the same time, we now understand the importance of continuing this essential work. We see the immense importance of a better understanding of cultural differences and their influences and strategies that give us a better ability to engage and recognize diverse talent, together with effective tools to guide women and girls throughout the maze of educational and career decisions in the growing world of Informatics and technology.

When starting EUGAIN, we began with an ambitious set of questions we intended to answer (see Table 2.1). Now, four years later, while we have shed light on all these questions, we find them far from answered. We have understood how hard it is to measure progress and how multifaceted the progress can be, moving us into technology that is inclusive for everyone, not only women and girls.

Over the duration of EUGAIN, we have had the privilege to watch closely when the change was taking place in the institutions of our project members, which we have celebrated with the Minerva award and made sure to document as many of the efforts take time to bloom. As for now, we are excited that the seeds have been planted and will continue nourishing these ongoing activities in all our institutions. We hope our results and this book bring inspiration to the reader to do the same.

2.8 How You Use Our Results

All the deliverables of the EUGAIN project are and will continue to be available on our website https://eugain.eu—we encourage every reader of this book to download them and put them to use in their environment, whether in school, at university or at a company.

We picked the three personas from the preface of the book that seem most relevant to this chapter and actions that can be taken upon it. We encourage anyone affiliated with higher education to consider starting a similar networking action.

Kim, the university professor. Kim had a wonderful time with the EUGAIN network and made important connections across many countries. They decide to write a follow-up proposal with a subset of the members of EUGAIN.
Actions: They lead a group of people that they closely collaborated with during the Cost Action and that they feel they have common goals with and submit a second round Cost Action proposal to the European Union.

Bazyli, the industry manager. Bazyli was a visitor at the final EUGAIN conference and was very impressed with the results. They tool away the Deliverable 7 guidelines (described in detail in a later chapter in this book) and implement them at their company. They decide to join the proposal that Kim mentioned in that inspiring meeting.
Actions: Bazyli offers to host a series of workshops at their company and host one of the working group meetings for the envisioned future Cost Action. Their company is excited about the prospect of many highly qualified women coming to visit them.

Nicole, the activist. Nicole found out about EUGAIN on social media and are delighted about the hands-on guidance that the research outputs as well as the Deliverable 7 guidance provide. They decide to reach out to various members of the project.
Actions: Nicole invites them to join one of their campaigns for encouraging young women to look into Informatics as a possible future career.

References

1. ACM Women. ACM-W: Supporting, celebrating, and advocating for Women in Computing. women.acm.org, 2024.
2. M. Ali, P. Sapiezynski, M. Bogen, A. Korolova, A. Mislove, and A. Rieke. Discrimination through optimization: How Facebook's ad delivery can lead to biased outcomes. *Proceedings of the ACM on human-computer interaction*, 3(CSCW):1–30, 2019.
3. Anita Borg. Anita Borg. AnitaB.org, 2024.
4. C. R. Association. *Taulbee Survey*. Publications Office, 2019.
5. AWC. Association for Women in Computing. http://awc-hq.org/home.html, 2024.
6. S. L. Bem. Gender schema theory and its implications for child development: Raising gender-aschematic children in a gender-schematic society. *Signs*, 8(4):598–616, 1983.
7. CRA-WP. The Computing Research Association's Committee on Widening Participation in Computing Research (CRA-WP). https://cra.org/cra-wp/, 2024.
8. W. Damon, R. M. Lerner, and N. Eisenberg. *Handbook of child psychology, social, emotional, and personality development*. John Wiley & Sons, 2006.

9. J. Dastin. Amazon scraps secret AI recruiting tool that showed bias against women. In *Ethics of data and analytics*, pages 296–299. Auerbach Publications, 2022.
10. European Commission and Directorate-General for Research and Innovation. She figures 2021. 10.2777/06090, 2021.
11. EUROSTAT. ICT specialists - statistics on hard-to-fill vacancies in enterprises. https://tinyurl.com/yc377hn3, 2017.
12. EUROSTAT. More men with an ICT education employed than women. https://ec.europa.eu/eurostat/web/products-eurostat-news/-/ddm-20221011-1, 2021.
13. C. Frieze and J. L. Quesenberry. How computer science at CMU is attracting and retaining women. *Communications of the ACM*, 62(2):23–26, 2019.
14. J. L. Glass, S. Sassler, Y. Levitte, and K. M. Michelmore. What's so special about STEM? A comparison of women's retention in STEM and professional occupations. *Social forces*, 92(2):723–756, 2013.
15. L. Happe and B. Buhnova. Frustrations steering women away from software engineering. *IEEE Software*, 39(4):63–69, 2021.
16. IEEE. Women in computing. https://tinyurl.com/bdekpzkv, 2024.
17. Informatics Europe. Informatics education in Europe: Institutions, degrees, students, positions, salaries. Key data 2008–2013, 2009–2014, 2010–2015, 2011–2016, 2012–2017. https://tinyurl.com/299xvbz6, 2018.
18. Informatics Europe. Women in informatics research and education. https://tinyurl.com/j9h8f8d5, 2019.
19. L. Jaccheri, C. Pereira, and S. Fast. Gender issues in computer science: lessons learnt and reflections for the future. In *2020 22nd International Symposium on Symbolic and Numeric Algorithms for Scientific Computing (SYNASC)*, pages 9–16. IEEE, 2020.
20. V. A. Lagesen, I. Pettersen, and L. Berg. Inclusion of women to ICT engineering–lessons learned. *European Journal of Engineering Education*, 47(3):467–482, 2022.
21. U. of Bamberg. University of Bamberg, 2024.
22. N. U. of Science and Technology. Ada project. www.ntnu.edu/girls, 2024.
23. M. Razavian and P. Lago. Feminine expertise in architecting teams. *IEEE software*, 33(4):64–71, 2015.
24. E. Rubegni, B. Penzenstadler, M. Landoni, L. Jaccheri, and G. Dodig-Crnkovic. Owning your career paths: Storytelling to engage women in computer science. In *Gender in AI and Robotics: The Gender Challenges from an Interdisciplinary Perspective*, pages 1–25. Springer, 2023.
25. L. J. Sax. Anatomy of an enduring gender gap: The evolution of women's participation in computer science. *The Journal of Higher Education*, 88(2):258–293, 2017.
26. K. K. Silveira and R. Prikladnicki. A systematic mapping study of diversity in software engineering: a perspective from the agile methodologies. In *2019 IEEE/ACM 12th International Workshop on Cooperative and Human Aspects of Software Engineering (CHASE)*, pages 7–10. IEEE, 2019.
27. Statista. Share of software developers by gender in Europe 2020, by country, 2020.
28. Statista. Software developer gender distribution worldwide as of 2022, 2022.
29. B. Trinkenreich, R. Britto, M. Gerosa, and I. Steinmacher. An empirical investigation on the challenges faced by women in the software industry: A case study. In *Proceedings of the 2022 ACM/IEEE 44th International Conference on Software Engineering: Software Engineering in Society*, pages 24–35, 2022.
30. L. L. Wang, G. Stanovsky, L. Weihs, and O. Etzioni. Gender trends in computer science authorship. *Communications of the ACM*, 64(3):78–84, Feb. 2021.
31. M. West, R. Kraut, and H. Ei Chew. I'd blush if I could: closing gender divides in digital skills through education (UNESCO/EQUALS GLOBAL Partnership). https://unesdoc.unesco.org/ark:/48223/pf0000367416.page=1, 2017.

Open Access This chapter is licensed under the terms of the Creative Commons Attribution 4.0 International License (http://creativecommons.org/licenses/by/4.0/), which permits use, sharing, adaptation, distribution and reproduction in any medium or format, as long as you give appropriate credit to the original author(s) and the source, provide a link to the Creative Commons license and indicate if changes were made.

The images or other third party material in this chapter are included in the chapter's Creative Commons license, unless indicated otherwise in a credit line to the material. If material is not included in the chapter's Creative Commons license and your intended use is not permitted by statutory regulation or exceeds the permitted use, you will need to obtain permission directly from the copyright holder.

Part II
From School to University: Intervention Methods

Chapter 3
How Early Recruitment Helps Achieve Gender Diversity in Informatics

Rukiye Altin , Eliot Bytyçi , and Àngela Nebot

3.1 Personas

This chapter represents recruitment initiatives, which might be useful for different kind of personas. Thus before those initiatives are unfolded, two representatives that might find them useful, a school principal, named imaginatively Alex, and a school teacher, named Jamila, are described below.

> **Alex, the school principal.** Looking at the resources in this chapter, Alex the school principal takes the recommendations to their next school board meeting. Some of the teachers are enthusiastic about developing role models in the classroom, others are a bit more sceptical. So Alex starts a group activity where the teachers pair up with a partner, interview each other on what role models they have in their lives, and create role model descriptions for each other.

R. Altin (✉)
Kiel University, Kiel, Germany
e-mail: ral@informatik.uni-kiel.de

E. Bytyçi
University of Prishtina, Prishtina, Kosovo
e-mail: eliot.bytyci@uni-pr.edu

À. Nebot
Soft Computing Research Group at Intelligent Data Science, Artificial Intelligence Research Center, Universitat Politècnica de Catalunya, Barcelona, Spain
e-mail: angela@cs.upc.edu

© The Author(s) 2025
B. Penzenstadler et al. (eds.), *Actions for Gender Balance in Informatics Across Europe*, https://doi.org/10.1007/978-3-031-78432-3_3

> **Jem, school teacher.** Looking at the resources in this chapter, Jem is a school teacher has passion about STEM and wants to support their students being open to that direction. She needs suggestions about how to raise awareness on gender diversity in computer science so Jem starts a group activity where the teachers can rainstorm about inspiring activities for students from kindergarten to high school.

3.2 Introduction

The field of informatics is growing rapidly, with technology playing a significant role in almost every aspect of our lives. Even though this growth brings new career seats on the fields, women are still not involved enough in informatics which is a significant and ongoing problem. This imbalance slows down innovation and strengthens stereotypes, making it harder to build a more inclusive tech environment. Therefore, the primary research objective of this chapter is to examine strategies for achieving gender equality in informatics education, from kindergarten through university, with a focus on early intervention and recruitment initiatives. The chapter emphasizes the importance of encouraging gender diversity in informatics to enhance creativity and innovation in our technology-driven world.

To address this issue, we conducted systematic research and found that while some programs and strategies try to close the gender gap in informatics, most of them focus on later stages of education or hiring, often ignoring the important early years [12, 14, 16]. These approaches are limited by their reactive nature and lack of continuity from early education through higher education. Thus, in this chapter, we aimed to highlight the importance of starting early recruitment efforts that cover all stages of education to tackle social stereotypes that discourage young girls from choosing careers in computer science and related fields. The chapter is answering the key questions below:

- How can early education initiatives foster an interest in informatics among girls?
- What strategies can be used to sustain this interest through secondary and high school?
- How can universities create spaces that motivate and support women to study and succeed in informatics?

This study seeks to propose more effective and sustainable approaches to achieving gender parity in the field of informatics, and we believe this chapter will raise awareness among society, educators, and school administrators that informatics is for everyone.

3.2.1 Why Gender Balance in Informatics Is a Need

In today's fast-changing world of technology, it is important to give everyone equal chances to succeed. Although boys and girls have the same skills and abilities when it comes to using and learning technology, there is a big difference in how they see themselves and their future careers. Girls often think they aren't as good as they really are because of societal pressures and gender stereotypes, which can lower their confidence compared to boys [10, 11, 31]. This impacts their career goals and limits their interest in jobs in technology fields, like informatics. Addressing this issue requires several steps, starting in early education and continuing through higher education and beyond. Girls need to be encouraged to build self-confidence and develop a real interest in technology from a young age. This early support can help reduce the negative effects of gender stereotypes and societal expectations. Schools have the ability to create environments that not only support but actively encourage girls to get involved in technology. High schools, in particular, play a key role in this effort. By using focused strategies, they can have a big impact on the career choices of young women.

Recruitment actions aimed at increasing female participation in informatics within educational institutions, both at the K-12 and university levels, are crucial for fostering diversity and inclusion in the tech industry [12]. Historically, women have been underrepresented in the field of informatics, resulting in a significant gender gap that persists today. These lack of recruitment of women in the technology has significant and wide-reaching consequences. First, it contributes to a shortage of skilled professionals, leaving many tech jobs unfilled [62, 63]. This gap not only hinders innovation but also slows the progress of technological advancements. the underrepresentation of women in tech results in biased software and algorithms, as diverse perspectives are essential for creating fair and effective solutions. Moreover, excluding women from the tech workforce limits economic growth by reducing the potential for global wealth creation. By not fully utilizing the talents and abilities of half the population, we miss out on many opportunities for economic and social progress. Addressing this disparity requires strategic and innovative approaches to engage and support female students from childhood through university level education. Effective recruitment initiatives not only enhance the overall quality of the educational experience but also contribute to the development of a more inclusive, equitable, fair and powerful technology industry [63].

This section explores best practices, recruitment strategies and recommended actions for educational institutions at both the K-12 and university levels to effectively engage and support female students in technology fields. By examining successful outreach programs, mentoring opportunities, inclusive curricula and supportive policies, we aim to provide guidance for institutions for the recruitment of girls in informatics. The ultimate goal is to empower girls to recognise their potential, gain self-confidence and pursue careers in computer science, thereby contributing to a more diverse and innovative technological future.

3.3 Recruitment Initiatives

Studies on students' perceptions of computer science (CS) in K-12 have shown a gap in knowledge about CS education [9–11]. Even though boys and girls have the same abilities in learning and using CS-related topics, programming, gender stereotypes often suggest that men are more capable in CS fields than women [10]. Therefore, it's crucial to create an environment that boosts girls' self-confidence and increases their interest in CS from an early age, starting in school [10, 12]. This section will highlight best practices and recommend actions for K-12, focusing on how recruitment initiatives should include a strategy that extends from kindergarten to universities.

3.3.1 Initiatives in K-12 Education Level

In recent years, K-12 schools have been making remarkable efforts to integrate CS into their curricula because school directors are aware that future job markets will increasingly demand programming, problem solving and algorithmic thinking skills [16]. Yet, we are all aware that there is an issue about gender balance in CS fields and it's obvious achieving gender balance in the field of informatics requires an effort across all educational levels to change the stereotypes and make the environment serve for all. The strategic effort should be starting from a very early age through kindergarten to universities. The importance of teaching CS topics at a young age lies in its ability to naturally enhance a variety of skills, including problem-solving, creative thinking, and computational thinking, which are valuable across all fields of study and careers [16, 17]. Addressing this issue early will help spark an interest in CS fields among girls and it will also help to break down the stereotypes that often prevent girls from pursuing careers in STEM (Science, Technology, Engineering, and Mathematics) fields, including informatics. Sustainable solutions are needed to foster gender balance in CS and that will be started with the help of CS curriculum in K-12 [13, 14]. The following sections highlight the detailed initiatives at the kindergarten, secondary school, and high school education levels.

3.3.1.1 Kindergarten

The integration of technology and CS into the curriculum at an early age can increase interest and demystify informatics for young children. As technology continues to grow and the need for computer scientists increases, countries are looking for ways to add informatics to their school programs to better prepare future generations for the modern world [15, 20]. This brings a new workload to the teachers because they need to incorporate age friendly activities that engage students with the new technology and sparks children's interest in computer science. Robinson [20] stated that resources such as Kodable, Scratch, Code.org and ScratchJr are great resources to get benefits from while having interactive game style lessons to the young learners. These activities can be both fun and educational, appealing to all children and helping to break the stereotype that technology is only for boys. According to Otterborn et al. [18], learning a skill at a young age is crucial for children's development, and including informatics in the early curriculum is important because it helps build computational skills such as critical thinking, algorithmic thinking, problem-solving, decomposition, evaluation, and abstraction. Scholars also agree that the skills gained through learning programming are essential for personal growth, as they enable the younger generation to develop a higher level of global awareness [10, 12, 15]. But the question that arises is how to integrate computer science at the kindergarten level? Educators have been looking ways to include computer science in kindergarten level and the most popular way is unplugged activities [20–22]. Studies highlight that integration of computer science into kindergarten should be with the integration of five crucial points as: unplugged computing activities, meeting with the technologies at early age, developing materials that focus on gender-neutral curriculum, professional training for educators and involving parents in the learning process [22–25].

Unplugged activities, which involve teaching computer science in lessons without the use of computers, offer an efficient approach to introducing kindergarten students to computer science as a subject. They are the most well-known examples of how to include computer science in an early age level of education. Unplugged activities are not only involving students to engage with CS content but it helps them to develop their computational thinking skills naturally [20]. According to Lemay et al., unplugged activities are helping students in kindergarten to have kinesthetic engagement which is important during their development [26]. Involving activities without computers into kindergarten curricula can be an important strategy to achieve gender balance in informatics because the awareness of gender issues in the field of computer science fields will begin to be stated in early ages. Patrick et al. [19] indicates that kindergarten boys and girls are perceiving the competence and enjoyment differently so when the activity related to computer science is developed, gender perspectives should be included. By addressing gender stereotypes and engaging both genders in unplugged activities can create a more inclusive environment that encourages all children to pursue interests in computer science from an early age. Implementing programming activities without using computers in kindergarten with gender diversity awareness requires a systematic curriculum design. Huang and Looi [27] state that designing a curricula for computer science in kindergarten with unplugged activities requires a diverse environment to access a wide range of students. Therefore, designing a curriculum that integrates unplugged computer science activities involves careful planning and consideration of the developmental stages of young children to spark students' minds that computer science is for all. Scholars [20, 28–30] stated key elements of an effective curriculum as follows:

- Activities should help cognitive and motor skills which is possible by including unplugged activities gradually and reinforced through repetition.
- Unplugged activities should be planned with focusing on different interests, learning styles and gender stereotypes.
- Interdisciplinary collaboration is an efficient way to be integrated in unplugged activities to make learning more easy and relevant.
- A sense of belonging environment should be included in the unplugged activities that will decrease the females' lower sense of belonging to computer science stereotypes.

We believe a positive curriculum that serves for all genders with an integration of unplugged computer science activities will help female students' confidence and their interest in CS subjects.

Meeting the new technologies at an early age has become increasingly popular as we are living in the modern digital age. The importance of integrating new technology at the early age education is critical to have an impact on students about the computer science field and how fast it's growing as it brings new marketing and job areas. According to Sullivan and Bers [31] to avoid long-lasting negative stereotypes that tells computer science is a masculine field, introducing new technology at a very early age is important because it shows a reduction in gender-based stereotypes related to STEM careers. Addressing gender stereotypes, providing equitable opportunities for all children, and engaging them with the new technology starting from the kindergarten level will create a pathway to more balanced representation in the field of computer science in the future. Scholars have several suggestions about how to include computer science into kindergarten level with introducing students to the new technology. ScratchJr is one of the tools that has been used in kindergarten level while introducing computer science to pupils. ScratchJr is a visual programming tool that allows users to code with a block-based approach. According to Louka and Papadakis [32] involving ScratchJr to the learning environment in kindergarten improves students CS skills and it helps students to understand basic concepts of programming easier. Their study also shows that there is no difference between girls and boys as both genders showed a similar performance. This is important to erase the stereotypes that boys are more successful in CS related topics than girls. Another study involving ScratchJr was conducted at the kindergarten level to assess its accessibility for novice users, while also providing opportunities for more experienced users to expand their knowledge [33]. The study found out that new learners were easily engage with the activities and students with the experiences kept learning about the programming. Thus, it is clear that ScratchJr fosters an inclusive learning environment for kindergarten students that can help students to engage in computer science in the future easily.

Professional training for educators plays a vital role in addressing the issue of gender diversity, as children's interests and self-perceptions start to develop during their kindergarten education. Such training will help to create a gender-balanced environment in computer science for the future. Kalogiannakis and Papadakis [35] designed a workshop for 23 pre-service teachers to train how to include

MakeyMakey and Scratch 3 in their lessons. Their case study found that interacting with pre-service teachers and teaching them how to include new technology tools in their lessons provides effective teaching skills by involving them directly in the process. It's obvious that teachers have an important impact on shaping students' attitudes and interests. Students, especially in their early age, can be directed to the thought that there is no bias or a gender stereotype in the field of informatics if teachers play a role in their perceptions during their education. Researchers indicate that students are mostly showing a positive reaction when teachers communicate with them with high expectations and this brings a positive self concept in science courses [34, 36, 37]. Therefore, teachers should have professional trainings about how to have effective teaching by understanding gender bias and stereotypes.

Developing materials that focus on gender-neutral curriculum in kindergarten is being recognized recently because of the importance of gender diversity for encouraging young women to choose computer science. Even though the studies are being made to make students achieve computer science contents starting from an early education stage, developing course materials that appeals to all genders is a big challenge for the teachers working in K-12 [32, 34]. Knupfer [38] stated that designing a material which should encounter gender bias is important to promote a diverse range of role models and encourage girls for computer related activities. However, it is not easy to create effective gender-neutral materials. According to Gulcicek [39] including gender-neutral activities to kindergarten level has an effective role in decreasing students gender stereotypes because such activities creates an inclusive and safe environment for all genders.

Involving parents in the learning process is the last important point that should be considered when integrating gender-neutral activities in kindergarten level. Parental involvement in this process has been recognized as a crucial factor in fostering children's early learning experiences because engaging parents in activities with their children naturally contributes to closing the gender gap, as students of this age often see their parents as role models [39, 40]. Hoover and Sandler [41] state that activities including parents to the activities of their children in kindergarten level supports students' learning because it also fosters a supportive home environment for learning which can help with gender balance. Thus, schools and educators should create an effective strategies for involving parents in kindergarten education to create opportunities for parental engagement both inside and outside the classroom. According to Dabney et al. [42] collaborative initiatives between schools and parents encourages students' involvement in science subjects and it establishes a clear communication channel between educators and parents that supports children's developments and learning. Therefore, parents being involved in kindergarten learning activities is a crucial movement for efforts to have a gender balance in computer science because this makes parents more supportive for CS subjects and it can increase the confidence of students towards the field.

Table 3.1 summarises the main ideas on the integration of computer science in kindergarten.

Table 3.1 Key points of integrating computer science in kindergarten

Topic	Key points
Early introduction to technology	Integrating CS into the curriculum at an early age increases interest and demystifies informatics. It is crucial for the development of computational skills. Learning CS at a young age develops skills such as critical thinking, problem-solving, algorithmic thinking, and decomposition
Challenges for teachers	Teachers need to incorporate age-appropriate activities that engage students with technology and spark interest in CS. Teachers need professional training to effectively integrate technology into lessons and address gender bias, playing a key role in shaping students' perceptions
Recommended resources	Kodable, Scratch, Code.org, and ScratchJr are effective tools for introducing CS in a fun, interactive way for young learners. For instance, ScratchJr is an effective tool for teaching programming in kindergarten, and studies show no significant gender differences in its use
Unplugged activities	Teaching CS without computers (unplugged activities) is an effective strategy for introducing the subject at the kindergarten level. Unplugged activities help develop motor and cognitive skills while fostering inclusivity and challenging gender stereotypes
Fostering equitable environments and gender-neutral materials	Early exposure to technology and addressing gender stereotypes are essential for balanced representation in CS in the future. Developing gender-neutral curriculum materials is crucial for promoting diversity and reducing stereotypes
Parental involvement	Parental involvement in learning is key to supporting gender balance in CS and creating a positive home environment that fosters confidence in the field

3.3.1.2 Secondary and High School

The gender imbalance in computer science brings critical issues not only to gender equity but the diversity in the working environment which lacks perspective and creativity. Addressing this imbalance in early age is important to raise an awareness on the issue and to encourage young women that CS is for all. Even though there is a significant effort to promote gender equality in all fields, the gender gap in CS continues to struggle. Studies mention that disparity usually begins in secondary and high school where boys tend to take CS related extracurricular activities more than girls [43–46]. Therefore, the need to include computer science in primary and secondary school curriculum is growing. According to the studies, how we teach CS to young students is as important as having it in the curriculum especially in secondary and high school level to make CS education effective [47–50]. Also, Phelps and Santo [51] suggest that the curriculum should be updated to be more inclusive and should have extracurricular activities to attract female students. Secondary school plays a critical role for transitioning programming from unplugged and block-based methods to text-based coding with step-by-step algorithms. During this time, students are also beginning to learn more advanced problem-solving techniques in core subjects such as math and science [52, 53]. Therefore, it is important that content and teaching materials be carefully designed to promote awareness of gender imbalances and encourage all students, regardless of gender, to consider CS as a viable career path. In order to understand why fewer women pursue CS, researchers have primarily focused on high school, as it is the final stage before students choose a career path. Scholars agree that female students may feel uncomfortable with CS in high school due to fewer opportunities to learn programming, lessons often being tailored more toward boys, and a lack of real-world examples [53, 55–58]. Additionally, schools may inadvertently perpetuate stereotypes that make girls feel as though CS is not for them. Understanding these root causes is crucial for creating effective recruitment initiatives.

Research suggests several strategies to promote a more diverse future in CS fields. These strategies include educational interventions that address gender imbalances by integrating informatics into the curriculum; extracurricular programs that offer informal environments for students to explore informatics outside of formal education; mentorship and role model activities to showcase successful women in the field; supportive learning environments that foster classroom cultures encouraging participation from all students; and partnerships with industry and higher education to offer internship programs that provide real-world CS experiences [46, 59, 60]. Together, these initiatives aim to close the gender gap in CS and create a more inclusive and diverse future in the field. Below, we highlight those aspects that we consider to be key and which we believe deserve further discussion.

Diverse and Inclusive CS Curriculum Integrating CS into primary and secondary school curriculum is crucial for preparing students for a technology-driven future. This requires embedding CS concepts across various subjects, offering diverse learning pathways, and emphasizing foundational skills like algorithms and computational thinking. Inclusive teaching practices, such as Universal Design for Learning [61] and culturally relevant materials, are essential to ensure that all students engage meaningfully with the content. Effective CS education also relies on professional development for educators, community involvement, and diverse assessment methods. Ongoing training and mentorship can equip teachers with the skills to deliver quality instruction. By providing continuous feedback and utilizing various assessment methods, educators can create an equitable learning environment that encourages reflection and growth. Promoting an inclusive environment in CS education not only benefits individual learners but also enriches the entire field by bringing diverse perspectives and talents to the forefront.

Making Extracurricular Activities Inclusive Supporting students through extracurricular activities is crucial for achieving gender balance in informatics. Creating an inclusive environment where all students feel welcome and valued can significantly enhance their participation and interest in technical fields. One effective approach to promote inclusivity is to organize and conduct international projects that can be carried out virtually. These initiatives can leverage technology to connect students from diverse backgrounds, allowing them to collaborate on meaningful projects without geographical constraints. For example, students can participate in robotics competitions like the FIRST LEGO League (FLL), which not only helps them develop technical skills but also encourages teamwork and problem-solving abilities. In addition, engaging students in informatics challenges like Bebras [49, 53, 54], can stimulate their critical thinking and algorithmic skills while providing a platform for them to showcase their talents. Furthermore, these activities can be designed to specifically target underrepresented groups in technology, ensuring that students from various genders, cultural backgrounds, and skill levels have equal opportunities to participate. By fostering an inclusive culture within these extracurricular programs, it is possible to inspire a new generation of diverse talent in the field of CS. Ultimately, such initiatives not only contribute to gender balance but also cultivate a rich tapestry of perspectives and ideas that drive innovation and creativity in technology.

Seamlessly Transitioning from Block Coding to Text-Based Coding To facilitate a seamless transition from block coding to text-based coding while actively engaging students of all genders during class, several effective activities can be implemented. One approach is to incorporate an inspiring success story of a female technology entrepreneur or a notable female figure in IT or ICT into the curriculum each term. This not only highlights the achievements of women in the field but also provides relatable role models for students, fostering a sense of belonging and encouragement among young girls. Additionally, distributing informative leaflets that showcase the accomplishments of prominent female technology figures can serve as a constant reminder of the diverse pathways available in technology and CS. These leaflets can be displayed in classrooms and shared during relevant lessons, sparking discussions and motivating students to explore their own interests in the field. Furthermore, integrating interdisciplinary collaborations within the curriculum can enrich the learning experience by connecting coding and CS concepts to other subjects such as mathematics, science, and art. This holistic approach not only deepens students' understanding of coding but also demonstrates its real-world applications, making the learning process more engaging and relevant for all students. Collectively, these initiatives can create a supportive and inclusive classroom environment that encourages every student to pursue their interests in technology and coding.

Supportive learning environment is key to fostering a classroom culture that encourages all students to participate. Teachers can cultivate this environment by promoting collaboration, offering constructive feedback, and recognizing individual contributions. A supportive atmosphere makes it easier for girls to take risks, ask questions, and explore new concepts without fear of judgment or failure, creating a more inclusive learning experience for everyone. Teachers play a pivotal role in cultivating this type of supportive environment. They can do so by emphasizing collaboration rather than competition, which can help girls feel more comfortable participating in group activities and contributing their ideas. Encouraging teamwork allows students to learn from each other, and it promotes a sense of belonging and shared purpose. In addition, providing constructive feedback is crucial for building

Table 3.2 Key points of integrating computer science in secondary and high school

Topic	Key points
Inclusive CS curriculum	A diverse curriculum that includes Universal Design for Learning and culturally relevant materials is needed. Continuous teacher development and diverse assessment methods are essential for effective teaching
Inclusive extracurricular activities	Inclusive extracurricular programs, such as robotics competitions (e.g., FIRST LEGO League) and informatics challenges (e.g., Bebras), can boost participation from students of all genders and cultural backgrounds
Transition from block-based to text-based coding	A smooth transition from block-based to text-based coding in secondary school is important. Including success stories of women in technology and interdisciplinary collaborations can enhance student engagement
Supportive learning environment	A collaborative, supportive learning environment where teachers encourage participation, offer constructive feedback, and recognize individual contributions is key to fostering girls' confidence and engagement in CS

confidence and helping students, particularly girls, recognize their strengths and areas for growth. Teachers should also make a conscious effort to acknowledge individual contributions, ensuring that the efforts and achievements of girls in CS are recognized and celebrated. By doing so, teachers empower their students.

Table 3.2 summarises the main ideas on the integration of computer science in secondary and high school.

3.3.2 Initiatives in University Level

The gender disparity in informatics in the University level, continues to be an issue. Even though there are no global statistics available, some research conducted in US indicate that around 21% of the field graduates were female in 2023 [3]. The situation is not welcomed and represents the challenges that female are facing within the field, but also highlighting a broader issues, that of insufficient diversity within technology and researchers. Thus, several initiatives are undertaken to support the female students studying informatics but also to support female professors to remain in the field.

3.3.2.1 Gaining and Retaining Females Studying in the Field of Informatics

Informatics should not be seen as a standalone field, where boys and girls come and study to become informatics scientists. It is ever more seen as interdisciplinary field, which intertwines with other fields such as health, arts, and humanities. Thus, when a promotion of informatics occurs, it should also mention the contribution of the informatics related to other fields. This might be seen as a motivator for the females to pursue informatics or at least connect it with their main field of interests.

For example, a health scientist can use data analytics to analyze health data and thus the scientist would have competences from both fields: health and informatics, and could be better fitted than other scientists belonging to one field one. In arts, female that would have also competences in informatics, most probably could use it to their advantage to create more beautiful art pieces. Moreover, it could encourage the staff of the universities, to think about double degree programs [5] which would involve informatics and other degree of interest for the females, specifically.

Besides, another good motivation tool for the girls to study in informatics, would be the promotion of the programs by female teachers, who could act also as mentors in the future or as role models for the girls willing to pursues informatics. These female teachers could arrange, in accordance with university bodies, to organize information sessions [6] throughput the secondary schools, and orient students in pursuing an informatics related degree. This would help also in breaking stereotypes and making the degree attractive for girls. Also, the promotion material, being of different colors, could help raise an interest in checking out the programs.

In the universities itself, the programs should use gender balanced literature, and also try to engage teachers in creating new literature, examples or lecture notes in more gender-neutral language. The course names could also be revised to make them more interesting, as the example of the University of California, renaming an introductory programming course as "The Beauty and Joy of Computing" [7]. Furthermore, the authors of the books should be encouraged to use more gender balance terms but also the instructors to use inclusive language in their communication with students.

University of Michigan has created a program called RENEW [4], as an initiative to enhance recruitment and retention of women in undergraduate courses. This program implements smaller class sizes and mentorship opportunities. Moreover, universities can create groups that belong only to women, in order to enhance self confidence.

Moreover, girls studying informatics could have an additional incentive of getting a scholarship when enrolled in the informatics programs. For example, in Kosovo, the government provides girls in STEM a yearly scholarship for their successful enrollment.

3.3.2.2 Gaining and Retaining Women University Professors in the Field of Informatics

In order to gain and retain women university professors in the field of informatics, universities could set up more rigorous criteria to help set up the gender balance, created in the upper level of management of the universities. For example, in the last few years, a number of universities have drawn also different kinds of strategies or plan for gender equality and as a specific topic, gender balance at the University level.

Such a proposal could be that universities make a gender inclusive recruitment process and thus ensure that the job advert reaches higher audience, initially. But, as in some specific cases, such of an university in Poland [1], they could propose to set up a secondary criteria for employment, that of gender criteria. This will not undermine the merit based criteria, which according to them remains fundamental, but will help university in creating gender balance by providing additional criteria. Moreover, they suggest also several other methods that might help women in keeping their positions or at least make it easier for them to gain work-study-life balance, by providing support for them and their families. Moreover, the process of the candidates review could be more gender balanced, by creating gender balanced evaluation committee.

In order to retain women in the universities, they should create an inclusive environment by organizing debates and training on anti-bias approaches [8]. Moreover, they should secure and distribute funding for promoting gender balance. In another specific comparison study on Scandinavian Universities, for governing and promoting gender equality, different approaches used [2] were investigated. It initially investigates the national legislation and policies, which obligate universities to develop gender equality plans. Moreover, they stress out the need and commitment from higher management to for getting the fund, drawing up strategies and overseeing the action plans.

Table 3.3 summarises the main ideas on the gaining and retaining computer science girl students and women professors in the university.

Nevertheless, trying to close the gender gap in computer science at the university level, it is essential to implement strategies based on issues contributing to this disparity.

Table 3.3 Key points of gaining and retaining computer science female students and female professors in the university

Topic	Key points
Advocate CS as an interdisciplinary field	Computer science should be seen as an interdisciplinary field, and thus motivate girls to take classes in computer science
Promotion of the programs by female teachers	Female professors would not only promote the field but also maybe serve as mentors for future female students. Also, these female mentors, could set up smaller classes, working with fewer female students, to engage even more
Gender balance literature/courses	Encourage professors to create gender balance literature and gender balanced course names
Gender inclusive recruitment process	Not undermining merit based criteria but creating additional criteria to encourage gender balance
Create inclusive environment	Promote discussion, round tables, debates and conduct anti-bias trainings

3.4 Challenges and Future Possibilities

Many examples are provided in the preceding sections, but there are many obstacles to their optimal application as well. A few of these obstacles may arise when talking about the possibilities for kindergartens, including the possibility of incorporating computer science-related age-appropriate tools. To get the most out of the kids, staff training is just as important as equipment.

As we move on to primary school, the difficulties would lie in starting clubs outside of the classroom. This begs the questions of who would organize them, if they would be required, and if there would be gender parity.

Some of the obstacles in secondary education would have to do with the teacher's readiness to welcome or incorporate, if it isn't already included in the curriculum, success stories of female scientists or technology entrepreneurs. It would be impossible for some schools to print flyers, and it would probably be difficult to locate appropriate interdisciplinary partnerships. International initiatives could be helpful, even though they are difficult to write about and considerably harder to carry out.

Creating appropriate two-subject degree programs at the institution may be difficult because of bureaucratic and accrediting concerns.

Staff training on gender balance in professional growth could be a future possibility. Kindergartens, schools, and education agencies should also look at the availability of licenses and training programs for various technologies, since these could facilitate early computer science engagement for kids. Families could participate as well, either by starting clubs outside of the classroom or by sharing their knowledge of a particular accomplished woman in technology.

It is recommended that educators participate in global projects and receive specialized training in project writing and management. The governing bodies of the universities should encourage and support the personnel in pursuing the creation of two subject-degrees. Furthermore, employing more gender-balanced language and reading literature should be encouraged by leadership. The usage of artificial intelligence tools could be used to help teachers in creating lessons more gender balanced.

3.5 Reflections and Insights

Gender equality in informatics is crucial for fostering innovation and creativity, as diverse perspectives and experiences are essential for addressing today's technological challenges. It is important to first acknowledge how initiatives advance recruitment efforts aimed at achieving gender balance in informatics. We found out that recruitment initiatives to achieve gender balance in informatics must span all educational levels, from kindergarten to universities because current gender imbalances in the field of informatics are not only a challenge to equitable representation but also a significant barrier to innovation and creativity. This work provides a structured, comprehensive approach that addresses the issue from its roots, offering strategies that span across various educational levels, from kindergarten through to universities. By doing so, it bridges a crucial gap in the current landscape of recruitment initiatives for women in informatics.

3.5.1 Observations and Lessons Learned

In the current technological era, equal opportunities for all individuals are imperative for progress and innovation. Despite possessing equal skills and abilities, girls often underestimate their competencies due to societal pressures and gender stereotypes. This results in lower self-esteem and professional aspirations in technology-related fields. To counteract this, educational institutions must create supportive environments that encourage girls to develop self-confidence and a genuine interest in technology from a young age. High school institutions, in particular, play a critical role in influencing the career choices of young women. One important observation from this chapter is that gender stereotypes take root early in a child's education, often well before they are introduced to subjects like science, technology, engineering, and math (STEM). The strategies we discussed in this chapter emphasize the importance of starting recruitment efforts as early as kindergarten, where introducing informatics concepts can demystify the subject for both boys and girls. In K-12 education, early introduction to technology through age-appropriate activities can spark interest and break down stereotypes. Early exposure to computer science with the integration of tools like ScratchJr, Kodable, and unplugged computing activities, helps break down the stereotypes that often associate computer science with males. By including programming activities into early childhood curricula will create a gender-balanced environment in informatics for the future. Furthermore, this work highlights the pivotal role of schools in shaping student attitudes towards informatics, particularly in secondary and high school. Current studies state that efforts in secondary and high school should focus on maintaining and growing the interest developed in early education [44–46, 48]. By inviting positive female role models in classrooms or including their success in the curriculum, encouraging teamwork across different subjects, and offering activities like robotics competitions or programming challenges, schools can help raise girls interested and confident in informatics. This well-rounded approach tackles the big drop in female participation in informatics during high school, a time when students often decide on their future careers. In this chapter, we focused on the university level and found out that the gender imbalance in informatics became more visible. It becomes clear that informatics makes more sense when integration of interdisciplinary collaboration not only makes the field more appealing to women but also opens up new avenues for engagement. Universities should promote their programs through female role models and mentors, organize information sessions, and use gender-balanced literature and course materials. Offering scholarships to girls in informatics and implementing strategies for gender equality, such as secondary gender criteria for employment, can also help in achieving balance. Universities should take action, like providing scholarships and creating plans for gender equality, to make sure they focus on recruiting and keeping more women in their programs.

3.5.2 Future Vision

The new generation is our future so we need to take care of them well and provide opportunities to have a strong future. The vision for having a gender diverse environment in informatics will sustain an engagement in a wide range of areas which includes not only educators but policy makers, industry leaders, families and communities. How to have this future vision? First of all, the informatics education must be inclusive, accessible, and engaging for all students, regardless of gender. By this, we mean educators and school managers should continue to develop a gender friendly curricula which collaborates with the other disciplines to promote active learning and increase the sense of belonging for girls in informatics.

We believe it is important for universities to provide special programs that welcome all genders to informatics and remove the stereotype that informatics is only for men. This can involve adapting gender-inclusive language in course materials, including more diverse examples of success in informatics, providing support programs for female students to make them feel more welcome. In the long term, addressing the gender imbalance in informatics will also require a cultural shift, both within the education system and in society at large. Families, initiatives, communities should be as one as they play a crucial role in shaping children's interests and self-perceptions. Children's perceptions change more when parents are involved in the learning process because it helps build positive attitudes toward informatics. Also, as more women succeed in informatics and become visible leaders, the idea that informatics is only for men will start to change, making it easier for future generations of girls to see themselves in these roles.

By working together to follow the strategies in this work, we can build a more inclusive and creative future where informatics is a field for everyone. The journey may take time, but with steady effort, commitment and having more projects like EUGAIN, we can start to close the gender gap in informatics and help our tech workforce reach its full potential.

References

1. Rectors Office, http://www.aps.edu.pl/media/fkofxqsw/gender-equality-plan-for-aps.pdf. Cited 06 Jun 2024
2. Nielsen, Mathias Wullum: Scandinavian approaches to gender equality in academia: a comparative study, Scandinavian Journal of Educational Research, 61, 3, 295–318, (2017)

3. https://www.womentech.net/women-in-tech-stats
4. https://sites.google.com/umich.edu/renewcs/home
5. Cronhjort, Mikael, Samuel Bengmark, Linda Kann, and Viggo Kann: "Leadership and Pedagogical Skills in Computer Science Engineering by Combining a Degree in Engineering with a Degree in Education". In: 2020 IEEE Frontiers in Education Conference (FIE), pp. 1–9, (2020)
6. Stevenson, Monica L (2020). "The gender gap in STEM and computer science jobs: a study investigating job abandonment rates of women in computer science". PhD thesis. Northcentral University. url: https://www.proquest.com/dissertations-theses/gender-gapstem-computer-science-jobs-study/docview/2354843269/se-2?accountid=28955
7. Harvey, Brian (2012). "The beauty and joy of computing: Computer science for everyone". In: Proceedings of Constructionism, pp. 33–39. url: https://bjc.berkeley.edu/documents/2012/Constructionism The Beauty and Joy of Computing Computer Science for Everyone.pdf
8. Motogna, Simona, Lenuţa Alboaie, Ioana Alexandra Todericiu, and Catrinel Zaharia. "Retaining women in computer science: the good, the bad and the ugly sides." In Proceedings of the Third Workshop on Gender Equality, Diversity, and Inclusion in Software Engineering, pp. 35–42. 2022.
9. Kaya, E., Newley, A., Yesilyurt, E. & Deniz, H. Nature of Computer Science: Identification of K-12 Accessible Nature of Computer Science Tenets and Development of an Open-Ended Nature of Computer Science Instrument. *Proceedings Of The 17th ACM Conference On International Computing Education Research.* pp. 426 (2021), https://doi.org/10.1145/3446871.3469784
10. Gretter, S., Yadav, A., Sands, P. & Hambrusch, S. Equitable Learning Environments in K-12 Computing: Teachers' Views on Barriers to Diversity. *ACM Trans. Comput. Educ.* **19** (2019,1), https://doi.org/10.1145/3282939
11. Goldberg, D., Grunwald, D., Lewis, C., Feld, J., Donley, K. & Edbrooke, O. Addressing 21st century skills by embedding computer science in K-12 classes. *Proceeding Of The 44th ACM Technical Symposium On Computer Science Education.* pp. 637–638 (2013), https://doi.org/10.1145/2445196.2445384
12. Ibe, N., Howsmon, R., Penney, L., Granor, N., DeLyser, L. & Wang, K. Reflections of a Diversity, Equity, and Inclusion Working Group based on Data from a National CS Education Program. *Proceedings Of The 49th ACM Technical Symposium On Computer Science Education.* pp. 711–716 (2018), https://doi.org/10.1145/3159450.3159594
13. Vivian, R., Falkner, K. & Szabo, C. Can everybody learn to code? computer science community perceptions about learning the fundamentals of programming. *Proceedings Of The 14th Koli Calling International Conference On Computing Education Research.* pp. 41–50 (2014), https://doi.org/10.1145/2674683.2674695
14. Polycarpou, I., Andreou, P., Laxer, C. & Kurkovsky, S. Academic-Industry Collaborations: Effective Measures for Successful Engagement. *Proceedings Of The 2017 ACM Conference On Innovation And Technology In Computer Science Education.* pp. 250–251 (2017), https://doi.org/10.1145/3059009.3095098
15. DeClue, T. Computer science in kindergarten? Of course! the ABC'S of the K-12 CSTA model curriculum in computer science. *Journal Of Computing Sciences In Colleges.* **23**, 257–262 (2008)
16. Carter, L. Why students with an apparent aptitude for computer science don't choose to major in computer science. *ACM SIGCSE Bulletin.* **38**, 27–31 (2006)
17. Clarke-Midura, J., Silvis, D., Shumway, J., Lee, V. & Kozlowski, J. Developing a kindergarten computational thinking assessment using evidence-centered design: the case of algorithmic thinking. *Assessing Computational Thinking.* pp. 5–28 (2023)
18. Otterborn, A., Schönborn, K. & Hultén, M. Investigating preschool educators' implementation of computer programming in their teaching practice. *Early Childhood Education Journal.* **48**, 253–262 (2020)

19. Patrick, H., Mantzicopoulos, P. & Samarapungavan, A. Motivation for learning science in kindergarten: Is there a gender gap and does integrated inquiry and literacy instruction make a difference. *Journal Of Research In Science Teaching: The Official Journal Of The National Association For Research In Science Teaching*. **46**, 166–191 (2009)
20. Robinson, A. Unplugged Learning in the Kindergarten Computer Science Classroom. (2022)
21. Tadeu, P. & Brigas, C. Computational thinking in early childhood education: an análisis through the Computer Science Unplugged. (Universidad de Zaragoza, Asociación Universitaria de Formación del ..., 2022)
22. Hufad, A., Faturrohman, M., Rusdiyani, I. & Others Unplugged coding activities for early childhood problem-solving skills. *Jurnal Pendidikan Usia Dini*. **15**, 121–140 (2021)
23. Kim, J., Leftwich, A. & Castner, D. Beyond teaching computational thinking: Exploring kindergarten teachers' computational thinking and computer science curriculum design considerations. *Education And Information Technologies*. pp. 1–37 (2024)
24. Pollard, S. & Duvall, R. Everything I needed to know about teaching I learned in kindergarten: bringing elementary education techniques to undergraduate computer science classes. *ACM SIGCSE Bulletin*. **38**, 224–228 (2006)
25. Kandlhofer, M., Steinbauer, G., Hirschmugl-Gaisch, S. & Huber, P. Artificial intelligence and computer science in education: From kindergarten to university. *2016 IEEE Frontiers In Education Conference (FIE)*. pp. 1–9 (2016)
26. LeMay, S., Costantino, T., O'Connor, S. & ContePitcher, E. Screen time for children. *Proceedings Of The 2014 Conference On Interaction Design And Children*. pp. 217–220 (2014)
27. Huang, W. & Looi, C. A critical review of literature on "unplugged" pedagogies in K-12 computer science and computational thinking education. *Computer Science Education*. **31**, 83–111 (2021)
28. Master, A., Cheryan, S. & Meltzoff, A. Computing whether she belongs: Stereotypes undermine girls' interest and sense of belonging in computer science. *Journal Of Educational Psychology*. **108**, 424 (2016)
29. Margolis, J. & Fisher, A. Unlocking the clubhouse: Women in computing. (MIT Press, 2002)
30. Brennan, K. & Resnick, M. New frameworks for studying and assessing the development of computational thinking. *Proceedings Of The 2012 Annual Meeting Of The American Educational Research Association, Vancouver, Canada*. **1** pp. 25 (2012)
31. Sullivan, A. & Bers, M. Gender differences in kindergarteners' robotics and programming achievement. *International Journal Of Technology And Design Education*. **23** pp. 691–702 (2013)
32. Louka, K. & Papadakis, S. Enhancing computational thinking in early childhood education through ScratchJr integration. *Heliyon*. **10** (2024)
33. Blake-West, J. & Bers, M. ScratchJr design in practice: low floor, high ceiling. *International Journal Of Child-Computer Interaction*. **37**, pp. 100601 (2023)
34. Badillo-Perez, A., Badillo-Perez, D., Coyotzi-Molina, D., Cruz, D., Montenegro, R., Vazquez, L. & Xochicale, M. Piloting Diversity and Inclusion Workshops in Artificial Intelligence and Robotics for Children. *ArXiv Preprint ArXiv:2203.03204*. (2022)
35. Kalogiannakis, M. & Papadakis, S. Preparing Greek Pre-service Kindergarten Teachers to Promote Creativity: Opportunities Using Scratch and Makey Makey. *Children's Creative Inquiry In STEM*. pp. 347–364 (2022)
36. Beilock, S., Gunderson, E., Ramirez, G. & Levine, S. Female teachers' math anxiety affects girls' math achievement. *Proceedings Of The National Academy Of Sciences*. **107**, 1860–1863 (2010)
37. Beilock, S., Gunderson, E., Ramirez, G. & Levine, S. Reply to Plante et al.: Girls' math achievement is related to their female teachers' math anxiety. *Proceedings Of The National Academy Of Sciences*. **107**, E80-E80 (2010)
38. Knupfer, N. Gendered by design. *Educational Technology*. **37**, 31–37 (1997)
39. GÜLÇİÇEK, T. Investigating the effect of gender-neutral activities on preschool children's gender stereotypes. (Middle East Technical University, 2023)

40. Crowley, K., Callanan, M., Tenenbaum, H. & Allen, E. Parents explain more often to boys than to girls during shared scientific thinking. *Psychological Science*. **12**, 258–261 (2001)
41. Hoover-Dempsey, K. & Sandler, H. Parental involvement in children's education: Why does it make a difference?. *Teachers College Record*. **97**, 310–331 (1995)
42. Dabney, K., Tai, R. & Scott, M. Informal science: Family education, experiences, and initial interest in science. *International Journal Of Science Education, Part B*. **6**, 263–282 (2016)
43. Wang, M. & Degol, J. Gender gap in science, technology, engineering, and mathematics (STEM): Current knowledge, implications for practice, policy, and future directions. *Educational Psychology Review*. **29**. pp. 119–140 (2017)
44. Vilner, T. & Zur, E. Once she makes it, she is there: gender differences in computer science study. *Proceedings Of The 11th Annual SIGCSE Conference On Innovation And Technology In Computer Science Education*. pp. 227–231 (2006)
45. Altín, R. Secondary school students' programming and computational thinking skills: traditional and interdisciplinary approaches to teaching programming. (Middle East Technical University, 2021)
46. Altin, R. & Mühling, A. Why Female Students Are Dropping out of CS Programs. *Proceedings Of The 2024 On Innovation And Technology In Computer Science Education V. 1*. pp. 304–310 (2024), https://doi.org/10.1145/3649217.3653635
47. Falkner, K., Sentance, S., Vivian, R., Barksdale, S., Busuttil, L., Cole, E., Liebe, C., Maiorana, F., McGill, M. & Quille, K. An international comparison of k-12 computer science education intended and enacted curricula. *Proceedings Of The 19th Koli Calling International Conference On Computing Education Research*. pp. 1–10 (2019)
48. Goode, J. Increasing diversity in k-12 computer science: Strategies from the field. *Proceedings Of The 39th SIGCSE Technical Symposium On Computer Science Education*. pp. 362–366 (2008)
49. Oleson, A., Xie, B., Salac, J., Everson, J., Kivuva, F. & Ko, A. A Decade of Demographics in Computing Education Research: A Critical Review of Trends in Collection, Reporting, and Use. *Proceedings Of The 2022 ACM Conference On International Computing Education Research-Volume 1*. pp. 323–343 (2022)
50. Sax, L., Newhouse, K., Goode, J., Nakajima, T., Skorodinsky, M. & Sendowski, M. Can computing be diversified on "principles" alone? Exploring the role of AP Computer Science courses in students' major and career intentions. *ACM Transactions On Computing Education (TOCE)*. **22**, 1–26 (2022)
51. Phelps, D. & Santo, R. Student leadership, systems change: Opportunities and tensions for youth impact on district-wide computer science initiatives. *ACM Transactions On Computing Education (TOCE)*. **21**, 1–39 (2021)
52. Prahani, B., Rizki, I., Nisa, K., Citra, N., Alhusni, H. & Wibowo, F. Implementation of online problem-based learning assisted by digital book with 3D animations to improve student's physics problem-solving skills in magnetic field subject. *JOTSE*. **12**, 379–396 (2022)
53. Jua, S. & Others The profile of students' problem-solving skill in physics across interest program in the secondary school. *Journal Of Physics: Conference Series*. **1022**, 012027 (2018)
54. Čujdíková, M. & Jašková, L. Unsolved tasks in the bebras challenge for upper secondary blind pupils. *EDULEARN23 Proceedings*. pp. 1791–1797 (2023)
55. Vachovsky, M., Wu, G., Chaturapruek, S., Russakovsky, O., Sommer, R. & Fei-Fei, L. Toward more gender diversity in CS through an artificial intelligence summer program for high school girls. *Proceedings Of The 47th ACM Technical Symposium On Computing Science Education*. pp. 303–308 (2016)
56. Larsen, E. & Stubbs, M. Increasing diversity in computer science: Acknowledging, yet moving beyond, gender. *Journal Of Women And Minorities In Science And Engineering*. **11** (2005)
57. Wee, C. & Yap, K. Gender diversity in computing and immersive games for computer programming education: a review. *International Journal Of Advanced Computer Science And Applications*. **12** (2021)

58. Cohoon, J., Cohoon, J. & Soffa, M. Focusing high school teachers on attracting diverse students to computer science and engineering. *2011 Frontiers In Education Conference (FIE)*. pp. F2H-1 (2011)
59. Franklin, D. A practical guide to gender diversity for computer science faculty. (Morgan & Claypool Publishers, 2013)
60. Martin, A. & Fisher-Ari, T. "If We Don't Have Diversity, There's No Future to See": High-school students' perceptions of race and gender representation in STEM. *Science Education*. **105**, 1076–1099 (2021)
61. Rose, D. Universal Design for Learning. Journal of Special Education Technology, 15(4), 47–51 (2000)
62. Tapia, A. & Kvasny, L. Recruitment is never enough: Retention of women and minorities in the IT workplace. *Proceedings Of The 2004 SIGMIS Conference On Computer Personnel Research: Careers, Culture, And Ethics In A Networked Environment*. pp. 84–91 (2004)
63. Morris, L. Women in Information Technology Literature Review: Recruitment, Retention and Persistence Factors. (ERIC, 2002)

Open Access This chapter is licensed under the terms of the Creative Commons Attribution 4.0 International License (http://creativecommons.org/licenses/by/4.0/), which permits use, sharing, adaptation, distribution and reproduction in any medium or format, as long as you give appropriate credit to the original author(s) and the source, provide a link to the Creative Commons license and indicate if changes were made.

The images or other third party material in this chapter are included in the chapter's Creative Commons license, unless indicated otherwise in a credit line to the material. If material is not included in the chapter's Creative Commons license and your intended use is not permitted by statutory regulation or exceeds the permitted use, you will need to obtain permission directly from the copyright holder.

Chapter 4
Students' Activities from Elementary to High School

Rukiye Altin, Ozge Mísírlí, Irene Zanardi, Claudia Maria Cutrupi, Sunny K. O. Miranda, Valentina Dagiene, and Monica Landoni

4.1 Personas

This chapter represents recruitment initiatives, which might be useful for different kind of personas. Thus before those initiatives are unfolded, two representatives that might find them useful, a school principal, named imaginatively Alex, and a school teacher, named Jamila, are described below.

R. Altin (✉)
Kiel University, Kiel, Germany
e-mail: ral@informatik.uni-kiel.de

O. Mísírlí
Eskisehir Osmangazi University, Eskisehir, Turkey

I. Zanardi · M. Landoni
Università della Svizzera italiana, Lugano, Switzerland
e-mail: irene.zanardi@usi.ch; monica.landoni@usi.ch

C. M. Cutrupi
Norwegian University of Science and Technology, Trondheim, Norway
e-mail: claudia.m.cutrupi@ntnu.no

S. K. O. Miranda
University of Coimbra, Coimbra, Portugal
e-mail: sunnymiranda@dei.uc.pt

V. Dagiene
Vilnius University, Institute of Data Science and Digital Technologies, Vilnius, Lithuania
e-mail: valentina.dagiene@mif.vu.lt

> **Alex, the school principal.** Looking at the resources in this chapter, Alex the school principal takes the recommendations to their next school board meeting. Some of the teachers are enthusiastic about developing role models in the classroom, others are a bit more sceptical. So Alex starts a group activity where the teachers pair up with a partner, interview each other on what role models they have in their lives, and create role model descriptions for each other.

> **Jamila, school teacher.** Looking at the resources in this chapter, Jamila is a school teacher has passion about STEM and wants to support their students being open to that direction. She needs suggestions about how to raise awareness on gender diversity in computer science so Jamila starts a group activity where the teachers can rainstorm about inspiring activities for students from kindergarten to high school.

4.2 Introduction

In this chapter, We focus on school-based activities. We explain the experience of teaching Informatics in elementary to high schools, whether viewed as a specific or transversal subject and discuss the impact of gender differences on students' and instructors' attitudes toward it.

Recently, primary, middle and high schools have been striving to integrate Informatics into their curricula, recognizing the increasing demand for programming and algorithmic thinking skills in the future job market. Educating students in Informatics from a young age is essential because it naturally enhances various skills, including problem-solving, creative thinking, and algorithmic/computational thinking, thereby preparing students for diverse fields of study and careers. Researchers assert that, given Informatics' potential to become central to a technologically advanced society, every student should have the opportunity to engage with it [73].

Promoting computing education for primary and middle school students involves implementing engaging, age-appropriate activities that stimulate interest and understanding of fundamental computing concepts. Effective education in Informatics requires considering students' learning levels, employing effective pedagogical approaches, and incorporating interdisciplinary, real-life collaborative examples [51, 53].

Despite the increasing incorporation of Informatics in primary and middle schools and its growing popularity in academia, girls remain underrepresented. To achieve gender diversity in Informatics, it is essential to encourage girls from an early age to pursue this field [73]. Certain activities are particularly effective for teaching computer science to girls. These activities are designed not only to convey computer science concepts but also to engage and inspire girls, fostering an inclusive and stimulating learning environment. Effective approaches include hands-on programming and robotics experiences, narrative-driven and project-based learning, game playing and design, interdisciplinary projects, long-term school-based interventions, and strong support systems [73]. We start by reporting on a long-term study that aims to find out what children think a software engineer looks like to better understand children's mental models and the role played by gender. Then, the following section provides suggestions for effective types of activities widely recognised in academic literature organised according to whether these are to be administered in elementary or high school. We present various after-school programs divided according to suitable age, that are available to children to help them understand the possibilities of Informatics in a playful environment. By implementing these interventions in schools, we believe that it is possible to foster a sustained interest in IT among girls and contribute to reducing the gender gap in the IT field, whether it is viewed as a specific or a transversal subject, and we discuss the impact of gender differences in students' and instructors' attitudes toward it. In the last section, we present the various after-school programs

> **! Attention**
>
> In this chapter, we will talk about elementary, middle, and high schools. We are aware that there are national variations in these designations. Here, we are talking about kids in elementary school, who are typically six to eleven years old; middle schoolers, who are typically twelve to fourteen years old; and high schoolers, who are typically fifteen to eighteen years old.

4.3 Draw a Software Engineer

Perhaps because it is not usual to come across a woman computer scientist in college or the workplace, one may wonder what the secret is to the successful career paths of these women. How did they arrive here? And why did they stay when others left? Some have followed a straight path, albeit not without challenges, drawn by personal interest. Others moved into computing after studying and working in other fields, owing to the multidisciplinary nature that technology's ubiquity brings. Regardless of the route taken, self-reliance and perseverance have been critical. In fact, one reason why women do not stay in computing is the difficulties of working in a field perceived as masculine [8, 31, 35, 49]. These challenges have little to do with skills, talents, or predispositions, but rather with the ingrained gendered perception of the field [49]. This perception is distorted by stereotypes and mental models, which are important decision-making items, particularly regarding career choices. Our childhood aspirations heavily influence our interests, and in turn, they are influenced by what we deem to be socially appropriate and rewarding [34]. As a result, when an activity is perceived as masculine, those who do not align with masculine characteristics can almost hear a quiet warning that it is not for them.

Before sharing information about school and after-school activities, we examine children's perceptions of people working in the computing sector to determine which stereotypes exist and when they emerge.

4.3.1 Aspirations and Gender in Children

Among the models that explain how we form aspirations, Gottfredson proposed the theory of circumscription and compromise [34], where they identified socioeconomic status, ability, and gender as constructs of career aspiration. **The perception of job-self compatibility is specifically linked to self-concept and occupational images** (Fig. 4.1). The self-concept is one's perception of who they are, who they want to be, and who they are not. As a result, it is influenced by factors such as social class, intelligence, interests, values, personality, and even one's social standing. More interestingly to the current topic, the self-concept includes one's gender, as in its individual cultural dimension gender influences the beliefs one holds about oneself [61]. Occupational images are generalizations about a profession, such as what the job entails, how prestigious it is, and what personal characteristics are appropriate for the worker. Also in this case, gender plays a role, but this time we have to consider its interactional cultural dimension [61]: gender stereotypes, cognitive biases, and expectations shape our understanding of the world and influence how we conceptualize things.

Let us look at two examples. If we see ourselves as feminine and caring, and we see nurses as feminine-typed and caring, there will be an alignment, resulting in a high perception of job-self compatibility, which will lead to a job preference. If there is a high level of compatibility, low barriers, and abundant opportunities, the occupation is socially acceptable. If we regard the nurse title as prestigious, nursing can become our occupational aspiration. In this case, nursing would be classified as

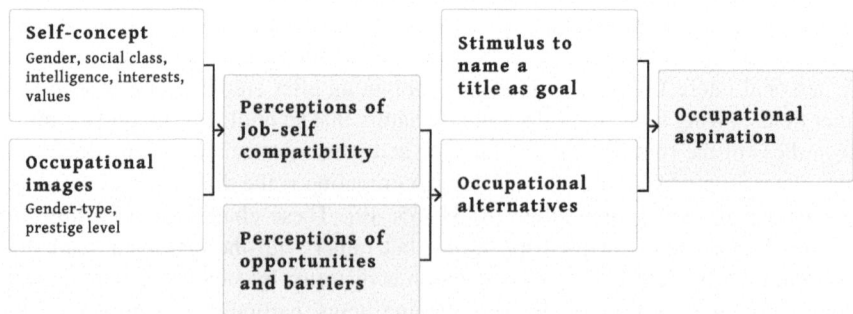

Fig. 4.1 Constructs relations in theory of circumscription and compromise, adapted from [33]

highly feminine and quite prestigious on our cognitive map of occupations, which develops along prestige and gender typing. If we consider computing, the outcome would be different.

> **Important**

For someone to be interested in computing as a possible career field, there must be a correspondence with the characteristics they believe are required for the field: computing is perceived as masculine and thus has masculine characteristics, which may act as a barrier to people with more feminine attributes.

To delve deeper into Gottfredson's theory, the process of circumscription and compromise of aspirations begins in childhood and progresses through four stages. The first three stages focus on excluding unacceptable options (circumscription), while the fourth stage focuses on selecting the most feasible occupations from among the preferred ones (compromise) (Fig. 4.2). The first stage begins in preschool, when children recognize occupations as roles and stop expressing their desire to become animals or fantasy characters. In the second stage, from six to eight years old, children categorize people as good or bad, with this distinction primarily guided by what is appropriate (good) for one's gender. They begin categorizing activities into feminine and masculine categories. This aligns with the timeline proposed by Bem's theory of gender schemata: children hold mental representations about what is feminine and what is not, and perform their gender based on their position on the spectrum [6]. Then, in the third stage, from nine to thirteen, they assess the prestige of the occupation, recognizing that there is a hierarchy in terms of professional status. They have now a variety of potential careers that they will rank in the fourth stage.

Gottfredson's theory of circumscription and compromise makes it easy to see that **gender matters and plays a significant role early on in the process of selecting an aspiration**. Not surprisingly, kids who identify more strongly with one gender tend to have more gender-typical goals [25]. Aspirations can be classified based on gender, depending on whether the job subjects are things or people. By categorizing occupations into people-oriented and things-oriented, we can see that women prefer the first category and men prefer the second [26, 74]. Informatics is considered a

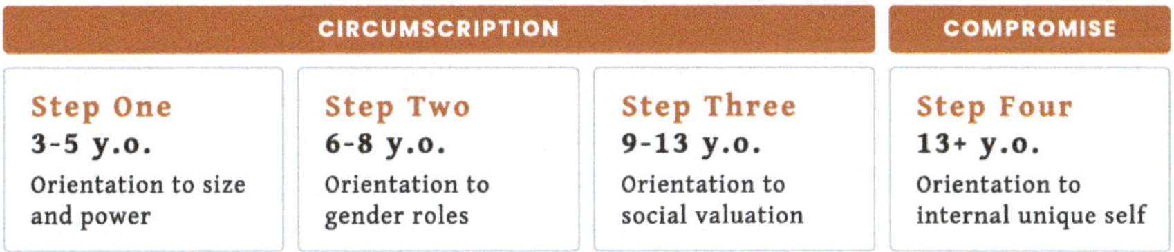

CIRCUMSCRIPTION			COMPROMISE
Step One **3-5 y.o.** Orientation to size and power	**Step Two** **6-8 y.o.** Orientation to gender roles	**Step Three** **9-13 y.o.** Orientation to social valuation	**Step Four** **13+ y.o.** Orientation to internal unique self

Fig. 4.2 Stages of circumscription and compromise on aspirations

things-oriented occupation [37], with no human contact [10], making it look more compatible with boys.

Interestingly, Gottfredson points out that **the narrowing of options must be considered irreversible, because rejected options are not reconsidered spontaneously; rather, children reconsider them only when prompted to do so**. This emphasizes the importance of first understanding the computer scientist's mental models, or occupation images, as defined by Gottfredson, and then taking action to avoid rejecting or reconsidering this career. While there are few actions we can take to improve a person's self-concept, we can change how the field is presented to demonstrate how much variety exists and, as a result, open up to more traditionally feminine characteristics. One way to investigate the occupational image that children hold of a profession is with drawings.

4.3.2 Years of Drawing Occupational Images

Drawings can aid in visualizing children's implicit associations when thinking about a certain thing. In some ways, asking to draw a professional figure gives us insight into that figure's identity: what they look like, what they wear, what they do, and how they do it. Moreover, because we are talking about children, drawing has the advantage of being more accessible and less cognitively demanding than verbal description, which would still require some awareness of the associations.

Drawing as a tool was initially used to investigate the scientist, when Chalmers et al. [17] developed the Draw a Scientist Test (DAST), an art-based tool for gathering images of STEM professionals. Because of its ease of use and flexibility, this tool has been widely used over the years to highlight the presence of stereotypical elements in drawing representations. Given that the task is the same, it is possible to track potential shifts in participants' perceptions as our society changes. Furthermore, the DAST task's ease of translation promotes cross-national research. As a result, it is feasible to compare drawings from various countries and investigate contrasts and similarities that may be influenced by cultural differences [30, 52]. In Informatics, these investigations focused on the computer scientist (DACST), the programmer (DAPT), and the computer user (DACUT) (Fig. 4.3).

We can trace the history of children's perceptions of people in Informatics since 1994 [9] (Fig. 4.4). MacOS Classic and Windows have been around for about ten years, with their innovative graphical user interfaces; Tim Berners-Lee published the first website three years prior, and Mosaic, the first web browser, was released to the public one year earlier. The year 1994 saw an impressive number of developments. The new web browser Netscape popularized the web, which became free of commercial restrictions and increasingly interoperable thanks to the World Wide Web Consortium (W3C), which was founded the same year. Yahoo! and Amazon were founded, and PlayStation appeared to revolutionize videogames, which later became an industry closely linked to boys' programming ambitions. Approximately 20 million people were online [40]. In this exciting time for computing, Barba

Fig. 4.3 Child drawing a software engineer

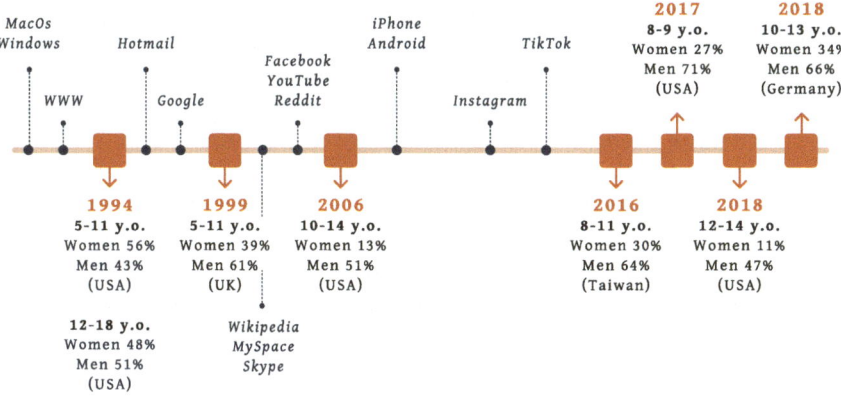

Fig. 4.4 Timeline of depiction of women and men as people working with computers

et al. asked children to draw someone they thought was a computer user. While elementary school children provided no stereotypical representation, from grade 7 onwards, an increasing number of drawings depicted them as a "nerd". According to the teenagers, nerds are thin and pale teenage boys who part their hair in the middle, wear eyeglasses, carry mechanical pencils in their pockets, and dress in oversized clothes and high-waters trousers. Interestingly, elementary school children drew more women as computer users, whereas middle and high school children drew more men.

Five years later, in 1999, Google and Hotmail were already established, Windows had progressed from W95 to W98, Apple had introduced the iMac, Wi-Fi had revolutionized internet connectivity, and Napster had only recently appeared. In just five years, the users grew from 20 million to 280 million [40]. Despite the growing popularity of computers, men did not account for the vast majority of drawings (60%). However, boys were less likely to draw women than girls, with 30% of girls drawing a man and only 4% of boys drawing a woman [11]. This means that computers were perceived as "boys' things" by boys.

By 2006, the biggest web players entered the arena, and the number of online users was over 1 billion [40]. In chronological order, Wikipedia, LinkedIn, MySpace, WordPress, Skype, Facebook, Gmail, YouTube, GoogleMaps, Reddit, and Twitter all made their debuts laying the groundwork for the modern online world. In this context, computer users' occupational images included their gender (men) and eyeglasses. Some individuals exhibited negative social characteristics and abnormal body weight, which are associated with the nerd stereotype [48]. Similarly to the previous study, men are depicted in slightly more than half of all drawings. However, also in this case, boys were less likely to draw a woman (6th grade 10%, 8th grade 3%) than girls a man (6th grade 53%, 8th grade 67%).

Ten years later, online users tripled [40] and too many advancements should be listed. A few notable events include the release of iPhone in 2007 and Android in 2008, the founding of Instagram in 2010, and the launch of TikTok in 2016. In 2016, 1.5 billion smartphones were sold, up from 122 million in 2007 [67]. Between 2016 and 2018, four studies looked into the occupational images of people in computing. In 2016 in Taiwan [16], elementary school children drew people in computer science smiling, wearing glasses, a hat and a tie, and carrying a toolbox. Approximately 73% of computer scientists were men. Similarly, in the USA in 2017 [35], men were depicted more often than women (71%). Fewer stereotypes were present, the main ones were about eyeglasses and baldness. The following year, still in the USA [58], middle school students drew more men than women (80%), depicting them with eyeglasses. At the same time, in Germany, children's perception was the same [12]: more men were depicted and boys were more definitely less likely to draw a woman than girls drawing a man.

There were no significant changes in the depicted gender, though a slight improvement can be seen. Four years after the previous results, and following the 2019 pandemic, we proposed a new study to determine whether anything happened.

4.3.3 How Informatics Is Imagined Now

Through the EUGAIN network, an empirical study was conducted using the Draw-A-Picture method to investigate children's perceptions of software engineering figures [21], called Draw a Software Engineer test (DASET). Specifically, the study aimed to understand how children perceive software engineers and the stereotypical elements in their representations, examining variations based on gender and age.

The investigation was conducted in Milan, Italy, involving 371 elementary school students from diverse socioeconomic and cultural backgrounds. The sample included 192 girls, 166 boys, and 13 children identifying as "other," with an average

age of around 8 years. Participation was voluntary, with parental consent obtained beforehand. The children's gender identification and grade level were recorded, while other information was kept anonymous.

During the activity, children were asked to draw a person working in the software engineering field (Fig. 4.3), ensuring the terminology used did not influence the result. Before starting the activity, the children were asked if they knew what software engineering was, with children associating it with concepts like computers, hackers, videogames, and robots. To maintain engagement, the activity included a storytelling element featuring a human-controlled robot named CYB, which responded to the drawings, providing a rewarding interaction for the children.

The sessions, conducted in groups of 15–20 children, lasted 30 minutes, with clear instructions and measures to avoid peer influence on the results. Children used pencils and markers, and their drawings were analyzed based on a coding scheme developed from existing literature [17]. This scheme included several parameters such as the validity of the drawings, generalities like gender and skin color, appearance (beard, clothes, eyeglasses, etc...), environment, and technical equipment. The coding was performed by three authors and the findings of the study were published in a full paper at ICSE 2023, in Software Engineering in Society track [21].

At first glance, compared to the occupational images depicted in the past, there are no big and exciting differences (Table 4.1). Men appeared slightly more often than women in children's drawings, and the only traditional stereotype was eyeglasses, but in less than a fourth of the cases. We can also add that non-binary children included in the study were aligned with girls and boys. What is interesting, though, is that the depicted gender was balanced for girls, boys, and non-binary children alike. We saw earlier that while around half of the girls used to portray men, boys were extremely skewed and did not draw women. That showed a lack of open-mindedness and a clear typing of programming and computers as exclusively masculine. With the years, it seems that something changed: almost half of the boys drew a woman. Informatics then is less masculine and more egalitarian (Figs. 4.5 and 4.6). The hope is that it is becoming so common and fundamental in our society that it is not a man's prerogative anymore, but everyone should be concerned with it.

Fig. 4.5 Drawing of women in software engineering

Fig. 4.6 Drawing of men in software engineering

The occupational images we collected were analyzed in terms of tools and environment to get a glimpse of the context children imagine for the software engineer (Table 4.1). Usually, the person is at the desk either standing up or sitting on a chair. Rarely there are references to videogames and science and almost no signs of junk food and coffee. Usually, there is a computer or a robot, sometimes a keyboard. Appearance-wise, the software engineer has normal hair and rarely a beard; no acne or other elements against beauty standards, and no geek shirts. In the end, the person who works in computing is not seen as a "nerd" as described in the first study of 1994.

If we look at age differences, we can also observe another interesting detail, even though less encouraging. The older the children were, the more men were depicted (Table 4.1). Not only that, but drawings contained more details: contextual elements were richer. This seems to point out that they got to know better what Informatics was and with that knowledge, they began to associate it with masculinity. This shift, which is still not dramatic, can be especially seen between grades 4 and 5.

4.3.4 How to Apply DASET

As it was mentioned above, one of the interesting characteristics of this type of study is its nature of replication. However, in order to ensure that results from different investigation are comparable, it is necessary to draw replication patterns. In the following, we will present the lessons learned from our research and provide information for those who wish to conduct the same experiment.

The present content was also presented during a workshop with EUGAIN network members and conducted by the authors of the paper [21].

Tips

To avoid reinforcing stereotypes, you can frame the activity as a collaborative effort to assist a robot in learning how to draw. This approach fosters a neutral and inclusive environment, encouraging children to freely express their ideas without regard for gender stereotypes.

Table 4.1 Parameters percentages

Parameter	Other (NB) (n = 13)	Girls (n = 192)	Boys (n = 166)	Total (n = 371)
Man Software Engineer	P = 0.54	P = 0.46	P = 0.56	P = 0.51
Woman Software Engineer	P = 0.46	P = 0.48	P = 0.39	P = 0.44
No gender Software Engineer	P = 0.00	P = 0.06	P = 0.05	P = 0.05
Pink skin	P = 0.54	P = 0.66	P = 0.60	P = 0.63
Brown skin	P = 0.00	P = 0.00	P = 0.00	P = 0.00
Unshaded skin	P = 0.46	P = 0.34	P = 0.40	P = 0.37
White lab coat	P = 0.00	P = 0.04	P = 0.05	P = 0.04
Elegant clothes	P = 0.00	P = 0.02	P = 0.04	P = 0.03
Geek shirt	P = 0.00	P = 0.04	P = 0.02	P = 0.03
Glasses	P = 0.15	P = 0.15	P = 0.19	P = 0.17
Beard	P = 0.08	P = 0.05	P = 0.08	P = 0.06
Acne	P = 0.00	P = 0.00	P = 0.01	P = 0.01
Crazy hair	P = 0.08	P = 0.03	P = 0.03	P = 0.03
Desk	P = 0.69	P = 0.58	P = 0.57	P = 0.58
Chair	P = 0.23	P = 0.29	P = 0.27	P = 0.27
Office chair	P = 0.00	P = 0.04	P = 0.11	P = 0.07
Bookshelf	P = 0.15	P = 0.02	P = 0.02	P = 0.02
Production machine	P = 0.00	P = 0.04	P = 0.06	P = 0.02
Secrecy symbols	P = 0.00	P = 0.03	P = 0.01	P = 0.01
Toys	P = 0.00	P = 0.01	P = 0.02	P = 0.01
Videogames	P = 0.08	P = 0.02	P = 0.06	P = 0.04
Food	P = 0.00	P = 0.01	P = 0.01	P = 0.01
Drinks	P = 0.08	P = 0.03	P = 0.03	P = 0.03
Computer	P = 0.62	P = 0.54	P = 0.52	P = 0.54
Robot	P = 0.31	P = 0.45	P = 0.37	P = 0.41
Earphones	P = 0.08	P = 0.01	P = 0.06	P = 0.03
Keyboard	P = 0.08	P = 0.16	P = 0.16	P = 0.16
Mouse	P = 0.00	P = 0.07	P = 0.07	P = 0.07
Smartphone	P = 0.00	P = 0.07	P = 0.11	P = 0.08
Tablet	P = 0.00	P = 0.02	P = 0.02	P = 0.02
Console	P = 0.00	P = 0.01	P = 0.04	P = 0.02
Controller	P = 0.00	P = 0.05	P = 0.04	P = 0.04
TV	P = 0.08	P = 0.03	P = 0.01	P = 0.02
Laboratory tools	P = 0.00	P = 0.02	P = 0.01	P = 0.01
Mechanic tools	P = 0.08	P = 0.05	P = 0.02	P = 0.04

Specify the Task To start the activity, the researchers need to present the tasks that are essentially required for the activity. At this point, the researchers can ask the group if they know who a software engineer is. We urge not to suggest any kind of association. It is possible that their understanding includes details not pertaining to the software engineer alone. In this case, it is important to take note of it.

Choose a Gender-Neutral Language When delivering the main instruction, it is critical to avoid using gendered language, if present, ensuring that the guidance remains neutral and inclusive.

Plan the Questionnaire Finally, we recommend that the children write a unique code on their drawing paper. This code will also be included in the survey to ensure a connection between their drawing and responses while maintaining anonymity. The team can collect the drawings after 30 minutes. Before accepting the drawing, we recommend that the child report the code. To avoid any potential influence on the children's responses, the survey should be administered after the drawing activity. It is critical that the children be asked to enter the same code that they used for their drawings, as this will help maintain the link between their artwork and survey responses.

4.4 School-Based Activities

Informatics integrated into education should not only cover the fundamentals of computers and programming, but also promote a direct connection with twenty-first-century skills such as problem-solving, algorithmic thinking, creativity, and so on [19, 68].

The literature recommends the following activities as best practices for integrating Informatics into the school curriculum. The specific activities within each topic may vary depending on the curriculum, how teachers implement it, and the student's interests and needs.

Unplugged Activities
Topic: Computational Thinking Concepts, Algorithms
Description: Teaching about Algorithms, Events, Loops [68].
Activities:

1. Students might engage in activities involving sequencing steps to complete a task, such as writing instructions for a partner to follow or creating a flowchart for a simple process (e.g., making a sandwich).
2. Activities could involve identifying cause-and-effect relationships, simulating event-driven actions (e.g., clapping hands to trigger a specific response), or creating simple "if-then" scenarios.
3. Students might participate in activities that involve repeating instructions, such as creating a dance routine with repeating movements or simulating a loop using physical objects.

Visual Programming with Block-Based Languages

Topic: Programming, Problem-solving, Creativity

Description: Programming languages like Scratch and Blockly are highly recommended for girls as they offer a visual and intuitive introduction to programming. These tools remove the complexity of syntax, allowing students to focus on logic and design.

Activities:

1. Storytelling and Animation—Girls often show interest in narratives and stories. Tools that allow the creation of interactive stories or animations, such as Alice or Scratch, are effective for teaching programming concepts for girls [41, 51].
2. Creating interactive stories, animations, or games using visual programming blocks. This could involve designing characters and backgrounds and programming character movements, interactions, and dialogue.

Educational Robotics

Topic: Computational thinking, Programming, Robotics, Problem-solving, Creativity.

Description: Robotics can effectively introduce CS concepts to elementary school students and foster engagement with STEM [29]. The robotics programming course significantly improved computational thinking and creativity in students [56]. Girls demonstrated a significantly more significant improvement in creativity [56] and performed slightly better than boys in combining CS concepts during robot programming [51]. Students learn programming concepts by designing, building, and programming robots to perform specific tasks. Kits like LEGO Mindstorms, Bee-Bots, Arduino, Micro:bit, Makey Makey are popular choices.

Activities:

1. Use Scratch programming to control electronic components such as Arduino, Micro:bit, Makey Makey to create interactive projects that respond to physical inputs [36]. This could involve using everyday objects (e.g., fruits, toys) as conductive materials to control Scratch programs.
2. Use block-based language to teach basic programming concepts while students explore robot functionalities [56].
3. Use a multilanguage robot programming platform for students to discover new CS concepts [51].

Presenting Role Models
Topic: Women Encouragement and Inspiration, Fight Bias and Stereotypes.
Description: Exposing girls to women role models in computer science can significantly increase their interest and confidence in this field, besides awakening new perceptions of STEM careers and professionals [4].
Activities:

1. Promote activities to expose students to women STEM professionals and their work [13] This can be accomplished by showing videos, films or the presence of women STEM professionals at the school.
2. Create a booklet that features women role models and their innovative work in Computer Science. The creation of booklets gives visibility to women role models in Computer Science and makes girls feel inspired and motivated [5]CS4FN, 2024.

Serious Games
Topic: Fight Bias and Stereotypes, Problem-solving.
Description: Girls prefer gender-oriented play. Using women models in games triggers greater interest among girls in technical subjects [2].
Activity: Promote serious games with women protagonists and women role models in games to teach school subjects.

Integrated Curriculum Project Using Project-Based Learning (PBL) Activities
Topic: STEAM Area Awareness, Computational Thinking, Problem-solving.
Description: Collaborative projects that integrate computer science with other topics effectively engage girls. The project-based learning approach allows students to see computer science's practical and multidisciplinary relevance. This encourages students to use digital skills while learning, increasing the motivation of students to STEAM area [19].
Activities:

1. Math and Coding: Using programming to solve maths problems.
2. Science Experiments: Using sensors and programming to collect and analyse data.
3. The ICT-integrated English lessons and activities are prepared and conducted to prepare the students for real-life experiences.

(continued)

4. Promote a collaborative STEAM activity event yearly. The school can ask teachers from different departments related to the STEAM area to prepare an event together. It can be planned as a competition [15].
5. Developing an app or website related to a personal or social theme, such as sustainability or health.

Game-Based Learning
Topic: Logical thinking, Problem-solving, Programming.
Description: Educational games that teach programming concepts fun and engagingly have been shown to be effective for girls [71].
Activities:

1. Solving programming puzzles in Lightbot.
2. Promote challenges using Code.org resources.

Involve the Parents
Topic: Parental support, Awareness, Encouragement.
Description: Engaging parents as advocates for computer science can be highly beneficial. By informing parents about the opportunities and importance of computing, and demonstrating how it can empower their children, we can encourage them to support their daughters' exploration of this field [45, 63].
Activity: The school can proactively engage girls and their parents through informative sessions and other activities. Including parents in activities, workshops, or information sessions related to computer science can inspire them to become active participants in their children's learning journey and encourage their daughters to consider Informatics a viable and exciting career path.

Collaborative Learning Environments
Topic: Programming, Problem-solving, Collaboration, Teamwork.
Description: Activities that promote collaboration and teamwork are particularly effective for girls, as they create a supportive and encouraging environment [7].

(continued)

Activities (Examples):

1. Pair Programming: Students work in pairs, taking turns writing code and providing feedback to each other.
2. Peer Feedback Activities: Students share their projects with classmates, providing constructive criticism and suggestions for improvement.

Inquiry-Based Activities
Topic: Problem-solving.
Description: Providing students with opportunities to engage in hands-on, inquiry-based activities that reflect real-world STEM applications is crucial for sparking interest [13].
Activities (Examples):

1. Create a Tourism Information System.
   - *Subtopic:* Programming, Information Systems, Time Management.
   - *Description:* Students developed a tourism information system using Micro:bit to help tourists plan their trips. They learned about coding, data display, and calculating travel times.
2. VR Panorama.
   - *Subtopic:* Virtual Reality, Tourism Promotion, Design Thinking.
   - *Description:* Students created VR panoramas using Google Cardboard to showcase Hong Kong tourist attractions. They explored VR technology and its application in tourism marketing.
3. Micro:bit Flood Warning System
   - *Subtopic:* Sensor Technology, Flood Warning Systems, Engineering Design.
   - *Description:* Students designed and built a flood warning system using Micro:bit or Mbot to simulate real-world applications. They learned about sensor technology, programming, and designing solutions for environmental challenges.

4.4.1 Coding with XLogo in Elementary Schools in Ticino

Getting a better understanding of how children perceive a software engineer is a great starting point when planning how to help them be more aware of implicit stereotypes and their influence of future job and study careers. Besides, when running the DASET study described above it emerged also that children did not really have a clear idea of what a software engineer did and this is a good argument to advocate for early intervention when it comes to introduce elements of Informatics to elementary school children. Here we describe an ongoing effort in Ticino, one of Switzerland cantons, where elementary school teachers, university professors and students of Informatics have come together to provide children a taste of coding. Started in 2022, the initiative has involved three schools and five different classes in primary 3, 4, and 5, engaging children in a 10/8 weeks long introduction to coding with XLogo, via an online platform and the related paper textbook [39]. The textbook is divided into 4 chapters that cover 3 essential topics of programming:

1. Writing codes to define and control computer's operations.
2. Using parameters, cycles, and conditional functions for the development and implementation of real programs.
3. Introduction to modular programming to solve problems in a structured and comprehensive method.

Each chapter has a brief theoretical explanation and practical examples of the new concepts and commands introduced, it offers numerous exercises for the reader to practice and explore. The exercises do not give out the code, just the expected visual output. This allows the reader to experience and explore the "Trial and Error" method, very common in programming fields, that is considered fundamental in developing problem-solving skills. The result of each exercise consists of a drawing that can represent just a straight line, a polygon, a circle, or a combination of all of them that can reproduce a common object such as stairs, a country's flag, or a humanoid face. The textbook is using the programming environment XLogo which is based on the educational programming language Logo, which first appeared back in 1967 and is now at the core of many programming languages developed for children.

In our initiative, after consulting also with the school teacher, we decided to use interactive teaching methods to teach programming as a natural way to involve children and make the subject fun. Overall, the purpose of a command is to make a turtle move in a certain direction and in doing so tracing a line that would compose a drawing, simple as a square in the beginning to become more complex while acquiring more commands. Commands are quite intuitive with simple syntax for children to follow. Also, the textbook is introducing each command one by one and allows the users to get confident with one command before moving to the next one.

The teaching team was composed by university professors, PhD, Master and bachelor students according to availability so that plenty of technical support was available when needed.

Children were working in pairs, organised by their teachers, sharing one laptop, and consulting their copy of the textbook. Each of the chapters of the textbook was divided in two parts to be administered separately, and each lesson would start with a recap. The teacher would act as facilitator and made sure children were comfortable and stayed focused. Each lesson lasted two teaching units, of 45 plus 45 minutes, with children too engrossed in the activity to give up their afternoon break and ask for exercises to take home. One child also asked her parents to move her regular doctor appointment to a different slot not to miss the lesson.

By gathering feedback from children and teachers, via interviews, open discussion, written assessments and direct observations, during this three years, we could appreciate how introducing coding via Xlogo in a hand-on fashion, provided a fun and engaging activity. Having the possibility to work in a classroom weekly for 8–10 weeks, let us observe changes in children's attitude but even after the novelty effect waived off, enthusiasm was always very high. Even reluctant participants got involved and enjoyed the experience of learning by doing. Girls were a bit more cautious in the beginning as less used to the tinkering paradigm adopted naturally by boys, but with a little extra encouragement, soon became very keen and proficient. Boys were more likely to go for the fun and even if in each class we made sure the textbook was read aloud and each new command explained by the tutor, boys liked best to experiment on their own, proud to share their drawings specially when different than the one mentioned in the textbooks. Quite on the opposite, girls would take pride when achieving exactly what the textbook exercise required, and would be careful to follow the sequence of activities proposed in the class. Teachers expressed their satisfaction too, with one commenting on how one of the "intellectual girls" in the classroom, spending her spare time during school break reading books, got captured by the simple exercises and enjoyed them too. Another teacher remarked on how a girl in her class had made great progress in mathematics once she got enticed with Xlogo. We also noticed how independent children grew in using both textbook and the programming environment as soon after the second meeting instead of asking for help, when raising their hands they were showing off their achievements. Our hope is that when growing up these children, and in particular the girls in these classes, will keep fond memories of their first encounter with Informatics, by associating it with a rewarding challenge they proved able to take on and achieve.

4.5 After School Activities

After-school computer science activities, ranging from elementary to high school, play an important role in addressing imbalance in Informatics because these activities provide early exposure, foster interest, and build confidence among girl students, which are essential for increasing gender diversity in computer science. According to Mouza et al. [54], CS knowledge is increasing with the after-school programs because students do not see it as assignments but practice it for fun. Early exposure to Informatics concepts is crucial for developing sustained interest and confidence in the subject, particularly among girls. Research has shown that integrating playful learning activities in after-school programs can effectively engage young students [23, 57, 72]. No One Left Behind (NOLB) Project is developed to involve young girls in programming and project results show that after-school coding courses had a significant impact on girl students' engagement and made them feel comfortable towards computer science [66]. Such projects can inspire students to engage more with computer science. Therefore, collaborations with the initiatives and including more projects are needed to encourage young girls to be in the computer science field just like how boys are doing. **After-school programs in elementary schools** are suggested as creating a playful learning environment, bringing role models in class to create a communication area for students and engaging competitions in the activities [47, 60, 62]. The following suggestions show how to include Informatics in after-school programs for the elementary school level to help gender balance in Informatics.

1. **Playful Learning Environment**: Game-based learning can make computer science fun and engaging for young students. Integrating educational games that teach Informatics to high school students boosts learning motivation and improves students' problem-solving, programming and critical-thinking skills [43]. Such activities make students more comfortable towards Informatics. For instance, Code.org activities can be integrated in after-school activities which offer a variety of coding games that incorporate popular themes and characters from movies and cartoons [1, 44, 46].
2. **Role Models in Class**: Having women role models in the classroom who have careers in Informatics can inspire young girls and show them that they belong in the field. Providing access to women role models and mentors in after-school activities can have a valuable impact on young girls' perception of computer science because the presence of women who are successful in the field can inspire and motivate students. According to Chen et al. [18], role models have an impact on students' career choices, so bringing women role models into the classroom at an early age can help remove the stereotype that Informatics is a men-dominated field. Cooperation with organizations or initiatives can be included in after-school activities to bring in women engineers and computer scientists to share their experiences and mentor students.
3. **Competitions**: Creating inclusive and supportive environments, these programs help to normalize the idea that Informatics is for everyone, regardless of gender. Therefore, competitions with the level of elementary schools can be included in the programs. Jr FLL: Junior FIRST LEGO League can be held to inspire students. FIRST® LEGO® League introduces children ages 4–16 to science, technology, engineering and maths (STEM) in an engaging and fun way that promotes hands-on learning experiences [55]. Through a dynamic global robotics programme, participants develop real-world problem-solving skills, helping students and educators work together for a better future. These competitions require students to work in teams to design, build, and program robots to complete specific tasks [70]. Research has shown that participation in robotics competitions can positively impact girls' perceptions of their abilities in STEM fields [55, 70].

After-school programs in high schools is important for shifting from simple, visual programming to text-based programming with written algorithms. At this stage, students begin to learn problem-solving in maths and science classes more seriously than in elementary school. After-school Informatics related activities offer several advantages over traditional classroom instruction. These programs are often more flexible, allowing for creative and hands-on learning experiences that can be tailored to the interests and needs of the students. Additionally, after-school programs can provide a more inclusive and supportive environment, which is particularly important for girls who may feel marginalized or discouraged in a men-dominated classroom [57]. A strategy should be developed in middle and high schools' after-school programs to promote gender diversity because by providing an engaging environment, these programs can encourage more girls to pursue Informatics, thereby helping to close the gender gap in this critical field [59, 64]. The following suggestions show how to include computer science in after-school programs for the elementary school level to help gender balance in Informatics.

1. **Hands-On Projects and Competitions**: Organizing coding clubs and hackathons that focus on collaborative projects rather than individual competition can raise the eagerness of students towards Informatics. This can reduce the intimidation factor and encourage participation from all students. Project-based learning (PBL) is an educational approach that involves students in complex, real-world projects through which they develop and apply skills and knowledge. PBL can be integrated into after-school programs to engage students because it increases students' motivation as a hands-on project [42]. Students can prototype an application that addresses real-world problems and works on the topic they are passionate about. Also, robotics activities can be included as an exciting way for students to apply their programming skills. Robotics projects often involve teamwork and problem-solving, which can be particularly appealing and empowering for female students[50]. Different competitions can be involved such as FLL: FIRST LEGO League can be held Bebras Challenges are organised. FLL is an international robotics competition that addresses students from 9 to 16 years old which takes place in lots of countries [27]. Usart et al. [69] indicates FLL increases students' problem solving skills which enables them to have twenty-first century skills naturally. On the other hand, competitions like Bebras, which is an international challenge in Informatics running for elementary and middle school students, increases students' motivations towards computer science [24].

After-school programs in high schools is important because despite ongoing efforts to address this issue, the disparity remains, particularly in high school education where foundational interests and skills are developed. To increase the awareness about Informatics for all genders, after-school programs present a valuable opportunity to engage girl students, fostering a diverse and inclusive environment that can lead to greater gender equity in the tech industry [32, 38]. To understand why there are fewer girl students in Informatics, researchers mainly look at high school education. They found that girls often feel uncomfortable with

Informatics in high school due to limited access to programming, a men-focused curriculum with abstract programming concepts, lack of real-world applications, and both subtle and obvious stereotypes from school staff [28]. The activities listed below are considered the best ways to incorporate Informatics into the high school after-school programs. The aim is to show that Informatics is more than just computers or coding by integrating it into all subjects, which can help change the "geek" stereotype of men role models for girl students.

1. **Providing Mentorship and Role Models**: Mentorship programs can play a significant role in encouraging girls to pursue computer science. Women mentors and role models can inspire students by sharing their experiences and providing guidance [22]. After-school programs can facilitate mentorship through guest speakers, workshops, and one-on-one mentoring sessions.
2. **Real-World Opportunities**: Connecting Informatics concepts to real-world applications can make the subject more appealing to female students [3]. Schools can collaborate with the initiatives to have projects after-schools with the students where students can work with a real client to see how Informatics is in the real world. Also, after-school programs can include activities such as field trips to tech companies, virtual tours, and guest lectures from industry professionals [14, 20]. These experiences can help students see the relevance of Informatics in various fields and inspire them to explore further.
3. **Promoting the Competition**: Effective promotion of competitions is vital in attracting students to after-school computer science programs [50]. This can be achieved through school announcements, flyers, social media, and events. Highlighting the benefits of participation, such as skill development, college preparation, and career opportunities, can motivate students and their families to get involved. Student teams for FRC: FIRST Robotics Competitions and WRO: The World Robot Olympiad can be formed to encourage more students. Also, science fair, hackathons per term can be organized to facilitate increased internet usage and technologies. Families can be involved during the process of competitions because involving parents and community members, such as coding nights, exhibitions, and competitions can raise awareness about the importance of gender diversity in Informatics and garner support for students' participation [65].

Promoting gender diversity in Informatics through after-school activities from elementary to high school is a multifaceted approach that requires commitment, collaboration, and creativity. Schools should work not only with teachers but with initiatives, parents and local committed to raise more awareness about the gender balance issue in computer science. By creating inclusive curricula, providing mentorship, fostering hands-on learning, addressing stereotypes, and involving families and communities, K-12 schools can create a supportive environment that encourages girl students to pursue Informatics. Successful implementation of these programs can lead to a more diverse and innovative tech industry, benefiting society as a whole.

4.6 Open Questions

In this chapter we started from elaborating on children's perception of Informatics as a profession and highlighted the presence of stereotypes at an early age. We then build on those insights, that were providing us with a better understanding of children's mental models, to ground a strong motivation for supporting the introduction of activities to engage girls with Informatics at school and after-school. Open questions stay on how to measure the effects of these activities and their effectiveness not only in terms of career choices but perhaps more importantly towards the overall objective of fighting against the obstacles that girls and women away from Informatics. For that we need to further explore the role played by the culture and society that are heavily influencing career choices of both boys and girls. Therefore, open questions stay on how families and educators as well as policy makers could better support and encourage girls in their choices. Next chapters will further elaborate on these open questions and add more, while providing evidences and pointing to relevant research directions.

References

1. Eunice Agyei. How to design activities for learning computational thinking in the context of early primary school in an after-school code club. Master's thesis, E. Agyei, 2019.
2. S. AlSulaiman and M. S. Horn. Peter the fashionista? computer programming games and gender-oriented cultural forms. In *CHI PLAY 2015 - Proceedings of the 2015 Annual Symposium on Computer-Human Interaction in Play*, pages 185–196. ACM, 2015.
3. Rukiye Altin and Andreas Mühling. Why female students are dropping out of cs programs. In *Proceedings of the 2024 on Innovation and Technology in Computer Science Education V. 1*, pages 304–310. 2024.
4. F. K. Bailie. Women who make a difference: Role models for the 21st century. *ACM Inroads*, 6(2):63–67, 2011.
5. J. Black, P. Curzon, C. Myketiak, and P. W. McOwan. A study in engaging female students in computer science using role models. In *Proceedings of the 16th annual joint conference on Innovation and technology in computer science education*, pages 63–67. ACM, 2011.
6. Sandra Lipsitz Bem. Gender schema theory and its implications for child development: Raising gender-aschematic children in a gender-schematic society. *Signs*, 8(4):598–616, 1983.
7. P. S. Buffum, M. Frankosky, K. E. Boyer, E. N. Wiebe, B. W. Mott, and J. C. Lester. Collaboration and gender equity in game-based learning for middle school computer science. *Computing in Science & Engineering*, 18(2):18–28, 2016.
8. Anne-Jorunn Berg and Merete Lie. Feminism and constructivism: Do artifacts have gender? *Science, Technology, & Human Values*, 20(3):332–351, 1995.
9. Robertta H Barba and Cheryl L Mason. The emergence of the "nerd" an assessment of children's attitudes toward computer technologies. *Journal of Research on Computing in Education*, 26(3):382–390, 1994.
10. Valeria Borsotti. Barriers to gender diversity in software development education: actionable insights from a danish case study. In *Proceedings of the 40th International Conference on Software Engineering: Software Engineering Education and Training (ICSE-SEET)*, pages 146–152. ACM/IEEE, 2018.

11. Mark Jeremy Brosnan. A new methodology, an old story? gender differences in the "draw-a-computer-user" test. *European Journal of Psychology of Education*, 14(3):375–385, 1999.
12. Philipp Brauner, Martina Ziefle, Ulrik Schroeder, Thiemo Leonhardt, Nadine Bergner, and Birgit Ziegler. Gender influences on school students' mental models of computer science: a quantitative rich picture analysis with sixth graders. In *Proceedings of the 4th Conference on Gender & IT*, pages 113–122, 2018.
13. Yu Chen, Stephen Cheuk Fai Chow, and Winnie Wing Mui So. School-stem professional collaboration to diversify stereotypes and increase interest in stem careers among primary school students. *Asia Pacific Journal of Education*, 42(3):556–573, 2022.
14. Sapna Cheryan, Benjamin J Drury, and Marissa Vichayapai. Enduring influence of stereotypical computer science role models on women's academic aspirations. *Psychology of women quarterly*, 37(1):72–79, 2013.
15. J. Century, K.A. Ferris, and H. Zuo. Finding time for computer science in the elementary school day: a quasi-experimental study of a transdisciplinary problem-based learning approach. *IJ STEM Ed*, 7(20):–, 2020.
16. Ching-Ching Cheng and Kuo-Hung Huang. Stereotypes and technology education: Different perceptions of computer career among elementary school students. *Journal of Baltic Science Education*, 15(3):271–283, 2016.
17. David Wade Chambers. Stereotypic images of the scientist: The draw-a-scientist test. *Science education*, 67(2):255–265, 1983.
18. Chen Chen, Jonathan Rothwell, and Pedrito Maynard-Zhang. In-school and/or out-of-school computer science learning influence on cs career interests, mediated by having role-models. *Computer Science Education*, pages 1–25, 2023.
19. Jord. Clarke, Deborah Silvis, Jessica F. Shumway, Victor R. Lee, and Joseph S. Kozlowski. *Assessing Computational Thinking*, chapter Developing a kindergarten computational thinking assessment using evidence-centered design: the case of algorithmic thinking. Routledge, 2023.
20. Sapna Cheryan, John Oliver Siy, Marissa Vichayapai, Benjamin J Drury, and Saenam Kim. Do female and male role models who embody stem stereotypes hinder women's anticipated success in stem? *Social psychological and personality science*, 2(6):656–664, 2011.
21. Claudia Maria Cutrupi, Irene Zanardi, Letizia Jaccheri, and Monica Landoni. Draw a software engineer test-an investigation into children's perceptions of software engineering profession. In *2023 IEEE/ACM 45th International Conference on Software Engineering: Software Engineering in Society (ICSE-SEIS)*, pages 37–47. IEEE, 2023.
22. Wendy DuBow, Alexis Kaminsky, and Joanna Weidler-Lewis. Multiple factors converge to influence women's persistence in computing: A qualitative analysis. *Computing in Science & Engineering*, 19(3):30–39, 2017.
23. Jill Denner, Jacob Martinez, Julie Adams, and Heather Thiry. Computer science and fairness: Integrating a social justice perspective into an after school program. *Science Education and Civic Engagement*, 6(2):49–62, 2015.
24. Valentina Dagienė and Sue Sentance. It's computational thinking! bebras tasks in the curriculum. In *Informatics in Schools: Improvement of Informatics Knowledge and Perception: 9th International Conference on Informatics in Schools: Situation, Evolution, and Perspectives, ISSEP 2016, Münster, Germany, October 13–15, 2016, Proceedings 9*, pages 28–39. Springer, 2016.
25. Joice J. Endendijk and Christel M. Portengen. Children's views about their future career and family involvement: Associations with children's gender schemas and parents' involvement in work and family roles. *Frontiers in Psychology*, 2022.
26. Organisation for Economic Co-operation and Development. *Why Do More Young Women Than Men Go on to Tertiary Education?* OECD Publishing, 2021.
27. https://www.firstinspires.org/. FIRST Lego League
28. Allan Fisher and Jane Margolis. Unlocking the clubhouse: the carnegie mellon experience. 34(2), 2002.

29. Yesharim Mor Friebroon and Ben-Ari Mordechai. Teaching computer science concepts through robotics to elementary school children. *International Journal of Computer Science Education in Schools*, 2(3):–, 2018.
30. Donna Farland-Smith. How does culture shape students' perceptions of scientists? cross-national comparative study of american and chinese elementary students. *Journal of Elementary Science Education*, 21(4):23–42, 2009.
31. Sarah Fox, Rachel Rose Ulgado, and Daniela Rosner. Hacking culture, not devices: Access and recognition in feminist hackerspaces. In *Proceedings of the 18th ACM conference on Computer supported cooperative work & social computing*, pages 56–68, 2015.
32. Joanna Goode. Increasing diversity in k-12 computer science: strategies from the field. In *Proceedings of the 39th SIGCSE Technical Symposium on Computer Science Education*, SIGCSE '08, page 362–366, New York, NY, USA, 2008. Association for Computing Machinery.
33. Linda S Gottfredson. Circumscription and compromise: A developmental theory of occupational aspirations. *Journal of Counseling psychology*, 28(6):545, 1981.
34. Linda S. Gottfredson. *Gottfredson's theory of circumscription, compromise, and self-creation*, chapter 4, pages 85–148. Jossey-Bass, 2002.
35. Alexandria K Hansen, Hilary A Dwyer, Ashley Iveland, Mia Talesfore, Lacy Wright, Danielle B Harlow, and Diana Franklin. Assessing children's understanding of the work of computer scientists: The draw-a-computer-scientist test. In *Proceedings of the 2017 ACM SIGCSE technical symposium on computer science education*, pages 279–284, 2017.
36. H. S. Hsiao, Y. W. Lin, K. Y. Lin, C. Y. Lin, J. H. Chen, and J. C. Chen. Using robot-based practices to develop an activity that incorporated the 6e model to improve elementary school students' learning performances. *Interactive Learning Environments*, 30(1):85–99, 2019.
37. John L Holland. *Making vocational choices: A theory of vocational personalities and work environments*. Psychological Assessment Resources, 1997.
38. Hoffman, B., Morelli, R. & Rosato, J. Student Engagement is Key to Broadening Participation in CS. *Proceedings Of The 50th ACM Technical Symposium On Computer Science Education*. pp. 1123–1129 (2019), https://doi.org/10.1145/3287324.3287438
39. Juraj Hromkovic. *Semplicemente Informatica*. Klett und Balmer AG, Baar, 2018.
40. Our World in Data. Number of people using the internet, 2022.
41. Sharin Rawhiya Jacob, Miranda C. Parker, and Mark Warschauer. *Integration of computational thinking into English language arts*, page 55–63. Association for Computing Machinery, New York, NY, USA, 2022.
42. Dimitra Kokotsaki, Victoria Menzies, and Andy Wiggins. Project-based learning: A review of the literature. *Improving schools*, 19(3):267–277, 2016.
43. Bolganay Kaldarova, Bakhytzhan Omarov, Lyazzat Zhaidakbayeva, Abay Tursynbayev, Gulbakhram Beissenova, Bolat Kurmanbayev, and Almas Anarbayev. Applying game-based learning to a primary school class in computer science terminology learning. In *Frontiers in Education*, volume 8, page 1100275. Frontiers Media SA, 2023.
44. Christopher Levy. *Elementary teacher professional development for computer science and digital game-based learning*. PhD thesis, Concordia University (Oregon), 2019.
45. Adam Lloyd, Jennifer Gore, Kathryn Holmes, Max Smith, and Leanne Fray. Parental influences on those seeking a career in stem: The primacy of gender. *International Journal of Gender, Science and Technology*, 10(2):308–328, 2018.
46. Dragan Lambić, Biljana orić, and Saša Ivakić. Investigating the effect of the use of code.org on younger elementary school students' attitudes towards programming. *Behaviour & Information Technology*, 40(16):1784–1795, 2021.
47. José Miguel Merino-Armero, José Antonio González-Calero, and Ramón Cózar-Gutiérrez. The effect of after-school extracurricular robotic classes on elementary students' computational thinking. *Interactive Learning Environments*, 31(6):3939–3950, 2023.
48. Emma M Mercier, Brigid Barron, and KM O'connor. Images of self and others as computer users: The role of gender and experience. *Journal of computer assisted learning*, 22(5):335–348, 2006.

49. Allison Master, Sapna Cheryan, and Andrew N Meltzoff. Computing whether she belongs: Stereotypes undermine girls' interest and sense of belonging in computer science. *Journal of educational psychology*, 108(3):424, 2016.
50. Allison Master, Sapna Cheryan, Adriana Moscatelli, and Andrew N Meltzoff. Programming experience promotes higher stem motivation among first-grade girls. *Journal of experimental child psychology*, 160:92–106, 2017.
51. M. Martínez, M. Gomez, and Benotti. A comparison of preschool and elementary school children learning computer science concepts through a multilanguage robot programming platform. In *Proceedings of the 2015 ACM Conference on Innovation and Technology in Computer Science Education*, pages 159–164. ACM, 2015.
52. Florence F McCann, Edmund A Marek, et al. Achieving diversity in stem: The role of drawing-based instruments. *Creative Education*, 7(15):2293, 2016.
53. J. MWang and Hejazi Moghadam. Diversity barriers in k-12 computer science education: Structural and social. In *Proceedings of the 2017 ACM SIGCSE technical symposium on computer science education*, pages 615–620. ACM, 2017.
54. Chrystalla Mouza, Alison Marzocchi, Yi-Cheng Pan, and Lori Pollock. Development, implementation, and outcomes of an equitable computer science after-school program: Findings from middle-school students. *Journal of Research on Technology in Education*, 48(2):84–104, 2016.
55. Yuxin Ma and Douglas C Williams. The potential of a first lego league robotics program in teaching 21st century skills: An exploratory study. *Journal of Educational Technology Development and Exchange (JETDE)*, 6(2):2, 2013.
56. J. Noh and J. Lee. Effects of robotics programming on the computational thinking and creativity of elementary school students. *Educational Technology Research and Development*, 68:463–484, 2020.
57. Tom Neutens and Francis Wyffels. Bringing computer science education to secondary school: A teacher first approach. In *Proceedings of the 49th ACM technical symposium on computer science education*, pages 840–845, 2018.
58. Katarina Pantic, Jody Clarke-Midura, Frederick Poole, Jared Roller, and Vicki Allan. Drawing a computer scientist: stereotypical representations or lack of awareness? *Computer Science Education*, 28(3):232–254, 2018.
59. Viera K Proulx. Computer science in elementary and secondary schools. In *Informatics and Changes in Learning*, pages 95–101, 1993.
60. Kiki Prottsman. Computer science for the elementary classroom. *ACM Inroads*, 5(4):60–63, 2014.
61. Barbara J. Risman. *Gender as a Social Structure*, pages 19–43. Springer International Publishing, Cham, 2018.
62. Alpaslan Sahin, Mehmet C Ayar, and Tufan Adiguzel. Stem related after-school program activities and associated outcomes on student learning. *Educational Sciences: Theory and Practice*, 14(1):309–322, 2014.
63. Mara Šimunović and Toni Babarović. The role of parental socializing behaviors in two domains of student stem career interest. *Research in Science Education*, 51(4):1055–1071, 2021.
64. Sue Sentance, Mark Dorling, and Adam McNicol. Computer science in secondary schools in the uk: Ways to empower teachers. In *Informatics in Schools. Sustainable Informatics Education for Pupils of all Ages: 6th International Conference on Informatics in Schools: Situation, Evolution, and Perspectives, ISSEP 2013, Oldenburg, Germany, February 26–March 2, 2013. Proceedings 6*, pages 15–30. Springer, 2013.
65. Linda J Sax, M Allison Kanny, Tiffani A Riggers-Piehl, Hannah Whang, and Laura N Paulson. "but i'm not good at math": The changing salience of mathematical self-concept in shaping women's and men's stem aspirations. *Research in Higher Education*, 56:813–842, 2015.
66. Bernadette Spieler and Wolfgang Slany. Female teenagers and coding: Create gender sensitive and creative learning environments. *arXiv preprint arXiv:1805.04366*, 2018.
67. Statista. Number of smartphones sold to end users worldwide from 2007 to 2023, 2024.

68. D. Scott, A. Zou, S. R. Jacob, D. Richardson, and M. Warschauer. Comparing boys' and girls' attitudes toward computer science. *Journal of Computer Science Integration*, 6(1):1–17, 2023.
69. Mireia Usart, Despoina Schina, Vanessa Esteve-Gonzalez, and Mercè Gisbert. Are 21st century skills evaluated in robotics competitions? the case of first lego league competition. In *CSEDU (1)*, pages 445–452, 2019.
70. Terri E Varnado. *The effects of a technological problem solving activity on FIRST™LEGO™League participants' problem solving style and performance*. PhD thesis, Virginia Polytechnic Institute and State University, 2005.
71. Maja Videnovik, Tone Vold, Linda Kiønig, Ana Madevska Bogdanova, and Vladimir Trajkovik. Game-based learning in computer science education: a scoping literature review. *IJ STEM Ed*, 10(54):–, 2023.
72. Timothy J Weston, Wendy M Dubow, and Alexis Kaminsky. Predicting women's persistence in computer science-and technology-related majors from high school to college. *ACM Transactions on Computing Education (TOCE)*, 20(1):1–16, 2019.
73. J. Wang, H. Hong, J. Ravitz, and Hejazi Moghadam. Landscape of k-12 computer science education in the us: Perceptions, access, and barriers. In *Proceedings of the 47th ACM technical symposium on computing science education*, pages 645–650. ACM, 2016.
74. Alexandra Wicht, Ai Miyamoto, and Clemens M Lechner. Are girls more ambitious than boys? vocational interests partly explain gender differences in occupational aspirations. *Journal of Career Development*, 49(3):551–568, 2022.

Open Access This chapter is licensed under the terms of the Creative Commons Attribution 4.0 International License (http://creativecommons.org/licenses/by/4.0/), which permits use, sharing, adaptation, distribution and reproduction in any medium or format, as long as you give appropriate credit to the original author(s) and the source, provide a link to the Creative Commons license and indicate if changes were made.

The images or other third party material in this chapter are included in the chapter's Creative Commons license, unless indicated otherwise in a credit line to the material. If material is not included in the chapter's Creative Commons license and your intended use is not permitted by statutory regulation or exceeds the permitted use, you will need to obtain permission directly from the copyright holder.

Chapter 5
Mentoring as a Tool for Better Gender Diversity in Informatics

Anna Szlavi, **Serena Versino**, **Daniel Raffini**, **Tuva Cornelia Oppenhagen**, and **Letizia Jaccheri**

5.1 Introduction

Despite its importance, gender imbalance in the informatics field, where women comprise only 24% of the software development industry, requires further exploration and greater attention [32]. In addition to under-representation and high dropout rates, women face challenges such as stereotypes, lack of role models, and impostor syndrome on a daily basis [32]. Two-thirds of children aged 6 to 11 show an interest in science, but the share of women willing to consider the field decreases when they enter middle and high school [34]. The lack of women in the field has led to bias in software systems, which affects several segments of the society, such as health care, job prospects, and criminal justice [33], and this calls for increasing gender balance in informatics. Diverse teams tend to deliver software that is closer to the customers' needs compared to non-diverse teams [32].

In addition, research shows that gender diversity in software teams yields a healthier work environment by increasing innovation, problem-solving, and wider perspectives [32]. Therefore, it is essential to both attract women to the field and retain the ones that are already pursuing an informatics education or career. However, studies show that it is harder to retain women than men in the field, and that 50% of women resign from technical careers before the age of 35 [20].

A. Szlavi (✉) · T. C. Oppenhagen · L. Jaccheri
Norwegian University of Science and Technology, Trondheim, Norway
e-mail: anna.szlavi@ntnu.no; tuva.c.oppenhagen@ntnu.no; letizia.jaccheri@ntnu.no

S. Versino
University of Pisa, Pisa, Italy
e-mail: serena.versino@phd.unipi.it

D. Raffini
Sapienza, University of Rome, Rome, Italy
e-mail: raffini@diag.uniroma1.it

© The Author(s) 2025
B. Penzenstadler et al. (eds.), *Actions for Gender Balance in Informatics Across Europe*, https://doi.org/10.1007/978-3-031-78432-3_5

Mentoring is one of the main tools used to attract and retain women in the field and reduce the challenges that lead to under-representation. It can help empower women, support work-life balance, promote women's groups, and support women's career growth [32]. Following Kitchenham's framework [16], this study began with a planning phase that involved a preliminary review of literature on mentoring programs, leading to the identification of two main research questions addressed through a systematic literature review (SLR).

This chapter aims to provide an overview of how mentoring promotes gender balance in informatics at various stages of education and career development. Additionally, the research seeks to provide actionable guidelines to various stakeholders interested in promoting greater involvement of women in informatics.

5.2 Background

This section explores the impact of diversity on innovation and its associated challenges, and how mentoring supports effective diversity management and career advancement, especially in the context of gender balance and intersectional inclusion.

5.2.1 Diversity

Diversity is considered essential to foster creativity, innovation, and flexibility, due to the increase in points of view and the amount of information [25]. However, diversity implies differences in values, beliefs, and attitudes as well, which can reduce the cohesiveness and task performance, potentially leading to more conflicts between people working together [25]. In addition to its positive impact on creativity and innovation, diversity may also lead to prejudices, stereotypes, and biases people can have against others [24].

It is important to highlight that the potential negative effects of diversity are not due to diversity itself, but rather to people's lack of education about diversity and their attitudes towards working in a diversified environment. The negative impact, therefore, stems from a cultural problem: people are not accustomed to managing diversity. That is why techniques dedicated to bringing people together and empowering them, such as mentoring, might be useful in making people more aware of the value of diversity and acceptance, while also exposing them to collaborate in working environments where more social groups are represented. When working with diversity, the concept of intersectionality [6] is vital to keep in mind: people's different identity segments are indivisible from one another when it comes to systemic challenges. In other words, embracing diversity and overcoming gender barriers in informatics requires recognizing that women are not a homogeneous group, but are also influenced by factors such as ethnicity, sexual orientation, and socioeconomic background, among others [30].

Diversity is an ideal goal to achieve in informatics, as it can increase a team's performance and the product's accuracy. However, it is important to recognize that this comes with challenges. On one hand, being prepared to address potential issues is essential. On the other hand, research indicates that the impact of diversity on team performance is time-dependent, meaning the effects of diversity should be evaluated over an extended period [25].

5.2.2 Mentoring

Mentoring has proven to be an effective tool at critical stages of one's academic career, such as the transition from high school to university, from university to industry, or during promotions [2]. It is one of the main strategies to empower marginalized groups within a field, such as women in informatics [32].

The process of mentoring mainly consists of a mentor and a mentee, where the mentor is a person who has gained experience and knowledge within the given field, and the mentee is the person or group of people that are being advised [26]. In addition to being an advisor and counselor, mentors often take on the roles of friends, psychological support, and role models [2]. Being a role model is often associated with being a mentor; however, there are differences between the concepts of a mentor and a role model, the latter being broader.

Mentoring programs provide benefits for not only the mentees, but for the mentors and the organization as well. Within the academic context, the students that are mentored can receive academic, professional, and personal guidance. Whereas the mentors can gain new skills such as leadership, planning, communication, and decision making. The university can experience increased student or employee satisfaction, which can decrease dropout rates [10]. Similar to educational environments, mentoring programs have shown their value in the industry. Experienced colleagues can advise and support less experienced colleagues, and both mentors and mentees can experience the same benefits as those experienced in an educational setting. Organizing mentoring programs among office colleagues is also a cost-effective tool and a way to use the in-house experience in an organization [21]. Similar to other interventions for diversity, mentoring relationships should be long term in order to be truly effective [14]. In addition, intersectional mentoring has shown to be specifically fitting for minoritized groups [31].

Mentoring programs can be categorized along several dimensions. The categories that will be used in this study are location, activities, mentor-mentee relationship, delivery method, duration, and the gender and level of experience of the participants.

5.3 Methods

This SLR investigates mentoring programs in informatics that target the inclusion of women. We began by defining RQs related to the topic, then we conducted a literature search, screened for relevant studies, and finally extracted and analyzing data from relevant studies.

5.3.1 Systematic Literature Review

To establish foundational knowledge and identify research gaps, RQs were initially formulated to guide the collection of primary studies from electronic databases and through bibliographic screening. Then, studies were selected using specific inclusion and exclusion criteria and assessed for quality based on their ability to minimize bias and enhance validity. The process also involved creating data extraction forms to gather relevant information from these studies. Finally, the collected data was synthesized to answer the RQs [16].

5.3.1.1 Research Questions

After several iterations, two RQs were formulated, focusing on the phenomenon of interest. The first one (**RQ1**): "What mentoring programs focusing on gender diversity in informatics exist?" seeks to identify existing initiatives for women in informatics, providing insights in the methodology and dimensions used in the different programs, while also pinpointing gaps in the current literature to aid in the design of new programs.

The second one (**RQ2**): "What are the impacts of mentoring programs focusing on gender diversity in informatics?" aims to assess the outcomes of the programs identified in (**RQ1**). This includes categorizing the effects to understand which challenges these initiatives address effectively.

5.3.1.2 Search Strategy

After defining the RQs, the search string was refined through several iterations, as detailed in Table 5.2 in the Appendix. The third and final version of the search string, yielding 366 studies, focused on three main areas: mentoring programs, gender equality, and informatics. A study was considered relevant if it intersected all these areas. Terms related to gender equality such as "inclusion," "gender equality," and "women" were combined with "diversity" to encompass broader dimensions. The search aimed to identify informatics articles written in English and published between 2013 and 2023.

The electronic database, Scopus, and its "Advanced document search" functionality was used to search for primary studies. Scopus' integrated operators and field codes were used to create the string based on the main areas of interest. The final search string, presented in the third row in Table 5.2 in the Appendix, resulted in 366 studies.

5.3.2 Study Selection

Relevant papers were identified from the 366 retrieved by reviewing titles and abstracts according to the predefined criteria outlined in Table 5.1.

The screening process focused primarily on papers that describe mentoring programs aimed at reducing the gender gap in informatics. Based on a preliminary review of titles and abstracts, the keywords "mentor," "mentee," and "mentoring" were identified as relevant to this study. Therefore, only studies that included these keywords and focused specifically on gender diversity were selected for inclusion. Papers addressing other types of diversity or multiple diversity aspects were excluded. Initially, 366 studies were reduced to 16 papers after screening. One additional study was included for background information, and four more were added from snowballing—examining references of relevant studies to find more pertinent publications. A total of 21 papers were included in the final analysis. Figure 5.1 reports the number of studies incorporated at each stage of the SLR.

	Inclusion criteria	Exclusion criteria
Table 5.1 Inclusion and exclusion criteria	• The paper describes a mentoring program. • The mentoring program focuses on gender diversity. • The mentoring program operates in the informatics field. • The paper is written in English. • The paper is published after 2013.	• The mentoring program focuses on other perceptions of diversity. • The mentoring program addresses multiple diversity aspects with a minor emphasis on gender. • The paper focuses on several interventions to achieve gender diversity, where a mentoring program is one of them.

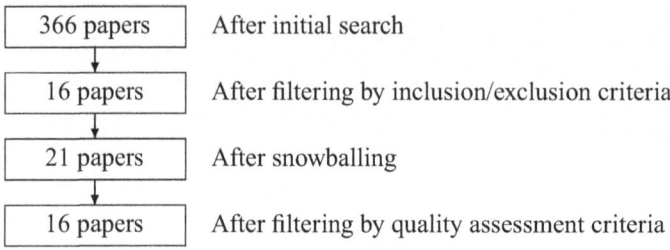

Fig. 5.1 Number of papers after each step in the SLR

5.3.3 Study Quality Assessment

The quality of the 21 papers was assessed using the following checklist, involving a more detailed review than the initial screening to mitigate bias and enhance validity [16].

- The paper is an empirical study.
- The goal of the study is related to attracting and/or retaining women in informatics.
- The study draws on pertinent theories concerning the under-representation of women in informatics.
- The paper presents the findings of the study.
- The paper provides enough information to get an overview of the whole study.

This step sought to eliminate studies potentially introducing bias, including those discussing identical mentoring programs or lacking robust theoretical foundations and detailed descriptions. Following this quality assessment, 16 papers satisfied the criteria and were included, as detailed in Table 5.3 in the Appendix. Methodological limitations are discussed in the Discussion section.

5.4 Results

The following section presents the data extracted from the 16 studies found in the SLR. One section for each of the two research questions is used to separate the data according to whether it is related to the overall description of the mentoring program (**RQ1**) or the impact of the mentoring program (**RQ2**). Table 5.3 in the Appendix gives an overview of the title of each study retrieved from the SLR.

5.4.1 RQ1: What Mentoring Programs Focusing on Gender Diversity in Informatics Exist?

5.4.1.1 Countries

Eight of the studies were conducted in the United States, two in Germany, two in Spain, one in Austria, one in Australia, one in Saudi Arabia, and one in Latin America. Chile, Colombia, Costa Rica, Ecuador, Spain, and Mexico are the countries included in the study conducted in Latin America [9]. Figure 5.2 shows the distribution of the areas where the studies were conducted. The United States is classified under North America, Saudi Arabia under the Middle East, and European nations under Europe. This categorization aids in understanding the cultural and developmental contexts within which the mentoring programs were implemented, given the differences in the sizes and characteristics of these regions. Figure 5.2 shows that 88% of the mentoring programs were executed in developed areas, including North America, Europe, and Australia.

5.4.1.2 Mentoring Activities

In this study, mentoring activities are defined as the interactions and work that occur during sessions between mentors and mentees. Several activities were identified from the studies extracted from the SLR. To get an overview of the pursued activities, four categories of activities are identified and used to classify the 16 studies: meetings, interactive activities, presentations, and forums.

- The first category identified is meetings, which was an activity used in nine of the 16 studies (56%) [1–3, 9, 10, 15, 22, 28, 29]. Meetings between mentors and mentees, conducted either face-to-face or virtually, often follow a structured agenda. These sessions are typically focused on discussions and activities designed to achieve objectives like enhancing confidence and learning strategies for success [2]. Other meetings were tailored to provide guidance based on the specific needs of the mentees. For instance, first-year female students received

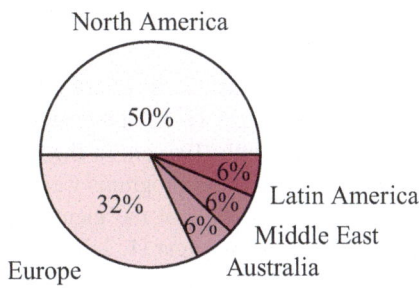

Fig. 5.2 Location of the mentoring programs

social, administrative, and academic support to facilitate their integration into university life [10].
- Interactive activities are the second type of mentoring activity. This category involves the mentoring sessions where the mentees were exposed to hands-on projects and tasks, which often involved creating software and hardware. Half of the studies, that is eight out of 16, incorporated interactive activities into the mentoring program [5, 8, 14, 15, 18, 28, 34, 35]. Clarke-Midura et al. [5] introduces an app camp where the mentees created phone apps [5], and [18] describes a program where the mentees built dancing robots. Whereas in [15], the sessions were used to teach the mentees programming languages and other aspects related to informatics [15].
- The third identified activity used in the mentoring sessions is presentations, which is used in six of the 16 studies (38%) [8, 9, 11, 14, 22, 35]. Presentations involve delivering a topic to a mentee. In some instances, mentors conducted presentations, such as in [8], where mentees received lectures about university life and various computer science programs. Alternatively, other presentations were delivered through lecture videos and slides for independent viewing by mentees, as described in [35].
- The least common activity identified was participation in forums (6%), utilized solely by the program described in [29]. This program featured a members-only community platform where mentors and mentees could engage in discussions about STEM-related topics.

The matching process between the mentors and mentees was a technique used in six of the 16 studies (38%) [1, 3, 8, 15, 22, 29] that involved identifying the best suited mentor for the mentee based on factors such as gender, location, area of interest, and availability. In [8], the mentees made interest profiles, in order to create groups with similar needs and interests. Another approach is shown in [1], where the mentors posted a description of what they did for a living, and the mentees chose the best suited mentor for themselves. Stoeger et al. [29] described a program with 312 mentees, where manual matching would be a challenging job. Therefore, the program used a matching algorithm that matched mentors with mentees based on personal and STEM related interests (Fig. 5.3).

5.4.1.3 Duration

Three time intervals were established to report the duration of the mentoring programs (see Fig. 5.4). The first category includes mentoring programs that lasted less than one month. Two out of the 16 mentoring programs fall into this category (12.5%). Both of these programs were informatics summer camps for children and teenagers [5, 34]. Half of the mentoring programs (50%) lasted for more than a month, but less than a year [1, 2, 8, 10, 15, 18, 22, 35]. Anazco and Zurn-Birkhimer [2] is an example of a study presenting a mentoring program that falls into this category. The program lasted for six months and consisted of both one-on-one

Fig. 5.3 Activities used in the mentoring programs

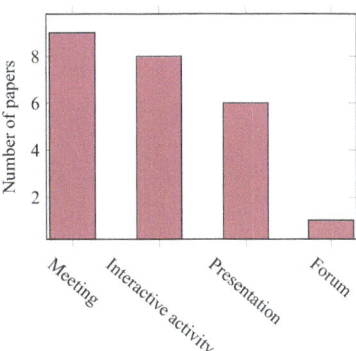

Fig. 5.4 Duration of the mentoring programs

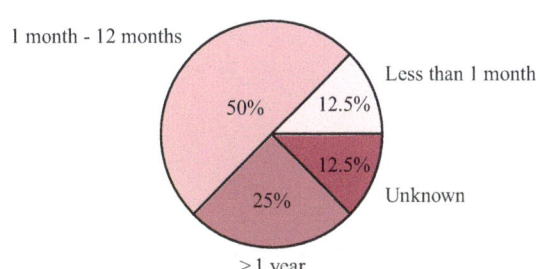

mentoring and group mentoring where the participants were part of a network, and the participants' role as mentor and mentee varied depending on the topic that was discussed [2]. Four programs, that is 25%, lasted for one year [3, 14, 28, 29]. An example is the mentoring program described in [29], where mentees received weekly emails, engaged on a community platform with chats and forums, and accessed a monthly magazine with STEM-related information. The duration of the mentoring programs was not provided by two studies [9, 11]. Three studies [1, 3, 8] reported multiple iterations of their mentoring programs, spanning several years. These iterations were part of a continuous improvement process, where adjustments were made based on observations and feedback from participants. In [3], participants who were mentees in initial iterations transitioned to mentor roles in subsequent cycles, reflecting a sense of empowerment and contribution gained through their involvement in the mentoring program. However, no individual mentoring relationships, defined as direct mentor-mentee pairings, extended beyond one year.

5.4.1.4 Mentor-Mentee Relation Types

Figure 5.5 shows the distribution of relationship types across the 16 studies analyzed in this study. One-on-one mentoring was the predominant model, implemented in six programs (37.5%) [1, 10, 15, 22, 28, 34], with meetings identified as a frequent

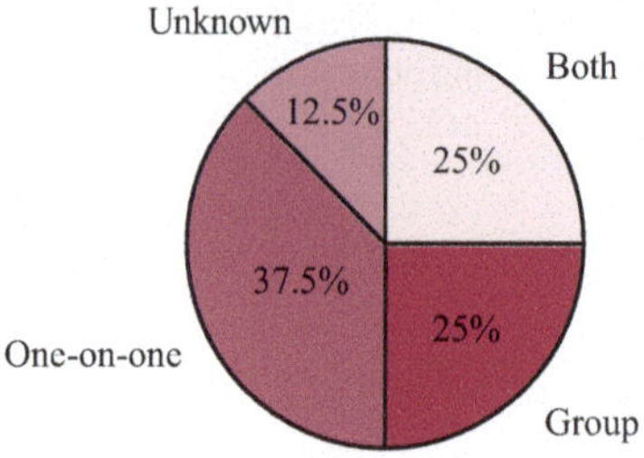

Fig. 5.5 Mentor-mentee relation types

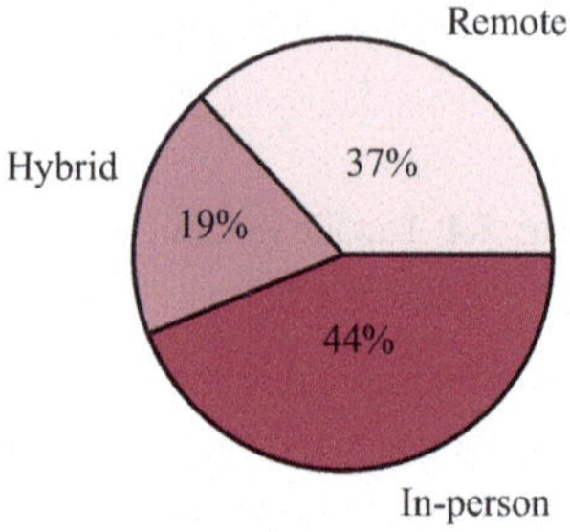

- Unknown 12.5%
- Both 25%
- Group 25%
- One-on-one 37.5%

Fig. 5.6 Delivery method of the mentoring programs

- Remote 37%
- In-person 44%
- Hybrid 19%

activity in five of these programs (83%) [1, 10, 15, 22, 28]. Group mentoring was employed in four programs (25%) [8, 11, 14, 18] and was typically used for interactive activities and presentations. All programs that used group mentoring incorporated either interactive activities, presentations, or both. For instance, in [8], mentees were engaged in presentations about university life, computer science programs, and the job market, alongside participation in projects and workshops. Four studies (25%) provided a hybrid approach of both group and one-on-one mentoring [2, 9, 29, 35], where individual online sessions were complemented by group discussions or hands-on projects. Two studies (12.5%) did not specify the mentoring format [3, 5]. Notably, no university-level mentoring programs exclusively used group mentoring, whereas this approach was common for younger mentees in elementary through high school.

5.4.1.5 Delivery Method

Seven of the mentoring programs were conducted in-person (44%) [5, 8, 9, 11, 14, 18, 34], six were remote (38%) [1, 2, 10, 15, 28, 29], and three utilized a hybrid approach (19%) [3, 22, 35], as shown in Fig. 5.6. The adoption of remote or hybrid methods in some programs was prompted by the COVID-19 pandemic [2, 10], leading to a marked increase in e-mentoring. Additionally, certain programs opted for remote or hybrid formats to overcome geographical barriers; for example, [3] implemented a hybrid model to accommodate mentees from 21 different colleges and universities. Other programs selected remote or hybrid approaches to capitalize on the advantages these methods offer in terms of flexibility and accessibility.

Several online communication platforms were utilized in the nine hybrid or remote mentoring programs, including Discord [35], Skype [15], Google Hangouts [15], phone conversations [15], Facebook [22], email [22], and Zoom [28]. Meetings were consistently conducted across all remote mentoring programs. For in-person programs, interactive activities were the most prevalent type of activity, employed in five out of the seven studies (71%).

5.4.1.6 Mentors and Mentees

Three categories were established based on gender and level of experience to characterize the participants in informatics mentoring programs. Gender-wise, participants were classified into female, male, or both genders if the program was inclusive. Regarding experience level, the categories are K-12 (encompassing kindergarten through high school), higher education, and industry. This classification helps delineate the demographic and professional backgrounds of mentors and mentees within these programs. Several programs encompass participants from various educational stages, leading to their grouping into a single category. "Higher education" includes participants who are in college or university, while "industry" pertains to individuals actively pursuing a career in the informatics field. Figure 5.7 provides the distribution of the mentors' genders across the 16 mentoring programs. Seven programs (44%) exclusively employed female mentors [1–3, 5, 15, 29, 34], while eight programs (50%) included both female and male mentors [8–11, 14, 18, 22, 28]. One program (6%) did not specify the gender of the mentors [35]. Notably, [8] underwent three iterations by the time of publication, starting with only female mentors and mentees in the first iteration and expanding to include both genders by the third to enhance diversity (Fig. 5.8).

The majority of the mentoring programs engaged college or university students as mentors, while others included industry professionals. As shown in Fig. 5.9, ten programs (59%) utilized mentors from higher education [2, 5, 8–10, 18, 28, 29, 34, 35], six programs (35%) involved mentors from the industry [1, 3, 11, 14, 15, 29], and one program (6%) did not specify the mentors' level of experience [22]. Most programs exclusively employed mentors from a single category; however, [29] provided a unique setup where mentees could interact with mentors from both STEM academic

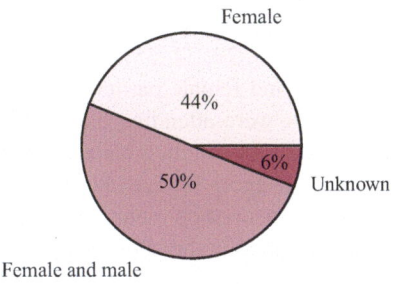

Fig. 5.7 Gender of the mentors

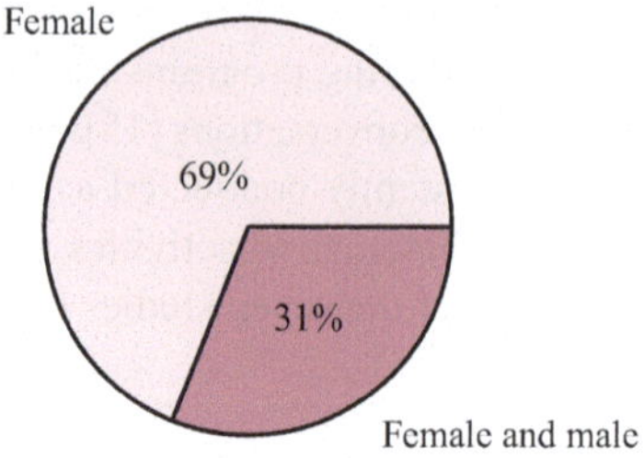

Fig. 5.8 Gender of the mentees

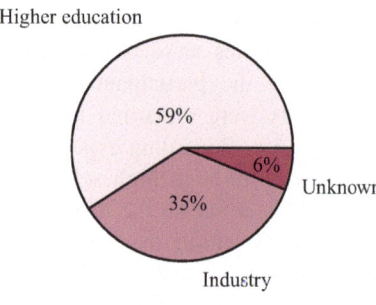

Fig. 5.9 Mentors' level of experience

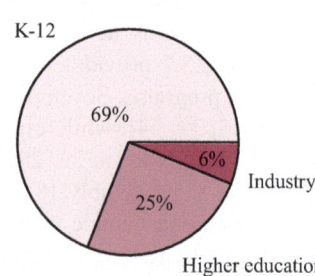

Fig. 5.10 Mentees' level of experience

fields and the industry via a members-only community platform. Additionally, some programs incorporated mentor training sessions to equip mentors with the necessary skills and knowledge, such as [10]. García-Holgado et al. [9] implemented a tutor system to ensure mentors fostered an inclusive environment and adhered to principles of gender equality. A common characteristic among mentors in most studies was their active involvement in informatics or the broader STEM field, whether through academic pursuits or professional endeavors in tech companies.

About 11 of the programs (69%) were offered to female mentees [2, 3, 9, 10, 14, 15, 22, 28, 29, 34, 35], while five programs [5, 8, 11, 18, 28] (31%) included both male and female participants (Fig. 5.8). Figure 5.10 shows that the majority of mentees were attending elementary, middle, or high school, or the equivalent educational stage in their respective countries, with 11 programs (69%) falling into this K-12 category [1, 5, 8, 11, 14, 15, 18, 28, 29, 34, 35]. Four programs [2, 9, 10, 22] (25%) focused on mentoring higher education students, and one program (6%) targeted women in the industry [3].

Eight of the programs mentoring K-12 students (73%) included interactive activities, such as coding camps where mentees created robots and phone apps. However, none of the programs dedicated to higher education students or industry professionals offered interactive activities. For these groups, meetings were more prevalent, occurring in five of the six programs (83%) aimed at higher education students or individuals who had already graduated. This activity was only identified in four of the 11 programs (36%) for K-12 students, often observed in combination with an interactive activity. Meetings were not utilized with mentees from elementary school; they were exclusively conducted with mentees in higher educational stages, such as middle and high school.

5.4.2 RQ2: What Are the Impacts of Mentoring Programs Focusing on Gender Diversity in Informatics?

Although the studies used different methods to collect the results and measured different effects, some similarities are identified. These similarities are used to create two categories and several subcategories that were used to measure the impact of the mentoring programs. The subcategories are presented in Fig. 5.11.

The first category which mentoring helped with is self-inflicted challenges, which pertains to obstacles arising from an individual's own thoughts and actions. This category encompasses six keywords, grouped into three subcategories: knowledge and skills, confidence and self-efficacy, and interest and motivation. "Knowledge and skills" refers to understanding STEM topics, informatics, career opportunities, and related areas. These keywords were observed in the results of eight of the 16 studies (50%). Of these, seven studies reported positive changes [1, 9, 11, 15, 29, 34, 35], while one study reported no significant change [5]. For instance, [29] reported improvements in knowledge of STEM topics, educational opportunities, and career choices. Similarly, [11] reported enhanced awareness regarding women in STEM.

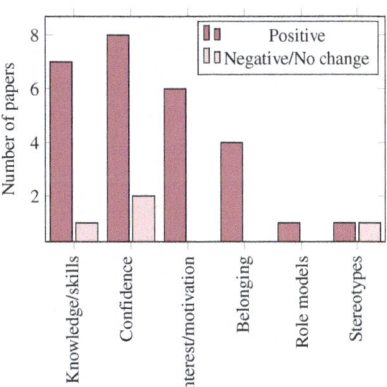

Fig. 5.11 Identified challenges

However, [5] assessed the program's impact on participants' skills through a technical multiple-choice test but found no significant changes in knowledge. Confidence and self-efficacy pertain to how participants evaluate their own abilities in the field. These keywords were mentioned in ten studies (62%). While two studies reported no change [11, 29], the remaining studies documented positive changes [3, 5, 14, 15, 22, 28, 34, 35].

Lastly, interest and motivation pertain to participants' enthusiasm for learning about informatics and STEM topics, as well as their intent to pursue a degree or career in the field. Six of the papers (37%) reported positive changes in participants' interest or motivation [2, 5, 8, 14, 18, 35]. For instance, [35] reported that girls exhibited greater interest than boys in engaging with other engineering programs.

Social challenges pertain to factors beyond the individual's control, such as role models and stereotypes. The first subcategory, sense of belonging, refers to the extent to which participants feel included and integrated within the informatics community. Four studies (25%) reported keywords related to this subcategory, where all experienced a positive effect [2, 3, 34, 35]. One example is [35], where the girls' sense of belonging was strengthened after the summer camp. Similarly, [3] reported that women in the program experienced reduced isolation after connecting with other women in the field. The second subcategory, role models, was mentioned in [8] (6%), where nearly half of the mentees identified their mentors as role models. Lastly, stereotypes, the third subcategory, were mentioned in [8, 11]. In [8], mentees indicated that the mentoring program corrected their perception of computer science as a male-dominated field with isolated work. However, [11] reported no significant change in participants' gender stereotypes after the mentoring program.

Long-term effects from mentoring programs were observed in only one study [3]. This one-year program, which had undergone five iterations, mentored women in STEM academia. The results showed that nearly all participants remained in STEM academia and advanced in their careers while feeling less isolated. Another significant finding came from [28], which examined whether the gender of the mentor influenced tutoring style or mentee experience. The study found that female mentors were more likely than male mentors to adopt a dictating rather than supportive tutoring style. However, mentee participation did not vary based on the mentor's gender. The study concluded that tutoring style was more critical to the effectiveness of the mentoring session than the mentor's gender.

In one study [1], girls had regular online discussions with a mentor about career opportunities. After the program concluded, some mentees participated in focus groups and interviews, offering insightful feedback. They found communication through text messages challenging and suggested using familiar digital platforms instead of new technology. Additionally, they recommended allowing the flexibility to change mentors and incorporating group mentoring sessions to benefit from peer questions. They likened these group sessions to Instagram's live feature, where users can broadcast and interact with followers' questions [1].

5.5 Discussion

In this section, the results related to the two RQs are presented, along with applicable actions and guidelines for implementing mentoring to promote gender balance in informatics.

5.5.1 RQ1: What Mentoring Programs Focusing on Gender Diversity in Informatics Exist?

Countries Section 5.4.1.1 provided an overview of the geographical areas where the mentoring programs featured in the literature were offered. 88% of programs retrieved from the SLR were offered in the Global North,[1] whereas only 12% were offered in less developed areas, which reveals a gap. Similarly to diversity in the participant's gender, diversity in national backgrounds, connected to ethnicity and race, can yield benefits due to multiple points of views, availability in knowledge and skills, and constructive conflicts [24]. Therefore, including research and results from mentoring programs outside of the Global North, may yield new, relevant findings in the research area. Additionally, UN's Sustainable Development Goal 5, involving gender equality, aims to empower all girls and women [19]. Therefore, including various nationalities and cultures in mentoring all across Europe and beyond is necessary to close the gender gap on both an EU and a global level.

Delivery Method An almost equal distribution of in-person and remote/hybrid mentoring programs has been found. Figure 5.6 shows that 56% of the studies use a remote or hybrid mentoring program, whereas 44% exclusively use in-person mentoring sessions. The equal distribution of remote/hybrid and in-person mentoring programs can be due to the benefits e-mentoring yields; however, many mentoring programs were made remote or hybrid due to the COVID-19 pandemic when in-person activities were restricted. This increase in remote and hybrid mentoring programs can lead to both positive and negative consequences. As aforementioned, e-mentoring offers several benefits, including communication across large geographical distances, reduced costs [22], and asynchronous communication [27]. On the other hand, there are drawbacks with the increase of e-mentoring programs. This includes needs of skills to handle technology [22] and the importance of structure and follow-up [27]. Therefore, it is important to keep in mind that while online mentoring can be more inclusive, it does call for special efforts to make it successful.

---

[1] Global North is defined by the Cambridge Dictionary as "the group of countries that are in Europe, North America, and the developed parts of Asia".

Duration Mentoring programs often report disappointing results due to the lack of mentor training and follow-up after the matching of mentor and mentees, which is especially important in remote and hybrid solutions to promote engagement and involvement from the participants [27]. An example from the SLR is the remote mentoring program presented in [1], where the only follow-up the mentors got was weekly emails with reminders to stay in touch with the mentees, as well as suggestions on topics for discussion. The study reported surprisingly low engagement and interaction between the participants, which can be a result of not enough follow-up and training for the mentors. Moreover, the authentic impact of diversity within a team becomes observable only when the group has reached a mature stage [25]. This also applies to mentor-mentee relations, which means that the relations should be long term to effectively influence participants [14]. The results in Sect. 5.4.1.3 report that 62.5% of the studies found in the SLR presented mentoring programs lasting for less than a year, and 25% of the programs lasted for a year. While some of the programs included several iterations, which together lasted for several years, none of the mentor-mentee relations lasted for more than a year. This reveals a major gap and need for creating long-term mentoring programs. The goal is to reach a critical mass of female students, which in return will create a community of women and lead to further enrollment of female students. A community of women will reduce the risk of stereotyping, sexism, and unwanted attention, because they are no longer a small minority [17]. In addition, continuous efforts over time addressing important inclusion needs are necessary to create a more gender diverse field.

Mentors and Mentees An important result presented in Sect. 5.4.1.6 is the higher share of mentees from K-12 education compared to mentees from higher education and industry. Figure 5.10 shows that only 6% of the programs were offered to mentees from the industry, and 25% were offered to women in informatics study programs in higher education. Socio-cultural challenges and gender-related incidents in IT companies can result in women leaving projects and jobs [32], so it would be vital to offer mentoring programs to women who are already or currently in the field. Gender stereotypes and impostor syndrome lead to high dropout rates in technical study programs as well [10]. Therefore, it is just as important to retain women in education and at the workplace, as it is to attract new women to the field [32]. Moreover, Sect. 5.4.1.6 outlined the lack of interactive activities in mentoring programs for mentees in higher education and industry, which might be more engaging and personal. An explanation might be that women studying or working in informatics are already thought to be engaged in such activities, but offering mentoring programs that include interactive activities can be effective to explore new technologies and areas in the field. This is especially important for women, because women tend to have lower confidence than men when doing unfamiliar informatics tasks [33]. It is also common for women to avoid using new technologies because they risk spending extra time [33]. Additionally, tinkering with software is more frequently observed for male developers, while women tend to aim for a more process-oriented learning style [33]. This indicates that women already pursuing a informatics education or career could benefit from mentoring programs involving interactive activities, in order to be exposed to new technologies.

Mentor-Mentee Relation Types The distribution of relationship types between mentors and mentees is balanced, as illustrated in Fig. 5.5. However, none of the programs that exclusively use group mentoring are offered to women in higher education or industry, while the approach is frequently observed for K-12 students. This indicates another gap in mentoring programs offered to women above the K-12 educational stage. One-on-one mentoring may seem more appropriate for mentees in university or a higher level, because stereotypes related to informatics tend to increase with age, especially for girls [7]. However, group mentoring can be more efficient than one-on-one mentoring in certain cases, because it offers multiple viewpoints and cross-disciplinary examination of the discussed topics. Group projects and activities are also an opportunity group mentoring can offer [4]. Additionally, group mentoring can be efficient for mentoring programs using a hierarchical approach, i.e. when the mentors have more experience than the mentees. In these circumstances, group mentoring tends to create a safe space for mentees who are uncomfortable having one-on-one mentoring sessions with someone considered higher up in the hierarchy [4, 13]. The differences in the power dynamics between a senior mentor and a junior mentee can often be experienced as problematic and lead to a feeling of isolation for mentees belonging to a marginalized group [13]. Therefore, it may be worth exploring the possibility of offering group mentoring for women in higher education and industry as well.

Furthermore, research indicates that women tend to exhibit more caring characteristics when providing help compared to men, which may be reflected in their mentoring approach [23]. However, the findings in [28] contradict this theory, showing that male mentors employed a more supportive approach than female mentors. The study concluded with the statement that the mentee's participation was independent of the mentor's gender. On the one hand, this statement supports the idea of gender diversity. Finzel et al. [8] did several iterations of a mentoring program, where they first only included female mentors and mentees, but later decided to include both male and female participants to provide diversity. On the other hand, males mentoring females in informatics can drive the mentoring program away from its initial goal of creating a more diverse field, by developing a feeling of isolation for the mentees [4]. Thus, experimenting with all-female or mixed-gender mentors may be beneficial to explore what works better with the specific pool of mentees involved in the program.

Finally, peer mentoring, in which participants share a similar level of expertise and social identity, such as gender, often creates communities and counter-spaces. These supportive environments are crucial for participants to share challenges, identify opportunities for growth, and develop career-related skills [12].

5.5.2 RQ2: What Are the Impacts of Mentoring Programs Focusing on Gender Diversity in Informatics?

The main impact of participating in a mentoring program, as observed and reported by participants, involves improvement in self-confidence in informatics. Measuring participants' feelings and experiences related to being mentored is relatively straightforward. However, questionnaires, the most frequently used data collection method in these studies, only capture information at a conscious level. Given that participants self-report their experiences, data accuracy may be compromised, as deeply embedded social phenomena like stereotypes often operate subconsciously and are not easily captured by questionnaires. While it is challenging to measure how effectively a mentoring program can change the stereotypical image of a computer scientist, it is clear that most participants feel they have gained more confidence and skills in informatics. Moreover, the interest in determining whether mentees perceive an increase in female role models through participation in the mentoring program has been explored in Finzel et al.'s [8] study. Our analysis, as depicted in Fig. 5.7, reveals that 44% of programs utilized exclusively female mentors, while 50% employed both genders. This indicates significant exposure of participants to female professionals in informatics. Such exposure is crucial for providing role models, enhancing female mentees' sense of belonging, and potentially improving retention rates within the field.

5.5.3 Personas

This study aims to provide targeted, practical guidelines to empower a wide range of stakeholders to significantly enhance women's participation in informatics. The following stakeholder examples are selected based on the EUGAIN Book Personas; below are three examples associated with this work.

> **Kim/Kimmy/Kymi, the university professor.** Looking at the resources of this chapter, Kim, the university professor takes the recommendations to the next departmental meeting. Some of the professors are enthusiastic about the idea of mentoring, recalling how useful it was for them as mentees. But they are skeptical about the workload, so Kim proposes that higher year students get involved as peer mentors, and professors only take the responsibility of supervising student mentors twice a semester.

> **Brandy/Bazyli/Bo, the industry manager.** Looking at the resources of this chapter, Bo, the industry manager takes the recommendations to the next leaders meeting. Some of the managers are thrilled about the idea of mentoring, because they want to keep as many of their women employees as possible. But they think it is problematic that there are not many senior women at the company to serve as mentors. So Bo proposes to create mentoring groups, this way one mentor could manage multiple mentees, and women could also benefit from peer discussions.

> **Des/Deniz/Derya, student about to graduate.** Des, the student about to graduate, is now aware of what mentoring is and wants to discuss it with classmates. So Des creates a social community to share experiences with other students and to publicize new mentoring opportunities. After a few mentoring experiences, Des and other students consider officially proposing their social community as a channel for mentoring initiatives for younger students.

5.5.4 Limitations

Our study has some limitations. Firstly, the impacts of the mentoring programs were based on participants' self-reports, which can lack objectivity. Figure 5.10 in Sect. 5.4.1.6 shows that 69% of the mentoring programs involved K-12 students, including children as young as 10 years old. For example, [34] reported that girls in 6th grade felt learning about informatics influenced their future career aspirations. Similarly, in [18], all mentored 5th and 6th graders considered engineering as a potential career. While the programs may have impacted the participants, the validity of these results can be questionable due to the participants' young age. Moreover, the short duration of some mentoring programs can be a limitation in evaluating the results. Indeed, long-term programs are needed to observe the true effects of the intervention [14]. Some programs analyzed in this SLR were relatively short, such as [34], which lasted only one week, and [5], which lasted two weeks. The brief duration may not be sufficient to yield robust results. Lastly, the perception of diversity, stemming from our search query as presented in Sect. 5.3 can affect results. Indeed, diversity encompasses differences not only in gender but also in nationality, ethnicity, age, and more [24]. The binary perception of gender used in this study can be a limitation, too. For simplicity, the study focused on women and men, but it must be acknowledged that gender diversity extends beyond the binary classification.

5.6 Conclusion

The SLR presented in this chapter retrieved 16 papers about mentoring programs that aim to reduce the gender gap in informatics. Results related to **RQ1** show a variety in the dimensions of the mentoring programs, such as activities, relation types between mentor and mentees, and delivery method. The analysis, however, identified important gaps too. All but two mentoring programs were carried out in the Global North, which indicates that little focus is paid to mentoring programs in less developed countries. It calls for a broader acknowledgement and implementation of mentoring programs outside of the most advanced countries. Further, the duration of the mentoring programs ranged from one week to one year, which poses a challenge to observing the long term impact of mentoring programs. It is also important to note that mentor training is important to ensure engagement and interaction between the participants, especially due to the increase in remote and hybrid interventions after the COVID-19 pandemic.

Of the 16 mentoring programs analyzed, 11 were offered to K-12 mentees, indicating an under-representation of programs for women in informatics university programs and the IT industry. This suggests that current studies and interventions are primarily focused on attracting women to the field rather than retaining those already pursuing careers, which reveals an opportunity for university professors, heads of departments, HR offices, and managers.

Regarding **RQ2**, mentoring programs in this study were assessed based on the participants' self-reported experiences after participating in the mentoring program, rather than on statistics showing the long term effects of the initiatives, such as an increase in women in the field. Based on these self-reports, improvements in the participants' confidence, knowledge, skills, motivation, and interest came up most often, which can further imply positive changes in the participants' sense of belonging and perceptions of stereotypes. In addition, a better exposure to relatable role models can be another benefit of mentoring programs.

However, in further research it would be interesting to observe the long term effects of mentoring programs for women in informatics. Such long term effects can include statistics over the share of women and drop out rates in informatics education and companies before and after running the mentoring program. For a sustainable change, long term efforts and interventions are required, as women's barriers are deeply entrenched.

Appendix

Tables 5.2 and 5.3.

Table 5.2 Search strings

Iteration	Search string	Result
1	TITLE-ABS-KEY(mentor*) AND TITLE-ABS-KEY ("inclusion" OR "gender equality" OR "women" OR "female") AND SUBJAREA(comp) AND PUBYEAR > 2015	256 papers
2	TITLE-ABS-KEY(mentor*) AND TITLE-ABS-KEY ("inclusion" OR "diversity" OR "gender equality" OR "women" OR "female") AND SUBJAREA(comp) AND PUBYEAR > 2015	317 papers
3	SUBJAREA(comp) AND TITLE-ABS-KEY(mentor* AND ("inclusion" OR "diversity" OR "gender equality" OR "women" OR "female")) AND PUBYEAR > 2013 AND (LIMIT-TO (LANGUAGE, "English"))	366 papers

Table 5.3 Studies retrieved from the SLR

Study	Title	Year
[10]	Mentoring for future female engineers: pilot at the Higher Polytechnic School of Zamora	2021
[34]	A Coding/Programming Academy for 6th-Grade Females to Increase the Knowledge and Interest in Computer Science	2019
[14]	An Effective Industry-Based Mentoring Approach for the Recruitment of Women and Minorities in Engineering	2017
[5]	Investigating the Role of Being a Mentor as a Way of Increasing Interest in CS	2016
[2]	Adapting to an unexpected hybrid campus: e-mentored female engineering students' intrinsic motivation, sense of belonging, and perception of campus climate	2022
[18]	Dancing Robots: A collaboration Between Elementary School and University Engineering Students	2017
[9]	Definition and Implementation of W-STEM Mentoring Network	2023
[35]	Engaging Girls in Learning Engineering through Building Ubiquitous Intelligent Systems	2022
[8]	From Beliefs to Intention: Mentoring as an Approach to Motivate Female High School Students to Enrol in Computer Science Studies	2018
[3]	Social Enterprise Model for a Multi-Institutional Mentoring Network for Women in STEM	2018
[11]	The Impact of Female Role Models Leading a Group Mentoring Program to Promote STEM Vocations among Young Girls	2022
[15]	Remote Mentoring Young Females in STEM through MAGIC	2013
[22]	Balancing the Equation: Mentoring First-Year Female STEM Students at a Regional University	2016
[29]	The effectiveness of a one-year online mentoring program for girls in STEM	2013
[28]	"RemoteMentor" Evaluation of Interactions Between Teenage Girls, Remote Tutors, and Coding Activities in School Lessons	2020
[1]	Exploring e-mentoring: co-designing and un-platforming	2019

Acknowledgments This study was partially supported by COST Action CA19122 EUGAIN (European Network for Gender Balance in Informatics) and the Erasmus+ Women STEM Up project (2022-1-SE01-KA220-HED-00008623).

References

1. A. Alhadlaq, A. Kharrufa, and P. Olivier. Exploring e-mentoring: Co-designing & un-platforming. *Behaviour & Information Technology*, 2019.
2. M. I. S. Anazco and S. Zurn-Birkhimer. Adapting to an unexpected hybrid campus: E-mentored female engineering students' intrinsic motivation, sense of belonging, and perception of campus climate. In *CoNECD (Collaborative Network for Engineering & Computing Diversity)*, 2022.
3. S. A. Atwood, R. McCann, A. Armstrong, and B. S. Mattes. Social enterprise model for a multi-institutional mentoring network for women in stem. In *2018 CoNECD - The Collaborative Network for Engineering and Computing Diversity Conference*, 2018.
4. B. N. Carvin. The hows and whys of group mentoring. *Industrial and Commercial Training*, 2011.
5. J. Clarke-Midura, V. Allan, and K. Close. Investigating the role of being a mentor as a way of increasing interest in cs. In *The 47th ACM Technical Symposium on Computer Science Education*, 2016.
6. K. Crenshaw. Demarginalizing the intersection of race and sex: A (black) feminist critique of antidiscrimination doctrine, feminist theory and antiracist policies. *University of Chicago Legal Forum*, 1989(1):139–167, 1989.
7. C. M. Cutrupi, I. Zanardi, L. Jaccheri, and M. Landoni. Draw a software engineer test - an investigation into children's perceptions of software engineering profession. In *IEEE/ACM 45th International Conference on Software Engineering: Software Engineering in Society*, 2023.
8. B. Finzel, H. Deininger, and U. Schmid. From beliefs to intention: Mentoring as an approach to motivate female high school students to enrol in computer science studies. In *GenderIT '18: Proceedings of the 4th Conference on Gender & IT*, 2018.
9. A. García-Holgado, S. Segarra-Morales, A.-B. González-Rogado, and F. J. García-Peñalvo. Definition and implementation of w-stem mentoring network. In *XIV Congress of Latin American Women in Computing 2022*, 2022.
10. A.-B. Gonzalez-Rogado, A. García-Holgado, and F. J. Gracía-Peñalvo. Mentoring for future female engineers: Pilot at the higher polytechnic school of zamora. In *XI International Conference on Virtual Campus (JICV)*, 2021.
11. M. Guenaga, A. Eguíluz, and A. Mimenza. The impact of female role models leading a group mentoring program to promote stem vocation among young girls. *Sustainability*, 2022.
12. C. Horner-Devine. Peer mentoring circles: A strategy for thriving in science. https://blogs.biomedcentral.com/bmcblog/2017/05/18/peer-mentoring-circles-a-strategy-for-thriving-in-science/. Accessed: 2024-10-03.
13. M. C. Horner-Devine, T. Gonsalves, C. Margherio, S. J. Mizumori, and J. W. Yen. Beyond hierarchical one-on-one mentoring. *Composite Materials*, 2018.
14. A. Illumoka, I. Milanovic, and N. Grant. An effective industry-based mentoring approach for the recruitment of women and minorities in engineering. *Journal of STEM Education Innovations and Research*, 18(3), 2017.
15. R. Khare, E. Sahai, and I. Pramanick. Remote mentoring young females in stem through magic, 2013.
16. B. Kitchenham. Procedures for performing systematic reviews. Technical Report TR/SE-0401, Keele University, 2004.

17. V. A. Lagesen, I. Pettersen, and L. Berg. Inclusion of women to ict engineering - lessons learned. *European Journal of Engineering Education*, 2020.
18. M. McLean, D. Harlow, T. Susko, and J. Bianchini. Dancing robots: A collaboration between elementary school and university engineering students. In *Proceedings of the 7th Annual Conference on Creativity and Fabrication in Education*, 2017.
19. U. Nations. Achieve gender equality and empower all women and girls. https://sdgs.un.org/goals/goal5#overview. Accessed: 2024-10-03.
20. J. D. Patón-Romero, S. Block, C. Ayala, and L. Jaccheri. Gender equality in information technology processes: A systematic mapping study. *Lecture Notes in Networks and Systems*, 2023.
21. J. Ramalho. Mentoring in the workplace. *Industrial and Commercial Training*, 2014.
22. J. Reid, E. Smith, N. Iamsuk, and J. Miller. Balancing the equation: Mentoring first-year female stem students at a regional university. *International Journal of Innovation in Science and Mathematics Education*, 2016.
23. J. Rhodes, S. R. Lowe, L. Litchfield, and K. Walsh-Samp. The role of gender in youth mentoring relationship formation and duration. *Journal of Vocational Behavior*, 2007.
24. G. Rodríguez-Pérez, R. Nadri, and M. Nagappan. Perceived diversity in software engineering: A systematic literature review. *Empirical Software Engineering*, 2021.
25. G. Sauberer, J. Maj, and V. Senichev. How to leverage the potential of diverse and virtual teams and benefit from diversity management. In *Communications in Computer and Information Science*, 2018.
26. A. Shah. What is mentoring? *The American Statistician*, 2017.
27. P. B. Singe and C. B. Muller. When email and mentoring unite: The implementation of a nationwide electronic mentoring program, 2001.
28. B. Spieler, J. Mikats, S. Valentin, L. Oates-Indruchová, and W. Slany. "remotementor": Evaluation of interactions between teenage girls, remote tutors, and coding activities in school lessons. In *Learning and Collaboration Technologies. Designing, Developing and Deploying Learning Experiences*, 2020.
29. H. Stoeger, X. Duan, S. Schirner, T. Greindl, and A. Ziegler. The effectiveness of a one-year online mentoring program for girls in stem. *Computers & Education*, 2013.
30. A. Szlavi, M. F. Hansen, S. H. Husnes, and T. U. Conte. Intersectionality in computer science: A systematic literature review. In *IEEE/ACM 4th Workshop on Gender Equity, Diversity, and Inclusion in Software Engineering (GE@ICSE)*. Association for Computing Machinery (ACM), 2023.
31. A. Szlavi, M. F. Hansen, S. H. Husnes, T. U. Conte, and L. Jaccheri. Designing for intersectional inclusion in computing. In *Universal Access in Human-Computer Interaction*, pages 122–142. Springer, 2024.
32. B. Trinkenreich, R. Britto, M. A. Gerosa, and I. Steinmacher. An empirical investigation on the challenges faced by women in the software industry: A case study. *Software Engineering in Society*, 2022.
33. M. Vorvoreanu, L. Zhang, Y.-H. Huang, C. Hilderbrand, Z. Steine-Hanson, and M. Burnett. From gender biases to gender-inclusive design: An empirical investigation. In *Proceedings of the 2019 CHI Conference on Human Factors in Computing Systems (CHI '19)*, 2019.
34. S. Wang, S. Andrei, O. Urbina, and D. A. Sisk. A coding/programming academy for 6th-grade females to increase knowledge and interest in computer science. *Frontiers in Education Conference*, 2019.
35. M. Yang, B. Tiwari, R. Gutam, E. Ma, S. Zhang, and V. Muthukumar. Engaging girls in learning engineering through building ubiquitous intelligent systems. In *2022 IEEE International Conference on Teaching, Assessment and Learning for Engineering (TALE)*, 2022.

Open Access This chapter is licensed under the terms of the Creative Commons Attribution 4.0 International License (http://creativecommons.org/licenses/by/4.0/), which permits use, sharing, adaptation, distribution and reproduction in any medium or format, as long as you give appropriate credit to the original author(s) and the source, provide a link to the Creative Commons license and indicate if changes were made.

The images or other third party material in this chapter are included in the chapter's Creative Commons license, unless indicated otherwise in a credit line to the material. If material is not included in the chapter's Creative Commons license and your intended use is not permitted by statutory regulation or exceeds the permitted use, you will need to obtain permission directly from the copyright holder.

Part III
From Bachelor/Master Studies to PhD

Chapter 6
Voices of Female Informatics Students Across Universities

Özge Büyükdağlı, Miguel Goulão, Milena Vujošević Janičić, and Amal Mersni

6.1 Introduction

Pursuing a PhD is a challenging and life-changing decision, requiring consideration of many factors. Some factors encourage the decision to start a PhD, while others discourage it. These factors are relevant to all potential doctoral candidates, but some challenges may differ depending on the candidate's gender. Women, especially in fields like Informatics, often face additional hurdles that complicate their academic journey as they transition from bachelor's and master's degrees to PhD programmes [1, 3, 4, 18].

These challenges include balancing personal and professional responsibilities, managing financial constraints, and navigating societal expectations in male-dominated fields. The lack of visible female role models and mentors can add to these challenges, sometimes making the PhD journey feel more isolating and discouraging.

Despite these difficulties, many women are motivated to pursue a PhD. The factors driving them range from career advancement and professional growth to the

---

Ö. Büyükdağlı (✉) · A. Mersni
Faculty of Engineering and Natural Sciences, International University of Sarajevo, Sarajevo, Bosnia and Herzegovina
e-mail: obuyukdagli@ius.edu.ba; amersni@ius.edu.ba

M. Goulão
NOVA School of Science and Technology, Caparica, Portugal
e-mail: mgoul@fct.unl.pt

M. Vujošević Janičić
Faculty of Mathematics, University of Belgrade, Belgrade, Serbia
e-mail: milena.vujosevic.janicic@matf.bg.ac.rs

© The Author(s) 2025
B. Penzenstadler et al. (eds.), *Actions for Gender Balance in Informatics Across Europe*, https://doi.org/10.1007/978-3-031-78432-3_6

desire to contribute to meaningful research or achieve personal fulfilment. Access to strong mentorship and support systems is essential in helping women overcome these challenges and continue on their academic path. Understanding these factors provides valuable insights into why some women persist in their academic journey while others may be discouraged.

Some women are motivated by external factors, such as the desire to build an academic career. They see a PhD as the first step to achieving this goal, often choosing academia over industry [11]. Others may choose an academic career path for the convenience of work-life balance. They value the work environment, flexible schedule, and possible part-time positions [13]. Additionally, some candidates may view a PhD as a chance to develop professionally and gain valuable knowledge. It allows them to improve their competence in keeping pace with fast-evolving industry standards and gives them a competitive advantage over peers with lower degrees. For some, a doctorate opens doors to higher-level positions or more financially rewarding careers [8, 10, 15]. Furthermore, a PhD can lead to increased salary expectations, job security, and a more attractive benefits package. On the other hand, women may be passionate about the practical experiences they gain in the industry and consider academia too theoretical for their interests [1]. For these women, the hands-on nature of industry work aligns more closely with their professional goals and ambitions.

In addition to career goals, research interest is a crucial factor that can increase a student's motivation to pursue a PhD, especially if the student was involved in research during master's studies and had positive experiences [11]. Personal fulfilment motivates students who may have professional interests combined with a passion for research and gaining more knowledge. Thanks to this deep connection, such students may wish to contribute to the advancement of the field and not need extra motivation to continue progressing and excelling in their studies [8, 10, 11, 13, 15].

In contrast, financial concerns can be a significant factor discouraging women from pursuing a PhD. Research indicates that women are more likely to self-finance their studies, while men are more frequently offered paid positions in academia [12]. As a result, women may hesitate to start a PhD due to concerns about career and financial constraints, particularly if they plan to start a family. The financial burden of raising a family can force them to choose between supporting their children and advancing their academic careers [13].

Beyond financial concerns, women tackle unique psychological challenges in academia. They may perceive themselves as less capable and skilled than they are, a phenomenon known as the *impostor syndrome*, leading them to seek higher qualifications to compensate for these perceived shortcomings [7]. This psychological burden can lead some women to leave the field [9]. The confidence gap underlying *impostor syndrome* is reported to be more frequently experienced by women than men, who are often found to be overconfident in their abilities [2, 9].

Additionally, research has shown that men, in particular, may sometimes present themselves as experts, even when lacking the necessary knowledge and skills, as observed in programming courses [7]. There is also an unfounded perception among women that leadership roles in technical fields should belong to men [17].

Furthermore, hostility or micro-aggressions in academic environments may contribute to feelings of discouragement among women pursuing advanced degrees. While women often prefer collaborative work and learning, classrooms, especially in computer science, are frequently structured around a male-centric perspective [18], making them feel unwelcoming to many females [5].

Other factors that draw a candidate to an Informatics PhD may be related to seeing successful role models. This motivation becomes stronger when observing the accomplishments of other PhD holders in the labour market, boosting the desire for similar success and recognition [13, 15]. They may also be encouraged by their families and peers to pursue an advanced degree [8, 10, 11, 13, 15].

On the other hand, since role models play a significant role in inspiring young people, the lack of visible female representation in Informatics may itself become a negative factor. Young girls may be unable to imagine themselves as professors or in managerial positions if they do not experience this through real-life models [7].

Sexism and stereotyping also continue to impact women negatively [6, 7], from girls being told STEM is nerdy to implicit biases that project boys as being more technically capable. Women in STEM programmes experience sexism and typecasting in class and in the workplace by their male peers, teachers, and managers [6, 7].

Why Voices?
We collected women's perspectives on these factors via two surveys targeting women studying or working in Informatics. The collected testimonies include perspectives from Bachelor, Master, and PhD students, post-docs, and faculty. These testimonies provide relatable, compelling examples that potential and current PhD candidates may learn from, with the side effect of increasing their sense of belonging as they identify with the experiences of others.

Overview of the Chapter Section 6.2 presents our data collection and analysis method. Section 6.3 presents women's testimonies on their decision to start a PhD. Section 6.4 highlights the insights and lessons learned during their PhD studies, while Sect. 6.5 concludes the chapter with final remarks.

Who Can Benefit from This Chapter and How?
This chapter is aimed at students, professors and school teachers.

> **Derya, a student about to graduate.** Derya has many questions about her future career in Informatics, including whether or not to pursue a PhD. After reading this chapter, she will see that it is completely normal and that many other female students and PhD holders have had similar concerns. She will also read about different motivating and demotivating stories, and hopefully, this will help her make decisions at this important point in her life.

> **Kymi, a university professor.** Kymi, as an enthusiastic university professor teaching in Informatics, wants to motivate more female students to continue their studies in Informatics at the PhD level. Even though she was also a PhD student years ago, she feels the new generation may have different concerns and perceptions about pursuing a PhD in this field. After reading this chapter, she will better understand the motivations and concerns of female students in Informatics, which will help her improve her communication with them and design better programmes and approaches to support and encourage their academic and professional growth.

> **James, a school teacher.** James loves to encourage and guide his students to study in different or sometimes unconventional fields based on their strengths and interests. He is not very knowledgeable about the Informatics field, which is one of his students' most popular interests. However, he is aware that fewer females are working in this field. He wants to learn more about the challenges and motivations of females in Informatics so that he can better prepare for in-class activities and share more realistic stories about having a career in IT.

6.2 Methodology

This chapter is part of a series of inquiries we conducted on the data from a large-scale survey on current, past and prospective PhD students in Informatics. The large-scale survey which incorporates a mixture of open and closed questions, was dedicated to understanding why female students pursue a PhD in Computer Science, with participants from all genders included to enable a comparative analysis. For this study, a subset of the original dataset, which includes only female participants, was used. The goal was to gain a comprehensive understanding of the factors influencing the perceptions and decisions of female students in Informatics regarding pursuing a PhD and to share their firsthand comments to present an authentic and detailed picture. A mixed-methods approach was applied to analyse and present this data, incorporating both quantitative and qualitative methods (see Sect. 6.2.1), with a primary focus on qualitative methods such as sharing quotes. Additionally, supportive descriptive statistics are presented to highlight interesting results of the survey. We complemented that survey with a second one, of a smaller scale, aimed at collecting lessons learned by female students who decided to do a PhD in Informatics. This second survey was analysed using only qualitative methods (see Sect. 6.2.2).

6.2.1 Survey A: Why Do Women Pursue a PhD in Computer Science?

We conducted a large survey to answer the overarching question: *"Why do women pursue a PhD in Computer Science?"*. This survey combined a set of quantitative and qualitative answers. We used an *open invitation strategy* [16] by advertising our survey in several channels, namely mailing lists, personal contacts, classes and seminars at universities, conferences, workshops and summer schools. The target population for the survey was Informatics students, researchers, and practitioners in Europe. In the case of participants who already have a PhD, they were encouraged to reflect on their experience during their PhD. We leveraged the contacts of the EUGAIN COST Action and Informatics Europe. By the end of our data collection campaign, on May 30, 2023, the survey received 867 responses from 53 countries. We filtered out 280 of those, as they contained no relevant information.

The large-scale survey collected answers from people of all genders to contrast the answers provided by female respondents with those provided by respondents of other genders. We addressed the more quantitative aspects of the survey, and some high-level qualitative concerns in [1], where a more detailed discussion of the survey design can be found. Here, we focus only on the responses from female participants, primarily on qualitative questions but not exclusively, addressing a concern not explored in [1]. Of the 587 valid survey responses, 309 of the respondents identified as female which is the population we used in this study. The current occupation of all 309 female participants is graphically illustrated in Fig. 6.1. Note that some participants hold more than one position, such as being a PhD student while working in industry. Additional statistics about this population are presented in the following sections of the study.

We focus our qualitative analysis in this chapter mainly on 2 qualitative open questions of our survey, as answered by participants who identify as females. The two questions were:

1. Do you have any insights on what encourages students to start a PhD in computer science?
2. Do you have any insights on what discourages students from starting a PhD in computer science?

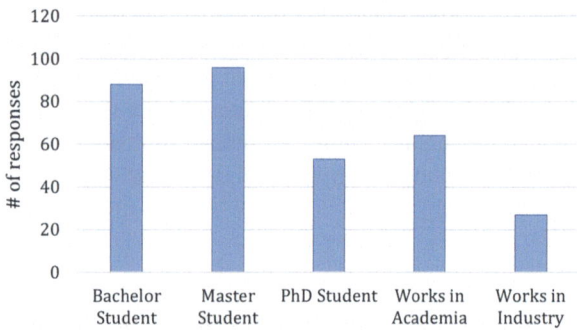

Fig. 6.1 Current occupation of participants

Among 309 female participants, 101 responded to the first question, while 114 responded to the second one once we removed empty and invalid answers (neither of the questions was mandatory in our survey). As such, we have 101 respondents for our first question, concerning *encouraging factors* for doing a PhD in Computer Science, and 114 respondents for our second question, concerning *discouraging factors* for doing a PhD in Computer Science.

The participants' responses are shared in this chapter using a specific notation format, as given in this example: [P107 MS DE]. This notation consists of three parts: **Participant ID** is a unique identifier assigned to each participant who participated in Survey A. **Education Status** indicates the last degree they obtained, in case they are not a student currently, or the degree they are studying. Considering the education status of all participants, we used a two-letter coding: the first letter indicates the study level, bachelor(B), master(M) and PhD(P), second letter, and the second letter indicates whether they are still a student (S) or degree holder(H). Lastly, **Country Code** represents the participant's country using a two-letter code, as defined by international standards. As a result, [P107 MS DE] refers to a participant with ID 107, who is a Master's student from Germany. This detailed notation offers context for the quotes presented in the following sections, enhancing the reader's understanding of the participants' backgrounds and perspectives.

Thematic analysis was conducted on these survey answers by two of the authors, who read through all the comments and categorised them into three main categories: *Career and Professional Development*, *Support and Mentorship*, and *Personal and Environmental Factors*. We identified common subcategories that appeared in both questions, where *encouraging* and *discouraging* factors were mentioned. For example, for the first question (encouraging factors to pursue a PhD), *lack of interest in industry jobs* was identified as a subcategory mentioned by some group of participants, whereas for the second question (discouraging factors), *preference for practical experience and industry* identified as another subcategory. Therefore, these subcategories were grouped under *Career and Professional Development* main category. We will analyse their results in Sects. 6.3.1, 6.3.2, and 6.3.3 in more detail.

Additionally, selected comments from another general open-ended question, "Do you have any further comments?", along with relevant statistics from other questions of the survey, are presented where appropriate to support the analysis.

6.2.2 Survey B: Lessons Learned from a PhD in Informatics

We complement these findings with the survey results we designed to collect testimonials from female PhD students in Informatics. These testimonials aim to provide relatable examples from current and recent PhD students to our readers (such as Derya, a student about to graduate), complementing the body of knowledge in this area with illustrative examples. The survey instrument contained 10 questions. Of those, 2 are contextual questions concerning the country in which the respondents are doing, or did, their PhD, and whether they have already completed their PhD. The remaining 8 questions include 5 relevant questions for this chapter and 3 questions for chapter 3.c.[1] The 5 questions relevant to this chapter are:

1. What are the advantages of being a woman in doctoral studies?
2. What are the challenges/disadvantages of being a woman in doctoral studies?
3. What lessons have you learned during your doctoral studies, working on your dissertation, and in your career so far, that you would like to share?
4. What advice would you offer to future doctoral students?
5. Is there anything else you consider important and would like to share about your experience in doctoral studies?

Our *target population* was women currently doing (or who recently completed) a PhD in Informatics in Europe. Our *sampling strategy* aimed to collect representative testimonials from women with this profile. We recruited our respondents through a convenience sample strategy. We disseminated our survey among the young researchers within EUGAIN COST Action and via the authors' contacts and Informatics PhD students' mailing lists. We were looking for participants from several countries and universities, most doing their PhD, but some having recently completed it, so they could reflect on our questions in hindsight. Achieving a large number of participants was **not** a priority here, as we wanted these personal opinions to serve as *illustrations* of existing findings in the literature, with much larger sample sizes, but not necessarily so specific to our population. The collected testimonials were then presented in a narrative format to provide a comprehensive view of the participants' experiences and viewpoints.

By the end of our data collection campaign, on June 28, 2024, we collected 20 responses, which we will refer to throughout this chapter as R1 to R20. We use the same notation (described in Sect. 6.2.1) which includes the participant's ID, education status and country code. All our respondents identify as women. Five of

---
[1] Chapter entitled "The Impact of Peers, Mentors and Role Models on Successful PhD Studies".

our respondents recently finished their PhD; the remaining 15 are working on their PhD. We received answers from Serbia (6), Portugal (5), Germany (3), Bosnia and Herzegovina (3), Cyprus(1), Italy (1) and Turkey (1).

To avoid language barriers, we created a base questionnaire in English and then translated it into the languages of the contacts we made using our sampling strategy so PhD students could express themselves in a language they are comfortable with. We distributed these versions of questionnaires to our contacts via Google Forms. The questionnaires were completely anonymous, so respondents would feel free to answer without concerns about social norms or other constraints that could otherwise occur. The answers were all translated into English before being analysed.

6.3 Perceptions of Female Respondents

Our perceptions are shaped by various factors such as our past experiences, the influence of those around us, our family, cultural and educational background, expectations, and current emotional state. Depending on the topic of interest, the weight or impact of these factors on an individual's perceptions may vary. In this section, we aim to investigate the perceptions of female students studying Informatics or related fields regarding pursuing a PhD in Informatics, using their own words.

Understanding and categorising this wide range of perceptions provides insights into the motivations and barriers female students face when considering continuing their studies at the PhD level. This analysis will enable us to identify common categories, ultimately helping us formulate strategies and tools to support and encourage more women to pursue advanced studies in this field.

As outlined in Sect. 6.2, these perceptions have been grouped into three main categories: *career and professional development*, *personal and environmental factors*, and *support and mentorship*. Career and professional development involve students' aspirations, the opportunities they see ahead, and their expectations about how a PhD might shape their future career paths. It reflects their hopes for growth and advancement in their chosen fields. Personal and environmental factors consider the influence of individual circumstances, such as family responsibilities or financial concerns, alongside broader societal and cultural influences that affect their decision-making process. Lastly, support and mentorship highlight the guidance and encouragement students receive from their academic and professional networks, which plays a significant role in shaping their confidence and motivation to pursue advanced studies.

In the following subsections, we explain and illustrate (see Fig. 6.2) these categories in more detail, addressing both the encouraging and discouraging factors through selected quotes to authentically represent our respondents' views. We quoted the students' responses without edits to ensure their perspectives were captured accurately. After presenting them, we analysed and interpreted the key

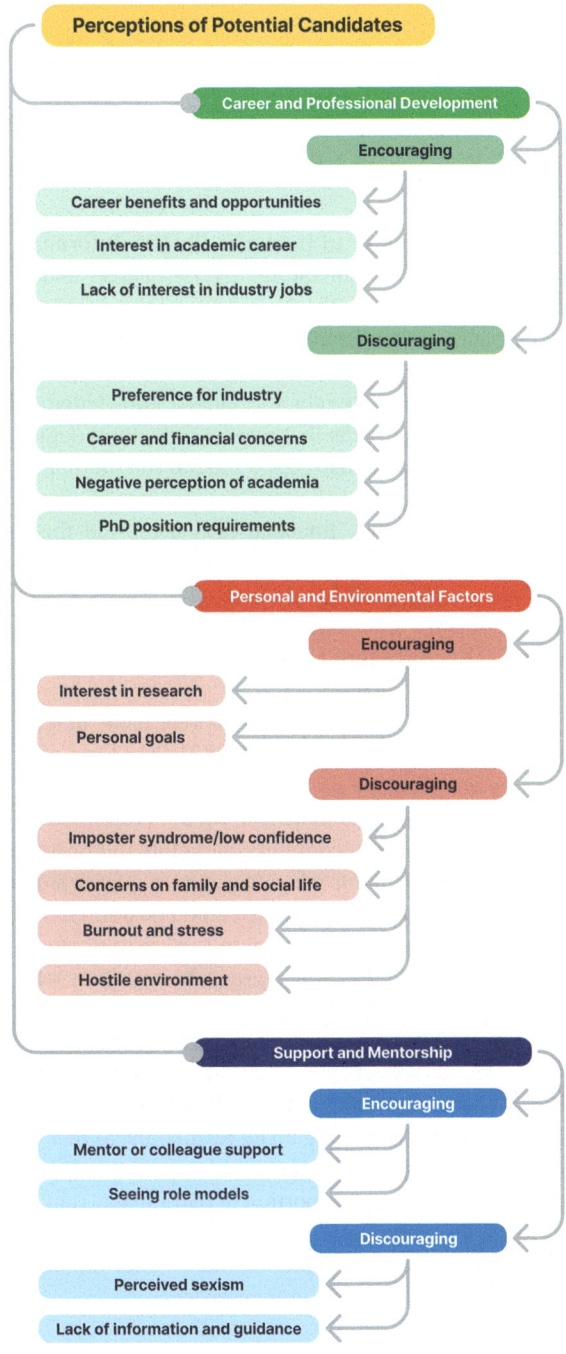

Fig. 6.2 Main factors shaping the female perception of PhD in Informatics

categories, offering insights into how these perceptions shape female students' experiences in Informatics.

6.3.1 Career and Professional Development

Women may choose to pursue a PhD in Informatics for many reasons. One of the most important motivating drivers is career and professional development. This decision can significantly shape future opportunities in both academia and industry. Participants in our study identified a range of factors "both encouraging and discouraging" that influenced their decision to pursue a PhD. Many are motivated by the opportunity to gain specialised knowledge, advance in their chosen fields, and access career paths that require a doctoral degree. Intellectual fulfilment and a passion for research also play a crucial role in their decision-making. However, the decision is not without challenges. Concerns about the length and demanding nature of PhD programmes, financial pressures, and the availability of more attractive prospects in the industry often make this choice more complex.

6.3.1.1 Encouraging Factors

The flexibility to pursue different career paths in research, education, or industry is appealing for some students: [💬 P821 PH IT] *"[...]make a great career doing PhD in Computer Science so that anyone can have three paths: in a research area or educational area or an industrial area."* Preferring the university atmosphere, some women enjoy more freedom in conducting their research: [💬 P82 MS DE] *"Having more independence on what to conduct own research in (compared to industrial jobs)."* The prospect of securing a good position in the industry or the non-academic public service fields is a reason to further their studies: [💬 P362 MS DE] *"Aimed jobs that require a doctoral degree."* Many others who start a PhD can expect higher salaries and better benefits and climb the career ladder faster: [💬 P481 MS BA] *"Better work opportunities after PhD qualification."* Additionally, the participants were asked to reflect on how a PhD might influence their future career prospects, responding to the statement "A PhD would improve my future career." on a Likert scale, as shown in Fig. 6.3. The results reveal that most respondents believe that a PhD would benefit their career, either strongly ("definitely yes") or to some extent ("rather yes"). A notable portion of participants remained neutral. Only a minority of respondents expressed less favourable views ("rather not" and "not at all"). Overall, these results highlight a predominant belief among participants in the benefits of earning a Ph.D. for their future careers.

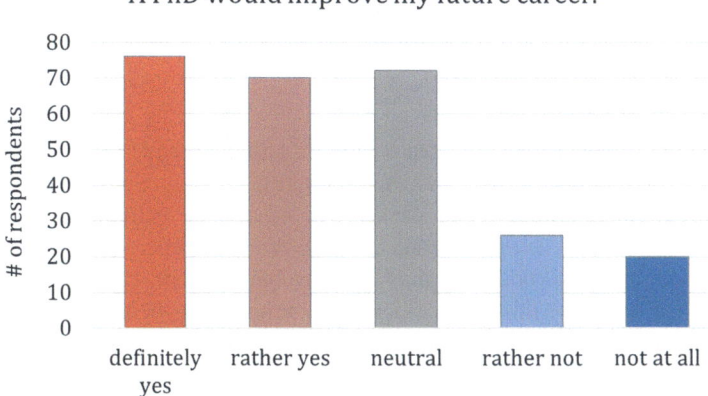

Fig. 6.3 Responses to the statement "A PhD would improve my future career"

Career Benefits and Opportunities
A PhD is seen as a sign of expertise in a chosen field and a valuable pathway to advance in science, research, and academia. For some, the appeal lies not only in gaining knowledge but also in the flexibility it offers to pursue different career trajectories, whether in research, education, or industry. Additionally, it provides greater independence in conducting research, especially in academic settings. For others, a PhD is a means to secure better work prospects, whether in academia or professional fields that require a doctoral qualification. Some participants are motivated by career progression and view a PhD as a necessary step to achieve specific goals. In contrast, others approach it more transactionally, pursuing it for higher salaries and improved benefits. As a long-term commitment, candidates may face challenges staying on course, especially when the PhD is seen primarily as a stepping stone for career advancement rather than a passion for research or teaching.

Some students see the PhD as the first step to a position as a university professor: [💬 P418 PH NL] *"Sometimes as a path to an academic career[...]"*, and their perception of what it entails goes beyond merely obtaining a degree. It involves devoting significant time and effort to research and contributing to developing new knowledge within their field, as one student explained: [💬 P668 MH NL] *"Having the drive. Wanting to spend time researching specific problems you think are important. Wanting to keep learning new things. Not being content, just continuing."* Commitment to rigorous academic research and professional development is essential for those aspiring to academic careers: [💬 P637 MS IT] *"I believe that the most prominent reasons for students to pursue the PhD studies in computer science are the passion they feel for their profession but also the curiosity and desire to push their abilities further."*

> **Interest in Academic Career**
> A PhD is a fundamental first step to building a higher-education career for someone who chooses academia as their primary goal. Some candidates may have an inborn love and passion for academia, including academic responsibilities such as research and teaching activities. Interacting with their students and sharing knowledge may be enjoyable for them. Thus, a doctorate is a means to pursue this career track. For some others, their willingness to grow intellectually and improve professionally is crucial in enrolling in a doctoral programme. In addition, the nature of the academic environment and the way of working may attract some other candidates to pursue a PhD.

Some students prefer academia over industry. The stressful environment and the long working hours of industry positions may be challenging. After working in industry, some students return to university. As noted by a former PhD student, [💬 P418 PH NL] *"I have had a PhD student who had worked in industry and concluded that this was not for her."* These students may face the long process of obtaining a doctoral degree with more determination than candidates who only see a PhD as a gateway to advance in their careers. Some others prefer academic research over industry work, feeling that industry focuses more on short-term practical outcomes: [💬 P321 PS NL] *"Industry is mostly interested in very practical fast-paced development."* Experience in the industry can make academic work seem more appealing, particularly due to the increased flexibility and freedom it provides: [💬 P80 MS DE] *"[...] freedom in the work I choose to do [...]"* and the desire to stay longer in the university environment: [💬 P812 MS DK] *"[...] Want to stay in the university bubble a little longer."*

> **Lack of Interest in Industry Jobs**
> While industrial jobs may offer financial benefits, they often come with constraints on research freedom and autonomy. Research in these settings is typically driven by commercial interests and financial gains rather than pure scientific inquiry. In an academic environment, students can freely engage in research activities valued and driven by curiosity and the aspiration to add knowledge and contribute to the field. That is why academia appeals to candidates who want to explore their research interests without being limited or having to consider the financial outcomes of their work. Career changes are another reason candidates apply for doctoral studies. They often have several

(continued)

years of working experience in the industry before deciding to pursue a PhD, as the industry may not meet their expectations. However, Informatics offers excellent opportunities for growth and change, making a PhD a promising path for those seeking to advance their careers.

6.3.1.2 Discouraging Factors

Even if one can choose to do a PhD, it is not for everyone. Many students prefer not to pursue a PhD for several reasons. For instance, many prefer gaining hands-on experience: [🔍 P80 MS DE] *" Preferences for more practical experience."* and see better and more diverse job opportunities in the industry: [🔍 P427 MH NL] *"better opportunities in the industry - can't find a project that aligns with your interest"*, and [🔍 P110 MS DE] *"Industry [...] different areas to work in."*

For some, the academic environment feels disconnected from practical applications and is seen as overly theoretical: [🔍 P456 PH AT] *" [...] too theoretical and thus not relevant for industry...."* Beyond these perceptions, concerns about job insecurity in academia also influence students' decisions. Many find the stability and financial benefits of the industry more attractive: [🔍 P232 PH SI] *" A long commitment, no prospects of a stable job in academia after finishing the PhD, competitive environment (and low self-esteem), better salary and more stability in industry."*

Participants were also asked to respond to the statement, "I have better job opportunities in the industry than at university." on a Likert scale, as shown in Fig. 6.4. The distribution of responses shows a significant inclination towards industry, with many participants acknowledging it as offering better job prospects.

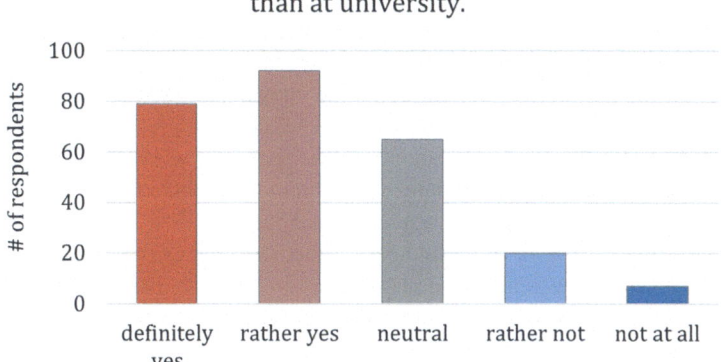

Fig. 6.4 Responses to the statement "I have better job opportunities in the industry than at university"

> **Preference for Industry**
> Industrial jobs may offer diverse and different opportunities, especially for those passionate about practising and working with technology. Thus, the industry may appeal more to these candidates who would not consider starting a PhD. They love solving real-life problems and deploying their hands-on skills to develop tangible products that are useful and impactful for humanity. They may perceive a PhD as a purely theoretical endeavour, even if this is far from necessarily the case.

Others express concerns about whether a PhD will advance their career goals: [💬 P369 PS IE] *"I feel like doing a PhD in computer science doesn't help in career. Using that time to work in a company is much better if you seek to advance your career...".*

Some also doubt the job opportunities and the challenges of securing a stable, long-term academic career: [💬 P541 PH SI] *"[...] uncertain job prospects (moving from postdoc to postdoc after completing PhD)[...] prolonging studies and not being able to settle down for a few more years."* and [💬 P528 MH IT] *"Uncertainties about a future in Academia"*.

Indeed, the payment gap is a recurring concern: [💬 P107 MS DE] *"Especially in computer science, the payment outside of the university is way higher. It feels like a waste of possible income staying at the university."* This sometimes leads to students giving up on their PhD and switching over to the industry: [💬 P659 MS FI] *"Usually, the salary of a PhD student is very low, and it doesn't allow them to live decently[...]. This adds extra stress, and many people cannot cope with it, so they leave for the industry where the salaries are much higher."*

> **Career and Financial Concerns**
> Many students believe that pursuing a PhD offers fewer career advancement opportunities than industry positions. Another obstacle that may prevent a PhD candidate from embarking on this journey is that career prospects are not always clear. After graduation, the candidate may need to find a post-doctoral position, which may not immediately lead to a secure, long-term appointment. The student may then have to search for other academic work. Such a lengthy process may scare some candidates from pursuing a PhD. Additionally, the significant salary gap between academia and industry is a key reason why students choose to work in the industry rather than pursue a long PhD. The stress caused by low PhD stipends and the inability to maintain a decent standard of living further motivates students to transition to industry roles, where financial rewards are much higher.

6 Voices of Female Informatics Students Across Universities 119

Some students negatively perceive academia and its stringent requirements, making a career in industry seem more attractive. They may find a PhD in Informatics irrelevant to industry needs and less valuable than actual industry experience: [💬 P120 MS DE] *"I always saw an academic career as a fallback option for people who didn't find anything else. In IT, if you have actual skills, you don't need degrees."*

They may also find the PhD process too demanding, with a stressful work-life balance that requires sacrifices and constant availability at the cost of their overall wellness: [💬 P112 MS DE] *"the long time in which you have to work a lot of hours without getting paid much when at the same time I can start my career nearly as well without a PhD."*, and the [💬 P96 MS DE] *"'work is life' mentality with working on weekends, always reachable, and so on."* Some others see doctoral studies as too long and exhausting, requiring accomplishing multiple tasks at the same time:[💬 P115 MS DE] *"You need about 5 years to get the PhD and have to do a lot besides from your PhD project (like teaching)."*

> **Negative Perception of Academia: Workload, Stress, and Mental Health Challenge**
> Some candidates doubt starting a PhD because of their negative perception of academic careers. To them, such a career may feel stressful and challenging to manage due to the high workload involving teaching, research, and administrative duties. Strict promotion requirements, together with tight deadlines and the demand to be constantly available, can cause burnout. Furthermore, the time and effort required to apply for research funding, with no guarantee of success, adds another layer of stress, complicating the already demanding academic journey.

Some others think finding a good PhD position may be challenging, with the pressure to publish often being a source of anxiety. They are also frustrated by their work falling behind paywalls, making it less accessible. This leads to a feeling that the effort may not be worth it, except for the academic recognition: [💬 P120 MS DE] *"[...] the conditions for getting a PhD in any field seem ridiculously constraining [...] like having to have published an official paper at least three times [...]it just doesn't seem worth the effort, except for the title itself."*.

Enrolling for a PhD requires family sacrifices like moving abroad: [💬 P524 PH SI] *" Requirement to move abroad to get a PhD."* Many others may struggle to have good academic records and high grades since a good PhD position may have rigorous application requirements, such as a high CGPA: [💬 P93 MS DE] *" [...] high requirements on grades."*

> **PhD Position Requirements**
> One more point of discouragement is the stringent requirements for a PhD position, such as a high CGPA and the expectation of novel research ideas. Outstanding recommendation letters and substantial past research records are also required. When considered alongside the competition to find a doctoral position, these barriers may deter students from starting a PhD. Another challenge is finding the right mentor whose research interests are compatible with the student's own. This matters because having a supportive mentor is vital throughout the long years of the doctorate.

6.3.2 Personal and Environmental Factors

Personal factors, such as desires, plans, and preferences, are important influences when making decisions in life. Deciding to pursue a PhD is particularly challenging, as it has impacts on various aspects of one's life. In this section, we share the personal and environmental factors that were mentioned by our participants in pursuing a PhD, again under two categories: encouraging and discouraging factors. It is interesting to observe that the most encouraging factors are either the motivations to begin a PhD, such as a passion for research or the potential rewards upon its completion, including the prestige of the title, personal fulfilment, and the achievement of success. On the other hand, discouraging factors mostly centre around the challenges encountered during the PhD process, such as concerns over stress and potential burnout, the environment they will be working in, and the possible negative impacts on their family plans or social life.

6.3.2.1 Encouraging Factors

Some of the participants highlighted the importance of having a strong interest and passion in doing research in this area: [💬 P637 MS IT] *"I believe that the most prominent reason for students to pursue the PhD studies in computer science is the passion they feel for their profession but also the curiosity and desire to push their abilities further."*. [💬 P445 PS NL] *"For me, it was the beauty of logic and mathematical proofs with applications that kept being neat while having an impact"*.

One PhD holder mentioned her specific memories of how she realised she enjoyed doing research, and it was the main reason she decided to start doing PhD: [💬 P439 PH IT] *"The main reason why I decided to start a PhD was that I enjoyed a lot the course on Algorithms I took during my Master's studies. I asked the teacher of that course to be my master's thesis supervisor, and she gave me an open problem to solve. In this way, I realised how fun it was to do research. In general, I believe that the motivation given by good and enthusiastic teachers is essential.".* This comment is a good example of supporting and encouraging students during their early studies.

> **Interest in Research**
> Pursuing a PhD, by definition, demands extensive research efforts in addition to other academic requirements. Without a passion for research, the process can become burdensome and challenging. Some participants mentioned that their interest in research developed during their bachelor studies. This observation suggests that increasing the early research experiences by including bachelor students in projects or interesting studies could be a valuable strategy to encourage female participation in PhD programmes.

Many participants mentioned personal factors as motivational drivers in choosing the PhD path. For example, [💬 P91 BS DE] mentioned clearly what she wants in her life and how starting a PhD would provide it to her: *"Knowing how it could help me to achieve my personal goals specifically, would encourage me to start a PhD. By personal goals I mean things like independence, freedom in the work I choose to do, expertise, the opportunity for my work to be acknowledged, financial stability, opportunities to do different interesting and important things, and developing my skills and soft skills. [...]"* . Other various needs and desires are also mentioned such as [💬 P708 PH AT] *"freedom, learn something new every day to dig deep into things that interest you"*, [💬 P496 MS BA] *"[...] status in society"* and [💬 P235 MS RS] *"Becoming an expert in a field which you are excited about. Experiencing highest level work and getting to know talented peers."*.

> **Personal Goals**
> Choosing to pursue a PhD is a demanding and challenging path that requires resilience, self-discipline, creativity, and patience. It is a long journey with many potential challenges. To complete this journey joyfully and successfully, one needs strong motivation. One of the strongest motivations in life comes from personal goals, dreams, or targets because they bring passion and ambition which can make the journey more enjoyable, "the light at the end of the tunnel", namely the rewards at the end, is often mentioned by many voices, varying individually: status in society, independence, freedom, financial stability, becoming an expert etc.

6.3.2.2 Discouraging Factors

Various personal reasons may lead individuals to avoid or dismiss the idea of pursuing a PhD. This section will explore the factors beyond a lack of interest in PhD studies. Specifically, we focus on the barriers to pursuing a PhD even if they have considered it as a potential path. Low self-confidence, *impostor syndrome* [14], family restrictions, concerns about social life, or not having enough information about PhD can be listed as some of these factors.

Many participants are worried about the difficulties and challenges that might occur while pursuing their PhD. [💬 P47 MS PT] *"Burn-out. Stressful and anxiety-inducing deadlines."*. [💬 P321 PS NL]*"It is quite a commitment, known to be long hours, hard work, lots of smart people, impostor syndrome [...]"*. [💬 P363 PH NL] *"wrong expectations and wrong picture in media, film and school. Academia has become a rather hostile and stressful working environment with much too high expectations considering the pay. Only the very dedicated idealistic persons still pursue it. Work-life balance has become a big issue and students see and feel it as well."*.

> **Impostor Syndrome and Low Confidence**
> Lower self-confidence, diminished self-esteem, and the belief of not being good enough are some of the most negatively influential personal factors in the decision-making process of pursuing a PhD. The study [1] shows that the female participants who decided not to pursue a PhD had significantly less self-confidence compared to male participants. Similarly, female participants are less confident than males in their interaction with other students. These results put female students in a more vulnerable position in terms of the negative effects on their success through their studies and decisions. It raises the importance of organising support and mentorship programmes to provide support to help them cope with these feelings.

Some participants are worried about family planning and the impact of the long study duration of a PhD on their plans. [💬 P235 MS RS]*"Possibly having to give up or postpone many decisions in your personal life [...]"*. [💬 P581 MS IT] *"[...] the fact that the majority of Italians finish university at 25/26 discourages them from studying more, since at that age you generally want to start a family and your own life [...]"*. One participant shared her concerns about pregnancy and potential problems that can occur during it, [💬 P229 PS IE] *"[...] if you are a woman who is planning a family when going on maternity leave (which is very short in Ireland) you will lose your scholarship when you take a break, and for Ireland, many would not be eligible for state support because for that you would have to have paid taxes before going on leave. This could be very discouraging [...]"*. The work-life balance is another highlighted concern by the survey participants. [💬 P481 MS

BA] *"Additional study and research time which is hard to keep up with considering they want to work and earn and support their lifestyles."*

> **Concerns on Family Plans and Social Life**
> The potential impact of long study duration on family plans and intense work schedules due to deadlines raises concerns for potential PhD candidates about their future family and social lives. It is essential to be fully aware of the expectations and demands of PhD studies in advance. Being prepared and making detailed plans ahead of time can help balance the requirements of PhD studies with maintaining a healthy and fulfilling social life. This includes understanding time management, how to deal with strict and short deadlines, and how to manage intense study and work periods. Additionally, it can be beneficial to find a support system that can help during difficult times and find various approaches to manage stress.

Also, some negative experiences during their bachelor's or master's studies can lead to discouragement. These negative experiences can be either personal, such as burnout, or environmental, such as the hostile or sexist environment they experienced during their earlier studies. A few participants mentioned burnout and the difficulties they had during their earlier studies in their field: [💬 P275 PH NL] *"You are smashed after bachelor and masters"* and [💬 P855 MS DK] *"[...] exhausted from studying, burned out, wanting to get away from the university"* and [💬 P369 MS IR] *"Usually, the salary of a PhD student is very low and it doesn't allow them to live decently, at least in an expensive city like Dublin. This adds extra stress and many people are not able to cope with it, so they leave for the industry where the salaries are much higher."*.

> **Burnout and Stress**
> Burnout and stress are common challenges discouraging female students from pursuing a PhD in Informatics. Academic overload can leave students feeling incapable of reaching their educational goals. Financial pressures, particularly in high-cost cities, add to the burden, often pushing students toward more stable, better-paying jobs in the industry. These challenges highlight the need for more robust support systems to help students manage academic demands and financial stress, allowing them to continue their studies confidently.

Other reasons mentioned by some of the female students were related to their negative experiences or observations of the work environment. [💬 P275 PH NL] *"As a female PhD student in CS, I faced rude male Masters students when I was a TA (teaching assistant). During my first year as a TA, they were always trying to undermine me, asking a male TA a question which I set in the assignment [...]".* [💬 P708 PS AT] *"time-limited contracts, 75% or 50% contracts, some Professors and how they treat PhDs"* [💬 P96 MS DE] *"male dominated field..."*

> **Hostile Environment**
> Some female students described facing hostility in their academic work environments. Some felt their authority was undermined in teaching roles, with male students bypassing them and seeking answers from male teaching assistants instead. Others mentioned job insecurity due to short-term contracts and how some professors treated PhD students. Additionally, the male-dominated culture, with expectations of always being available and working weekends, added to their stress and pressure. Addressing these issues requires fostering a more inclusive work environment, with better support for female students in teaching roles and improved job security.

It is also important to highlight that many of our female voices mentioned that the lack of female researchers in the field and their potential or existing work environment would not concern them. [💬 P93 MS DE] *"[...] I know that I am going to be one of the only females in my group, but I am not afraid of it. This is how it has been during my complete studies, so I am used to this and comfortable with it. Still, I would love to have at least a few other females with me."*. The participants were also asked if they agree or disagree with the statement, "I am afraid of being one of only a few females in a PhD group." the resulting Likert scale answers are given in Fig. 6.5. Most respondents indicated that they are "not at all" afraid, while smaller groups

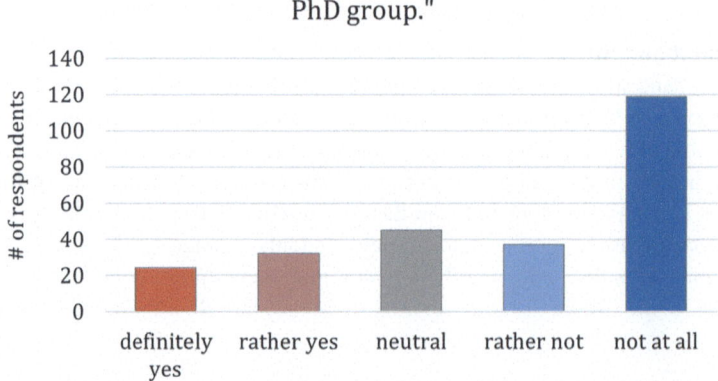

Fig. 6.5 Responses to the statement "I am afraid of being one of only a few females in a PhD group"

expressed varying levels of agreement. This suggests that a significant portion of participants do not have concerns about being one of the few females in a PhD group.

As a female Informatics student or engineer who experienced gender unbalanced work environment, it is mentioned that it would not be difficult or something new for them: [💬 P668 MH NL] *"[...] I was already convinced I wanted to do this and am (unfortunately) quite used to a gender imbalance, both for study and work. This does not influence my plans much as it does not matter which direction I go. [...] I had no idea what the balance would be. But I have been used to being one of the few or even the only female in a company. This would not stop me."* and [💬 P47 MS PT] *"I don't think someone with a master's in computer science would be averse to getting a PhD just because of gender imbalance. They already have a master's, they've experienced it before."*. On the other hand, it is important to highlight that some voices shared their negative experiences during their studies or in the work environment and mentioned how it negatively affected their perceptions.

6.3.3 Support and Mentorship

According to the survey results presented in [1], female participants who choose not to start a PhD have lower self-confidence than males. Rosenstein et al. [14] also surveyed graduate and undergraduate computer science students, and they show that women (71%) are experiencing *impostor syndrome* more frequently than men (52%). Positive encouragement and support from professors, family, or peers are crucial factors in students' decision-making, particularly among women, and help to mitigate the lower self-confidence observed in female students. Encouragement and support can be provided in various ways: direct mentorship, engaging students in research projects during their undergraduate or master's studies, offering or directing them to available positions and opportunities, providing a safe and supportive environment and organising informative sessions on the PhD process, seminars and events where students can find their role models are some examples of supportive activities.

6.3.3.1 Encouraging Factors

Many participants shared their positive experiences with their mentors, peers, and role models: [💬 P421 PH DE] *"My professor was my role model. The way she included us in the projects encouraged me a lot."*. Direct invitation or encouragement from the mentor is mentioned to be one of the most influential factors in a student's decision to pursue further academic opportunities. [💬 P232 PH SI] *"A personal invitation from the professors is a big encouragement and often a deciding factor. Even if there are no available options at their research group/department, there is always the option of helping your students get in contact with other universities and researchers from the international scientific community..",* [💬 P541 PH SI] *"Explicit invitation/encouragement from a mentor/professor, nice research project (possibly involving the student).".* Some believe that it can even help to boost and improve self-confidence and [💬 P33 MS DE] *" I think encouragement from a professor or researcher would help a lot to build confidence.".*

> **Encouragement from Mentors and Colleagues**
> Encouraging, motivating, and supporting female students during their studies and decision-making processes are crucial in shaping their future career choices, especially in academia. Research indicates that female students in the Informatics field often experience lower self-confidence than their male colleagues, highlighting their particular need for and benefit from such support. This assistance, whether provided by professors or colleagues, helps them improve their skills, boost their confidence, and gain valuable guidance. Additionally, personal experiences shared by female PhD students and holders serve as an important source of inspiration and confidence-building for prospective PhD candidates.

Role models not only motivate and increase one's confidence in future decisions on pursuing a PhD but can also influence earlier choices in life and give the courage to start a new journey such as this example: [💬 P275 PH NL] *"I was highly inspired by my supervisor at X institution (during my Masters thesis project) to pursue PhD. That along with the fact that I found an approachable Computer Science professor who enjoyed teaching (as opposed to the majority of the school teachers and teachers from the Bachelor I had who taught because they were getting paid for it). This CS professor intrigued my interest in the working logic of machine learning models so much that I switched from Biomedical Engineering (both Bachelor and Master) to CS (for PhD).".*

They also want to hear more about personal experiences from PhD students or PhD holders: [💬 P131 MS DE] *"more information events, role models, insights in the work and life of other PhD".* Including role models and real-life insights can provide a more relatable perspective: [💬 P187 PH AT] *"Challenge-driven and example-based stories on what a PhD can be like and why PhD@CS is good to do. In addition, sharing personal experiences helps.".* Hearing specific experiences from the current PhD students can provide a clearer picture of what to expect during the PhD journey: [💬 P778 MS DK] *"Talking to current PhD students who can tell about specific experiences.".*

> **Seeing Role Models**
> Seeing a successful woman with a PhD in Informatics, hearing about her experiences and challenges, and learning how she overcame them can be highly motivating for a young female at the start of her career. It creates a strong belief that "I can do it" and shows that even successful and strong women in this field have faced similar challenges. This perspective can be invaluable during difficult times and while making important life decisions. Organising seminars and talks given by these successful female researchers and PhD holders would help female students meet various role models and create an environment where they can freely address their questions and concerns.

6.3.3.2 Discouraging Factors

As outlined in earlier sections, a lack of information about PhD process is observed in many comments in the survey. Some are unaware of the application requirements or process, while others are concerned about the PhD process, expectations, responsibilities, or their future career opportunities after completing their PhD: [💬 MS73DE] *"Unclear how to apply, unclear what I would do after the PhD. Unclear on family and relationship in the future.."* and [💬 P39 MS DE] *"not enough information about what a PhD in computer science looks like"*. Some participants highlighted the difficulty of reaching detailed well-organized information about PhD process. [💬 P447 PS NL] *"Poor organisation of information around the PhD process. If the prospective PhD student must expend huge effort to find all the relevant information, some will give up beforehand."*. And there are some assumptions about what the future holds based on their negative experiences today: [💬 P126 BS DE] *"We don't even get a lot of information on what we have to do for the upcoming Bachelor thesis. You have to ask other students for that, and I don't know a lot of older students in computer science, so that's already an issue. So getting information on a PhD seems difficult."*.

To further investigate how much the participants know about the aims and requirements of a PhD, two different statements were given to them as part of the survey. The participants were then asked if they agreed or disagreed with these statements using a Likert scale with five levels: "I am aware of the aims and contents of PhD studies." and "I am aware of the requirements for starting a PhD". The results show that (Fig. 6.6) almost half of the participants were either uninformed or unsure about the PhD process. Additionally, more than 80% of survey participants indicated that they had never attended any informative session or programme about studying for a PhD, as shown in Fig. 6.7.

Forty-nine participants who stated that they attended an informative event were also asked about the specific events they participated in. The events they attended

Fig. 6.6 Awareness of PhD process

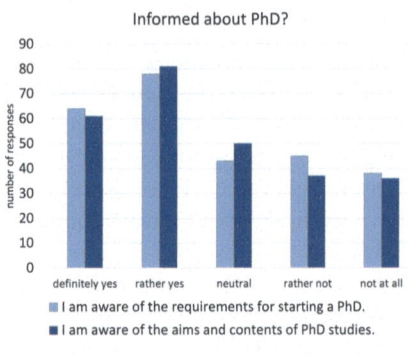

Fig. 6.7 Attendance to informative events

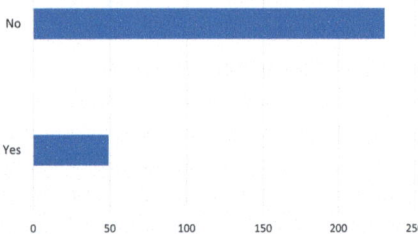

were in various formats and structures. Some attended specific workshops and programmes that offered mentorship and advice on pursuing a PhD where current PhD students, professors, and post-docs also shared their experiences and career paths: [💬 P232 PH SI] *"Our department at the university had an information event at which PhD studies were presented. We were encouraged to talk to PhD students, professors and post-docs about what doing a PhD looks like."*. Some mentioned their attendance at the invited speakers' seminars and how they benefited from Q&A sessions at the end. There are also no positive experiences with some of these events: [💬 P285 PS NL] *"I enrolled in an honours programme that would prepare you for starting a PhD. I quit after the first course though because I didn't like the courses and how things were organised."*. Organising more well-designed information sessions, activities, or events to inform students about the PhD process, and providing a safe and open environment for them to ask questions to clarify their concerns or uncertainties, would be beneficial for them to have a clearer opinion about the PhD process.

Survey participants provided valuable suggestions and practical tips. One participant emphasised the importance of awareness and clear information: [💬 P447 PS NL] *"Knowing that it's an option at all is the basic prerequisite. If prospective PhD students are actively informed of what it is and how it works, the interest among them will be naturally attracted. A good working relationship with their promoter is also a big plus."*. Another participant highlighted the misconceptions and the need for proper information and guidance process about the PhD process and gave some practical suggestions: [💬 P835 PS IS] *"Students usually are afraid that they will not succeed in PhD, as it will be much harder than what they are doing (which is not true at all). Educate them about what is research and PhD might help them to consider enrolling. This can be by including them in research projects, and papers, providing research methodology as a course for them."*

> **Lack of Information and Guidance**
> One of the biggest challenges in the decision process of pursuing a PhD is the lack of clear and detailed information and guidance. Well-organised information sources are crucial for providing prospective PhD students with up-to-date and relevant details on what a PhD is like. Additionally, organising meetings between candidates and current PhD students can provide personal insights and mentorship, helping to clarify any uncertainties and build confidence in their decision.

Participants also suggested that more direct interaction with experienced individuals could be beneficial: [💬 P581 MS IT] *"It would be helpful if the university organised meetings with professors and PhD students (even ones that have finished it and now work in companies or the university) to tell their experience and give students enrolled in a degree more information."*. Additionally, one participant pointed out the need for better and clearer information on the structure and objectives of a PhD programme: [💬 P871 MH DE] *"It only informs about PhD is better after MSc than going into the industry. Not about aims and organisation and planning a PhD."*.

6.4 Insights from Current and Former PhD Students

This section presents testimonials collected via survey B (introduced in Sect. 6.2.2). These testimonials provide valuable insights from current and former PhD students. Although coming from different countries and backgrounds, these insights have many things in common.

6.4.1 Advantages and Disadvantages

There are not many advantages of being a woman in doctoral studies. Some respondents noticed advantages that are not gender related: [💬 R1 PH CY] *"That you push science forward"*, [💬 R10 PS RS] *"The possibility of engaging in research work that encourages creativity and the search for new ideas and solutions, which leads to constant advancement and self-improvement in all aspects of one's personality"* and [💬 R18 PS BA] *"Freedom, accomplishment despite all the challenges".* Other respondents noticed a possibility of becoming a role model and decreasing the current underrepresentation status: [💬 R11 PS PT] *"Inspire future generations of women to pursue academic careers."* and [💬 R2 PS IT] *"The chance to prove women are powerful and active contributors in science for society".* Practical advantages include dedicated events and quotas: [💬 R19 PH BA] *"There are dedicated conferences and workshops for women"*, [💬 R13 PS DE] *"[...] I see it as an advantage to be able to take part in them."* and [💬 R15 PS PT] *"Maybe quotas in some situations are an advantage..."*

Some respondents find that there are no advantages, saying that simply as: [💬 R14 PS PT] *"None"* and [💬 R5 PS RS] *"I wouldn't say there are any :)"*, while others explicitly say that there are disadvantages: [💬 R6 PS RS] *"In my opinion, there are no advantages, only disadvantages."* and [💬 R7 PH RS] *"Haha... well, there are no advantages. A woman in science, especially in engineering... it wasn't exactly easy."*

The underrepresentation affects the visibility: [💬 R4 PH DE] *"Getting attention. Positive or negative, but I feel visible."* and [💬 R16 PS PT] *"In a room full of men, it is easier for people to remember me and my name, given the existing minority of women."* However, some women find this an important disadvantage: [💬 R13 PS DE] *"As you are less represented, you are automatically different and receive more attention and criticism."*

When talking about disadvantages and challenges, all the respondents had much longer answers and the number of disadvantages was bigger. Disadvantages start with simply having more work to do: [💬 R1 PH CY] *"That you often need to undertake additional load/tasks"* and [💬 R9 PS RS] *"I have noticed that female colleagues are often more meticulous and responsible in working on some secondary tasks, so they are more frequently assigned administrative tasks not necessarily related to their doctoral studies. "*. The problem of more work also arises from fake gender equality solutions: [💬 R4 PH DE] *"Being asked to be on a million service roles for "equal" gender representation."*. On the other hand, this also introduces another kind of problem: [💬 R4 PH DE] *"Getting told that we only got something because we were a woman."*

Disadvantages continue with the necessity women face to prove themselves: [💬 R13 PS DE] *"I think that as a woman you have more of a feeling of having to prove something."*, [💬 R7 PH RS] *"My feeling is that we are generally less appreciated compared to our male colleagues."*, [💬 R4 PH DE] *"The old cliches of having to prove ourselves more than anyone else."*, [💬 R5 PS RS] *"[...] there is still a perception that some areas and topics are more 'male,' and often female colleagues need more time to prove themselves in the same things and gain attention."* and [💬 R16 PS PT] *"I feel some pressure and insecurity in having a "good" academic performance and as a researcher. I try to keep a mask of self-confidence in my abilities, expressing myself through clothes and makeup. I feel that, if I don't, I will not be "taken seriously" professionally."*

The problems women face when balancing family and doctoral studies are the most common and are widely discussed: [💬 R18 PS BA] *"Balancing family and doctoral studies is complicated, especially with kids."* There are two kinds of problems. One is related to society's pressure to start a family and the other is the lack of wider support: [💬 R10 PS RS] *"If a woman has a family (husband, child/children), or intends to have one, the challenges are much greater. The organisation of the studies (both institutional and personal through research work and collaboration with a mentor) can significantly affect a woman's family life, which should not suffer due to any shortcomings in this area."* Society pressure was mentioned in different contexts: [💬 R19 PH BA] *"Prejudice of society, motherhood (pregnancy)"*, [💬 R20 PS BA] *"The societal pressure to start my own family as soon as possible created unnecessary stress and caused anxiety. Additionally, after deciding to have a family, my previous mentor's attitude and the prejudice of people who believe one should not start a family before finishing studies put great pressure on me and became a breaking point for my psychology."* and [💬 R6 PS RS] *"The pressure from family and surroundings to start my own family as soon as possible indirectly creates pressure to complete my doctoral studies as quickly as possible, which further causes anxiety and destroys my motivation to work."* Similarly, starting a family imposes different burdens on women, starting from uncertainty as: [💬 R5 PS RS] *"inevitably many things are beyond our control."* to practical issues on getting paid maternity leave: [💬 R15 PS PT] *"The scholarship is not a proper work contract, which delays the start of a taxpayer's life. Someone teaching in Portugal cannot pay taxes on her scholarship. For women, who may need a maternity leave earlier than most men, this is a problem."*.

There are also some neutral opinions about having no advantages, or disadvantages: [💬 R8 PH RS] *"I did not notice any special advantages or disadvantages compared to my male colleagues."* [💬 R9 PS RS] *"I am not sure if there are any advantages or if being a woman in any way facilitated or hindered my doctoral journey."* [💬 R17 PH PT] *"None, I think it is the same as when a man does a PhD."*.

> **Advantages and Disadvantages**
> Our respondents highlighted disadvantages related to family planning and support for women having children. They also mentioned the enforced need to prove themselves and the issue of receiving additional workload not directly connected to their PhD studies. On the other hand, advantages were not addressed, and many respondents do not believe there are any.

6.4.2 Lessons Learned and Advice to Share

Females find support in both teamwork and within themselves: [💬 R1 PH CY] *"You need a team to support you"*, [💬 R2 PS IT] *"Surround yourself with people supporting you. Self-confidence plays a crucial role in achieving goals."*, [💬 R4

PH DE] *"Academia is mostly about endurance and trusting ourselves that we can forge our path."*, [💬 R7 PH RS] *"It's tough to work alone; it's much easier, better, and more interesting in a team, and you achieve results faster."* and [💬 R3 PH TR] *"I realised that receiving support at the right times and places can significantly enhance a person's success, motivation, and contributions to society and science [...] While it may not always be a time when we feel our best, it is crucial to pick ourselves up when we fall and to access the support we need during those times."*.

External support may come from peers and different networks: [💬 R4 PH DE] *"Invest in your relationships. We spend a lot of time with colleagues, so it is worth making those relationships good. And networks will serve you well in the long run, so there is a career pay-off as well if you stick around."*, [💬 R1 PH CY] *"Join as many networks as possible, find a mentor and ask advice "*, [💬 R3 PH TR] *"I would advise future doctoral students to create a peer support group for this challenging process. Such a group can be invaluable for academic success and psychological well-being."* and [💬 R12 PS DE] *"My experience has also been that it's especially fun when you go down this path together with others."*.

Supervisors and mentors are of crucial importance for successful PhD studies. [💬 R8 PH RS] *"...choose a mentor who suits you, even if you have to change them after realizing they are not a good fit"*, [💬 R11 PS PT] *"Choose your supervisors well..."*, [💬 R20 PS BA] *"Find a mentor who will support you psychologically and not undermine you"*, [💬 R12 PS DE] *"The relationship with the doctoral supervisor is crucial for the progress and outcome of a PhD. You should feel that you are in good hands. Ideally, the supervisor is a role model, motivator and most critical voice at the same time. "* and [💬 R7 PH RS] *"If the mentor is bad, then you're in trouble."*.

Our respondents highlight the following important personal characteristics: [💬 R11 PS PT] *"Consistency and resilience are of the utmost importance throughout the process."*, [💬 R17 PH PT] *"Resilience, perseverance, and focus."*, [💬 R18 PS BA] *"Dedication is important, but not to overdo things to avoid burnout."*, [💬 R19 PH BA] *"Persistence is the key to success."*, [💬 R10 PS RS] *"... openness and honesty in collaboration with the mentor and other colleagues, obedience, patience, strong faith, and will... "*, [💬 R12 PS DE] *"... being stubborn..."* and [💬 R9 PS RS] *"... be honest with yourself and listen to your priorities."*

To keep going, it is crucial to choose PhD research topic wisely: [💬 R5 PS RS] *"It is crucial to do what inspires us and what we look forward to every Monday :)"*, [💬 R7 PH RS] *"You shouldn't choose a PhD topic based on the mentor you want to work with, but according to your interests and the relevance of the field – it's very difficult if you find yourself in a field that doesn't interest you"*, [💬 R19 PH BA] *"Study what you are passionate about, in the sense that you could spend days and nights working on it because of your curiosity and not any external motivators. Do not hurry to enrol for a doctorate if you haven't found such an interesting problem to study"*, [💬 R20 PS BA] *"... choose a topic that will make you happy and eager to dive deep into the research."* and [💬 R12 PS DE] *"Above all, doing a PhD means pursuing a passion. That doesn't mean it's always easy, but it helps enormously to keep going."*.

Self-care is recognised as very important for successful PhD studies: [💬 R5 PS RS] *"Most importantly, take care of yourself and your health, because no career is worth it."*, [💬 R3 PH TR] *"It's crucial to take good care of your health, including maintaining healthy eating habits and regular exercise."*, [💬 R20 PS BA] *"Avoid any unnecessary stress! Health comes first, and unfortunately, after losing it, it is hard to recover."*, Mental health should particularly be considered seriously. [💬 R19 PH BA] *"My mental health suffered a lot"*, [💬 R15 PS PT] *"Get an appointment with a psychologist just like you would visit a dermatologist when you find a case of skin cancer in the family. It is the new routine, once or twice a year. Don't just stand there waiting for a crisis, or a burnout. "* and [💬 R4 PH DE] *"I always make sure to spend enough time with people who uplift me, because it is too easy to commiserate with others and then I feel depleted."*.

> **Main Recommendations**
> is important to surround yourself with knowledgeable individuals who possess professional competencies and can provide emotional support. Choosing a good mentor and selecting a topic that inspires you are crucial steps. Since pursuing a doctorate is a lengthy process, it is essential to take care of your physical and mental health.

Some respondents had negative experiences and therefore recommend: [💬 R14 PS PT] *"It is not worth doing a PhD."* and [💬 R6 PS RS] *"Carefully consider whether a doctorate is necessary for your career. If it's not, don't start it."* However, other respondents shared different positive experiences: [💬 R13 PS DE] *"Many things that I didn't believe I could do always turned out well in hindsight."*, [💬 R20 PS BA] *"This is a process, a long but not endless journey. Study and work daily, but don't see it as a burden; see it as a way to develop yourself. Take life easy and just do your part. Everything will eventually bear fruit."* and [💬 R17 PH PT] *"Never give up, the path is long and full of highs and lows, but in the end, all the personal effort pays up."*.

6.5 Conclusions

As an underrepresented group in this field, female students in Informatics face many challenges and concerns and have different perceptions about pursuing a PhD. It is crucial to hear their voices to better understand what influences their decisions. This chapter presented their opinions firsthand, using their comments. These comments will help female students in Informatics realise they are not alone and that their concerns and positive and negative experiences are common among students from different countries.

By analysing the voices across universities, we can conclude that the most important encouraging factors that motivate women to pursue PhD in Informatics include career benefits and opportunities, interest in research and fulfilling personal goals. Additional motivation comes from mentors, peers and role models. However, there are many discouraging factors. While some of these factors, such as a preference for an industry career path over academia, are beyond our influence, many discouraging factors, like imposter syndrome, low confidence, and concerns about family plans and social life, should be carefully considered and addressed through personal communication and different kinds of programmes. One such programme is discussed in chapter *WoCa Lunch: A Program for Female Students to Get Informed about PhD Studies*.

Raising awareness of these issues, particularly among male mentors, is essential for fostering better support for women during their doctoral studies. A greater understanding of the specific challenges women face is a critical step toward achieving gender equality in the field. Moving forward, the academic community— including mentors, institutions, and policymakers—must take action to address these barriers. Mentorship programmes can provide essential guidance and role models, helping female students build confidence and overcome feelings of imposter syndrome. Confidence-building workshops can also play a key role in addressing these challenges, while creating more inclusive academic environments can help reduce concerns about balancing family plans with academic life. Although the path to gender equality in Informatics remains challenging, joint efforts can accelerate progress and lead to more equitable outcomes.

References

1. E. Abraham, M. Goulão, M. Vujošević Janičić, S. J. Delany, A. Mersni, O. Yeremenko, O. Buyukdagli, K. Boudaoud, C. Oehlhorn, U. Schmid, C. Büsing, L. Schmid, H. Bolke-Hermanns, K. Köhnle, M. Pato, D. Sunar Cerci, and L. Schmid. Why do women pursue a PhD in Computer Science? Manuscript under review, 2024.
2. A. Adamecz-Völgyi, J. Jerrim, J.-B. Pingault, and D. Shure. Overconfident boys: The gender gap in mathematics self-assessment. *IZA Discussion Paper*, 2023.
3. S. Beyer. Why are women underrepresented in computer science? gender differences in stereotypes, self-efficacy, values, and interests and predictors of future cs course-taking and grades. *Computer Science Education*, 24(2–3):153–192, 2014.
4. S. Beyer, K. Rynes, J. Perrault, K. Hay, and S. Haller. Gender differences in computer science students. In *Proceedings of the 34th SIGCSE technical symposium on Computer science education*, pages 49–53, 2003.
5. J. Cohoon. Must there be so few? including women in CS. In *25th International Conference on Software Engineering, 2003. Proceedings.*, pages 668–674. IEEE, 2003.
6. J. M. Cohoon, Z. Wu, and J. Chao. Sexism: toxic to women's persistence in CSE doctoral programs. *ACM SIGCSE Bulletin*, 41(1):158–162, 2009.
7. A. Denisco. The state of women in computer science: An investigative report. *Tech Republic*, 2017.
8. S. Diogo, A. Gonçalves, S. Cardoso, and T. Carvalho. Tales of doctoral students: Motivations and expectations on the route to the unknown. *Education Sciences*, 12(4):286, 2022.

9. S. M. Hyrynsalmi. The underrepresentation of women in the software industry: Thoughts from career-changing women. *2019 IEEE/ACM 2nd International Workshop on Gender Equality in Software Engineering (GE)*, pages 1–4, 2019.
10. J. London, M. F. Cox, B. Ahn, S. Branch, T. Zephirin, A. Torres-Ayala, and J. Zhu. Motivations for pursuing an engineering PhD and perceptions of its added value: A US-based study. *International Journal of Doctoral Studies*, 9:205, 2014.
11. M. d. C. C. Moreno and S. Kollanus. On the motivations to enroll in doctoral studies in computer science—a comparison of PhD program models. In *2013 12th International Conference on Information Technology Based Higher Education and Training (ITHET)*, pages 1–8. IEEE, 2013.
12. B. Moskal. Female computer science doctorates: what does the survey of earned doctorates reveal? *ACM SIGCSE Bulletin*, 34(2):105–111, 2002.
13. S. Motogna, L. Alboaie, I. A. Todericiu, and C. Zaharia. Retaining women in computer science: the good, the bad and the ugly sides. In *Proceedings of the Third Workshop on Gender Equality, Diversity, and Inclusion in Software Engineering*, pages 35–42, 2022.
14. A. Rosenstein, A. Raghu, and L. Porter. Identifying the prevalence of the impostor phenomenon among computer science students. In *Proceedings of the 51st ACM Technical Symposium on Computer Science Education*, pages 30–36, 2020.
15. A. Tarvid. Motivation to study for PhD degree: Case of Latvia. *Procedia Economics and Finance*, 14:585–594, 2014.
16. S. Wagner, D. Mendez, M. Felderer, D. Graziotin, and M. Kalinowski. Challenges in survey research. *Contemporary Empirical Methods in Software Engineering*, pages 93–125, 2020.
17. Y. Wang and D. Redmiles. Implicit gender biases in professional software development: An empirical study. *2019 IEEE/ACM 41st International Conference on Software Engineering: Software Engineering in Society (ICSE-SEIS)*, pages 1–10, 2019.
18. J. Yates and A. C. Plagnol. Female computer science students: A qualitative exploration of women's experiences studying computer science at university in the UK. *Education and Information Technologies*, 27(3):3079–3105, 2022.

Open Access This chapter is licensed under the terms of the Creative Commons Attribution 4.0 International License (http://creativecommons.org/licenses/by/4.0/), which permits use, sharing, adaptation, distribution and reproduction in any medium or format, as long as you give appropriate credit to the original author(s) and the source, provide a link to the Creative Commons license and indicate if changes were made.

The images or other third party material in this chapter are included in the chapter's Creative Commons license, unless indicated otherwise in a credit line to the material. If material is not included in the chapter's Creative Commons license and your intended use is not permitted by statutory regulation or exceeds the permitted use, you will need to obtain permission directly from the copyright holder.

Chapter 7
WoCa Lunch: A Program for Female Students to Get Informed About PhD Studies

Milena Vujošević Janičić ⓘ **, Erika Ábrahám** ⓘ **, Amal Mersni** ⓘ **, Oleksandra Yeremenko** ⓘ **, and Miguel Goulão** ⓘ

7.1 Introduction

The doctorate (PhD) or doctor of philosophy is the highest academic degree in most fields of study, including informatics and computer science. During doctoral studies, students learn to conduct independent research and contribute new insights and knowledge to their field of study. Doctoral graduates often pursue academic careers as professors and researchers, but may also work in industry, government and other fields where advanced research skills are valued.

The number of women opting to pursue a PhD in informatics is low, with around 19% of PhDs awarded in Europe [24], and 24% in the United States of America [36], making women an underrepresented minority. The impact of this is far-reaching: with a small number of female professors, researchers, and mentors, the number of role models decreases, decreasing further interest of females in informatics at

---

M. Vujošević Janičić (✉)
Faculty of Mathematics, University of Belgrade, Belgrade, Serbia
e-mail: milena.vujosevic.janicic@matf.bg.ac.rs

E. Ábrahám
RWTH Aachen University, Informatik 2, Aachen, Germany
e-mail: abraham@cs.rwth-aachen.de

A. Mersni
International University of Sarajevo, Ilidža/Sarajevo, Bosnia and Herzegovina
e-mail: amersni@ius.edu.ba

O. Yeremenko
Kharkiv National University of Radio Electronics, Kharkiv, Ukraine
e-mail: oleksandra.yeremenko@nure.ua

M. Goulão
NOVA School of Science and Technology, Caparica, Portugal
e-mail: mgoul@fct.unl.pt

© The Author(s) 2025
B. Penzenstadler et al. (eds.), *Actions for Gender Balance in Informatics Across Europe*, https://doi.org/10.1007/978-3-031-78432-3_7

all levels. Different initiatives exist to inform, encourage, and support women if they decide to pursue a PhD. Supporting initiatives include financial incentives and support [44], mentorship and networking [22, 30], guidance and outreach [5, 10, 30], online learning support [19, 47], and creating an inclusive environment [39, 55].

In this chapter, we present the Women Career Lunch (WoCa Lunch) program [1], a supporting initiative to help female students make informed decisions about enrolling in a PhD program. The program is crafted to explain the journey of pursuing a PhD with all its benefits and drawbacks. The program's topics are thoughtfully selected to address the challenges and considerations women may face in their academic careers. It gives guidelines through informing female students about others' successes, problems, and experiences. The program has a broad range of positive impacts, including an increased number of female PhD students, their improved success rate, and an increased awareness of gender inequality in informatics, and it contributes to establishing a network of women in informatics.

⊙ **Personal Experience Sharing: The WoCa Lunch Story**
The idea for this program came up through contacting female students with PhD offers and recognising the diversity of their questions. After maintaining regular but unstructured discussions with them for a while, it has become obvious that we need to define and structure the topics to be discussed clearly for effectivity and repeatability.

Based on our first experiences and careful considerations of further relevant topics, a survey has been designed to identify typical areas of uncertainties which might hinder gifted students from enrolling in a PhD program, keeping an eye also on gender-based differences. Evaluating more than 850 answers from 53 countries served as an excellent basis for the topical design of a program, which we named *Women Career Lunch*, or short *WoCa Lunch*.

Although PhD requirements are similar everywhere, they also have specificities depending on the country and the university. Different educational contexts may require tailored approaches, and the opportunities after completed studies change dynamically. Therefore, different adaptions of the program implementation might be necessary to accommodate diverse backgrounds, institutions, and cultural settings.

Who Can Benefit from This Chapter and How?
This chapter is aimed at teachers to assist in launching the program and students who do not have a WoCa Lunch program organised at their university.

Kim, the university professor. Kim wants to encourage outstanding female students to enrol in PhD studies. Kim reads about the impacts of the WoCa Lunch program and the different ways the program can be adapted to her environment. Kim is pleased to have a catalogue of questions, answers and practical instructions about organising the program. The decision of whether to enrol in doctoral studies is not easy. Thanks to this program, female students will make informed decisions!

Deniz, the student about to graduate. Deniz does not like that her university does not organise programs or initiatives supporting the transition to doctoral studies. Fortunately, she comes across this article and decides to read the questions, answers, and personal experiences listed in the article. After reading, she understands better the essence of a doctorate and its opportunities. She knows which questions to seek further answers to and whom to approach. She feels encouraged by the new insights.

Instructions on How to Read This Chapter

To make the text easier for teachers and students, we marked paragraphs concerning specific topics in the following way.

- ⊗ *Questions and answers*
  Each module's questions and answers are given in paragraphs marked with ⊗ sign.
- □ *Questions for a personal experience discussion*
  Questions for personal experience sharing are in paragraphs marked with □ sign.
- ⊙ *Personal experience sharing*
  Personal experiences examples are given in boxes marked with ⊙ sign.
- △ *Impact of the program*
  Different impacts of the program are given in paragraphs marked with △ sign.
- ○ *Instructions for organising the program*
  Organisational instructions are given in paragraphs marked with ○ sign.

Overview of the Chapter

Section 7.2 starts with an overview of existing supporting initiatives. Section 7.3 provides all the necessary information and instructions to assist teachers considering launching the WoCa Lunch program at their institution. We describe in detail the modules of the WoCa Lunch program, each module's purpose, relevant questions and some possible answers for an interview-style discussion, supplemental questions for personal experience discussion, and examples of individual experiences. Section 7.4 discusses the program's broad range of long-term and short-term effects. Section 7.5 explores various options for adjusting the program. Finally, Sect. 7.6 concludes and outlines open questions and possible directions for further work.

7.2 Encouraging Initiatives

Despite the efforts made to smooth the transition from undergraduate and master's studies to PhD programs, female PhD students are still underrepresented in informatics, especially those belonging to ethnic minority groups, candidates with children, candidates with special needs, or international students, to name a few subgroups. Studies have pointed out a few common reasons for this lack of participation, including but not limited to financial constraints, societal and familial obstacles, emotional and psychological barriers, and exclusionary practices such as stereotyping, sexism, and workplace hostility [1, 5, 17, 37].

In response to these challenges, various initiatives have been established globally to support females and underrepresented groups in their academic path in informatics. These initiatives can be grouped into four main categories (1) regulations, (2) pedagogy and education, (3) financial support, and (4) guidance and engagement. Each category offers distinct strategies and advantages tailored to specific aspects of the problem.

Regulations focus on creating long-term structural change within institutions by promoting equity and non-discrimination through policy reform. Pedagogy and education initiatives target immediate improvements in teaching methods, curricula, and educational practices to make learning environments more inclusive and supportive. Financial support addresses economic barriers by providing scholarships and grants, allowing students to focus on their studies without financial stress. Lastly, guidance and engagement programs offer mentorship and networking opportunities to help students navigate academic and professional challenges.

This section explores various initiatives designed to address these challenges, each dedicated to resolving specific barriers faced by females and underrepresented PhD students in informatics. Figure 7.1 provides a visual overview of the initiatives mentioned.

7.2.1 Regulations

Regulations that provide an inclusive institutional culture can support minority involvement in informatics. Fostering a supportive and gender-neutral atmosphere involves creating policies such as gender equality in the institution, anti-discrimination, and unbiased recruitment. The hoped-for result is higher recruitment and retention rates. This understanding has encouraged many European institutions to approach exclusion and discrimination proactively. Universities have initiated policy- and strategy-building projects to create an inclusive and diverse atmosphere where women feel supported. An example is the gender-sensitive code of conduct that the Norwegian University of Science and Technology (Norway) created to follow a systemic approach towards building anti-discrimination practices in its teaching and learning methods [51].

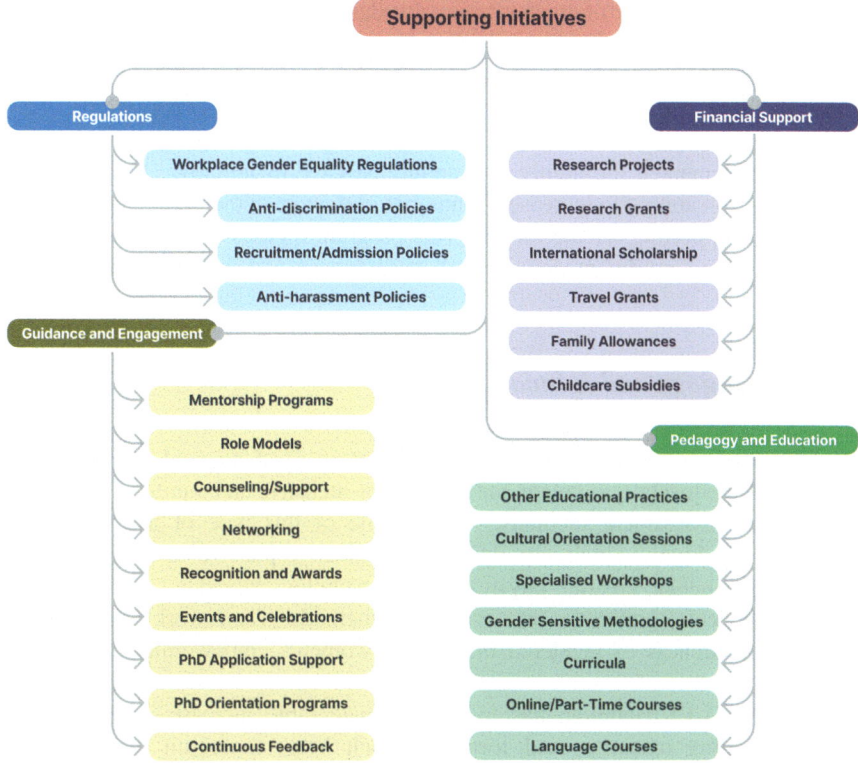

Fig. 7.1 Supporting initiatives for underrepresented groups in informatics doctoral programs

Another way European universities have chosen to fight against harassment and gender bias is by setting up various anti-bias committees. For example, the LIS Computer Science Lab, Aix Marseilles University (France) has a Gender Equality and Anti-Harassment Committee, with the mission to address stereotyping and fight sexism. The Committee aims to support their lab staff in removing barriers to promotion and offer legal and psychological support [31]. Similarly, the University of Rennes (France) established the gender-equality Committee at IRISA and the Anti-harassment Committee at Inria [29].

The Institute for Computing and Information Sciences of the Radboud University in Nijmegen (Netherlands) has implemented effective recruitment initiatives. Their best practices include hiring female researchers as a stepping stone to later promotion, broad-based recruitment for a diverse student body, and providing academic and psychological support to female staff and students. These strategies have proven successful in increasing the representation of women in their programs [27].

Chalmers University of Technology (Sweden) implemented gender equality practices with the Gender Initiative for Excellence. A university foundation considers it the highest individual contribution to affect academic culture through systemic changes in recruitment and procedural practices to achieve gender parity [55].

The Computer Science Department at the Technical University of Dublin (Ireland) implemented the highly outstanding SUCCESS initiative. It is a seven-year-long action aiming to increase the number of women in their computer science program by supporting female faculty. This program focuses on achieving gender parity, including recruitment, career, work environment, and support [28].

7.2.2 Pedagogy and Education

In addition to regulatory actions, enough attention must be paid to improving pedagogy and education to create and implement inclusive and equitable teaching, learning, and assessment methods. An example of this type of action is Koc University (Turkiye), which has developed gender-responsive strategies. Their best practices include creating physically and psychologically safe spaces through inclusive curricula, materials, and evaluation methods. Their work also focuses on raising awareness of gendered biases and women's empowerment as a skill area [41].

The COVID-19 pandemic has led to a considerable increase in the use of distance learning resources and formats, which helps to recruit more female doctoral students. Online PhD programs in fields like information technology [1, 47] highlight the growing need for such flexible educational models. Additionally, the opportunities for remote meetings and recorded lectures represent significant changes that could particularly benefit women with families, enhancing female participation in PhD programs. The best practice example for this is an online *Computer Science and Information Technology* program from the Sudan University of Science and Technology (Sudan). Due to the problem of finding qualified teaching staff, the program was designed to bring mentors from well-known universities and aspiring women PhD candidates from Sudan. In its sixth year, its success is evident in nine women and two men having already completed their degrees [47].

Since 2020, the Computer Science Department at Carnegie Mellon University (USA) has offered PhD students an open-access course named *CS-JEDI: Justice, Equity, Diversity, and Inclusion*, focusing on diversity, equity, and inclusion (DEI) in computer science. This course is a compulsory subject for first-year PhD students, and its content is created and curated by PhD students based on their personal and institutional knowledge. Instructors, carefully chosen to suit DEI's theme and the underlying principles, complement the course [32]. Also, the Norwegian University of Science and Technology offers a course on gender equality called *TDT10— Gender and Diversity in Software Development*. The course aims to explore the place of gender and diversity in software development and how the field can be enriched through increased inclusivity [49].

7.2.3 Financial Support

Financial support is crucial for many women considering an advanced degree, as the time for a PhD often coincides with starting or raising a family. A woman with family responsibilities might hesitate to allocate the time and finances needed to start and sustain a PhD in various fields, including informatics [1, 43].

In recent years, many financial incentives and support in terms of scholarships, research grants, and, in some cases, stipends have been introduced to cover the tuition fees and other costs for women [1, 44]. Google PhD Fellowship program [35] and Microsoft Research Women's Fellowship [46] are two of those, as well as the Diane Lemaire Scholarship [58] offered to women in IT to enhance their research capabilities.

Koc University (Turkiye) has a scheme to help women academicians who take a break to start a family get back on their academic career track. The scheme provides financial and social support for a smooth transition into teaching and research [59].

Another way to support women in informatics is through various research projects. A few notable examples include the European Network for Gender Balance in Informatics (EUGAIN) [25], which aims to promote gender parity in informatics. The "Making Early Career Investigators' Voices Heard for Gender Equality" (VOICES) [8] project focuses on the challenges faced by young researchers and innovators, specifically those inequalities reinforced by disparities within academia linked to other social determinants, such as origin, socioeconomic status, sexuality, or ability. It promotes dialogue among various stakeholders to address the inequalities experienced in the field. *LIBRA* [20], *EQUAL-IST* [53], *FemTech.dk* [60], and *IDUN* [50] are examples of projects aiming to achieve gender equality in informatics and increase the representation and participation of women in leadership positions in life sciences.

7.2.4 Guidance and Engagement

Guidance and engagement through mentorship, role modelling (including both contemporary and historical role models), outreach events, and networking opportunities are instruments to draw women to a PhD and keep these women in the field after graduation. Some successful examples include EUGAIN Summer Schools, designed to train and assist PhD students in their research journey [26]. On a smaller scale, many universities and programs host guidance and engagement events, such as PhD-specific orientations. Many young women may not truly understand what a PhD involves and believe it is too complicated to apply for. To answer such concerns, the Department of Computer Science at Stanford University (USA) allows young women to interact directly with PhD students and professors. Potential candidates freely ask questions that relate directly to them and understand the application and study processes [57]. Brown University (USA) takes a slightly different approach. The faculty students create a tailor-made application program for underrepresented groups and assign an application mentor to candidates who seek help [10].

Stony Brook (USA) has an outreach event where their successful PhD candidates are celebrated to inspire other young women [23]. *AnitaB.org* [6], *ACM-W* [4], *CRA Women* [21], National Center for Women and Information Technology [48], Association for Women in Computing [9], and many more, are holding similar engagement activities, all in hopes of increasing visibility and enthusiasm among young researchers to make informatics their career choice. The 2018 Grace Hopper Celebration was a landmark event for this type of action. The event brought together an international group of 20,000 representing more than 70 countries [55]. The mostly female participants represented a cross-section of ages and stages of a career in informatics. They had the opportunity to socialise and network to enhance their career prospects and be inspired by the examples set by the other participants [55].

While these initiatives are most welcome, they remain shining examples rather than the norm. The number and depth must increase to attract more young women to informatics PhD programs and into the long-term career track.

7.3 Women Career Lunch

The *Women Career Lunch (WoCa Lunch)* program was developed in the context of the European COST Action EUGAIN, to provide an effective yet low-cost, low-effort, and easily adaptable program to support female students in career advancement opportunities through PhD studies.

> ⊙ **Personal Experience Sharing: Pilot Executions**
> The program has been executed for the first time at the Computer Science Department of the RWTH Aachen University (Germany). We have received highly positive feedback. After completion, the participants all felt well informed about PhD studies and beyond that, they reported under others increased self-confidence, and strengthened connections to other female students.
>
> Based on the positive experiences, two further executions have been carried out at RWTH Aachen University for mathematics and informatics students, and a compressed form has been implemented at the Department of Computer Science, Faculty of Mathematics, University of Belgrade. Also, these program

(continued)

> instances ended with highly positive participant feedback. An execution at the Computer Science Department of the *Universidade Nova de Lisboa* (Portugal) is in preparation.
>
> The authors highly welcome notice from everyone inspired to try the program. We will be happy to give additional support or hear about experiences.

The program was developed based on findings from a comprehensive survey [1], designed to provide potential female PhD candidates with important information in a structured, engaging, and collaborative manner. The program is structured into modules, each of which is a cohesive unit suitable for a one-hour discussion. Participation in these modules aims to encourage students and equip them with the necessary information to make well-informed decisions about pursuing a PhD.

To facilitate dissemination and aid implementation, a multi-language version of the WoCa program is publicly available [2]. It includes detailed guidance on the structure and format, practical procedures and a comprehensive catalogue of questions for discussion within each module. This catalogue can be accessed currently in English, French, German, Portuguese, Serbian, Spanish, Turkish, and Ukrainian.

The program contains eight modules, with the first and last edge modules held in person, and six topical modules between them conducted either in person or virtually. Each module occurs during lunchtime and lasts approximately one hour. A guest is invited and interviewed within each of the six topical modules. These guests can be either members of the hosting institution or external experts. The purpose is to address the topics from a question catalogue in a friendly and familiar setting, while also providing insights into the career development of female role models.

- *Organising Group* The team organising the program ideally includes two moderators and administrative support. The moderators should hold PhDs and be part of the academic staff. Optimally, moderators include at least one female and one senior researcher.
- *Inviting Guests* Each module is held by at least one moderator and a guest experienced in the given topic. Ideally, each guest should be female, with at least one being an early-stage researcher. Guests should be partly local to the hosting department or institute, and partly external from other universities. To reduce the required effort, external guests typically participate online. Guests should be suitable role models, demonstrating enthusiasm, motivation, communication skills, and openness. They should speak the local language, as the modules are conducted in the local language. To ensure adequate preparation, each guest should receive the catalogue of questions they will be asked at least two weeks before their module.
- *Number of Participants* The optimal number of participants is between 10 and 20. A too-small group puts a too-strong focus on each student, and a too-large group makes it hard to establish a familiar atmosphere.

◯ ***Inviting Participants*** A program execution can be announced publicly, based on a personal invitation, or a combination of both.

- Since the program targets female students as potential PhD candidates, participants should possess relevant abilities. Personal invitations can be targeted to students with good grades in relevant subjects. It eases the invitee selection if the organisers have available students' accomplishments. Otherwise, invitees can be identified through interaction in lectures and courses.
- Open calls for participation can be sent to department-local mailing lists for students, or announced via posters. A slide with the call can be prepared and sent to all teachers in the department, asking them to show it to the students in their lectures.

In smaller departments, though the focus is on female students, one can also consider mixed groups. For an optimal environment, however, we stress the importance of maintaining a balanced composition and avoiding an underrepresentation of women.

⊙ **Personal Experience Sharing: Inviting Participants**
During the first implementations, we felt that one of the most important factors to raise the female students' interest in the program was *personal contact*. The first time we announced the program, the result of sending an email to a list was a relatively low number of registrations. However, talking to female students after a lecture and inviting them to join was very effective. Once joined, nearly all students attended all modules till program completion.

◯ ***Time and Location*** To reduce conflicts with courses and other events, good experiences were made by scheduling the modules at lunchtime, with one-hour duration each, every other week on the same day. Email reminders the day before each module are meaningful. A smaller seminar room or lecture hall is well-suited when a module is in person. If funds are available, pizza or similar easy-to-order-easy-to-share food contributes to a friendly atmosphere. If no funds are available, e.g. coffee and tea can be offered during the modules. There are no additional costs for online sessions.

◯ ***Scalability and Cost*** WoCa requires almost no funding. Funds are welcome for in-person meetings but are not necessary. There are no additional costs for online sessions. As the number of participants should be between 10 and 20, this does not require special conditions so the program can be easily implemented at any institution.

7.3.1 Module 1: Kick-Off Meeting

The initial meeting aims to help students and moderators get to know each other, make students understand the essence of the entire program, and learn what to expect from it. This is an opportunity for moderators to introduce themselves and briefly present their career paths. To further engage and motivate the students to participate, it is beneficial to briefly introduce the guests who will be participating in the program.

The meeting should also allocate time for discussion, during which students can express what they are most interested in, and which questions intrigue them the most. Let them know if these topics and questions will be addressed in a specific module. If not, expand the questions within the best-matching module.

The discussion can be initiated by posing questions and expecting public answers (when the group is small enough). Each student takes two to three minutes to answer these questions. In the case of larger groups, one can ask them to fill out an online form and then read and discuss their answers.

☐ *Questions for a personal experience discussion*

- Could you briefly introduce yourself?
- Which topics did you like the most during your studies?
- Do you consider enrolling in PhD studies?
- What would you like to learn about PhD studies within this program?
- Tell us about your research experience (if you have some).

7.3.2 Module 2: What Is a PhD?

Students should learn the objectives of a PhD, the skills that will be developed during PhD studies, and the requirements for PhD admission and completion. They should also learn about the typical day-to-day life of a PhD student.

7.3.2.1 Objectives and Skills

While many practical requirements, personal experiences, and academic and industry opportunities can significantly vary through countries and universities, PhD objectives, elements of PhD research and skills to be developed are almost constant.

- ⊗ **What are the objectives of a PhD?** PhD programs aim to train students to conduct high-quality research independently, advance their field of study, and make noteworthy contributions to academia and society. Students prepare for future challenges by staying updated with the latest research trends and methodologies while developing problem-solving abilities and critical thinking.

⊗ **What are the elements of PhD research?** PhD research involves independent research, which includes understanding research methodology, managing data and information ethically, and effectively communicating findings through scientific writing and dissemination such as conferences and journal publications.

⊗ **What skills will be developed during PhD study concerning research, teaching, and leadership?** Various skills are gradually developed through the PhD process. Carrying out research effectively assumes creativity, innovation, and self-initiative. Students develop effective time management to balance research, teaching, and other commitments. Students enhance written and oral communication skills to present research findings to academic and non-academic audiences. Conflict management skills are developed while resolving disputes or disagreements arising during research or collaborations. Project work and the guidance of undergraduate and master students shape strategic thinking, teamwork abilities and leadership skills.

⊙ **Personal Experience Sharing: My Most Useful Lessons Learnt in PhD**

1. It is important to choose a supervisor who suits you, even if you have to change them after realising they are not a good fit.
2. It is important to talk with colleagues doing similar work to yours, even if such conversations initially seem exhausting or require preparation.
3. It is crucial to stay updated in your field through papers, conferences, workshops, and similar activities.

7.3.2.2 Practical Requirements

PhD admission and completion requirements can vary depending on the university and program. We give a common outline that should be discussed within this module, but filling the outline with the program-specific information is important. In addition, students should get links to official pages explaining the admission process, including necessary documentation and deadlines.

⊗ **What are the requirements for PhD admission?** PhD admission requires a bachelor's or, more often, a master's degree in a related field. Some programs may have additional requirements, such as specific prerequisite courses. The university or program usually specifies a minimum GPA (Grade Point Average) for enrolling in PhD studies. Application documentation may require a personal statement or a motivation letter which is a document outlining the applicant's research interests, academic background, career goals, and reasons for pursuing a PhD in that particular field. This should fit with the research interests of faculty members in the program. Previous research experience, such as undergraduate research projects, master's thesis, or relevant work experience, is often valued.

PhD programs may require taking standardised or subject-specific tests (like the Graduate Record Examination test) or acquiring letters of recommendation from professors or professionals who can attest to the applicant's academic abilities and potential for research. In some cases, applicants may be interviewed during the admission to discuss their research interests and fit with the program. For international students, proof of English proficiency is usually required through tests like TOEFL or IELTS unless the applicant has completed a degree in an English-speaking country.

⊗ *What is the typical day-to-day of a PhD student?* The life of a PhD student involves a mix of research, teaching and academic administration tasks (if applicable). More precisely, the most common activities are:

Research work —includes brainstorming, developing novel methods for problem-solving, programming, conducting experiments, collecting and analysing data.

Research dissemination —includes attending seminars, conferences, and workshops to present research, network and discuss with peers.

Writing and reading scientific literature —Writing includes writing and editing research papers, dissertation chapters, or reports. Reading includes finding relevant literature and studying the latest research in the field.

Meetings —with an advisor or research team to discuss progress, results, and next research steps.

Teaching (if applicable) —includes preparing for and delivering lab sessions, grading assignments, and providing guidance and feedback to students.

Administrative tasks —include responding to research- and teaching-related emails, completing paperwork concerning project or funding administration, contributions to group administration, or serving on departmental commissions.

PhD students often have flexible schedules and day-to-day activities may vary based on individual preferences and project requirements.

⊙ **Personal Experience Sharing: Finding Life Balance**
The hardest is balancing work, doctoral studies, and private life. While I don't have an answer, it's important to think about it daily. Strive to ensure that no aspect suffers too much.

○ *Discussion on everyday PhD life* Discussion should be based on the personal example given by the module's guest. In addition, inviting a current PhD student to present her experience on this topic is also a good practice.

⊙ **Personal Experience Sharing: The Essence of My Personal PhD Experience**

1. A doctorate (like any other scientific research) is often not a straightforward path to results but involves many ups and downs.
2. It is crucial to present your work often, through seminars, conferences, or similar events, even though this is the least appealing task for a doctoral student. Doing so provides valuable feedback regarding the work itself.
3. It is important during the doctorate (and any other research) to be proactive, meaning not waiting for tasks from the supervisor but showing initiative, proposing methodologies or activities, and similar actions.

⊗ *What are the requirements for finishing a PhD dissertation?* The requirements for finishing a PhD always include writing and defending a PhD dissertation. Different procedures and tasks should be completed before writing the dissertation. An initial task includes developing and defending a dissertation proposal that outlines the research objectives, methodology, literature review, and expected outcomes. This proposal is usually presented to a committee for approval before beginning the research and is written with the help of the PhD advisor. University regulations or the advisor may specify the number of published papers that should precede dissertation writing. Papers should be published at chosen scientific venues (conferences or journals). After enrolling in PhD studies, the student will learn the overall process and procedures. It is not necessary to understand them completely in advance.

☐ *Questions for a personal experience discussion*
- Why did you decide to do a PhD and what was your decision process?
- What were the elements of your PhD process?
- What did you learn through your PhD that was most useful to you?
- What advice would you give PhD students based on your experience?

7.3.3 Module 3: Why a PhD for an Academic Career?

A PhD provides the training and credentials necessary to work in academia and contribute to society. This module clarifies the process of selecting a research topic, research group, and supervisor for PhD studies, and the impact of these choices on the future career. Also, students should understand the evaluation processes of the quality of their work and the overall duration of their PhD studies.

7.3.3.1 Academic Career

Students usually see their professors only as teachers and do not completely comprehend the many other parts of professors' jobs.

- ⊗ *What does an academic career look like?* The educational pathway starts with undergraduate studies and continues through MSc and PhD studies. After earning a PhD, many academics undertake postdoctoral positions to gain further research experience and establish themselves in their field. Typically, the first full-time academic position is assistant professor, followed by associate professor and the final position is a full professor. Different university systems exist, and progressing from one level to another may depend on distinct factors. However, at all levels responsibilities include teaching, conducting research, and doing professional service. Teaching assumes designing courses, delivering lectures, leading seminars, and evaluating students. It also assumes guiding undergraduate and graduate students in their academic and research endeavours. Conducting research depends on the discipline and includes research dissemination, such as writing articles, books, and conference papers. It also assumes writing proposals to secure funding for research projects. University and professional service assumes participating in departmental and university committees, contributing to the governance and development of the institution, being involved in academic societies, peer reviewing for conferences and journals, organising conferences, writing assessments, and other professional activities.
- ⊗ *How does the PhD prepare you for an academic career?* PhD prepares for an academic career through rigorous training in many important aspects essential for conducting original research (e.g., experience in research methods, critical thinking and problem solving, teaching, academic writing and oral presentations).
- ⊗ *What is important to progress to the next step in an academic career?* After obtaining a PhD, further specialisation is possible through postdoctoral studies. Postdoctoral studies are necessary for advancement and achieving higher academic titles at some universities, while this is not the case at others. It is important to learn about opportunities and conditions at the desired university, adjust the PhD studies accordingly, plan the next steps and apply on time for suitable positions.

7.3.3.2 PhD Topic and Supervisor

Choosing a PhD topic requires careful consideration of personal interests, the feasibility of the research, and the expertise and mentoring style of potential supervisors. The PhD topic significantly influences the academic career, shaping the specialisation, research opportunities, and professional network.

- ⊗ *How do you choose a topic for your PhD?* The topic should hold significant importance for the community, and the research findings should potentially offer noteworthy new insights. Personal interests and the possibility of long-term engagement are of utmost importance. Students should choose a topic they are genuinely interested in and passionate about, as they will be working on it intensively for several years. It should be a topic for which the student can stay motivated over an extended period. It is also crucial that the topic aligns with the expertise of potential supervisors and faculty members in the respective department. Ensure the department has the necessary resources and support for the chosen topic.

> ⊙ **Personal Experience Sharing: Topic vs Supervisor**
> You shouldn't choose a PhD topic based on the supervisor you want to work with, but according to your interests and the relevance of the field—it's extremely problematic if you find yourself in a field that doesn't interest you. On the other hand, if the supervisor is bad, you're in trouble (I had a good supervisor, but I saw firsthand what it means to have a bad supervisor). So somehow a combination of both is necessary. Otherwise, you'll have to rely on sheer willpower.

- ⊗ *How do you choose a supervisor?* A supervisor should be supportive, accessible, and willing to provide regular feedback and guidance. To ensure a productive and supportive working relationship, the supervisor's research interest and expertise should match the chosen topic, and the mentoring style should match the working style and needs of the PhD student. A strong publication and funding record and the success of their former students in terms of completion rates indicate a successful and well-respected researcher.
- ⊗ *How does the PhD topic determine your career?* The PhD topic defines the area of expertise and often sets the direction for future research and (academic or industrial) career. This specialisation can influence eligibility for different types of positions. The research area determines potential collaborators and research networks. Certain topics may attract more funding and grant opportunities.
- ⊗ *Who are your partners throughout an academic career path?* The supervisor is the most important academic partner. They provide guidance, support, and feedback throughout the whole PhD. However, peers and colleagues are also substantial as direct collaborators and discussion partners in everyday activities. Finally, PhD students build their professional network by engaging with organisations and attending conferences. The professional network is also important for getting guidance and feedback. Collaborations with researchers from different fields widen this network for interdisciplinary topics.

> ⊙ **Personal Experience Sharing: Who Are Your Partners?**
> You have to be proactive, not wait for something to happen, but constantly look for solutions and be persistent. If you get stuck and don't know how to solve something, go and ask everyone you can think of. Of course, sometimes you have to figure things out on your own, but in today's times and society, it's better not to work alone but to ask for help. It's difficult to work alone; it's much easier, better, and more interesting in a team, and you achieve results faster.

7.3.3.3 Timeline and Quality Assessment

The exact duration of PhD process can vary depending on the program structure, complexity of the research project, available funding, and many different personal factors. The PhD dissertation must present original research that contributes new knowledge or insights to the field and must be validated by external experts.

- ⊗ *How long does a PhD take?* A PhD typically takes between 4 and 6 years to complete. Students usually complete coursework (if mandatory) within the first two years. The remainder of the program focuses on conducting original research, writing the dissertation, and defending it.

  The complexity and scope of the research project can significantly influence the duration. Projects involving experimental work or extensive data collection may take longer. Interdisciplinary research or projects requiring collaboration with other fields might also extend the timeline.

  The availability of research funding and resources can impact the pace of progress. Full-time students usually complete their PhD more quickly than part-time students, who may balance their studies with work or other commitments. Life events, health issues, or family responsibilities can also affect the time required to complete a PhD.

- ⊗ *How is the quality of PhD work assessed?* The supervisor guides the research, provides feedback, and ensures that the work meets academic standards. In addition, PhD students have to publish their research findings in peer-reviewed journals or present at conferences. This serves as an external validation of the quality and relevance of the research. At least two experts review the PhD dissertation. Typically, at least one expert is external.

☐ *Questions for a personal experience discussion*

- What is your career path and did you plan it explicitly?
- How did you choose your PhD topic?
- What did you learn during your PhD and academic career?
- From what mistakes did you learn and what would you do differently in hindsight?

7.3.4 Module 4: Why a PhD for a Career in Industry?

Pursuing a PhD in informatics is an excellent foundation for a successful career, offering numerous opportunities in academia, industry and government [45]. This advanced training hones discipline-specific expertise and cultivates a broad set of transferable skills essential for various career paths, both research-intensive and non-research-intensive [56]. Engaging with industry during a PhD enhances learning and fosters knowledge exchange, resulting in graduates who are well-integrated into the industry [11]. Additionally, the personal networks that PhD candidates build autonomously align their specialised knowledge with market needs, facilitating a smooth transition from academia to industry [34]. Ultimately, PhD training is a crucial bridge between academic and industry sectors, equipping students with valuable, marketable skills for real-world applications [40].

7.3.4.1 Career in Industry

PhD is not critical nor required for many industry jobs. However, for the most interesting and challenging industry jobs, PhD provides the necessary qualifications and enables employment in higher-level research positions. There are also possibilities for doing a PhD in collaboration with industry partners. Furthermore, the PhD work's outcomes can result in the creation of a spin-off company.

- ⊗ **What can a career in the industry look like?** An industry career for an informatics professional can be diverse and dynamic, encompassing a wide range of roles and responsibilities. Professionals often need ongoing education, certifications, and training to keep up with rapidly evolving technologies and industry trends and advance their careers.
- ⊗ **How important is the PhD topic for further career opportunities?** The topic of a PhD can profoundly impact career opportunities. In industry, the practical applicability of research is crucial, with topics addressing current technological challenges enhancing employability. Research and development roles prioritise innovation, valuing PhD topics that advance technology or explore new research avenues. Deep technical expertise gained from specific issues can be advantageous for specialised roles. For aspiring entrepreneurs, a PhD topic meeting a significant market need can underpin a viable business, attracting investors and customers. A strong foundation in cutting-edge areas offers a competitive edge in product development. Research relevant to public interest and policy issues is precious in government or policy-making. Given the rapid evolution of technology, selecting a flexible topic that fosters skill adaptation ensures long-term career benefits. Lastly, sustained passion and enthusiasm for research contribute to better outcomes and a more fulfilling career.
- ⊗ **Can I do a PhD with industrial participation?** Industry-focused PhD programs differ across countries, companies, and fields. Many companies partner with universities and research institutions, enabling employees to pursue a PhD

through joint research projects. Some universities provide part-time or evening PhD programs, allowing professionals to maintain their jobs while balancing work and research commitments. Research fellowships or grants from industry bodies, government agencies, or private foundations can also support PhD research in collaboration with industry partners. Typically, industry-sponsored PhDs offer funding for research, including stipends, tuition fees, and access to advanced facilities and technologies not commonly available in academic settings. However, challenges include balancing work and research responsibilities and potential restrictions on publishing findings. Among the requirements for an industry-focused PhD program are eligibility criteria (e.g., citizenship, prior PhD status), a relevant academic background, a research proposal aligned with industry needs, a collaboration agreement, intensive supervision and mentorship, and a practical project focus.

⊙ **Personal Experience Sharing: Obtaining PhD with Industry Collaboration**
A PhD in industrial collaboration has its advantages and disadvantages. The benefits include working on cutting-edge technologies and fresh and relevant data. Besides gaining academic experience, one acquires industrial experience which opens up further opportunities for career development in the industry. On the other hand, the solution that needs to be implemented is not a proof of concept but a production-ready solution of industrial quality, and therefore, significantly higher demands are placed, exceeding standard academic prototypes.

- *Can PhD research lead to a spin-off company?* PhD research with commercial potential can lead to the creation of spin-off companies. Key factors include establishing commercial viability, securing intellectual property protection, and obtaining support and funding from incubators or investors. Additionally, acquiring business skills and mentorship and building industry collaborations and networks are crucial. Numerous successful companies in fields such as biotechnology and informatics have originated from PhD research, demonstrating the potential for academic work to be transformed into marketable products and services. Creating a spin-off from academic research is a challenging but rewarding opportunity to bridge the gap between scientific discoveries and practical applications.
- *Which industry-relevant skills are acquired during a PhD?* A PhD program cultivates essential transferable skills applicable to industry roles. PhD candidates develop project management expertise from planning to execution. Research papers, report communication, and complex concept explanations sharpen writing proficiency. Critical thinking skills evolve through data analysis and informed decision-making. Adaptability is fostered by navigating diverse

challenges, and leadership abilities emerge from guiding teams and driving initiatives.

7.3.4.2 Benefits of Having a PhD in Industry

Having a PhD in industry offers significant benefits both to individuals and society. PhD holders contribute to societal advancement by generating foundational knowledge and enhancing the productivity of their colleagues [16]. Their training is also valuable in non-research workplaces due to their systematic and analytical thinking skills and ability to handle complex problems [42]. Collaborative doctoral education addresses industry skills and equips PhD students with practical, transferable skills and broad societal impact [7]. Industrial PhD students benefit from access to data, projects, networks, and contextual understanding, enhancing their academic research and workplace contributions [12–14]. Moreover, cooperation between companies and universities encourages the former to recruit PhDs, fostering innovation and stronger cooperative relationships [15, 33].

- ⊗ *What are the benefits of having a PhD towards a career in the industry?* A PhD benefits an industry career by offering advanced economic contributions and diverse career paths. PhD holders enhance productivity and contribute to knowledge creation. Their skills are valuable in research roles and non-research positions, while their varied work experiences prepare them well for career development.
- ⊗ *Is the salary with a PhD higher than that with a master's degree?* PhD can lead to higher earning potential in certain industries and roles, but it is not a universal rule. Some companies have policies or cultures that reward higher education with higher salaries, while others may prioritise skills and experience over academic qualifications. Many factors, including industry norms, job market conditions, location, and individual qualifications, contribute to determining salary levels. While a PhD may not always guarantee a higher starting salary, it can lead to faster career progression and access to higher-paying positions over time.
- ⊗ *Do domestic and foreign companies appreciate PhD training differently?* Domestic and foreign companies may have slightly different perspectives on the merits of having a PhD, but it largely depends on the industry, company culture, and specific job roles. Some IT jobs require highly skilled individuals, knowledge of the latest technologies, and strong problem-solving skills. On the other hand, some IT jobs are not as demanding, and therefore, not in need of PhD holders.

☐ *Questions for a personal experience discussion*

- What was your career journey?
- Would your career have been possible without a PhD?
- What skills did you gain during your PhD that are substantial for your job?
- What influence does the PhD have regarding your reputation in the company?

7.3.5 Module 5: How to Find a PhD Position?

The application process might include different steps and procedures that are not simple and require time and preparation. In addition, if a student wants to apply for a position at a university where they did not study, it might be difficult to find a suitable PhD position, a group, and a supervisor.

7.3.5.1 Finding a PhD Position

Finding a PhD position, if not within the department where the previous level of study was completed, requires serious effort and time. The search for the right position should begin at least a year in advance, as it is not easy to find a well-suited position. Once a position is found, it is necessary to prepare and submit documentation following the deadlines set by the given university or research institution.

- ⊗ **What can I do during my studies to qualify for a PhD position?** Requirements for academic qualifications differ depending on PhD programs but usually include outstanding results at the bachelor's and master's levels. Successful candidates demonstrate competency through well-structured research proposals, strong performance in PhD interviews, and a clear interest in the research area. Publications, conference presentations, positive references, and teaching experience are not required, but they enhance the applicant's profile.
- ⊗ **Where do I find PhD positions?** PhD positions can be discovered through various channels. Universities, research institutions and laboratories often advertise PhD positions on their websites and academic job boards. Professional networks like *LinkedIn* and *ResearchGate* with departmental announcements serve as valuable resources. Subscribing to email lists and newsletters in the field of interest provides timely updates on new opportunities. Attending academic conferences and workshops also uncover open positions. University graduate school offices offer additional information.
- ⊗ **What institute suits me?** The choice of the institute, and within it the group, is pivotal for a successful PhD experience.

  The institute should be aligned with the applicant's academic background and interests. Consulting tutors and academics helps to understand the institution's reputation and research strength.
- ⊗ **Which group suits me?** Understanding the research group before enrolling in PhD is crucial. If possible, a visit to the research group should be arranged, to attend seminars, lab meetings, and social events, and to observe the group's atmosphere, interactions, and dynamics among members. Conversations with current PhD students, postdocs, and faculty allow gaining insights into their experiences and ongoing research projects. If a visit cannot be arranged, research group members can be approached by email to arrange an online meeting.

Research group sizes vary. Some are small, fostering close collaboration, while others are larger and more diverse. Applicants should consider their preference, whether they seek a tight-knit community or prefer a broader network.

⊗ *Which topic suits me?* Determining the right topic is essential for a fulfilling research journey. For the choice of the research topic, genuine interests should be prioritised, reflecting on modules the applicant enjoyed during their undergraduate or master's degree. The research questions should be original and feasible within a reasonable time frame. PhD topics based on third-party-funded projects often have predefined content and aims, while others might offer more topic flexibility.

⊗ *How do I find a supervisor?* In the case of advertised projects, direct communication with the academic lead responsible for the project is imperative. Conversely, prospective candidates should meticulously examine faculty profiles and actively participate in conferences to identify potential supervisors whose research interests align with their own. The subsequent step is crafting a brief email expressing interest and inquiring about supervision availability.

7.3.5.2 Application Process and Funding

Applying for a PhD involves nontrivial steps that depend on the targeted position. The entry requirements should be met, and funding options to support the studies should be explored. The application should be prepared and submitted according to the university's guidelines, ensuring all necessary documents are included.

⊗ *What does the application process look like?* Once a position is identified, it is important to read carefully all the instructions and requirements. First, a thorough check should ensure that the basic conditions are met. If they are, the required documentation should be gathered with enough time allocated, as preparing the documentation often involves obtaining documents from various student services, getting letters of recommendation from professors, or translating documents into a foreign language. Additionally, the required documentation usually includes writing a motivation letter, a detailed CV, and descriptions of previous projects worked on. All of this requires dedicated effort and time to prepare well.

⊗ *What is important in the written application?* The cover letter is paramount in the written application for a PhD study. This document provides an opportunity to elaborate on the qualifications, highlight relevant achievements, and articulate why the applicant is the most suitable candidate for the program. Diligent attention to spelling, grammar, and punctuation is essential, as these details significantly impact the overall professionalism and application clarity. A well-crafted cover letter effectively conveys academic and research competencies, demonstrating attention to detail and unwavering commitment to excellence.

⊗ ***What does the PhD application interview look like?*** The format of the PhD application interview varies but typically includes several key components. It often begins with discussing academic interests, background, goals, and proposed projects, in a formal or informal setting. Presenting a research proposal or demonstrating expertise in a specific area might be required. Additionally, a one-to-one discussion with the prospective supervisor is expected, allowing for a more in-depth conversation about the fit for the program. The interview process may include orientation activities such as visits to research spaces and networking opportunities with current students and faculty.

⊗ ***What funding possibilities are available?*** Funding possibilities for PhD studies vary widely. Full-time positions are typically geared towards international students, providing comprehensive support, whereas part-time positions cater to working professionals who wish to combine their careers with doctoral studies. Funding can come from positions aligned with specific research projects or state-funded positions, which government agencies or institutions finance. Additionally, scholarships are available to cover tuition fees and living costs, alleviating financial burdens. Self-funding, where the student independently covers their expenses, remains an option for those who do not secure funding.

☐ *Questions for a personal experience discussion*

- How did you find your PhD position?
- What did the application process look like?
- From which mistakes during your application process did you learn most?
- What advice would you give to potential PhD applicants?

7.3.6 Module 6: How to Handle Doubts and Problems Before and During the PhD?

Concerns and emotional issues commonly arise during PhD studies and can be difficult to deal with. When one starts a PhD, it is often the same period as building a career or starting a family, so a student considering a PhD might question whether it is the right path. These conflicting ambitions may overburden the candidate throughout the years needed to complete their doctorate. That is why problem recognition and seeking help in the right place before they become critical are key to properly overcoming issues on time.

7.3.6.1 Personal Doubts, Concerns and Burnout

Doing a PhD is, among other things, a challenge to the student's resilience. Beyond the scientific challenge per se, PhD candidates need to cope with the *"impostor syndrome"* [54] leading the candidate to doubt their readiness to start, continue, and complete this professional and personal journey. Family challenges, mental health issues, financial constraints, and a work-life imbalance may all appear as the student progresses in their PhD studies.

- ⊗ **Am I capable of pursuing a PhD?** Doing a PhD is not as complicated as many candidates imagine. It requires research skills, intellectual capability, solid field knowledge, and resilience. Completing it successfully is possible if the student remains persistent and committed. For many PhD candidates, the *impostor syndrome* holds them back rather than the study itself. There will be challenges along the way, and the candidate must manage time and be disciplined in facing work and learning obligations. Some students only rely on their intellect. However, believing in yourself, possessing a strong work ethic, and having clear career goals are key to success.
- ⊗ **Will I have enough innovative ideas?** It is normal not to have (good) novel ideas at the first stage of the PhD process while the student gains expertise in the state of the art. Working under the supervision of a PhD mentor who shares the student's research interests can help formulate an innovative approach or solution. The candidate will also have many chances throughout their studies to refine their knowledge and understanding to reach their insights. That way, the student will create novelty in due time. A PhD process is a real-time learning and feedback loop so each step will inform the next. A PhD offers a huge potential for exploration and growth, professionally and personally.
- ⊗ **What do I do if I am unsure or have problems during my doctorate studies?** Doubts and problems are inevitable in the PhD process. The first step to facing these problems is to accept they will happen. If students are aware and mentally ready, their chances of facing the issue increase dramatically. There are mechanisms to help a struggling student, starting with mentorship. The first step is reaching out to the supervisor for help and guidance. Many universities have staff who help PhD students solve issues, such as counselling centres and financial aid programs. Academically, by attending conferences, training programs, and workshops, students may develop new skills and discover novel ideas or methods. This may inspire them if they feel stuck in their research or need to resolve the issues they encounter during their PhD journey. Lastly, taking good care of oneself through proper exercise and diet can also help the student stay focused and strong throughout the process.
- ⊗ **Is doing a PhD compatible with family planning?** Raising a family while pursuing a PhD is difficult but possible. Many universities have specific initiatives to support women PhD candidates in the process. The PhD supervisor can help. Flexible schedules, online meetings, and recorded lectures help tremendously to manage studies and family obligations. Childcare help and financial aid to support children also play their part, along with other on-campus child-friendly facilities. Time management and efficient planning will help complete all tasks academically and at home. This relies heavily on communication between spouses and the university staff and a supportive environment, which can help diffuse problems before they become bigger issues that may impact the studies.

⊗ ***What do I do if I "run out of breath" during the doctorate?*** Everyone knows this feeling. A PhD takes years of continuous effort, and it is normal to have highs and lows during such a long period. Because of the current lifestyle, people are increasingly driven by quick rewards. Accepting that a PhD is a journey is the first step to remaining focused on the process. Time and task management skills are crucial—working on a schedule, planning effectively, and sticking to the plan allow the student to feel in control. Self-care practices such as physical exercise, mindfulness, being kind to yourself, eating and sleeping well throughout the years help, as does taking breaks when needed. Asking for help when overwhelmed by a task or a problem is a skill. If the problem is mental or emotional burnout, there are counselling services and support groups. A PhD retreat with other doctoral students can be one way to get out of a down period. In a retreat, the PhD students write, rest, and discuss each other's progress, allowing them to network, collaborate, and recover psychologically with people going through the same process.

⊗ ***What are the typical concerns of students during their doctorate studies?*** Starting a PhD comes with many concerns because often candidates cannot access human or reference resources clearly explaining all the steps and details. Questions are on many different levels, starting with whether they can find a novel idea to research, to financial concerns throughout the PhD process, and whether they can build and maintain a good mentor-mentee relationship with a chosen supervisor. Writing the thesis and publishing articles in relevant, high-quality journals are other significant worries, along with academic milestones such as qualification exams, proposals, and thesis defence. Students are also anxious about job prospects during and after their studies. All these issues can lead to stress and burnout, so some students worry about how to take care of their well-being.

⊗ ***Where can I find advice and support if I have problems?*** Depending on the problem, who the student can contact will differ. The PhD supervisor is nearly always the first contact point, but there are also dedicated offices or groups for various issues. Secondly, administrative and graduate offices make life easier for PhD students, from a Career Centre to help with networking and potential work to residence and visa offices to guide international candidates with relocation questions. There are mental health support centres to help with psychological issues and writing centres to aid with problems with academic tasks such as research.

7.3.6.2 Topic and Supervisor

During a PhD, difficulties might appear related to changing research topics and disruptions in communication with the supervisor. However, solving these problems is directly related to an open dialogue with and constant feedback from the supervisor.

⊗ **Can I change, or adjust, my research focus during the PhD?** Although researchers usually choose a topic at the beginning of their PhD program based on personal interests, previous experience, or discussions with potential supervisors, it is possible to change it later. Indeed, new aspects and problems may emerge, and the focus may change during the research process. In this case, consultation with the supervisor is crucial to get advice and feedback. In addition, collaborating with colleagues, participating in scientific seminars and conferences, and exploring interdisciplinary work can help change the research direction. However, it should be borne in mind that specific changes may affect research funding, as some grants are designed for particular areas.

⊗ **What do I do if I am dissatisfied with my PhD supervision?** To prevent such a situation, PhD students should always be proactive, i.e., take the initiative, seek feedback, and actively interact with their supervisor. However, in the case of such a problem, only open communication will allow a solution. Of course, it is necessary to understand the root causes of dissatisfaction and determine whether the problem is related to time, support, or appreciation. In this case, expectations, roles and responsibilities must be clarified, and the need for timely feedback, guidance, and emotional support must be communicated in an open dialogue with the supervisor. As a last resort, advice can be requested from faculty or graduate school. The experience of other PhD students who have faced similar problems can also be helpful.

7.3.6.3 Sexist Remarks and Sexual Harassment

As in many other areas of society, inappropriate comments and sexual harassment remain prevalent in STEM. A 2018 report in the US refers to up to 50% of women in faculty and from 20% to 50% of women students state they encountered or experienced sexually harassing conduct in academia [52]. There is, however, an increasing awareness of this problem. Institutions are adopting concrete measures to prevent misconduct and promote equity within scientific organisations (see, for instance, [18]).

⊗ **Am I okay with being one of the few women in the group?** The current enrolment rates of women in informatics degrees suggest women will remain far from achieving parity in informatics in the next years or even decades. This does not necessarily imply a toxic environment for women. The community is increasingly aware and concerned about this problem, and it typically considers sexual harassment and gender-based discrimination a code of conduct violation.

⊗ **Where can I find help for sexual harassment?** Higher education institutions have channels for reporting misconduct. These channels often have an anonymity mechanism to protect the person making allegations from possible retaliations against victims or whistle-blowers. These allegations are then analysed by an independent inquiry committee, which determines if the alleged misconduct infringes the code of conduct and, if so, initiates an investigation into the allegations. Of course, false claims raised in bad faith are considered a serious offence [52]. Conferences and other scientific events typically also enforce codes of conduct. See, for instance, the policies from ACM [3] and IEEE [38].

⊗ **How are the dignity and respect rights of PhD students applied at universities?** Most higher education institutions have adopted codes of conduct and action plans to ensure gender equality. These aim to create a healthy space where all can thrive. The codes cover the behaviour of students, professors, and other staff and usually include recommendations on how to deal with any breaches of these policies.

☐ *Questions for a personal experience discussion*

- What obstacles/uncertainties did you face during your doctorate?
- Did you fear that you might not be smart enough for a PhD?
- How did you deal with any doubts you had?
- Who did you get support from?

7.3.7 Module 7: Considering a PhD Abroad?

Finding a proper PhD position may include considering applying for PhD studies abroad. Applying for a position abroad introduces different challenges, including the application process, administrative issues, financial issues, and differences compared to a PhD in a native country.

⊗ **What distinguishes a doctorate abroad from a doctorate in my country?** The differences between obtaining a doctorate abroad and in the home country can vary widely. Academic and institutional differences include the structure, duration, and specific requirements of doctoral programs. Practical issues, like tuition fees and living expenses, can also vary greatly. Some countries offer substantial scholarships, grants, or stipends for international students. One likely needs to navigate language barriers and adapt to a different culture, which can be challenging but enriching.

7.3.7.1 Finding a Position

When searching for the best-suited position, practical aspects such as required documentation, residence visa, language, and similar factors, can help to start narrowing down the list of countries and universities of interest.

⊗ **How do I find doctoral positions abroad?** Various academic job platforms and websites help in the search for doctoral positions abroad. Once potential universities according to the research interests have been identified, information can be gathered on the official websites of the universities and pages dedicated to research opportunities. Of course, participating in academic events and presenting research results at international conferences can also help to establish new connections, communicate with professors and researchers, and find opportunities for PhD positions abroad. It also opens up opportunities for direct contact with professors whose research coincides with the personal interests of the PhD candidate. At the same time, the recruitment agencies' services can also be used to find PhD vacancies.

- ⊗ **What to consider when applying for a doctorate abroad?** One should consider the required documents, prerequisite tests, and communication with potential supervisors. It should be clarified whether a student visa is needed. It should be understood what the general process for applying to PhD programs abroad is, which usually requires an online application, academic transcripts, a CV including relevant experience, a statement of purpose, letters of recommendation, and language proficiency test results.
- ⊗ **Can I ask doctoral candidates abroad for reports on their experiences?** Communicating with doctoral students who have studied abroad can provide valuable information about the research environment, workload, funding opportunities, etc. Such connections can be organised through existing online platforms, academic forums, and social media groups. In addition, contact information about the research team representatives can be found on the official university websites. It is advisable to ask for some advice based on their experience by email or direct message.

7.3.7.2 Practical Issues

The practical concerns for a PhD may be broadly grouped into three categories: before, during, and after a PhD. Before starting a PhD, students must find the right country, program and supervisor. Communicating with the country, region or university officials may require time and energy. Knowing the local language or using translation services may also be necessary. Diplomas must be translated and notarised, often submitted via mail, requiring payment. Making travel arrangements, securing housing and healthcare, and other practical matters are all part of starting a PhD abroad. During the PhD, students must adapt to living in a new culture and being far from their family and friends. They establish themselves in the local culture, as the PhD process is lengthy. Academic and social expectations may also require some adjustment for the candidate. After the PhD, the student may struggle to stay in the country of study due to legal barriers or experience reverse culture shock when returning to their home country. The diploma recognition process is also reversed, this time for the foreign qualification to be recognised by the home state.

- ⊗ **Do the requirements abroad differ from those in my country?** Each country or region has unique requirements for accepting a PhD candidate. Some universities demand standardised tests during recruitment, while others focus on the candidate's research background. PhD program prerequisites may also vary, as some universities recruit among undergraduate degree holders, whereas others only select potential candidates with master's degrees. Traditional PhD programs may last about 6 years and be more research-oriented, whereas newer programs are tighter and based more on coursework.

⊗ **Do I have to speak the local language?** Many international PhD programs are fully available in English. However, that is only one facet. Since a PhD involves living in a country for several years, it may be necessary to socialise or communicate often with locals who may not speak English, creating a language barrier. Personal and professional development may be difficult without understanding local customs and culture. As a PhD candidate, attending domestic conferences and scientific gatherings that require direct communication with local researchers may be hard. Without a translator, a candidate may be unable to broaden their networking opportunities and explore potential research collaborations.

⊗ **How do I finance my stay abroad?** A PhD may be financed in several ways. First, in some countries, a PhD position comes with a salary, and the candidate is a staff member and a student. Examples include Sweden, Germany, and Finland. Other countries, like the US or Canada, have available positions such as teaching assistants or part-time researchers. Hoping to attract bright young researchers, countries like China and Italy offer city or region-based grants and other benefits, such as family allowance. Institutes also provide project-based PhD positions. Many non-governmental organisations offer stipends, travel grants, incentives, and other financial awards to different groups, such as women of colour, students with specific needs, and more.

⊗ **Where can I get advice if I want to go abroad?** The best place for a PhD candidate to start is by asking for help from their professors, as these academicians know the student and have their networks. They can refer the student to a supervisor working in a university abroad who might be a good fit. Another source is the International Relations Office or Career Centre, as both offices have connections with other universities and can potentially recommend the student to a relevant program. The Erasmus+ Student Network, international study and exchange groups, international fairs, and summer programs are excellent for networking and gathering information.

⊗ **What do I have to think about administratively?** The key administrative requirements are properly translated and registered diplomas and certificates, a valid passport with enough time and pages to apply for visas and residence permits, and the appropriate health insurance. The candidate may be refused a visa or residence without ensuring these documents are in order, even if the PhD application is accepted.

Residency or a relevant visa is necessary for full-time study and financial support. Always verify specific eligibility criteria for each program. Many countries require proof of funds even when the student is offered a scholarship, and having the bare minimum in the bank statement may cause immigration officers to reject entry into the country. Proof of accommodation and a return ticket are required, so securing these before crossing the border into the host country is a good idea. Once in the country, internationals are expected to register at the local police station for legal purposes. Registering at one's embassy is also well-advised.

7.3.7.3 After the PhD

A degree from a prestigious foreign institution can enhance the CV and open international career opportunities. However, the recognition of the degree may require additional steps.

⊗ **Is the doctorate obtained abroad recognised in my country?** The recognition of a doctorate obtained abroad varies depending on the country and the specific institution where the degree was earned. Some countries have bilateral agreements for mutual recognition of academic qualifications. Degrees from highly reputable and globally recognised institutions are more likely to be accepted internationally. The Ministry of Education or the equivalent authority in the home country for information on recognising foreign degrees should be contacted before enrolment in a specific PhD program.

☐ *Questions for a personal experience discussion*

- Where have you been abroad, how did you organise your stay, and who did you get support from?
- What skills did you learn?
- Looking back: what were the pros and cons of your stay abroad?
- How important was the stay abroad for your career?

7.3.8 Module 8: Wrap-Up Meeting

The final module is dedicated to wrapping up the program and gathering participants' feedback. Participants are encouraged to share their experiences and insights about the previous modules. Additionally, they are asked to provide suggestions for improvement, ensuring that future program iterations can be refined and enhanced based on their valuable input.

Similar to the first module, the discussion can be held by participants answering the questions orally or through an online form. However, for this session, it could be better to discuss after the participants have filled out the form, as that way there is written evidence that can be referred to when necessary.

☐ *Questions for a personal experience discussion*

- How would you rate your level of satisfaction with your participation in this program?
- Is there any question that remained unanswered, and if so, which one?
- What did you find the most interesting or useful in this program?
- How could the program be improved?

7.4 Impact of WoCa Lunch

The central goal of the WoCa Lunch is to help female students make informed decisions about their career paths beyond master studies. This central goal is connected to diverse implicit effects in different dimensions.

7.4.1 Long-Term Impact

In general, this program is expected to increase the presence of women in informatics, especially at the PhD level.

- △ *Increased number of female PhD students* The program is designed to strengthen gifted female students, get their unfounded doubts out of the way, and motivate them to follow their scientific enthusiasm by enrolling in PhD studies. Thus the most obvious expected impact is increasing the number and percentage of female PhD students.
- △ *Improved success rate of female PhD students* We stress that this program does *not* aim at convincing female students to go for a PhD. Instead, the objective is to inform them about the diverse aspects of PhD studies, and thus to support them to identify the career path which best fits their interests and abilities. Therefore, besides increasing the percentage of female PhD students, another expected impact is avoiding disappointments due to wrong expectations, thus reducing the dropout during PhD studies.
- △ *Awareness for women in informatics* We expect an increased consciousness of Informatics/Computer Science departments for the needs of female students and the fact that gender-related differences need to be considered.
- △ *Further developing the program* Last but not least, collecting experience from WoCa Lunch executions allows us to understand better the reasons, motivations and fears that influence the career planning of female students, which will in turn help to adapt and further improve the contents and form of the program.

7.4.2 Short-Term Impact

In contrast to the long-term impact on the overall evolution of the representation and role of women in informatics, the program's short-term impact is mostly on the participants as individuals.

- △ *Informed career decision of participants* The program has been based on the answers of a carefully designed questionnaire, widely distributed in Europe. The evaluation of the answers helped us compose the program contents to cover all relevant topics, which were recognisable from the answers to lead to uncertainties, wrong assumptions, doubts or fears. The perhaps most direct impact is to allow, by discussing those topics, for informed decisions of the participants regarding their career paths.

△ *Network of women in informatics* The program is expected in general to increase the self-awareness and the self-confidence of the participants and to strengthen the networking and the exchange between them. Besides the impact on the participating students, networks get strengthened beyond university boundaries, between the organisers and the invited interview partners.

7.4.3 Measuring Impact

The factors determining the evolution of the number of PhD students and the representation of women under them are manifold and diverse. Each execution of this program influences this evolution, and monitoring the number, percentage, and success rate of female PhD students hopefully will show positive tendencies. However, from the observation of complex effects, we cannot reliably draw any conclusion regarding the different factors of cause, thus the concrete impact of this program as a single factor is hard to measure quantitatively.

Whereas it is hard to determine and measure long-term impact, the short-term effects are somewhat easier to assess. The last module, the wrap-up meeting, offers a valuable opportunity to help the students reflect on their impressions, exchange their experiences, and get feedback about the immediate program's impact.

A short questionnaire, based e.g. on the questions listed in Sect. 7.3.8, can be designed for this purpose. Given that the program profits from a familiar atmosphere, the number of participants per execution should be relatively low: both paper and online evaluations are well-suited and do not require much effort to be processed. We can also collect direct feedback comments in the wrap-up session, in a live discussion (Fig. 7.2).

In addition, getting additional feedback a few semesters later allows us to maintain statistics about the further career paths of the participants.

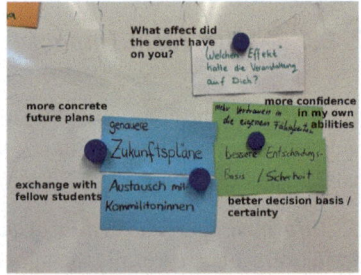

Fig. 7.2 Participants' feedback

7.5 Possible Adaptions to Different Environments

Considering diverse backgrounds, institutions, and cultural settings, joint lunches and discussions about the elements of PhD studies are not always feasible. For example, if students have varying commitments and do not have a standard lunch break, if there are not enough guest speakers or if there is a lack of support from the department, the program should be adapted to suit the local needs. The presented materials can be utilised in different ways.

- *Program Timing* The program is planned to last one hour every other week during lunchtime. However, the program can also be scheduled in the afternoon after lectures and other commitments, or at any time convenient to all the participants.
- *Program Format* The program consists of eight modules. If required, the number of modules can be reduced, or the program can be held as a full or half-day workshop, seminar, or simply as a two-hour lecture with discussion.
- *Choosing the Right Modules* Not all modules are equally applicable in every environment. For example, in countries with just a few universities or where students who go abroad do not return to their home country, modules related to finding positions and studying abroad might not be as relevant as other modules. Similarly, if the program is organised to motivate students to do the PhD at a given department, one might also want to skip these two modules. Additionally, modules related to academic and industrial careers can be combined. On the other hand, understanding what a PhD is and how to handle doubts and problems during the PhD always requires special attention.
- *Participants* The program can be adapted for different underrepresented minorities, considering their needs and problems. This means the module about personal doubts and obstacles should be carefully complemented, while other modules can mostly remain the same. Also, in some environments, the number of potential PhD students is too small to make it sensible to organise the program exclusively for women or any other underrepresented minority. In such environments, PhD students themselves are an underrepresented minority and should be given special encouragement and attention. The suggested questions do not have to be specially adapted when broadening the scope of participants.

> ⊙ **Personal Experience Sharing: Two-Hour Workshop**
> The simplest form of the program was conducted at the Department of Computer Science, Faculty of Mathematics, University of Belgrade. It was organised as a two-hour workshop with all interested students. There were no guest speakers. During the workshop, the organiser showed slides containing all the questions by modules and then discussed the answers to the questions that interested the students the most. Six students attended the workshop, and

(continued)

all were very pleased with the opportunity to hear, understand, and discuss the topic of doctoral studies.

The interactive nature of the workshop allowed students to engage deeply with the material and receive tailored advice based on their specific concerns and interests. The success of this simple yet effective format highlights the importance of adaptability and demonstrates that, even with limited resources, we can create meaningful learning experiences. This format can serve as a model for other departments or institutions facing similar constraints, emphasising the value of personalised interaction and focused discussion.

7.6 Conclusions

In this chapter, we presented the WoCa Lunch program and reported on the first executions, demonstrating its positive impact. We described in detail answers to questions of interest. These answers can help teachers focus on the main issues that should be discussed during sessions if they decide to implement this program. Also, these answers can help students at universities where such a program is not implemented to understand the PhD process better, and its advantages and disadvantages. Students should also get ideas about important topics and answers they should seek further.

The program can be extended in different directions, depending on the participants' feedback after each program's execution. Additionally, one important direction is the development of supporting tools needed for program participation of individuals with special needs.

The next step is to unfold the program's main potential, which lies in its repeatability. The structured contents and the observations and recommendations presented here and under [2] allow execution with little effort and low cost. The authors would highly appreciate hearing back experience reports from further executions.

Acknowledgments This work was supported by COST Action CA19122—EUGAIN (European Network for Gender Balance in Informatics). The authors also acknowledge the support by the Ministry of Science, Technological Development, and Innovation of the Republic of Serbia, grant number 451-03-47/2023-01/200104, and NOVA LINCS (UIDB/04516/2020) for their financial support.

References

1. E. Ábrahám, M. Goulão, M. Vujošević Janičić, S. J. Delany, A. Mersni, O. Yeremenko, O. Buyukdagli, K. Boudaoud, C. Oehlhorn, U. Schmid, C. Büsing, L. Schmid, H. Bolke-Hermanns, K. Köhnle, M. Pato, D. Sunar Cerci, and L. Schmid. Why do women pursue a PhD in Computer Science? *Journal of Systems and Software*, 2024. Submitted.
2. E. Ábrahám, M. Goulão, M. Vujošević Janičić, S. J. Delany, A. Mersni, O. Yeremenko, L. Schmid, A. Nebot, O. Buyukdagli, K. Boudaoud, and D. Sunar Cerci. Women's Career Lunch — Catalog of questions for the speakers. https://doi.org/10.5281/zenodo.10079419, Nov. 2023.
3. Policy Against Harassment at ACM Activities. https://www.acm.org/about-acm/policy-against-harassment, 2018.
4. ACM-W Supporting, celebrating, and advocating for women in computing. https://women.acm.org/, 2024.
5. B. F. André. Gender Balance in Computer Science: How do Women View the Transition into a PhD? Master's thesis, Universidade Nova de Lisboa, Lisbon, Portugal, June 2022. Available at https://run.unl.pt/bitstream/10362/155510/1/Andre_2022.pdf.
6. Paving the Way Forward for Women and Nonbinary Individuals in Tech. https://anitab.org/, 2024.
7. L. Assbring and C. Nuur. What's in it for industry? A case study on collaborative doctoral education in Sweden. *Industry and Higher Education*, 31:184–194, 2017.
8. Cost Association. VOICES. https://www.cost.eu/actions/CA20137/, 2021.
9. Association for Women in Computing. https://www.awc-hq.org/home.html, 2024.
10. Computer Science Department at Brown University. Helping Students From Underrepresented Groups Apply To CS PhD Programs. https://cs.brown.edu/degrees/doctoral/applications/helpful-resources-applying-computer-science-phd-programs/, 2023.
11. R. Barnacle, D. Cuthbert, C. Schmidt, and C. Batty. Vectors of knowledge exchange: The value of industry engagement to HASS PhDs. *Higher Education*, pages 1–15, 2020.
12. I. Bernhard and A. K. Olsson. University-Industry Collaboration in Higher Education: Exploring the Informing Flows Framework in Industrial PhD Education. *Informing Sci. Int. J. an Emerg. Transdiscipl.*, 23:147–163, 2020.
13. I. Bernhard and A. K. Olsson. Industrial PhD Education – Exploring Doctoral Students Acting in the Intersection of Academia and Work-Life. *InSITE Conference*, 2022.
14. I. Bernhard and A. K. Olsson. One foot in academia and one in work-life – The case of Swedish industrial PhD students. *Journal of Workplace Learning*, 2023.
15. J. Bröchner and A. Sezer. Effects of construction industry support for PhD projects: The case of a Swedish scheme. *Industry and Higher Education*, 34:391–400, 2020.
16. B. Casey. The economic contribution of PhDs. *Journal of Higher Education Policy and Management*, 31:219–227, 2009.
17. J. M. Cohoon, Z. Wu, and J. Chao. Sexism: Toxic to women's persistence in CSE doctoral programs. *ACM SIGCSE Bulletin*, 41(1):158–162, 2009.
18. Higher Education Commission and others. Policy on protection against sexual harassment in Higher Education Institutions. *The Higher Education Commission. Retrieved September*, 25:2022, 2020.
19. Ph.D. in Information Technology. https://www.computerscience.org/degrees/phd/online/information-technology/, 2023.
20. LIBRA - Unifying innovative efforts of European research centres to achieve gender equality in academia. https://www.eu-libra.eu/, 2015.
21. The Computing Research Association's committee on widening participation in computing research (CRA-WP). https://cra.org/cra-wp/grad-cohort-for-women/, 2024.
22. Grad Cohort Workshop for Women. https://cra.org/cra-wp/grad-cohort-for-women, 2023. 10.10.2023.

23. Department of Computer Science, Stony Brook University. Celebrating the Success of Women PhD Students in Computer Science. https://www.cs.stonybrook.edu/about-us/News/Celebrating-Success-Women-PhD-Students-Computer-Science, 2023.
24. E. Di Nitto, I. García-Varea, M. Jazayeri, D. A. Tamburri, and S. Tikhonenko. Informatics Higher Education in Europe: A Data Portal and Case Study. *Communications of the ACM*, 66:61–67, 2023.
25. CA19122 - European Network for Gender Balance in Informatics (Memorandum of Understanding). https://www.cost.eu/actions/CA19122/, Jun 2021.
26. 2nd International EUGAIN Summer Training School: Research Recharge (June 14-15, 2023 – Rome, Italy). https://eugain.training/, 2023.
27. Informatics Europe. Radboud wins 2017 Minerva Informatics Equality Award. https://www.informatics-europe.org/news/396-radboud-minerva-award2017.html, 2017.
28. Informatics Europe. SUCCESS @ TU Dublin Computer Science Wins 2019 Minerva Informatics Equality Award. https://www.informatics-europe.org/news/499-success-tu-dublin-computer-science-wins-2019-minerva-informatics-equality-award.html, 2019.
29. Informatics Europe. 2022 Minerva Informatics Equality Award. https://www.informatics-europe.org/society/minerva-informatics-equality-award/2022.html, 2022.
30. Informatics Europe. Best Practices in Supporting Women. https://www.informatics-europe.org/society/minerva-informatics-equality-award/best-practices-in-supporting-women.html, 2023.
31. Informatics Europe. Two Winners Honoured with the 2023 Minerva Informatics Equality Award. https://www.informatics-europe.org/news/850-two-winners-honoured-with-the-2023-minerva-informatics-equality-award.html, 2023.
32. B. Flanigan, A. A. Joshi, S. McAllister, and C. Vajiac. CS-JEDI: Required DEI education, by CS PhD students, for CS PhD students. In *Proceedings of the 54th ACM Technical Symposium on Computer Science Education V. 1*, pages 87–93, 2023.
33. J. García-Quevedo, F. Mas-Verdu, and J. Polo-Otero. Which firms want PhDs? An analysis of the determinants of the demand. *Higher Education*, 63:607–620, 2012.
34. E. Germain-Alamartine, R. Ahoba-Sam, S. Moghadam-Saman, and G. Evers. Doctoral graduates' transition to industry: Networks as a mechanism? Cases from Norway, Sweden and the UK. *Studies in Higher Education*, 46:2680–2695, 2020.
35. Google. Google PhD Fellowship Program. https://research.google/programs-and-events/phd-fellowship/, 2024.
36. K. Hamrick. Women, Minorities, and Persons with Disabilities in Science and Engineering. https://ncses.nsf.gov/pubs/nsf21321/report/field-of-degree-women, 2021.
37. S. M. Hyrynsalmi. The Underrepresentation of Women in the Software Industry: Thoughts from Career-Changing Women. *2019 IEEE/ACM 2nd International Workshop on Gender Equality in Software Engineering (GE)*, pages 1–4, 2019.
38. IEEE Computer Society. IEEE Policy Against Discrimination and Harassment. https://www.ieee.org/content/dam/ieee-org/ieee/web/org/about/corporate/ieee-policies.pdf, 2024.
39. L. Jaccheri, C. Pereira, and S. Fast. Gender issues in Computer Science: Lessons learnt and reflections for the future. In *2020 22nd International Symposium on Symbolic and Numeric Algorithms for Scientific Computing (SYNASC)*, pages 9–16. IEEE, 2020.
40. P. Johanesen, J. García-Bustos, and P. Wood. Training PhD students to bridge the Academia-Industry gap. *Microbiology Australia*, 37:73–75, 2016.
41. Koc University, Gender Equality Office. Teaching. https://geo.ku.edu.tr/teaching/, 2023.
42. S. Kyvik and T. Olsen. The relevance of doctoral training in different labour markets. *Journal of Education and Work*, 25:205–224, 2012.
43. R. Lindner. Barriers to Doctoral Education, Equality, Diversity and Inclusion for Postgraduate Research Students at UCL. https://www.grad.ucl.ac.uk/strategy/barriers-to-doctoral-education.pdf, 2020.
44. V. Lockett. Supporting Women in PhD Programs: Scholarships and Resources to Optimize Success. https://www.phds.me/financial-aid/scholarships-and-grants/women/, 30.03.2023.

45. M. Maxon. Getting a PhD in a STEM field is a great start to a winning career. *Molecular Biology of the Cell*, 30:2617–2619, 2019.
46. Microsoft. Microsoft Research PhD Fellowship. https://www.microsoft.com/en-us/research/academic-program/phd-fellowship/, 2024.
47. S. Munoz-Hernandez and I. Osman. Using a productive distance PhD program to empower women in academia. In *2016 IST-Africa Week Conference*, pages 1–7. IEEE, 2016.
48. National Center for Women and Information Technology. https://ncwit.org/, 2024.
49. NTNU. TDT10 - Gender and diversity in software development. https://i.ntnu.no/wiki/-/wiki/Norsk/TDT10++Gender+and+diversity+in+software+development, 2024.
50. Norwegian University of Science and Technology. IDUN - From PhD to professor. https://www.ntnu.edu/idun, 2019.
51. Norwegian University of Science and Technology. Gender equality and diversity at NTNU. https://www.ntnu.edu/genderequality, 2023.
52. National Academies of Sciences Engineering and Medicine. *Sexual Harassment of Women: Climate, Culture, and Consequences in Academic Sciences, Engineering, and Medicine*. National Academies Press, Washington, DC, 2018.
53. European Union's Horizon 2020 Research and Innovation Programme under Grant Agreement No 710549. EQUAL-IST. https://equal-ist.eu/, 2016.
54. A. Rosenstein, A. Raghu, and L. Porter. Identifying the prevalence of the impostor phenomenon among computer science students. In *Proceedings of the 51st ACM Technical Symposium on Computer Science Education*, pages 30–36, 2020.
55. E. Rubegni, B. Penzenstadler, M. Landoni, L. Jaccheri, and G. Dodig-Crnkovic. Owning Your Career Paths: Storytelling to Engage Women in Computer Science. In *Gender in AI and Robotics: The Gender Challenges from an Interdisciplinary Perspective*, pages 1–25. Springer, 2023.
56. M. Sinche, R. Layton, P. D. Brandt, A. B. O'Connell, J. D. Hall, A. M. Freeman, J. R. Harrell, J. G. Cook, and P. Brennwald. An evidence-based evaluation of transferrable skills and job satisfaction for science PhDs. *PLoS ONE*, 12, 2017.
57. Stanford Engineering, Computer Science. Incoming CS PhD students. https://www.cs.stanford.edu/student-services-overview/new-student-orientation/incoming-cs-phd-students, 2023.
58. The University of Melbourne, The Faculty of Engineering and Information Technology. Diane Lemaire Scholarship. https://eng.unimelb.edu.au/students/scholarships-prizes-and-awards/graduate-research-students/scholarships/scholarships/diane-lemaire, 2024.
59. Koc University. Return to Research Grant. https://geo.ku.edu.tr/return-to-research-grant-2-2/, 2024.
60. University of Copenhagen (DIKU), Computer Science Department. FEMTECH.DK. https://www.femtech.dk/, 2021.

Open Access This chapter is licensed under the terms of the Creative Commons Attribution 4.0 International License (http://creativecommons.org/licenses/by/4.0/), which permits use, sharing, adaptation, distribution and reproduction in any medium or format, as long as you give appropriate credit to the original author(s) and the source, provide a link to the Creative Commons license and indicate if changes were made.

The images or other third party material in this chapter are included in the chapter's Creative Commons license, unless indicated otherwise in a credit line to the material. If material is not included in the chapter's Creative Commons license and your intended use is not permitted by statutory regulation or exceeds the permitted use, you will need to obtain permission directly from the copyright holder.

Chapter 8
The Impact of Peers, Mentors and Role Models on Successful PhD Studies

Judith Knoblach, Ute Schmid, Miguel Goulão, Larissa Schmid, Milena Vujošević Janičić, and Karima Boudaoud

8.1 Introduction

> *If you want to go fast, go alone. If you want to go far, go together.*
>
> *African proverb*

PhD programmes in informatics are pivotal in shaping a resilient, versatile, and inclusive future for technology. Prioritising diversity and empowering women pursuing doctoral studies in informatics goes beyond addressing equality: it catalyses untapped potential, contributing to a more vibrant future for the industry and society.

J. Knoblach (✉) · U. Schmid
Otto-Friedrich-Universität Bamberg, Bamberg, Germany
e-mail: judith.knoblach@uni-bamberg.de; ute.schmid@uni-bamberg.de

M. Goulão
NOVA School of Science and Technology, Lisbon, Portugal
e-mail: mgoul@fct.unl.pt

L. Schmid
Karlsruhe Institute of Technology (KIT), Karlsruhe, Germany
e-mail: larissa.schmid@kit.edu

M. Vujošević Janičić
Faculty of Mathematics, University of Belgrade, Belgrade, Serbia
e-mail: milena.vujosevic.janicic@matf.bg.ac.rs

K. Boudaoud
Département Réseaux et Télécommunications, IUT de Nice Côte d'Azur - site de Sophia Antipolis, Sophia Antipolis, France
e-mail: karima.boudaoud@univ-cotedazur.fr

© The Author(s) 2025
B. Penzenstadler et al. (eds.), *Actions for Gender Balance in Informatics Across Europe*, https://doi.org/10.1007/978-3-031-78432-3_8

Doctoral researchers experience higher stress levels than the general population, with isolation and identifying as a female among the most prominent risk factors [21]. This feeling of isolation is prevalent among female informatics students [29]. The lack of visible role models and mentors in academia that female students identify with can discourage female students who may need help envisioning themselves succeeding in an academic career currently perceived as male-dominated [35]. The underrepresentation of female informatics students leads to a lower sense of belonging when compared to their male peers. Lower enthusiasm, self-confidence, and self-esteem are noteworthy factors which deter women from starting a PhD in informatics. A recent survey shows how the so-called *"impostor syndrome"* [26] is more frequent among female software engineers (60.6%) than among males (48.8%). This syndrome is also problematic concerning the decision to start a PhD in informatics: female students who decide not to pursue a PhD in informatics exhibit a significantly higher impostor syndrome than those who do it [6]. There is no such difference among male students. Interestingly, female students feeling well-prepared and accepted by their peers tend to perform at the same level as their male peers [18].

Motivating females to pursue a PhD in informatics is crucial to address the persistent underrepresentation of women in the field. By increasing female participation in Phd programs, we can foster diverse perspectives that are vital for innovation, and accelerate the societal shift toward gender equality in technology, where progress has been slow despite ongoing efforts across Europe. To do so, we need to mitigate the above mentioned sense of isolation. In this context, the role of peers, mentors and role models may be pivotal so that PhD students may embark on their PhD journey, knowing there will be allies there for them along the way.

In this chapter, we discuss the roles of peers, mentors, and role models and how they can help (female) PhD students on their path to a PhD. This discussion is centred around the EUGAIN network results, the available literature findings, and a qualitative survey conducted with current and recently graduated female PhD students in informatics. We use direct quotes from our respondents to illustrate some points throughout this chapter. For instance, to supplement our argument on the relevance of having a good support network, we quote a former PhD student in Germany who offered compelling advice to current and future PhD students, in the context of our survey: [💬 R4 PH DE] *"Invest in your relationships. We spend a lot of time with colleagues, so it is worth making those relationships good. And networks will serve you well in the long run, so there is a career pay-off if you stick around."*

The remainder of this chapter is organised as follows. Section 8.2 introduces the notions of peers, mentors and role models. Section 8.3 briefly describes our survey on female students' insights on doing a PhD in informatics. Sections 8.4, 8.5, and 8.6 discuss the role of peers, mentors and role models in the PhD process. Section 8.7 addresses who can benefit from the chapter. Finally, Sect. 8.8 summarises this chapter.

8.2 What Are Peers, Mentors and Role Models?

Gibson defines *role model* as a cognitive construction based on the attributes of people in social roles an individual perceives to be similar to her or himself to some extent and desires to increase perceived similarity by emulating those attributes [19]. Role models can also be negative. Individuals observe negative role models to learn how to avoid attributes or behaviours they perceive as negative. An individual actively observes, adapts and rejects attributes of multiple role models. These attributes help in defining role expectations as well as one's self-concept. Individuals often have multiple partial role models from which they select specific traits they identify to create a combination of influences that match their current needs.

A key element is that the relationship between the individual and the role model is often one-way. No direct interaction is required, as one can identify with the values and actions of distant role models with whom the individual interacts infrequently or not at all. Role models can also be close people with whom the individual interacts frequently, including people with a higher hierarchical status, peers or even subordinates within the same organisation, or other people with no clear hierarchical relationship.

Gibson contrasts this notion of a role model with the one of a *mentor*. He defines a *mentor* as a person who *"provide[s] advice and support to a protégé through an interactive relationship"*. Although a *mentor* can be a role model for a *mentee*, and *vice-versa*, that is not necessarily the case. Mentees tend to have just one or two mentors at any time. Kram and Isabella [24] discuss how mentor-mentee relationships are typically long-term, focused on helping the mentees advance their careers, as mentors offer sponsorship, coaching, increased exposure and visibility, challenging work and protection. Mentors also provide psycho-social functions, including role modelling, counselling, confirmation and friendship, that help the mentee develop their professional identity and competence. Unlike the relationship with role models, which is one-way, the relationship between mentor and mentee is usually explicit (both mentor and mentee are aware of it) and substantially shaped by context.

The two-way relationship between mentors and mentees is also beneficial for mentors, who gather technical and psychological support and leverage the successful development of young talent in the organisation for their reputation. There is also an element of internal satisfaction in supporting a younger colleague's growth and success. Eventually, the context changes and this (often symbiotic) mentoring relationship ends. This may occur due to organisational (e.g. the mentee completing their PhD) and/or personal changes (e.g. an increased sense of confidence or a growing need for independence) [24].

In an academic context, mentors are often the students' supervisors, establishing a hierarchical relationship between supervisors and their students. This hierarchical relationship may entail challenges with communication, mutual support, and collaboration. Boud defines *peers* as *"other people in a similar situation to each other who do not have a role in that situation"* [14]. A peer relationship can support some mentoring functions while mitigating communication, mutual support, and collaboration challenges. Peers can be helpful in academic information sharing, strategy and feedback, and psychosocial functions, including confirmation, emotional support, personal feedback, and friendship [24].

8.3 Survey

This chapter summarises research concerning the role of peers, mentors and role models during the PhD process. We complement these findings with the results of the survey we designed to collect testimonies from female PhD students in informatics. These testimonies aim to provide relatable examples from current and recent PhD students to our readers, complementing the body of knowledge in this area with more relatable testimonies. From the survey answers, we can learn women's opinions about their peers, mentors, and role models as they pursue a PhD in informatics.

The testimonies reported here were collected in the survey already described in Sect. 6.2.2 of Chap. 6 (entitled *Voices of Female Informatics Students Across Universities*). As a quick recap, that survey included responses from 20 women. Five of our respondents recently finished PhD in informatics; the remaining 15 are working on their PhD. We received answers from Serbia (6), Portugal (5), Germany (3), Bosnia and Herzegovina (3), Cyprus(1), Italy (1) and Turkey (1). We identify the respondents here as R1 to R20. For each respondent, we also add *education status* which indicates if the respondent is a PhD student (noted as PS) or a PhD holder (noted as PH). We also add *country code* which represents the respondent's country using a two-letter code, as defined by international standards.

The 3 questions from that survey which are relevant to this chapter are:

1. How important have your peers been to you, and how do (or did) they affect you and your doctoral studies?
2. How would you describe your relationship with your mentor?
3. Who were your role models during your doctoral studies and why?

In the second question, note that we use the word mentor rather than supervisor. Most of our respondents also used it in the same way. As mentioned above, for PhD students their supervisor usually also serves as a mentor.

In Sects. 8.4, 8.5, and 8.6 we will summarise these results, in context with the corresponding body of knowledge, to make this discussion more relatable for PhD candidates, future PhD candidates, and those who have already completed their PhD and may be considering becoming or already are mentors or role models.

8.4 The Role of Peers

Students often discuss things outside the scope of classes or formal group meetings, ask each other questions, and share knowledge and experiences, making the learning process more enjoyable. Boud [24] adds that the form of learning from peers is crucial in the sense that students need to develop vital skills of learning from each other, including the ability to discern the level of accuracy of the information they receive from their peers, which presumably may be more variable than the generally more accurate information received from a mentor.

Peers can complement formal mentoring relationships (e.g., between the PhD student and her supervisor(s)). Unlike formal mentoring relationships, which are asymmetric by nature, with a power relationship of the supervisor (the professor) over the mentee (the student), a peer relationship can form a two-way reciprocal relationship with students learning from and with each other in both formal and informal ways [14]. This has several variants, including senior students tutoring junior students and more levelled peer relationships. In addition, peers can engage in community activities that nurture social relationships, creating student support networks.

8.4.1 Peers Networking

Although several peer networking opportunities may arise organically, many Universities and Research Centres foster formal (e.g., reading groups, internal workshops) and informal (e.g., PhD students' get-togethers, and informal virtual groups) contexts for their PhD students to interact with their peers. These strategies can be particularly helpful for more junior students to start creating their support networks. The networks can effectively mitigate feelings of isolation. Effectively joining a research community significantly increases the likelihood of completing the degree successfully and in good time [11].

Peer networks like the one at Brown University can support students in different stages, starting from the application process for a PhD in informatics.

Once a student enrols in a PhD program, the next challenge is to navigate the PhD process to obtain a successful completion. There are several examples of female PhD students' networks see for example the network at KTH Royal Institute of Technology.

Brown University, US
At Brown University, United States of America, a student-led initiative aids applicants from underrepresented groups (including women) in applying to

(continued)

the Computer Science Doctoral program [7]. The goal is to bolster the diversity of the program students. The network provides individual feedback on students' applications and makes available a collection of useful resources, including guidance sessions, testimonials, blog posts on how to build strong applications, and links to other related initiatives in other top Universities.

KTH Royal Institute of Technology, Sweden
KTH Royal Institute of Technology has a network entitled *"Women PhD Candidates at KTH (WOP@KTH)"* [37]. This network provides a forum for discussing common challenges and strategies to overcome them, with the ultimate goal of helping students to fulfil their professional potential, while balancing career and personal life. The network organises workshops, seminars, testimonial talks by women in academia and industry, and social events.

Apart from these more generic peer networks, there are other more topic-specific possibilities a PhD student can explore. Internal research projects in the research lab can be a good starting point for interacting with peers working on a related topic. Most international conferences include doctoral symposiums, which offer a good opportunity to meet peers on relatively close topics and for scientific mentoring beyond that of supervisors. Participating in conferences (as a simple attendant, a student volunteer, or an author) is a great opportunity for networking with peers and a stepping stone towards success in doctoral work.

8.4.2 Personal Experiences

We collected the personal experiences of current and former female PhD students on the relevance of their peers to their trajectory. Several common themes emerged. Most participants consider their peers very important in their trajectory. [💬 R2 PS IT] *"My peers have been instrumental in my doctoral studies, providing a network for sharing information and collaboratively solving complex issues. Their diverse perspectives have enriched my research approach and contributed significantly to my academic development. Engaging with fellow doctoral candidates has not only enhanced my learning experience but also fostered a supportive academic environment."*.

Others are a bit less enthusiastic. [💬 R5 PS RS] *"At the beginning of the studies, the exchange of opinions and ideas, discussions about interests, and obtaining additional information depending on the field in which colleagues are doing their doctorate certainly means a lot. However, in the long run, only personal motivation and organisation help to continue further."* Sometimes, there is a barrier concerning the area of study which makes the interaction with local peers less productive, from a technical perspective. [💬 R2 PS IT] *"My colleagues [...] do not research in the field I am engaged in, so there was a lack of productive discussion and knowledge sharing. Nevertheless, their experiences, the challenges they face, and their support have been significant to me."*

Unfortunately, some students do go through a more lonely PhD process. [💬 R11 PS PT] *"They were not relevant."* On a more positive note, no respondent reported a generally negative effect of their interactions with their peers.

Finally, we also present the most neutral statement we collected from our respondents. This highlights that even for those who think interactions with peers are not too relevant, they were not negative either. [💬 R7] *"They didn't influence me much. Sometimes we discussed certain topics, but they didn't have an impact."*

8.5 Mentoring Programs

Mentors play a crucial role in the PhD process. They can support students in navigating the technical aspects of their work and help them cope with non-technical challenges they often struggle with. These may include career path issues, and mental health-related issues like anxiety, stress, or depression. Other common challenges include a lack of self-confidence, also known as *"impostor syndrome"*, and cultural and language barriers for students doing their PhD abroad.

Mentors listen to the student's concrete concerns and can offer constructive feedback, suggest relevant resources and alternative perspectives, and promote links for the student to extend their network. In addition, a mentor can offer valuable empathy to the student and build up the student's confidence and accountability, contributing to the student's academic growth. As discussed in Sect. 8.2, a healthy mentor-mentee relationship has mutual benefits.

PhD supervisors are usually among a PhD student's mentors but are not necessarily (or desirably) alone in the mentor role. Other faculty members can also help, as can more senior students, post-doctoral members of the team, and the wider research community.

No matter how well-intended mentors may be (while most are, sometimes the relationship with the mentor may become toxic), they will not always offer the best advice the student needs. Each mentor has a context governing their vision of what advice to offer. That context is, naturally, constrained by the mentor's personal and professional experiences. As such, it is useful for the student to build a mentoring network so the student can learn from different perspectives and make her judgement of the challenges she faces. It is part of the student's growth process to learn how to filter the advice they should follow and identify the advice that, for some reason, may not apply to her or fit her needs. As famously put by David Evans, a Computer Science Professor from the University of Virginia, US, *"Everyone*

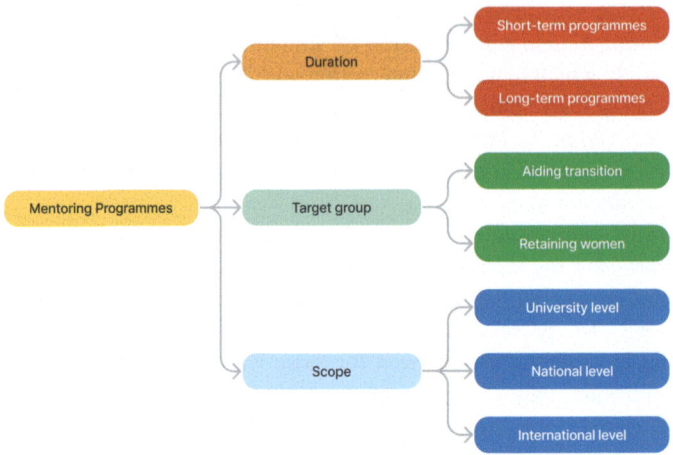

Fig. 8.1 Mentoring programmes categories

should [...] **read and listen to lots of advice from individuals**, *but* **ignore most of it.**" [17].

The chapter on *Mentoring as a Tool for Better Gender Diversity in Informatics* presents a systematic literature review on mentoring. The chapter *Breaking Barriers: Strategies for Achieving Equity in Academic Careers in ICT/Informatics/STEM* gives concrete suggestions on how to set up a mentoring program.

Mentoring programs can be categorised based on *duration*, *target group*, and *scope*, as presented in Fig. 8.1.

8.5.1 Duration of a Mentoring Program

Mentoring can be long-term or short-term in terms of duration. Long-term mentoring involves sustained relationships over months or even years, offering continuous support that allows mentees to build strong, trusting relationships with their mentors, e.g. the Coffee Code Break platform. University-based mentoring programs typically match students with faculty or industry professionals who provide ongoing guidance throughout their academic careers. PhD supervisors typically act as mentors for their PhD students. Still, it is not uncommon to have other faculty members acting as mentors for technical and non-technical issues beyond the specific PhD supervision.

In contrast, short-term mentoring, such es the one at The International Conference for High-Performance Computing, Networking, Storage and Analysis, provides quick, focused guidance often related to specific events or needs. Examples include conference mentoring, where participants can seek advice and network with experienced professionals before, during and after academic conferences, and online mentoring platforms like *Coffee Code Break* which facilitate single or limited interactions, allowing students and professionals to get quick answers to specific questions or advice on particular issues. Doctoral symposiums often include experienced faculty who will offer specialised feedback to PhD students.

> **Short-Term Mentoring at Conferences**
> The International Conference for High-Performance Computing, Networking, Storage, and Analysis (SC) has a mentoring program [3] aimed at students attending the conference. They match students with mentors based on a questionnaire about research and personal interests. While virtual one-on-one meetups are proposed shortly before and after the conference, an in-person event is scheduled during the conference.

> **Coffee Code Break**
> Coffee Code Break [1] is an online platform aimed at Women in Tech, showing available mentors and providing the possibility to book a meeting with any of them.

8.5.2 Target Group of a Mentoring Program

Mentoring programs also differ in their target groups. Some programs focus towards retaining women in graduate studies, while others aim to aid the transition to PhD programs and industry [6].

To ensure women remain in graduate programs, mentoring focuses on providing academic and emotional support. Peer mentoring involves experienced graduate students mentoring newcomers, helping them adjust to the demands of graduate school and fostering a supportive community. Faculty mentoring, on the other hand, involves professors and other academic staff providing guidance on research projects, career advice, and navigating the academic landscape.

For those transitioning to PhD programs, PhD students often mentor master's students [2, 5], helping them understand the transition process and what doing a PhD is like. This includes research guidance, where PhD mentors help master's students understand research and develop the skills needed for doctoral studies, as well as advice on PhD program applications, funding opportunities, and interviews. As students transition from academia to industry, mentoring focuses on career preparation, including interview preparation and understanding industry expectations, as well as networking opportunities, where mentors introduce mentees to industry contacts, helping them build a professional network.

8.5.3 Scope of a Mentoring Program

The scope of mentoring programs can vary from within a university, e.g., at ETH Zürich, to a national or international level. University-based mentoring programs are often more personalised and accessible, with departmental programs matching students with faculty or senior students within their department for regular mentoring sessions, and women in CS clubs organising mentoring circles, workshops, and networking events.

> **ETH Zürich, Switzerland**
> ETH Zürich has a mentoring program [4] for women doing a PhD in Computer Science. Its main goals are to help find a mentor within the faculty to share academic experience and establish connections with other researchers of the department, mitigating the difficulties from young women starting their PhD to know other, more senior female students, or post-docs, as there may not be many, or any at all within the same research group.

National mentoring programs create broader networks, with national organizations like the National Center for Women & Information Technology (NCWIT) in the U.S. offering extensive mentoring programs, scholarships, and resources. Some countries have governmental programs encouraging women in Science, Technology, Engineering and Math (STEM) fields, including mentoring components. International and online networks provide access to a global community, which can be especially valuable for women in regions with fewer local resources. Global organisations like the Association for Computing Machinery's Council on Women in Computing (ACM-W) provide international mentoring opportunities and resources, and online communities on platforms like LinkedIn offer virtual mentoring opportunities, connecting women with mentors worldwide.

8.5.4 Personal Experiences

We asked our participants to describe their relationship with their mentors. Unsurprisingly, these relationships are quite varied. In most cases, the respondents referred to their supervisors as their mentors, although other people (e.g. other PhD students) can sometimes play the mentor role. For example, [💬 R13 PS DE] *"I consider other doctoral candidates or my supervisor to be mentors."*

Most participants mention a good personal relationship with their supervisor [💬 R8 PH RS] *"Wonderful, throughout the entire doctorate and after it"*. This kind of relationship often goes beyond the technical support. For example, [💬 R11 PS PT] describes *[a] good working and supporting relationship.*

Others mention a more distant relationship, which can be associated with less available supervisors: [🗨 R7] *"Very formal. I had to send many emails to get a response from him or a meeting appointment."* This does not necessarily imply a bad relationship: [🗨 R7]*"when the mentor had time, the collaboration was quite useful and good, with plenty of guidance and help"*. Sometimes the relationship is even less personalised, as noted by [🗨 R4 PH DE] *"My supervisor was doing 'minimally invasive' work - we had about 5 meetings about my PhD topic over the entire course of my PhD. Plenty of project meetings, not so much personal research supervision."*. This more distant relationship can also be part of a pedagogic approach. For instance, [🗨 R3 PH TR] notes that her supervisor *"saw these challenges as opportunities for [her] personal and academic growth, so [she] received minimal help from [her supervisor's] side."*. Indeed, some PhD candidates have a maturity level that leads them to appreciate an [🗨 R5 PS RS] *"Excellent, non-intrusive, yet a great support and a push forward."*

Non-intrusiveness encourages the student's autonomy but entails some risks. [🗨 R9 PS RS] *"We had correct cooperation, and he cared about our visibility in the community, so my engagements were primarily directed towards conferences and project tasks. These tasks brought me many useful experiences, domain breadth, and valuable acquaintances, but they were quite divergent and did not bring me closer to completing my thesis."* This student needed a closer collaboration with the supervisor, and got it, with her second supervisor. [🗨 R9 PS RS] *"With my second mentor, I have a very pleasant and friendly collaboration. He can dedicate more time to me and is more open to discussing the details of my work. He is much more systematic and organised, giving me confidence that we will reach our common goal."*

Support from the mentor was a common theme. This support can be both technical and personal [🗨 R10 PS RS] *"The relationship was very fair, with a lot of understanding and support, especially when the research was progressing slowly and results were lacking. With creative suggestions, guidelines, and advice, the mentor's approach was generally stimulating and encouraging for me."*

8.6 The Impact of Role Models on Career Choices

Role models positively impact women's professional development and pursuit of STEM careers [8, 20, 31]. Their influence on women is significantly greater than that on men [36]. The presence of female role models promotes the construction of a possible future self in STEM fields: *"a female engineer may observe certain qualities about her supervisor that allow her to more accurately identify advantageous personal characteristics facilitating promotion or advancement in the field."* [27]. The success of others can be inspirational when one perceives the other's success as relevant to one's interests and believes that it is personally attainable [34].

8.6.1 The Stereotype Threat

The underrepresentation of women in informatics and engineering leadership results from interconnected factors. These include the marginalising experiences of young women and follow through to ongoing stereotypes that hinder women's success across academia [28]. The stereotype threat describes the phenomenon of women confronted with negative stereotypes in STEM fields, doubting their ability to succeed in these fields. Stereotype threat refers to the worry that one's performance might be evaluated based on a negative stereotype. This concern could impede performance in areas where negative stereotypes are prevalent [30, 32].

Stereotypical role models often arise in the young women's environment such as family and friends. To avoid being perceived as an oddity, young women may be inclined to choose careers that are seen as typically female, if there is a lack of support or even criticism for choosing a supposedly male-dominated career path. Women pursuing a career in informatics and perceiving themselves as too feminine may feel pressured to perform well now more than ever.

Role modelling could prevent the harmful effects of stereotype threat and protect women from under-performance and leaving the field [16]. Viewing female professors as positive role models is not only associated with pro-science career aspirations but also helps reduce the implicit stereotype that science is masculine [39].

8.6.2 Work-Life Balance

Graduate students want to model themselves after women who balance work with their lives [10]. Individuals with low professional role confidence could benefit from interaction with professionals with whom they can identify, as women still find themselves in a situation where they think that they have to choose between work and family [12]. Nowadays, however, the presence of a family is no longer the primary indicator of a stable work-life balance. Above all, it is about whether time is invested exclusively in increasing one's productivity at work, or whether there is still time left over to pursue activities that have no work-related objective, but for purely leisure's sake.

8.6.3 Critical Mass

The presence of female role models positively influences the performance of young women in STEM fields. There is a positive correlation between the retention of female students and the percentage of their science and mathematics classes taught by female faculty [25]. Women's colleges are particularly successful at cultivating women's interest in counter-stereotypical disciplines and professions due to the presence of a critical mass of role models in those disciplines—female faculty and other female students [13]. A third of women in private-sector technical jobs said that they felt extremely isolated at work. Additionally, four of 10 female engineers and computing professionals reported lacking role models [22]. Women in doctoral programs in STEM leave without finishing at higher rates than men and turn away from academic and research careers. The lack of female role models is one factor in the decreasing motivation to acknowledge one's identity as both a female and a scientist [9]. Promoting visible female role models positively impacts young women and supports female students in deciding to pursue a PhD in informatics.

We must also consider an opposing perspective. According to [23], *tokens* are members of a group in which they are perceived as representatives rather than individuals. In contrast, the numerically dominant types control the group. Theoretically, a simple increase in the number of tokens should compensate for the existing imbalance. The potential risks associated with this line of thinking in the context of policy issues are highlighted in [38]. This approach fails to acknowledge the role of other factors, such as sexual harassment, gender pay gaps and barriers to mobility, in influencing women's decisions to remain in male-dominated occupations. Policymakers must also consider that the existence of initiatives for underrepresented groups may give the impression that they are less competent than their dominant counterparts [15]. Despite this criticism, we argue that the promotion of role models in the field of informatics will positively impact female doctoral students.

8.6.4 Personal Experiences

We asked our participants who their role models were and why. Figure 8.2 summarises the number of respondents who identified each role model profile. Most role models come from informatics. Faculty members are the most cited category. Among these, PhD supervisors are almost as cited as other faculty members. Peers (colleagues from the same or other research groups) are frequent role models. Role models can be from other domains, or one's personal life, including family, friends, and former teachers. Figure 8.3 summarises role models by sex. Eight respondents did not mention the sex of their role models, 5 mentioned they have both male and female role models, and 4 mentioned only female role models. None explicitly mentioned only male role models, but it seems likely that some of the NA responses include male role models. One participant said she could not think of any role models.

Most participants are inspired by research community members, learning best practices for their work process. [💬 R8 PH RS] *"My role models were my mentor, certain colleagues from the Department, and some colleagues from abroad. From each of them, I saw something attractive that I tried to implement in my scientific*

Fig. 8.2 Role model's profile

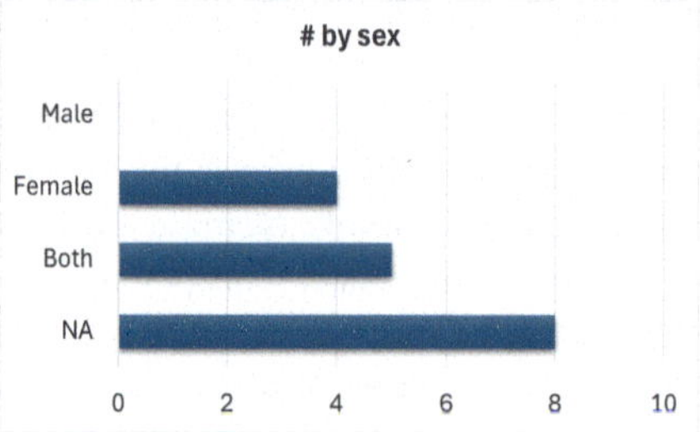

Fig. 8.3 Role models' gender

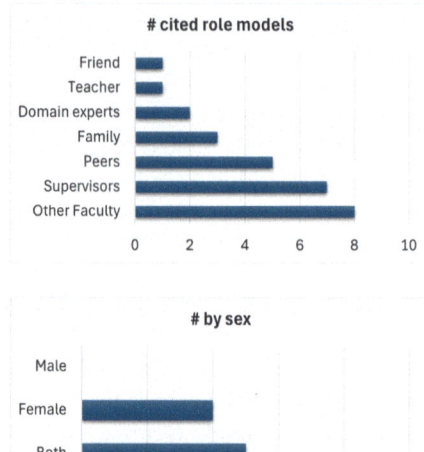

practice - the way of working, research strategies, relationships with colleagues, and so on."

PhD students draw different influences from several role models. Some of those influences are technical. [💬 R2 PS IT] *"During my doctoral studies, my role models have included both professional and personal influences. Professionally, my supervisor and his assistant, who also holds a PhD, have been exemplary role models. Their dedication to research excellence and their strategic approach to academic success have greatly influenced my work ethic and aspirations. On a personal level, my sister has been a significant role model. Her ability to combine academic achievements with a successful industry career inspires me to pursue a similar path of blending rigorous scholarly research with practical, real-world applications."* [💬 R4 PH DE] *"I had a few peers who were a couple of years ahead of me, some went to industry or founded their own company and some stayed in academia. Their work ethic and thoughtful feedback always inspired me."*

Others, have more personal takeaways from their role models, e.g. concerning work-life balance [💬 R5 PS RS] *"My mentor and the senior colleagues from the department. As a younger student, I primarily admired colleagues who had great success in the scientific community. However, over the years, I realised that my greatest inspiration is those who have balanced their private and academic/professional lives and reflect satisfaction with life :)."* The motivations for doing a PhD go beyond the research question one is answering. [💬 R12 PS DE] *"There were a few people who had a positive influence on me during my PhD. If I were to look for a common trait in these people, it would probably be their ability to pursue goals with determination and at the same time not lose sight of the bigger picture. A mixture of curiosity, determination and social responsibility."*

Pursuing a PhD is full of challenges. Role models may inspire resilience in overcoming them. [💬 R3 PH TR] *"I often thought of one of my friends during difficult times. She faced significant challenges and continued her PhD under time-restricted conditions. Her perseverance and dedication inspired me to push through my hardships."*

Even role models from one's past can have a pivotal effect. [💬 R16 PS PT] *"I often think of a violin teacher I had. I think of her as my first academic mentor. She was the first person who taught me how to study and, during my adolescence, we had many discussions about the importance of having dreams and pursuing them with courage and ambition. She had abandoned her medicine degree by the end of the second year, to study music and did so with determination, ambition, and passion. As a teacher, she was always demanding with me, but, at the same time, someone who wanted the best for me and motivated me to fulfil my potential."*

One can also learn from negative examples [💬 R6 PS RS] *"I don't have a positive role model; I only have a few negative examples whom I look at to know what not to do."*

Finally, some people cannot pinpoint their role models. [💬 R10 PS RS] *"I didn't have role models; enrolling in doctoral studies and their subsequent course were not inspired by others' examples. It somehow happened spontaneously."*

8.6.5 STEM Role Models in the Media

Social media provides a platform for individuals who may otherwise remain unheard. Numerous women in STEM have established themselves as influential figures in their respective fields through diverse formats such as YouTube, Instagram or TED Talks, thereby increasing the visibility of women in these fields. Girls identify media and influencers as an important source of STEM role models [33].

> **Media Examples**
> **Fei-Fei Li** is a leading researcher in artificial intelligence and presents widely attended TED Talks. **Nguyen-Kim** launched the YouTube channel *The Secret Life of Scientists* to challenge stereotypes about scientists and nerds and to communicate scientific topics to a young audience. She is currently active on German television and other YouTube channels. It is also worth looking at women with a smaller reach on Instagram and the like. **Quinn Dunki** demonstrates various technical topics, such as home-built computers and 3D printing, on the *Blondihacks* YouTube channel. Her videos significantly contribute to pushing the boundaries in a male-dominated field. **Dr Fatima** talks on her YouTube channel about research, politics and issues that can affect women in science.

8.6.6 Poster of Positive Role Models in Informatics

A positive role model in informatics can be a successful researcher and leader but, at the same time, should also be a person with their own private life, dreams, and hobbies. As the work-life balance is a crucial factor for women, this combination of a successful academic career with an attractive personal life can help.

However, a too-perfect life is not necessarily the best candidate for a role model, as it may appear as if it is out of reach. Real life is complicated. Role models with their struggles and even failures can be more relatable. One can get inspired to cope and transform those challenges into growth opportunities. This is particularly relevant for PhD students, as resilience is a key factor in the PhD process.

There are many different criteria for which someone can be a role model. To provide female role models with greater visibility, we recommend creating posters to showcase inspiring women. More visibility means increasing the critical mass of successful and happy women in informatics. We hope this will encourage more female students to pursue a PhD.

Figure 8.4 depicts an example of a role model poster developed in the scope of the EUGAIN project. Think of this as a template. How would you present yourself? We challenge you to imagine what your version of the poster would look like. Each part of this template includes a keyword defining the role model, a short description and some illustrations. This is designed to highlight how these role models are multi-dimensional. This could apply to any of the personas reading this book. This could apply to you. You can be someone's role model. Maybe you already are someone's role model. What would your poster look like?[1]

8.7 Who Can Benefit from This Chapter and How?

Here are concrete suggestions for the target audience on what they could do (referring to personas) as peers, mentors or role models.

> **Kim, the university professor.** Kim wants to help her PhD students persevere and complete their doctorates. Her assistance as a mentor and supervisor is invaluable, but she wants to know who else has influence and how they can contribute to the success of her students. After reading this chapter, Kim decided to strengthen the connections between the students in her group and to prepare posters that would serve as examples and role models for future students.

---

[1] The poster will be available on https://zenodo.org/records/13850762.

Fig. 8.4 Poster example

Deniz, the student about to graduate. Deniz decides to embark on the path of PhD studies. She is interested in knowing who her allies are on this journey and what she can expect from each of them. After reading this chapter, Deniz gets motivated to seek mentoring programs and then decides to try platforms for short-term mentoring programs and to make an effort to find and meet PhD students with whom she will collaborate.

> **Brandy, the industry manager.** Brandy wants to help achieve gender equality in informatics but doesn't know where to start. After reading this chapter, Brandy decided to get involved in mentoring programs and personally support young female students. Additionally, Brandy decided to financially support poster printing featuring role models because of the importance of role models and their influence on students' decisions to continue their education.

We hope these examples inspire you to leverage these possibilities.

8.8 Conclusions

Peers offer an informal opportunity to discuss issues during the PhD. There are networks for peers, often linked to a particular topic, to strengthen this valuable relationship. Universities should formalise peer networking opportunities through reading groups, workshops, and social events to help PhD students build support networks and reduce isolation. Peers can foster a collaborative environment by sharing diverse perspectives, providing emotional support, and welcoming students from underrepresented minorities. Collaborative problem-solving and knowledge-sharing are essential to academic success. Students who lack relevant local peer networks should explore broader, discipline-specific communities or international symposiums. Mentors should encourage students to engage in formal and informal peer interactions and guide them towards relevant academic communities. This guidance is crucial as it helps students find their academic niche and fosters a sense of belonging.

Mentoring programmes vary in terms of duration, target group and scope. Universities should establish formal and informal mentoring programs for female students, offering long-term support for technical and non-technical issues, like mental health and career advice. They should promote online mentoring platforms and peer-led initiatives for students needing more immediate access to faculty mentors. Mentors must offer technical advice and emotional support, helping students overcome impostor syndrome, anxiety, and cultural barriers. Mentors should tailor their guidance, recognising that one-size-fits-all advice may not always apply. Peers can serve as informal mentors, especially for junior PhD students, helping them adjust to academic life and share strategies for success. Students should actively seek mentorship beyond their primary supervisor, connecting with mentors in other departments or at conferences.

The visibility of female role models in informatics will positively impact female students pursuing and completing their PhDs. Seeing the number of women working successfully in informatics and leading fulfilling lives will break down negative stereotypes and encourage women to follow a similar path. We recommend creating posters to enhance the visibility of women working in this field. It is essential to avoid portraying a one-dimensional, successful woman and instead emphasise her vibrant character. Furthermore, universities should not only avoid portraying a one-dimensional, successful woman but also actively recruit and retain more female faculty in STEM. This will ensure they are visible as mentors and leaders, thereby increasing the presence of role models and helping combat stereotypes that STEM is masculine.

Mentors should emphasise work-life balance when guiding female PhD students, sharing professional strategies and personal experiences of managing career and personal life to offer a realistic and relatable path forward. Peers should foster an inclusive and supportive environment where achievements and challenges are openly discussed, which helps build confidence and a sense of belonging in male-dominated fields. Policymakers should create policies that ensure women in STEM fields have access to equal opportunities, addressing systemic issues such as gender pay gaps and barriers to mobility. Social media and online platforms should be leveraged to promote diverse voices in STEM, featuring women making significant contributions to the field and sharing their experiences with broader audiences. PhD students should be encouraged to seek multiple role models from various backgrounds, professionally and personally, to learn different strategies for success and resilience.

The personal experiences of our participants show that people often have several roles and act as peers, mentors and role models at the same time. Our aim was not to define exactly when a role is assigned to a person, but to emphasise their positive influence on female students.

Future research could benefit from a deeper exploration of how cultural context shapes the experiences of female PhD students. Specifically, investigating the varying influence of mentors, peers, and role models across different cultures and academic environments would offer a more nuanced perspective on these students' unique challenges and support systems.

References

1. Coffee Code Break, 2024.
2. CS PhD MentoRes, 2024.
3. Mentoring Program of SC, 2024.
4. Mentoring Programs at ETH, 2024.
5. Support for Women at Uni Muenster, 2024.
6. E. Abraham, M. Goulão, M. Vujošević Janičić, S. J. Delany, A. Mersni, O. Yeremenko, O. Buyukdagli, K. Boudaoud, C. Oehlhorn, U. Schmid, C. Büsing, L. Schmid, H. Bolke-Hermanns, K. Köhnle, M. Pato, D. Sunar Cerci, and L. Schmid. Why do women pursue a PhD in Computer Science? Submitted for publication, 2024.
7. C. S. at Brown University. Helping students from underrepresented groups apply to CS PhD programs. https://cs.brown.edu/degrees/doctoral/applications/helpful-resources-applying-computer-science-phd-programs/, 2023.
8. N. E. Betz and L. F. Fitzgerald. *The career psychology of women.* Academic Press, 1987.
9. M. Cabay, B. L. Bernstein, M. Rivers, and N. Fabert. Chilly climates, balancing acts, and shifting pathways: What happens to women in stem doctoral programs. *Social Sciences*, 7(2):23, 2018.

10. J. M. Cohoon and H. Lord. A faculty role in women's participating in computing. In *Encyclopedia of gender and information technology*, pages 297–303. IGI Global, 2006.
11. L. Conrad. Countering isolation: Joining the research community. In *Doctorates downunder: Keys to successful doctoral study in Australia and Aotearoa New Zealand*, pages 38–44. Acer Press, 2012.
12. C. Corbett and C. Hill. Solving the equation - AAUW, Mar 2015.
13. N. Dasgupta and S. Asgari. Seeing is believing: Exposure to counterstereotypic women leaders and its effect on the malleability of automatic gender stereotyping. *Journal of experimental social psychology*, 40(5):642–658, 2004.
14. B. David. Introduction: Making the move to peer learning. In *Peer learning in higher education*, pages 1–17. Routledge, 2014.
15. T. L. Dover, C. R. Kaiser, and B. Major. Mixed signals: The unintended effects of diversity initiatives. *Social Issues and Policy Review*, 14(1):152–181, 2020.
16. B. J. Drury, J. O. Siy, and S. Cheryan. When do female role models benefit women? the importance of differentiating recruitment from retention in stem. *Psychological Inquiry*, 22(4):265–269, 2011.
17. D. Evans. How to Ignore Advice.
18. A. J. Fisher, R. Mendoza-Denton, C. Patt, I. Young, A. Eppig, R. L. Garrell, D. C. Rees, T. W. Nelson, and M. A. Richards. Structure and belonging: Pathways to success for underrepresented minority and women phd students in stem fields. *PloS one*, 14(1):e0209279, 2019.
19. D. Gibson. Role models in career development: New directions for theory and research. *Journal of Vocational Behavior*, 65:134–156, 2004.
20. D. C. Hayden and E. L. Holloway. A longitudinal study of attrition among engineering students. *Engineering Education*, 75(7):664–68, 1985.
21. C. M. Hazell, L. Chapman, S. Valeix, P. Roberts, J. Niven, and C. Berry. Understanding the mental health of doctoral researchers: a mixed methods systematic review with meta-analysis and meta-synthesis. *Systematic Reviews*, 9, 2020.
22. S. A. Hewlett, C. B. Luce, L. J. Servon, L. Sherbin, P. Shiller, E. Sosnovich, and K. Sumberg. The athena factor: Reversing the brain drain in science, engineering, and technology. *Harvard Business Review Research Report*, 10094:1–100, 2008.
23. R. M. Kanter. Some effects of proportions on group life: Skewed sex ratios and responses to token women. *American journal of Sociology*, 82(5):965–990, 1977.
24. K. E. Kram and L. A. Isabella. Mentoring alternatives: The role of peer relationships in career development. *Academy of management Journal*, 28(1):110–132, 1985.
25. J. Robst, J. Keil, and D. Russo. The effect of gender composition of faculty on student retention. *Economics of Education Review*, 17(4):429–439, 1998.
26. A. Rosenstein, A. Raghu, and L. Porter. Identifying the prevalence of the impostor phenomenon among computer science students. *Proceedings of the 51st ACM Technical Symposium on Computer Science Education*, 2020.
27. A. F. Rudroff. *Success in the sciences: Potential influences of sex role conflict, self-efficacy, and role modeling on women's career aspirations*. Iowa State University, 2007.
28. L. Ryan, E. R. Daz, and A. P. Grow. Women in computer science and engineering: A transformational leadership approach to gender equity. *Advancing Women in Leadership Journal*, 40(1):39–47, 2021.
29. P. Sankar, J. Gilmartin, and M. Sobel. An examination of belongingness and confidence among female computer science students. *ACM SIGCAS Computers and Society*, 45:7—10, 2015.
30. T. Schmader, M. Johns, and C. Forbes. An integrated process model of stereotype threat effects on performance. *Psychological review*, 115(2):336, 2008.
31. J. E. Stake and M. Noonan. The influence of teacher models on the career confidence and motivation of college students. *Sex Roles*, 12:1023–1031, 1985.

32. C. M. Steele, S. J. Spencer, and J. Aronson. Contending with group image: The psychology of stereotype and social identity threat. In *Advances in experimental social psychology*, volume 34, pages 379–440. Elsevier, 2002.
33. A. Steffen and C. Hess. Exploration of girls' role models: Are there female stem role models in sight? In *International Conference on Gender Research*, volume 7, pages 370–377, 2024.
34. J. G. Stout, N. Dasgupta, M. Hunsinger, and M. A. McManus. Steming the tide: using ingroup experts to inoculate women's self-concept in science, technology, engineering, and mathematics (STEM). *Journal of personality and social psychology*, 100(2):255, 2011.
35. A. Szlávi. Barriers, role models, and diversity – women in it. *Central-European Journal of New Technologies in Research, Education and Practice*, 3(3), 2021.
36. J. Wang, H. Hong, J. Ravitz, and M. Ivory. Gender differences in factors influencing pursuit of computer science and related fields. In *Proceedings of the 2015 ACM conference on innovation and technology in computer science education*, pages 117–122, 2015.
37. WOP. Women PhD Candidates at KTH (WOP@KTH), 2024.
38. J. D. Yoder. Rethinking tokenism: Looking beyond numbers. *Gender & society*, 5(2):178–192, 1991.
39. D. M. Young, L. A. Rudman, H. M. Buettner, and M. C. McLean. The influence of female role models on women's implicit science cognitions. *Psychology of women quarterly*, 37(3):283–292, 2013.

Open Access This chapter is licensed under the terms of the Creative Commons Attribution 4.0 International License (http://creativecommons.org/licenses/by/4.0/), which permits use, sharing, adaptation, distribution and reproduction in any medium or format, as long as you give appropriate credit to the original author(s) and the source, provide a link to the Creative Commons license and indicate if changes were made.

The images or other third party material in this chapter are included in the chapter's Creative Commons license, unless indicated otherwise in a credit line to the material. If material is not included in the chapter's Creative Commons license and your intended use is not permitted by statutory regulation or exceeds the permitted use, you will need to obtain permission directly from the copyright holder.

Part IV
From PhD to Professor

Chapter 9
Good Practices for Promoting Gender Balance in Academia within Informatics: Evidence from Higher Education Institutions

Lili Nemec Zlatolas ⓘ, Petroula Mavrikiou ⓘ, Steve Kremer ⓘ, Brenda Murphy ⓘ, and Carla Teixeira Lopes ⓘ

> **Kim, a university professor.** Kim discovered this study and presented it to her career office, emphasising strategies for achieving gender balance in informatics. As a result, they formed a committee dedicated to implementing these measures to improve gender balance in the field.

> **Nicky, an activist.** Nicky aims to influence policies that promote gender balance and often require supportive data for her campaigns. She will soon give a talk at a higher education institution. The survey results from this study provide examples of practices that she can include in her presentation.

L. Nemec Zlatolas (✉)
Faculty of Electrical Engineering and Computer Science of University of Maribor, Maribor, Slovenia
e-mail: lili.nemeczlatolas@um.si

P. Mavrikiou
Frederick University, Nicosia, Cyprus
e-mail: p.mavrikiou@frederick.ac.cy

S. Kremer
Inria Centre at Université de Lorraine, Villers-les-Nancy, France
e-mail: steve.kremer@inria.fr

B. Murphy
Faculty of Arts & Humanities of South East Technological University, Waterford, Ireland
e-mail: brenda.murphy@setu.ie

C. T. Lopes
INESC TEC, Faculty of Engineering, University of Porto, Porto, Portugal
e-mail: ctl@fe.up.pt

© The Author(s) 2025
B. Penzenstadler et al. (eds.), *Actions for Gender Balance in Informatics Across Europe*, https://doi.org/10.1007/978-3-031-78432-3_9

9.1 Introduction

Women are still underrepresented in academia despite growing awareness of gender balance issues, especially in fields that are dominated by men like informatics and other STEM (science, technology, engineering, and mathematics) disciplines. For instance, the European Union's annual *She Figures 2021* report [10] highlights that only 20.8% of Information and Communications Technology (ICT) doctoral graduates are women. Moreover, a noticeable "glass ceiling" effect is observed, with the percentage of women decreasing significantly at higher academic ranks, such as full professorships. Additionally, women remain underrepresented in leadership positions within Higher Education Institutions (HEI), constituting only 23.6% in 2019 [10].

In response to these challenges, a European network of colleagues has been established to address gender balance in Informatics across countries and research communities. This initiative is organised as a European COST Action entitled European Network for Gender Balance in Informatics (EUGAIN), aiming to tackle the persistent under-representation of women at all levels within the field of Informatics.

Numerous HEI are actively addressing the under-representation of women. For example, universities in the UK are pursuing Athena Swan awards which recognises good practice in promoting gender equality in higher education to substantiate their commitment to this cause. In Europe the Minerva Informatics Equality Award recognises outstanding European initiatives and best practices that encourage women's careers in informatics research and education. Achieving gender balance in academia within informatics is critical across all career stages, from Ph.D. candidates to full professors, and requires a multifaceted approach that can also involve appreciation, visibility and support acquired from receiving the rewards.

Effective strategies such as mentorship programs, training in negotiation and leadership skills, acknowledgement of service contributions, and implementation of family-friendly policies can help mitigate barriers to female academic success. Institutions must actively combat implicit biases and foster diversity and inclusivity throughout academia. By adopting targeted practices, institutions can better support women in achieving success in academia.

One of the primary objectives of the EUGAIN COST action is to identify and recommend best practices related to gender balance. These practices are intended to address all aspects of the academic career path: recruitment, evaluation, promotion, and the creation of an inclusive, family-friendly work environment. To identify these practices, we developed a questionnaire that was distributed among HEI and research institutions. This paper presents the findings based on the responses we collected, addressing the following research questions (RQ):

RQ1: What recruitment, retention, and promotion practices are the most frequently used in achieving gender balance in informatics academia?

RQ2: What is the impact of institutional awareness and commitment to gender equality on the implementation and effectiveness of gender balance practices in informatics academia?

This paper addresses important topics relating to gender issues and our questionnaire. In Sect. 9.2, we review existing research on gender issues from Ph.D. level to Professorship. Section 9.3 outlines our approach to data collection, preparation, and analysis. In Sect. 9.4, we present the study participants and the questionnaire results. Finally, Sect. 9.5 discusses the results, and Sect. 9.6 presents concluding remarks.

9.2 Background

Gender balance in academia, especially in informatics, remains a significant issue that has garnered increasing attention over the years. Despite some progress, disparities persist across various fields, notably in informatics. This literature review examines good practices for promoting gender balance in academia within informatics, focusing on gender issues from Ph.D. to professors.

We organise this review by discussing different career stages, beginning with Ph.D. students. The specifics of academic career progression can vary between countries; therefore, we broadly categorise these stages as early-, mid-, and senior-career faculty positions. Depending on the country, early career stages may include roles like assistant professor or lecturer. Mid-career stages typically encompass positions such as associate professor, senior lecturer, or reader. Senior career stages typically pertain to (full) professors.

9.2.1 Research on Ph.D. Students

At the Ph.D. level, women in STEM fields such as informatics are underrepresented. In 2019, women comprised 23.1% of all ICT students at the doctoral level in the European Union, decreasing to 20.8% in 2021 [10].

Current research highlights mentorship as a key practice for promoting gender balance at the Ph.D. stage, creating a supportive environment crucial for women in informatics program. According to, mentoring helps female graduate students succeed in their Ph.D. studies by providing them with crucial support and direction. Mentors also help women connect with researchers in their profession by facilitating networking opportunities. Fisk et al. [12] suggest that both formal and informal mentorship relationships are valuable in this context. Research by Dutt et al. [9] on women in physics Ph.D. programs underscores how mentorship fosters a sense of belonging and helps navigate field-specific cultures and expectations.

Furthermore, amongst female graduate students, involvement in peer networks or workshops exclusively for women can improve community support and academic persistence [16].

9.2.2 Research on Early Career Stage Faculty

Women encounter significant challenges during the early career stages such as post-doctoral positions, lecturer roles, or assistant professorships. These challenges include the gender pay gap, the lack of opportunity for job growth, juggling work and home obligations, difficulty obtaining funding, and implicit bias [7, 15].

Effective strategies at this stage include implementing family-friendly policies. Research by Vacas-Soriano et al. [18] highlights the critical role of family-friendly policies, including parental leave and flexible work arrangements, in supporting women's success in informatics faculty positions. Research also shows that although female instructors experience higher levels of work-family conflict than their male colleagues, they are less likely to use flexible work schedules [3]. Therefore, implementing family-friendly policies can help alleviate these challenges and enhance the career prospects of female academics.

9.2.3 Research on Mid Career Stage Faculty

As women advance in their careers, they encounter challenges in the mid-career stage, such as senior lecturer positions, similar to those encountered in the early stages. Additionally, they face new barriers, including the gender pay gap, limited access to leadership positions [18], and obstacles to promotion and career advancement, often associated with the "glass ceiling" and "sticky floor" phenomena [5].

At this point, successful ways for fostering gender balance include putting in place family-friendly policies as well as leadership development and mentoring programs specifically designed for women. Research by Dopson et al. [8] demonstrates that participation in leadership development programs enhances the confidence of senior academic women in their leadership skills and improves their career prospects. Mentorship programs play a crucial role in offering support and guidance to women navigating academic challenges and seeking career advancement [1, 4]. Women's success has been proven to be greatly influenced by both official and informal mentoring and sponsorship; women who receive sponsorship are more likely to believe they have good employment prospects and want to stay in academics.

9.2.4 Research on Senior Career Stage Faculty

Women in the senior faculty career stage, such as full professors, encounter numerous challenges akin to earlier stages, including pressures to publish and secure research funding, implicit biases, and the absence of role models and supportive networks. In addition, obstacles like the "glass ceiling" and little prospects for leadership roles may face full professors.

At this stage, mentoring programs and specialised leadership training for women are effective ways to advance gender parity. Studies show that women who take part in leadership programs feel more confident in their leadership skills and are inspired to pursue leadership positions [2]. Institutions can further advance gender balance at the highest levels of academia by implementing diversity initiatives and setting targets or quotas for female representation [7]. In addition, discrepancies can be lessened by addressing implicit bias through impartial and open tenure and promotion evaluation procedures [14].

9.3 Methodology

In 2022, members of EUGAIN Working Group 3 developed a questionnaire to identify best practices promoting gender balance in academia within informatics. The questionnaire comprises 37 closed questions, many of which allow respondents to provide additional comments. It is structured into seven sections. The first section gathers information about the respondent's affiliated HEI (Q1–Q10). The rest follows the structure proposed by Bujdosó et al. [6], focusing on practices related to recruiting women (Q11–Q13), evaluating applications for hiring and promotion (Q14), retaining female talent (Q15–Q16), promoting women in academia (Q17–Q23), and mentoring practices (13 questions) as well as additional comments. The analysis of mentoring practices will be addressed separately, with this study focusing on recruiting, hiring, promotion, and retention practices for women. The detailed structure of the questionnaire is presented in the Appendix.

9.3.1 Data Collection

The survey was conducted using SurveyMonkey, launching on May 31, 2022, and closing on September 3, 2022. The survey link was initially distributed via email to members of the EUGAIN COST Action Management Committee, who further disseminated it to other Ph.D.-holding academics. Additionally, the survey link was shared with Informatics Europe and promoted on social media platforms such as LinkedIn and Twitter. On average, respondents spent approximately 17 minutes completing the survey. Most questions in the survey utilised ordinal scales, such as the Likert scale, and included nominal scales for Yes/No inquiries.

9.3.2 Data Preparation and Analysis

Before conducting the analysis, we performed data cleaning using IBM SPSS Statistics 29 and MS Excel 365. Three researchers were involved in employing the data cleaning and reached a consent on what data should be kept. Initially, we excluded two responses that were not associated with higher education or research institutions related to at least one informatics-related program. Additionally, for questions offering an "Other" option, we reviewed these responses to determine if they could be categorised into predefined answer choices. Responses classified as "Other" were removed, and appropriate responses were reassigned accordingly.

Following data cleaning, we derived four additional variables for subsequent analysis: the count of recruiting (Q11–Q14), retaining (Q15–Q16), and promotion practices (Q14, Q17, Q19–Q23) implemented by each institution, as well as the total count of practices (Q11–Q17, Q19–Q23). Specifically, for questions regarding the implementation of retention practices, responses categorised as "Agree" and "Strongly agree" were considered indicative of practice implementation, so we assigned a binary value (T/F) to those variables. Furthermore, we computed another variable capturing the number of gender representation awareness dimensions selected by each respondent (Q1, Q4–Q23). Percentages reported in the results section were calculated based on the total number of valid responses for each question, excluding missing values.

9.4 Results

In this section, we describe the characteristics of the questionnaire respondents. Subsequently, we analyse the gender distribution across different HEI and assess gender balance awareness within academia within informatics. At the end of the section, we examine the practices employed by HEI to promote gender balance in academia.

9.4.1 Participants

After cleaning the data, we obtained 57 valid responses out of 59 received responses. Regarding the roles of the respondents within their institutions (Q1), 55 participants provided answers: 12 (21.8%) hold managerial positions, 37 (67.3%) are faculty members, and 6 (10.9%) work as temporary staff. Participants (Q3)

Table 9.1 Distribution of number of respondents per countries

Country	No. of respondents
Portugal	14
Ireland	8
Slovenia	4
Austria	3
Italy	3
Serbia	3
Cyprus	2
Denmark	2
Estonia	2
France	2
Germany	2
Netherlands	2
United Kingdom	2
Belgium	1
Bulgaria	1
Czech Republic	1
Greece	1
Hungary	1
Norway	1
Romania	1
United States	1

were predominantly based in European countries, as depicted in Table 9.1, with one participant from the USA. All HEI (Q4) have departments of Informatics, while some also include other STEM departments such as Engineering or Mathematics.

9.4.2 Gender Distribution at Different Levels of the Career in Academia

The participants provided data on the percentage of female members in various staff positions at their institutions (Q5). For teaching assistants and Ph.D. students, there was an average of 25.88% females across 26 different institutions. Assistant professors had an average of 25.46% female representation across 37 institutions, while associate professors and full professors averaged 19.78% and 16.80%, respectively, across 40 institutions. It is noteworthy that higher positions within the institutions generally exhibited lower average percentages of female staff.

Figure 9.1 displays a boxplot illustrating these distributions, with some institutions appearing as outliers with higher proportions of full and associate professors than the majority of respondents. Notably, two outliers in the associate professor category were identified, with 66% female representation originating from Portugal

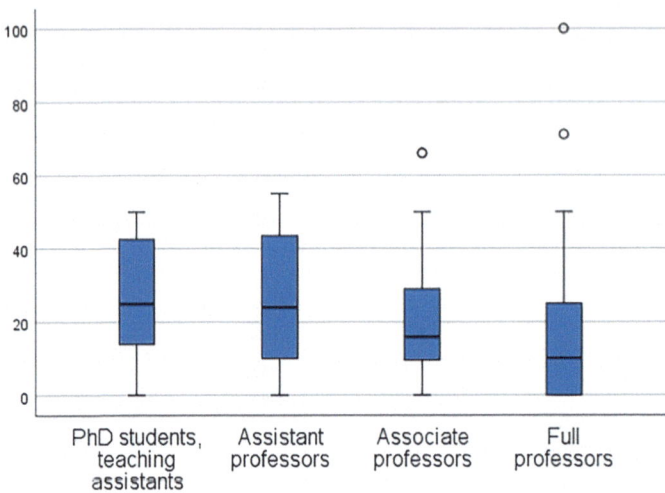

Fig. 9.1 Boxplots for the percentage distribution of women in various academic positions

and Cyprus. Additionally, two positive outliers were observed in the full professor category: one institution from Portugal, where all full professors were female, and another from Romania, where 77% of full professors were female.

Regarding part-time and full-time contracts, only 14 and 13 responses were received, respectively, so detailed numbers for these categories are not reported.

9.4.3 Gender Balance Awareness in Academia Within Informatics

The questionnaire encompassed five questions (Q6–Q10) aimed at evaluating various dimensions of an institution's awareness regarding gender balance representation. Each question provided respondents with options to answer Yes, No, or "I do not know." The distributions of these responses are visualised in the bar charts shown in Fig. 9.2.

As observed, a significant majority (65%) of respondents' institutions have implemented a Gender Equality Plan, and this is also expected since this is a requirement for institutions applying for various EU grants. Conversely, 43% of respondents indicated that their management teams lack members specifically responsible for gender representation. Additionally, a majority (54%) of respondents were uncertain whether gender figures are publicly accessible.

We further examined the number of gender representation awareness dimensions selected by each respondent. The data revealed that 33% of respondents selected only one dimension, while 17% reported none and another 17% reported all five dimensions. The respondents that reported selecting all five dimensions are identi-

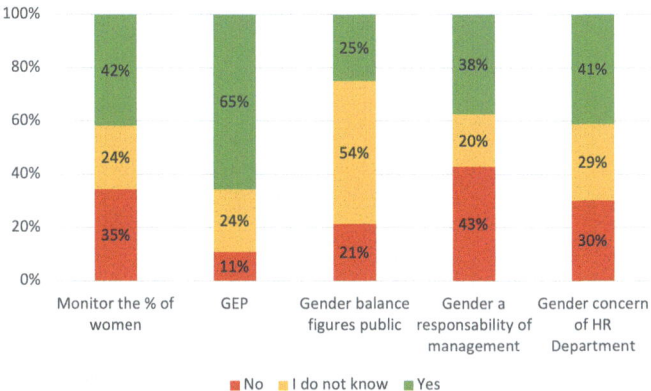

Fig. 9.2 Distribution of responses regarding gender balance awareness dimension

fied with the following institutions: INESC TEC, Portugal; Sapienza Università di Roma, Italy; South East Technological University, Ireland; University of Galway, Ireland; Technischen Universität Wien, Austria; and The French National Centre for Scientific Research (CNRS), France.

Our analysis did not uncover significant associations between these five awareness dimensions and the reported percentages of women across different positions (full, associate, assistant, and teaching assistants). Similarly, these percentages did not differ significantly among institutions with varying numbers of selected awareness dimensions.

9.4.4 Practices that Contribute to Gender Balance in Academia

In this section, we presented various good practices to the respondents and queried whether their institutions implement them. The questionnaire was structured into three categories of practices: recruiting women, retaining female talent and expertise, and promoting women.

For each category of practice, we calculated the total number of practices selected by participants. Question Q14 encompassed 12 items related to both hiring and promotion. Responses regarding hiring practices were categorised under recruiting women, while responses concerning promotion practices were categorised under promoting women. The total number of practices per category is illustrated in Fig. 9.3.

Items in the questionnaire were presented in different scales. Binary scales were used for recruiting and promoting practices, where selecting a specific practice was assigned a value of 1, and responses were summed accordingly. For retaining practices, a 5-point Likert scale was employed, with responses of "Agree" and

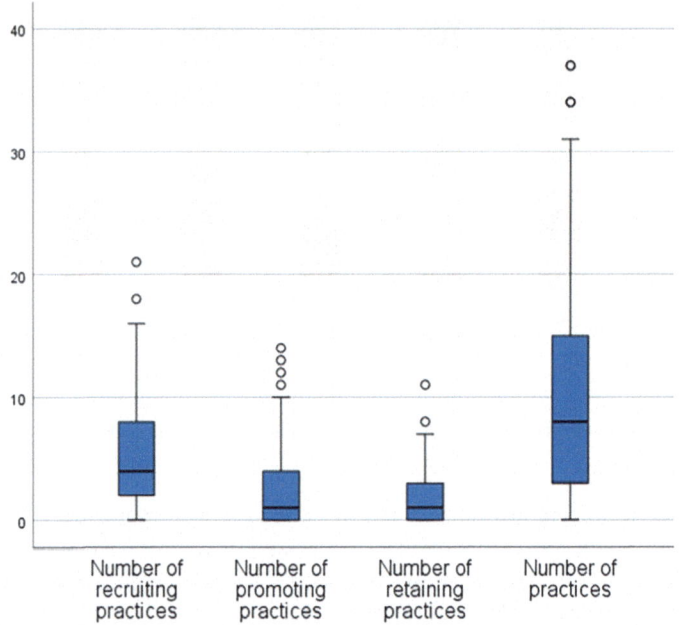

Fig. 9.3 Boxplots for the distribution of various practices in HEI

"Strongly agree" assigned a value of 1, which was then aggregated for all retaining practices.

Regarding recruiting women (Q11–Q14), out of the 25 practices available, respondents selected an average of 5.42 practices, with a maximum of 21 practices chosen. Notable outliers in this category included the Faculty of Informatics at TU Wien in Austria and CNRS—Univ Grenoble Alpes in France.

For promoting practices (questions Q14, Q17, Q19–Q23), there were 18 practices listed. On average, respondents selected 2.91 practices, with a maximum of 14 practices chosen. Positive outliers in this category were:

- University of Galway in Ireland,
- CNRS—Univ Grenoble Alpes in France,
- School of Informatics of the University of Edinburgh—UK,
- Computer Science Department in IT University of Copenhagen in Denmark.

For retaining practices (questions Q15–Q16), respondents had a choice of 13 listed practices. On average, institutions reported using 1.91 practices, with the maximum number of selected practices being 11. Positive outliers in this group were:

- Faculty of Informatics of TU Wien in Austria,
- Insight SFI Centre for Data Analytics/Data Science Institute of University of Galway in Ireland.

Out of all 56 possible practices, HEI use an average of 10.25 practices, with a maximum of 37 practices reported. Practices for recruiting women are the most commonly used, followed by practices for promotion, and lastly, practices for retaining women.

9.4.4.1 Recruiting Women

Participants in the survey were asked to indicate the types of practices their institutions use regarding recruitment advertisement. Table 9.2 provides a comprehensive list of these practices, which include activities such as writing the advert, advertising the position, evaluating the application, and other positive actions. The table also displays the number of respondents who selected each practice and the corresponding percentage of selections among valid answers.

The three most frequently used practices overall are related to writing the recruitment advertisement and evaluating applications: the use of inclusive language (34 HEI, 59.6%), stating that the institution is an equal opportunity employer (29 HEI, 50.9%), and implementing explicit evaluation criteria, such as having a list of requirements assessed by the hiring committee (27 HEI, 47.4%).

Conversely, the least adopted practices overall include: providing statistics in a multi-stage process, ensuring consistent female representation throughout each stage (3 HEI, 5.3%), redesigning position specifications (3 HEI, 5.3%), and emphasising STEM job opportunities for tele-commuting and tele-working compared to other fields (2 HEI, 3.5%).

9.4.4.2 Retaining Female Talent and Expertise

Using a Likert scale ranging from 1 to 5, where "1" signifies "Strongly disagree" and "5" indicates "Strongly agree", faculty and staff from HEI were surveyed regarding the implementation of practices aimed at retaining female talent and expertise (Q15–Q16).

Based on the mean ratings, the top three practices or policies prominently implemented are:

- Policies promoting disconnection, respecting the right to be offline outside the organisation (mean: 3.22),
- Gender and family-friendly strategies designed to support female talent (mean: 3.10),
- Creating an inclusive working environment, such as providing unconscious bias training for senior staff or allocating resources to initiatives such as promoting/encouraging women's networks within the institute, including secretarial support and a budget for holding events such as lunches (mean: 2.95).

Conversely, the three least popular policies include:

Table 9.2 Recruiting practices used by the collaborating institutions

Act	Description	#	%
W	Using inclusive language (e.g. use non-discriminatory language)	34	59.6
W	Advertise openly for all positions, stating that you are an equal opportunity employer	29	50.9
W	State that the Institution is committed to facilitating the combination of work and childcare in the recruiting ads	11	19.3
W	State that flexible terms of employment are possible, such as working part-time and flexible working hours	7	12.3
W	Are there any other best practices, which are practised in your Institution, that you are aware of?	4	7
W	Emphasise that jobs in STEM allow for more opportunities for tele-commuting and tele-working, compared to other fields	2	3.5
A	Distribute advertisements across a number of channels	22	38.6
A	Approach candidates indirectly (forward the advertisement)	14	24.6
A	Approach candidates directly (send the advertisement personally)	12	21.1
A	Allow a minimum of three months for applications to be submitted	11	19.3
E	Does your Institution have explicit evaluation criteria?	27	47.4
E	Do you ensure that the composition of the hiring committee is as balanced as possible?	25	43.9
E	Institution hosts open discussions around the issue of increasing the representation of women in the institution when interviewing?	16	28.1
E	Do you organise unconscious gender bias training in advance of interview?	14	24.6
E	Are career breaks (parental leave) taken into account with explicit identifications and rules?	13	22.8
E	Does your Institution forward guidelines to potential referees?	11	19.3
E	Do you appoint one member of the panel to be dedicated to monitoring gender issues and gender balance?	9	15.8
E	Does your Institution provide a gender sensitive template for applicants and/or referees?	7	12.3
E	Does your Institution provide help with solving the "dual career couples"?	7	12.3
E	Does your Institution invite women to interview also to give them experience of being interviewed?	6	10.5
E	Does your Institution provide/publish statistics in a multi-stage process?	3	5.3
O	Re-examine the applications and consider re-advertising if the initial list of candidates selected for interview does not include women?	9	15.8
O	Take action if too few suitable women apply	8	14
O	Use of quotas or dedicated positions?	5	8.8
O	Re-design the position specifications	3	5.3

The first column (Act) denotes the recruitment activities as follows: Write the Advert (W), Advertise Position (A), Evaluate Application (E), and Other Positive Actions (O)

9 Good Practices for Promoting Gender Balance in Academia within Informatics   211

Table 9.3 Retaining practices used by the collaborating institutions

Description	N	Mean
My institution has a Policy for disconnection	40	3.2
My institution utilises gender/family friendly strategies to facilitate female talent	40	3.1
My institution promotes an Inclusive working environment	39	3.0
My institution consults with women in the institution in order to gather opinions about the organisation, their role and their career ambitions and prospects	38	2.7
My institution has Family Friendly Guidelines in place for scheduling meetings	40	2.7
My institution provides visibility and self-promotion training for female researchers in permanent employment	39	2.4
My institution acknowledges and credits time spent on gender balance initiatives	39	2.4
My institution practices Positive Discrimination	39	2.4
My institution creates an 'Ambassador Program' or a personal development plan for researchers with high potential	40	2.4
My institution gives support to parents	40	2.2
My institution provides visibility and self-promotion training for female researchers in temporary employment	40	2.2
My institution ensure that at least 30% of the people on Ambassador Program are women	39	2.1
My institution distributes welcome packages with a booklet that lists childcare options as well as other useful info provided by institute members	40	2.0

- Visibility and self-promotion training for female researchers in temporary positions (mean: 2.18),
- Ensuring that at least 30% of participants in the Ambassador Program are women (mean: 2.08),
- Providing welcome packages that include information on childcare options and other useful resources from institute members (mean: 2.00).

A full list of recruiting practices is presented in Table 9.3.

9.4.4.3 Promoting Women

The two most frequently used practices (Q14) in application evaluation related to promoting women are:

- Implementing explicit evaluation criteria, such as having a defined list of requirements assessed by the promotion committee (22 HEI, 38.6%),
- Ensuring a balanced composition of the promotion committee, with at least 30% of its members being women (16 HEI, 28.1%).

Regarding best practices for promoting women in academia (Q17–Q23), the two most popular practices adopted by HEI are:

- Proposing suitable women for prestigious tasks, such as roles that are crucial for career advancement, like awards, representing the institution internationally, serving on Ph.D. committees, etc. (25 HEI, 75.8%),
- Implementing measures to ensure positive representation of women in decision-making positions and institutional committees, for example surpassing the proportion of women in the institution (16 HEI, 48.5%). The mean percentage of women in committees, reported by 9 HEI, is 25.17% (s.d. = 15.9%).

Other measures mentioned by participants that institutions employ when organising or supporting conferences are:

- Implement gender balance on Program Committees and among the conference leaders.
- Gender balance in keynote speakers/panels.
- Making sure a priori that the event program includes at least 1/3 female representation, and only then disseminate the event.

A full list of promoting practices is presented in Table 9.4.

9.4.5 The Impact of Gender Awareness on the Number of Implemented Practices

We assessed various dimensions of institutions' awareness regarding gender balance representation (Q6–Q10), including monitoring the percentage of women; having a Gender Equality Plan (GEP); publicising gender balance figures; designating a member of the management team responsible for gender representation; and integrating gender representation into the institution's HR Department concerns.

Following a descriptive analysis of the responses in Sect. 9.4.3, we examined the relationship between these awareness dimensions and the median number of implemented practices.

For this analysis, we employed inferential statistics to compare medians in two samples based on the Yes/No responses. Due to violations of t-test assumptions, we used the Mann-Whitney test. Table 9.5 presents the median number of practices across all HEI in each group and the p-value from the one-sided Mann-Whitney hypothesis test.

As depicted, the median number of practices is consistently higher in institutions that are aware of gender representation. However, statistically significant differences are observed only in the number of recruiting, promoting, and the overall total of practices across three dimensions: Monitoring the percentage of women, Gender responsibility within management, and Gender concern within the HR Department. The presence of a Gender Equality Plan and publicising gender balance figures do

Table 9.4 Promoting practices used by the collaborating institutions

Description	#	%
Does your institution propose suitable women for prestigious tasks?	25	75.8
Does your institution have explicit evaluation criteria?	22	38.6
Do you ensure that the composition of the hiring committee is as balanced as possible?	16	28.1
Are there any measures in place in your institution to ensure that there is a positive representation of women in Decision Making Positions and in Institutional Committees?	16	48.5
In your institution, are career breaks (parental leave) taken into account with explicit identifications and rules?	11	19.3
Does your institution host open discussions around the issue of increasing the representation of women in the institution when interviewing women and men, and ask how they would approach it?	11	19.3
Do you organise unconscious/implicit gender bias training in advance of interview?	10	17.5
Does your institution avoid overloading women with faculty service, specially related to student affairs, participating in voluntary commissions, and other purely administrative service?	9	25.7
Does your Institution ensure that female members are not overloaded with these functions?	7	23.3
Are you aware of any mechanisms—internal or external to the Institution—to increase the number of female applications/promotions?	7	17.5
Does your institution forward guidelines to potential referees?	6	10.5
Do you appoint one member of the panel to be dedicated to monitoring gender issues and gender balance?	5	8.8
Does your institution provide a gender sensitive template for applicants and/or referees?	5	8.8
When organising or supporting conferences, are there measures in place to ensure that there is positive female representation across the list of invited speakers and members of program committees?	5	17.2
Does your institution provide/publish statistics in a multi-stage process?	3	5.3
Does your institution invite women to interview also to give them experience of being interviewed?	3	5.3
Does your institution provide help with solving the "dual career couples"?	2	3.5

not show a significant relationship with the number of implemented practices. It is worth noting that the limited responses to the availability of gender balance figures may have influenced these findings.

Furthermore, we explored the relationship between the number of practices and the number of awareness dimensions per institution. As illustrated in Fig. 9.4, there is a discernible trend where the number of practices tends to increase with the inclusion of more awareness dimensions.

Table 9.5 Comparison of the median number of practices for institutions implementing the gender representation awareness dimension

		#recruiting		#promoting		#retaining		#all	
		Md	p	Md	p	Md	p	Md	p
Monitor the % of women	N	2	0.00**	1	0.02*	1	0.49	5	0.01**
	Y	7		3		2		14	
GEP	N	4	0.33	0.5	0.37	0.5	0.47	7	0.42
	Y	4.5		2.5		1		9	
Gender balance figures public	N	5	0.34	2	0.13	2.5	0.34	9.5	0.13
	Y	6		4		1		12.5	
Gender responsibility of management	N	3.5	0.01*	2	0.02*	1	0.15	6	0.00**
	Y	8		5		4		15	
Gender concern of HR Department	N	4	0.02*	1	0.04*	1	0.13	5	0.01**
	Y	7		3		2		14	

N denote institutions that do not implement the practice and Y institutions that do so. P-value for one-sided Mann-Whitney test. ** denote results significant at an $\alpha = 0.01$ and * results significant at an $\alpha = 0.05$

9 Good Practices for Promoting Gender Balance in Academia within Informatics 215

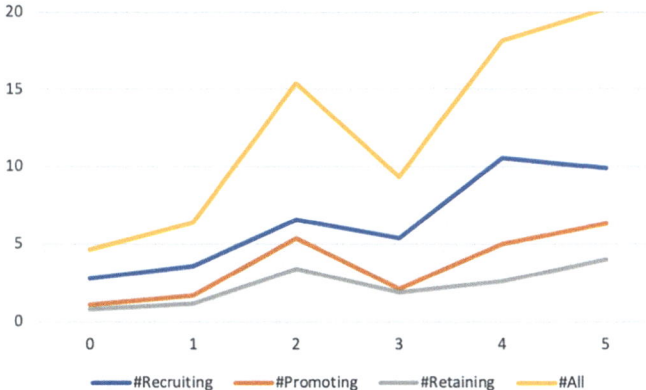

Fig. 9.4 Average number of practices per number of gender representation awareness dimensions

9.4.6 Comparison by Countries

We compared the number of recruiting, promoting, and retaining practices per country. Figure 9.5 illustrates the mean number of these practices, with each column representing the average of all practices used within each country. It is important to note that some institutions may have provided multiple responses in the survey.

Austria and the UK stand out with the highest mean number of recruiting practices (out of the 25 listed), averaging 13.33 and 13, respectively. For the 18 promoting practices, the highest average use was observed in the UK (9) and France (8.5). In terms of the 13 retaining practices, institutions from the UK reported the highest average at 6.5, followed by Austria at 5.33.

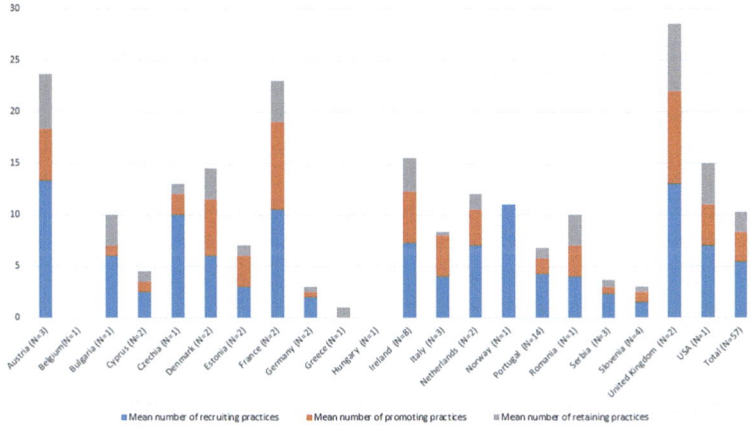

Fig. 9.5 Mean number of different practices per country

When considering the total number of implemented practices (out of the 56 listed), the UK leads with a mean of 28.5, followed by Austria with an average of 23.67.

9.5 Discussion of Results

To understand the factors contributing to gender balance in academia within informatics, we developed a comprehensive questionnaire and analysed the responses from 57 valid participants holding various positions within their institutions. The questionnaire consisted of 47 items (excluding 15 mentoring-related questions), all of which were optional for respondents.

We observed significant differences in the number of questions answered based on respondents' positions within their institutions. On average, individuals in managing positions answered the most questions (mean = 44.42), followed by faculty members (mean = 39.24), and temporary staff members answered the fewest (mean = 19.00).

As respondents held higher positions, they tended to answer more questions, potentially reflecting their deeper involvement or greater knowledge within their institutions. However, this could also be influenced by varying levels of familiarity with specific aspects covered in the questionnaire.

Respondents provided perceptions based on their institutional roles regarding the implementation of gender balance practices. While the exactness of these perceptions may vary, analysing them remains crucial. Institutions must not only implement these practices but also ensure effective communication regarding their initiatives and awareness of gender balance. For instance, if an institution publishes gender balance figures but lacks community awareness, the impact of such measures may be diminished.

As reported by the respondents from different institutions, the percentage of female members decreases as positions ascend from Ph.D. candidates to full professors. This trend underscores the persistent challenge of achieving gender balance at higher academic ranks, reflecting findings from research attributing this to unconscious stereotypes [17].

Most participating HEI have implemented a Gender Equality Plan, a requirement set by the European Commission for participation in its research framework programme [11]. However, few respondents indicated awareness of their institutions monitoring the percentage of women or making gender balance figures publicly available. Gender-related concerns typically fall under the purview of HR or management departments in many institutions.

Our analysis also focused on practices contributing to gender balance in academia within informatics, categorised into recruiting, retaining, and promoting women. Among 25 recruiting practices, HEI employed an average of 5.42 practices, with a maximum of 21. Retaining practices saw an average of 1.91 practices implemented, with a maximum of 11 in 13. For 18 promoting practices, HEI utilized an average of 2.91 practices, with a maximum of 14. Notably, top-performing institutions in this regard include CNRS—Univ Grenoble Alpes in France, Faculty of Informatics of TU Wien in Austria, University of Galway in Ireland, and School of Informatics of the University of Edinburgh—UK, each employing 37 out of 56 listed practices. TU Wien was also recognised with the 2022 Minerva award by Informatics Europe for developing the careers of female faculty [13].

In RQ1 we were looking into recruitment, retention, and promotion practices that are the most frequently used in achieving gender balance in informatics academia. The most frequently adopted recruiting practices include using inclusive language in recruitment advertisements and employing explicit evaluation criteria. Key retaining practices involve policies supporting disconnection rights and implementing gender/family-friendly strategies. Effective promotion practices include nominating women for prestigious roles and applying clear evaluation criteria for promotions.

Some of these practices are straightforward to implement, while others demand more substantial effort from the HEI. This discrepancy might explain why many institutions have adopted certain practices over others. Additionally, financial constraints could hinder some institutions from implementing more practices or recognising the necessity for measures to enhance the position of women in academia.

In RQ2 we were searching for the impact of institutional awareness and commitment to gender equality on the implementation and effectiveness of gender balance practices in informatics academia. Therefore, we examined the relationship between the implementation of these practices and the gender awareness dimensions within institutions. HEI that monitor gender percentages and assign gender responsibilities to HR and management tend to implement more practices, indicating a correlation between awareness and action. Similarly, institutions with higher levels of gender awareness dimensions tend to employ a greater number of gender balance practices, highlighting the importance of institutional commitment to addressing gender disparities in academia within informatics.

We summarise our main findings below:

- Across the participating institutions, the percentage of female members decreases as positions ascend from Ph.D. candidates to full professors.
- Most participating HEI have implemented a Gender Equality Plan.
- Few respondents indicated awareness of their institutions monitoring the percentage of women or making gender balance figures publicly available.
- Among 25 recruiting practices, HEI employed an average of 5.42 practices, with a maximum of 21.
- Retaining practices saw an average of 1.91 practices implemented, with a maximum of 11 in 13.
- For 18 promoting practices, HEI utilized an average of 2.91 practices, with a maximum of 14.

- Top-performing institutions regarding gender-balance practices are:
  - CNRS—Univ Grenoble Alpes in France,
  - Faculty of Informatics of TU Wien in Austria,
  - University of Galway in Ireland.
- The most frequently adopted recruiting practices are:
  - using inclusive language in recruitment advertisements and
  - employing explicit evaluation criteria.
- The most frequently adopted retaining practices are:
  - policies supporting disconnection rights and
  - implementing gender/family-friendly strategies.
- The most frequently adopted promotion practices are:
  - nominating women for prestigious roles and
  - applying clear evaluation criteria for promotions.
- We found a relation between institutions' awareness and action.

9.6 Conclusions

Gender disparity persists in academia within informatics, highlighting the need for heightened awareness and concerted efforts toward achieving gender balance. There is a noticeable trend of fewer women occupying higher positions from Ph.D. levels upward in this field. Our study aims to enhance understanding of the strategies employed by institutions to improve gender balance. The findings reveal that some institutions have already implemented diverse measures in recruiting, retaining, and promoting women, serving as positive examples. This research offers insights that can inspire other HEI to adopt effective strategies for achieving gender parity. Our forthcoming work will focus on publishing findings related to mentoring practices that foster gender balance in academia within informatics.

Acknowledgments This work has been partially supported by the COST Action CA19122—European Network for Gender Balance in Informatics (EUGAIN).

Appendix: Questionnaire

Welcome to a survey on Good Practices that Promote Gender Balance in Informatics Within the cost action CA19122 European Network For Gender Balance in Informatics (EUGAIN), we have developed a survey on Gender balance in Informatics.

Your participation in this survey is very much appreciated.

We will be more than happy to accept your best effort even if that means that some questions will have to go unanswered.

Your Institution

In the following we will use the word 'Institution' for the department, faculty, or institution for which you will provide the answers. We are interested in answers from STEM-related Institutes or Faculties, not from the whole University for example.

If you do not know the answer to some questions, you can skip them.

- Q1 What is your role in the Institution?
  ○ Managing Position ○ Faculty Member ○ Temporary Staff ○ Other (please specify) ....
- Q2 For what Institution are you answering this questionnaire (we are interested in STEM-related Departments, Institutes or Faculties)? *Example of an answer: "Department of..., Faculty of..., University of...."*
  ....
- Q3 In which county is your institution?
  ....
- Q4 What STEM disciplines are covered by your Institution?
  □ computer science □ information science □ chemical engineering □ mathematics □ electrical engineering □ civil engineering □ technology □ Other (please specify) ....
- Q5 What is the percentage of females at your Institution in these positions? academics ...., full professor ...., associate professor ...., assistant professor ...., other (assistant, PhD students,...) ...., holding a part-time contract ...., holding a full-time, not permanent contract ....
- Q6 Does your Institution monitor the percentage of women at all levels in the organisation *(e.g. doctoral, post-doc, lecturer, professor etc.)*?
  ○ Yes ○ No ○ I do not know.
- Q7 Is there a gender equality plan (GEP) at your institution or at a higher level (for example at the University, not at the Institute)?
  ○ Yes ○ No ○ I do not know.
- Q8 Are gender balance figures public (e.g. in Annual Reports)? (Provide URL)
  ○ Yes (add a link) .... ○ No ○ I do not know.
- Q9 Is gender representation a responsibility of a member of the management team?
  ○ Yes ○ No ○ I do not know.
- Q10 Is gender representation a concern for your Institute's HR Department?
  ○ Yes ○ No ○ I do not know.

1. Recruiting Women

Opening positions and collecting applications during the recruitment process. How is advertising executed?

We will be more than happy to accept your best effort even if that means that some questions will have to go unanswered.

Q11 When writing the Recruitment Advert is the process mindful of: [Tick as many as applicable]
☐ Using inclusive language (e.g. use non-discriminatory language).
☐ Advertise openly for all positions, stating that you are an equal opportunity employer.
☐ State that the Institution is committed to facilitating the combination of work and childcare in the recruiting media and in job descriptions.
☐ State that flexible terms of employment are possible, such as working part-time and flexible working hours.
☐ Emphasise that jobs in STEM allow for more opportunities for tele-commuting and tele-working, compared to other fields.

Q12 When advertising the position does your Institution consider any of the following [Tick as many as applicable]
☐ Allow a minimum of three months for applications to be submitted *(Time is needed for the advertisement to reach the right women, and they need time to respond).*
☐ Approach candidates directly *(e.g. Send the advertisement personally to (at least) three women you would like to see in the position and invite them to apply).*
☐ Approach candidates indirectly *(e.g. Invite colleagues to send the Call to three other women they think would be suitable for the post).*
☐ Distribute advertisements across a number of channels *(e.g. Send them to women's networks' email lists, such as national women in tech networks or networks of female professors).*

Q13 Does your Institution utilise any of the positive actions listed below? [Tick as many as applicable]
☐ Take action if too few suitable women apply. *(For example, extend the deadline for applications and readvertise the position (inter)nationally).*
☐ Re-examine the applications and consider re-advertising if the initial list of candidates selected for interview does not include any women.
☐ Use of quotas or dedicated positions? *(In a number of countries, the 'cascade model' is being introduced, following the German example. In this model, the institutions set targets for the proportion of women at each qualification level on the basis of the proportion of women at the level immediately below.)*
☐ Re-design the position specifications.

2. Application Evaluation for Hiring and Promotion

We will be more than happy to accept your best effort even if that means that some questions will have to go unanswered.

Q14 Choose as many as possible and please specify if your answers apply to both types of application: Hiring, Promotion or N/A—Not Applicable

(a) Do you ensure that the composition of the hiring committee is as balanced as possible? (for example, ensure that at least 30% of the committee consists of women)
☐ Hiring ☐ Promotion ☐ N/A
(b) Do you appoint one member of the panel to be dedicated to monitoring gender issues and gender balance?
☐ Hiring ☐ Promotion ☐ N/A
(c) Do you organise unconscious/implicit gender bias training in advance of interview/promotion boards for Interview/Promotion Panel Members?
☐ Hiring ☐ Promotion ☐ N/A
(d) Does your Institution forward guidelines *(around Unconscious Bias in recommendation letters)* to potential referees?
☐ Hiring ☐ Promotion ☐ N/A
(e) Does your Institution provide a gender sensitive template for applicants and/or referees *(for example, does it explicitly include a section on career breaks)*?
☐ Hiring ☐ Promotion ☐ N/A
(f) Does your Institution provide/publish statistics in a multi-stage process? *(for example, ensuring that you retain the same % of female representation at every level of the process)*
☐ Hiring ☐ Promotion ☐ N/A
(g) In your Institution, are career breaks *(parental leave)* taken into account with explicit identifications and rules? *(for example, some institutions allocate '18 months per child' when comparing female candidates who are Mothers, with other candidates)*
☐ Hiring ☐ Promotion ☐ N/A
(h) Does your Institution have explicit evaluation criteria *(for example, the institution has a list of requirements that are evaluated by the hiring commission)*?
☐ Hiring ☐ Promotion ☐ N/A
(i) Does your Institution invite women to interview not only to see whether they are best for the position, but also to give them experience of being interviewed and increase their status at their own institution?
☐ Hiring ☐ Promotion ☐ N/A
(j) Does your Institution provide help with solving the "dual career couples"? *(aka "two body problem")*, e.g. *helping to find a position for the applicant's partner.*
☐ Hiring ☐ Promotion ☐ N/A
(k) Does your Institution host open discussions around the issue of increasing the representation of women in the institution when interviewing women and men, and ask how they would approach it?
☐ Hiring ☐ Promotion ☐ N/A
(l) Are there any other best practices, which are practiced in your Institution, that you are aware of?
☐ Hiring ☐ Promotion ☐ N/A

3. Retaining Female Talent and Expertise

We will be more than happy to accept your best effort even if that means that some questions will have to go unanswered.

Q15 Please answer the questions on retaining female talent and expertise.

(a) My Institution utilises gender/family friendly strategies to facilitate female talent.
○ Strongly disagree ○ Disagree ○ Neither agree nor disagree ○ Agree ○ Strongly agree

(b) My institution has Family Friendly Guidelines in place for scheduling meetings (e.g. Only schedule meetings between e.g. 09:30 and 16:30 to allow compatibility with family commitments).
○ Strongly disagree ○ Disagree ○ Neither agree nor disagree ○ Agree ○ Strongly agree

(c) My institution has a Policy for disconnection (e.g. they honor the right to be offline outside working hours.).
○ Strongly disagree ○ Disagree ○ Neither agree nor disagree ○ Agree ○ Strongly agree

(d) My institution practices Positive Discrimination *(e.g. Overcompensating the imbalance of women in the institute by their overrepresenting at institute colloquia. For example, if 15% of the institution is female, women give at least 25% of the talks and external female speakers are invited./Upgrading a postdoc position to a tenure track position when there is an excellent female candidate and she meets the criteria specified./Including a mid-term review of progress against the criteria.)*
○ Strongly disagree ○ Disagree ○ Neither agree nor disagree ○ Agree ○ Strongly agree

(e) My Institution promotes an Inclusive working environment (e.g. Organises a course for all senior staff members on unconscious bias. These can cover all diversity issues, not just gender equality issues./Allocates resources to initiatives such as promoting/encouraging women's networks within the Institute, including secretarial support and a budget for holding events such as lunches.)
○ Strongly disagree ○ Disagree ○ Neither agree nor disagree ○ Agree ○ Strongly agree

(f) My Institution acknowledges and credits time spent on gender balance initiatives (e.g. it counts the hours female colleagues spend on support and network issues in the same way as all other departmental commitments and duties are accounted for and valued—does not assume that female employees can deal with this extra load in their spare time).
○ Strongly disagree ○ Disagree ○ Neither agree nor disagree ○ Agree ○ Strongly agree

Q16 Please answer the questions on retaining female talent and expertise.

(a) My Institution gives support to parents *(e.g. it funds childcare as part of conference travel expenses for participating faculty and researchers with young children/provides specific rooms for breastfeeding/funds travel expenses for a partner to go to the conference location during the breastfeeding period/promotes family-friendly measures with regard to travelling to conferences with children/inquires if conference venues have childcare facilities and personnel, and requests organisers to provide attendees with childcare and breastfeeding options and ensure that conferences organised by your Institution provide such facilities.)*
○ Strongly disagree ○ Disagree ○ Neither agree nor disagree ○ Agree ○ Strongly agree

(b) My Institution distributes welcome packages with a booklet that lists childcare options as well as other useful info provided by institute members.
○ Strongly disagree ○ Disagree ○ Neither agree nor disagree ○ Agree ○ Strongly agree

(c) My Institution creates an *'Ambassador Program'* or a personal development plan for researchers with high potential.
○ Strongly disagree ○ Disagree ○ Neither agree nor disagree ○ Agree ○ Strongly agree

(d) My Institution ensure that at least 30% of the people on *Ambassador Program* are women.
○ Strongly disagree ○ Disagree ○ Neither agree nor disagree ○ Agree ○ Strongly agree

(e) My Institution provides visibility and self-promotion training for female researchers in temporary employment.
○ Strongly disagree ○ Disagree ○ Neither agree nor disagree ○ Agree ○ Strongly agree

(f) My Institution provides visibility and self-promotion training for female researchers in permanent employment.
○ Strongly disagree ○ Disagree ○ Neither agree nor disagree ○ Agree ○ Strongly agree

(g) My Institution consults with women in the institution in order to gather opinions about the organization, their role and their career ambitions and prospects *(e.g., organise lunch once a month with a different woman, at a different level).*
○ Strongly disagree ○ Disagree ○ Neither agree nor disagree ○ Agree ○ Strongly agree

4. Promoting Women

We will be more than happy to accept your best effort even if that means that some questions will have to go unanswered.

Q17 Are there any measures in place in your Institution to ensure that there is a positive representation of women in Decision Making Positions and in Institutional Committees *(e.g. above the proportion of women in your institution)*?
○ Yes ○ No ○ I don't know.

Q18 What is the percentage of women in committees in your institution *(an estimated value will suffice if you do not have published figures)*?
....

Q19 Does your Institution ensure that female members are not overloaded with these functions (e.g. committees)?
○ Yes ○ No ○ I don't know.

Q20 Does your institution avoid overloading women with faculty service, specially related to student affairs, participating in voluntary commissions, and other purely administrative service?
○ Yes ○ No ○ I don't know.

Q21 Does your institution propose suitable women for prestigious tasks—i.e. tasks considered valuable for career advancement, such as prizes, representing the institution in informal meetings/internationally, PhD Committees etc.?
○ Yes ○ No ○ I don't know.

Q22 When organizing or supporting conferences, are there measures in place to ensure that there is positive female representation across the list of invited speakers and members of program committees *(e.g. withdraw funding if there is no reasonable gender balance in keynote speakers)*?
○ Yes (please list the measures below) .... ○ No ○ I do not know.

Q23 Are you aware of any mechanisms—internal or external to the Institution—to increase the number of female applications/promotions *(e.g., state initiatives; evaluate everyone that can be promoted at that stage)*?
○ Yes (please list the measures below) .... ○ No

5. Mentoring
The part of the questionnaire regarding mentoring was not analyzed in this paper (Q24–Q36).

6. Additional Comments
Q37 Please add any other comments
....

References

1. T. D. Allen, L. T. Eby, K. E. O'Brien, and E. Lentz. The state of mentoring research: A qualitative review of current research methods and future research implications. *Journal of vocational behavior*, 73(3):343–357, 2008.

2. S. Barnard, J. Arnold, S. Bosley, and F. Munir. The personal and institutional impacts of a mass participation leadership programme for women working in higher education: a longitudinal analysis. *Studies in Higher Education*, 47(7):1372–1385, 2022.
3. M. Beigi, M. Shirmohammadi, and J. Stewart. Flexible work arrangements and work–family conflict: A metasynthesis of qualitative studies among academics. *Human Resource Development Review*, 17(3):314–336, 2018.
4. V. Brizuela, J. J. Chebet, and A. Thorson. Supporting early-career women researchers: lessons from a global mentorship programme. *Global Health Action*, 16(1):2162228, 2023.
5. J. V. Brown, P. E. Crampton, G. M. Finn, J. E. Morgan, and P. Team. From the sticky floor to the glass ceiling and everything in between: protocol for a systematic review of barriers and facilitators to clinical academic careers and interventions to address these, with a focus on gender inequality. *Systematic reviews*, 9:1–7, 2020.
6. G. Bujdosó, C. Ghezzi, L. Hardman, J. Hillston, M. L. Jaccheri, H. Kirchner, and C. Pereira. More women in informatics research and education. Informatics Europe, 2016.
7. M. Carnes, P. G. Devine, L. B. Manwell, A. Byars-Winston, E. Fine, C. E. Ford, P. Forscher, C. Isaac, A. Kaatz, W. Magua, et al. Effect of an intervention to break the gender bias habit for faculty at one institution: a cluster randomized, controlled trial. *Academic medicine: journal of the Association of American Medical Colleges*, 90(2):221, 2015.
8. S. Dopson, E. Ferlie, G. McGivern, M. Fischer, J. Ledger, S. Behrens, and S. Wilson. The impact of leadership and leadership development in higher education': A review of the literature and evidence. 2016.
9. K. Dutt, D. L. Pfaff, A. F. Bernstein, J. S. Dillard, and C. J. Block. Gender differences in recommendation letters for postdoctoral fellowships in geoscience. *Nature Geoscience*, 9(11):805–808, 2016.
10. European Commission Directorate-General for Research and Innovation. *She figures 2021: gender in research and innovation: statistics and indicators*. Publications Office, 2021.
11. European Institute for Gender Equality. What is a Gender Equality Plan, June 2023. [Online; accessed 21. Jun. 2023].
12. N. Fisk, N. M. Kelly, and L. Liebrock. Cybersecurity communities of practice: Strategies for creating gateways to participation. *Computers & Security*, page 103188, 2023.
13. Informatics Europe. Minerva Informatics Equality Award: Best Practices in Supporting Women, June 2023. [Online; accessed 21. Jun. 2023].
14. K. L. Milkman, M. Akinola, and D. Chugh. What happens before? a field experiment exploring how pay and representation differentially shape bias on the pathway into organizations. *Journal of Applied Psychology*, 100(6):1678, 2015.
15. C. A. Moss-Racusin, J. F. Dovidio, V. L. Brescoll, M. J. Graham, and J. Handelsman. Science faculty's subtle gender biases favor male students. *Proceedings of the national academy of sciences*, 109(41):16474–16479, 2012.
16. K. O'Meara and N. P. Stromquist. Faculty peer networks: Role and relevance in advancing agency and gender equity. *Gender and Education*, 27(3):338–358, 2015.
17. C. Teelken, Y. Taminiau, and C. Rosenmöller. Career mobility from associate to full professor in academia: micro-political practices and implicit gender stereotypes. *Studies in Higher Education*, 46(4):836–850, 2021.
18. C. Vacas-Soriano, J. Hurley, and M. Bisello. Understanding the gender pay gap: What role do sector and occupation play? 2021.

Open Access This chapter is licensed under the terms of the Creative Commons Attribution 4.0 International License (http://creativecommons.org/licenses/by/4.0/), which permits use, sharing, adaptation, distribution and reproduction in any medium or format, as long as you give appropriate credit to the original author(s) and the source, provide a link to the Creative Commons license and indicate if changes were made.

The images or other third party material in this chapter are included in the chapter's Creative Commons license, unless indicated otherwise in a credit line to the material. If material is not included in the chapter's Creative Commons license and your intended use is not permitted by statutory regulation or exceeds the permitted use, you will need to obtain permission directly from the copyright holder.

Chapter 10
Good Practices for Improving Gender Balance and Diversity Throughout an Academic Career

Brenda Murphy, Carla Teixeira Lopes, Emanuela Merelli, Mara Gabriela Diaconu, Marie Gallais, Paloma Diaz, Paula Alexandra Silva, Petroula Mavrikiou, Silvia Ghilezan, and Steve Kremer

---

B. Murphy (✉)
South East Technological University, Waterford, Ireland
e-mail: brenda.murphy@setu.ie

C. T. Lopes
Universidade do Porto, Faculdade de Engenharia, INESC TEC, Porto, Portugal

E. Merelli
University of Camerino, Camerino, Italy

M. G. Diaconu
Norwegian University of Science and Technology, Trondheim, Norway

M. Gallais
Luxembourg Institute of Science and Technology, Esch-sur-Alzette, Luxembourg

P. Diaz
Universidad Carlos III de Madrid, Leganés, Spain

P. A. Silva
University of Coimbra, Coimbra, Portugal

P. Mavrikiou
Frederick University, Nicosia, Cyprus

S. Ghilezan
Mathematical Institute SASA & University of Novi Sad, Novi Sad, Serbia

S. Kremer
Inria Centre at Université de Lorraine, Villers-les-Nancy, France

© The Author(s) 2025
B. Penzenstadler et al. (eds.), *Actions for Gender Balance in Informatics Across Europe*, https://doi.org/10.1007/978-3-031-78432-3_10

> **Kim, the university professor.** Kim, the university professor, is concerned about the gender imbalance in their Informatics Department, and the low number of female full professors. Kim has scheduled a meeting with the Head of School to discuss this problem. The material in this chapter provides ideas for concrete actions to deploy that Kim can suggest to the Head of School.

10.1 Introduction

Despite growing awareness, women are still seriously under-represented in STEM (Science, Technology, Engineering, and Mathematics) areas. According to the She Figures 2021 report [6], the European Union (EU) has almost achieved gender parity among doctoral graduates (48.1% of women in 2018). Despite this progress, important gender gaps persist in certain broad fields of study.

Women are less likely to be employed as scientists and engineers. Similarly, they are under-represented among self-employed professionals in Science and Engineering (S&E) and Information and Communication Technology (ICT) occupations (24.9% of women in 2018). Women continue to be under-represented among Doctoral graduates in the majority of narrow STEM fields (Table 10.1: Physical Sciences (38.4%), Mathematics and Statistics (32.5%), ICT (20.8%), Engineering and Engineering trades (27%), Manufacturing and Processing (40.9%), and Architecture and Construction (37.2%)). A higher proportion of women researchers worked part-time (11.1% of women and 7.2% of men in 2019) and under precarious working contracts in the Higher Education Sector (HES) across the EU (9% of women researchers and 7.7% of men in 2019). Women are under-represented at the highest level of academia (grade A, i.e., equivalent to a full professorship), with minor improvements documented between 2015 and 2018—from 24.1% to 26.2%. While women are relatively well-represented among grade A staff in Humanities (35% in 2018), there is a minimal presence in the field of Engineering and Technology (17.9% in 2018) (Table 10.2). Women also remain under-represented among the heads of higher education institutions (23.6% in 2019) and as board members (31.1%) and leaders (24.5%) (Table 10.3).

Table 10.1 Woman Doctoral graduates [6]

General	48.1%
S&E and ICT	24.9%
Physical Sciences	38.4%
Mathematics and Statistics	32.5%
ICT	20.8%
Engineering and Engineering trades	27%
Manufacturing and Processing	40.9%
Architecture and Construction	37.2%

Table 10.2 Woman at Grade A [6]

General	26.2%
Humanities	35%
Engineering and Technology	17.9%

Table 10.3 Woman at leadership positions [6]

Heads of HEI	23.6%
Board members	31.1%
Leaders	24.5%

Research, in particular, requires creative thinking, and diversity is key to boosting creativity. In this chapter, we identify good practices that should be in place throughout an academic career—from PhD to Professor—which facilitate equal opportunities for women and other minority groups. We hope that this chapter can raise awareness of key issues and problems, explain why women remain under-represented, and provide detailed strategies to improving gender balance and diversity. In each section, we give examples of good practices that have been implemented, and we hope they can inspire deployment in other institutions. Finally, we wish to acknowledge that many recommendations of this chapter are inspired by the Informatics Europe booklet *"More women in informatics and education"* [2], and our chapter can be considered a revised version of their work.

The chapter is organised as follows. Section 10.2 discusses the importance of recruitment and selection policies, the composition and working methods of the selection committees and the language used and presents recommended best practices for recruiting women in higher eduction. Section 10.3 discuss the subtleties of gender bias that may occur in a hiring evaluation process and presents a good practice of application evaluation at Inria, France. Section 10.4 stresses the importance of ensuring conditions to retain female employees and gives the good practices at TU Dublin, Computer Science and Schloss Dagstuhl. Section 10.5 analysis the barriers and challenges that women face to advance in their academic career and presents some recommendations and strategies that can deal with these issues. Section 10.6 concludes the chapter.

10.2 Recruiting Women

The under-representation of women in senior and leadership positions in academia is a reality. European level data shows that in 2018, women represented more than 40% of academic staff but only occupied around a quarter (and only 17.9% in Engineering and Technology) of the equivalent full professorship positions [6]. Research shows that bias against women operates in recruitment and selection processes, affecting recruitment advertisements, the composition, and working methods of selection committees and the language used in evaluations [10]. Examples of such bias include the use of non-inclusive language such as male forms for a profession, even though female forms exist, or imprecise formulations about the required qualifications which is shown to attract less female applications, typically very careful to whether they meet the requirements. In [4], the authors suggest that the lack of gender parity is due to prevailing negative stereotypes that impact hiring discrimination and opportunities for advancement [4]. They argue that women in STEM have "lower social capital which limits opportunities; perceive their academic climate as unwelcoming, and report hostility in their work environments (for example, sexual harassment and discrimination)". They describe three factors that contribute to gender inequalities and women's departure from academic STEM fields: (a) numeric under-representation and stereotypes, (b) lack of supportive social networks, and (c) chilly academic climates. Below, we synthesise a list of recommended best practices for recruiting women in higher education.

- When writing a Recruitment Advert ensure that the process considers the following aspects:
  - Use inclusive language.
  - Advertise openly for all positions, stating that you are an equal opportunity employer.
  - State that the university/department/institute is committed to facilitating the combination of work and childcare in the recruiting media and job descriptions.
  - State that flexible terms of employment are possible, such as working part-time and flexible working hours.
  - Emphasise that jobs in Informatics allow more opportunities for tele-commuting and tele-working, compared to other fields.
- When advertising the position consider the following:
  - Allow 3 months for applications to be submitted. Time is needed for the advertisement to reach the right women, and they need time to respond.
  - Approach candidates directly. For example, send the advertisement personally to, at least three women you would like to see in the position and invite them to apply.
  - Approach candidates indirectly. Invite colleagues to send the advert to three other women they think would be suitable for the post.
  - Distribute advertisements across a number of channels. For example, sending them to women's networks' email lists, such as national women in tech networks or networks of female professors.
- Consider using positive actions:
  - Take action if too few eligible women apply. For example, extend the application deadline and advertise the position again (inter)nationally.
  - Re-examine the application and consider re-advertising if the initial list of candidates selected for the interview does not include any women.

- Use quotas or dedicated positions. Several countries introduced the 'cascade model' following the German example. In this model, the institutions set targets for the proportion of women at each qualification level based on the proportion of women at the level immediately below.

> **Application of the CASCADE Model, Germany**
> German research institutions, including the Friedrich-Alexander Universität Erlangen-Nürnberg (FAU), the Helmholtz Association, and the German Leibniz Association, have introduced flexible quotas for the shares of female employees according to a cascade model [21]. In this stepped model, the actual ratio of a career level becomes the ideal ratio for the next career level [7]. Such ratios help to battle the phenomenon, known as glass ceiling or sticky floor, where the ratio of women decreases the higher the position. Such ratios can also be used to achieve target ratios using more complex calculations that include the percentage at the previous career level [18].

10.3 Application Evaluation for Hiring and Promotion

Gender bias that may occur in an evaluation process is difficult to prove. However, a study by in [8] reported that the adoption of blind auditions increases the probability of women being hired in a previously male-dominated context of prestigious symphony orchestras, providing evidence of unconscious gender bias. Similarly, gender bias appears in recommendation letters which are often an important element when reviewing hiring or promotion applications. Researchers studied over 300 recommendation letters at a large medical school and have shown that the length, wording, and style significantly differ for male and female applicants favouring male applicants [25].

- Ensure that the composition of the hiring committee is as balanced as possible. For example, ensure that the committee consists of at least 30% of women.
- Appoint one or two members of the panel to be dedicated to monitoring gender issues and gender balance.
- Organise unconscious/implicit gender bias training in advance of interview/promotion boards for Interview/Promotion Panel Members.
- Forward guidelines around unconscious bias in recommendation letters to potential referees.
- Provide a gender sensitive template for applicants and/or referees. For example, does it explicitly include a section on career breaks?
- Provide/publish statistics in a multi-stage process (for example, ensuring that you retain the same % of female representation at every level of the process).

- Consider career breaks (maternity leave, parental leave) with explicit identifications and rules. For example, some institutions allocate '18 months per child' when comparing female candidates who are mothers, with other candidates to ensure that the perception of their productivity is unharmed.
- Consider explicit evaluation criteria. For example, do they value different or less typical profiles while evaluating applications, taking into account aspects such as software, interdisciplinary research, and research data.
- You may also consider:
  - Inviting women to interview not only to see whether they are best for the position, but also to give them the experience of being interviewed.
  - Providing help with solving the "two body problem", that is, helping to find a position for the applicant's partner.
  - Hosting open discussions around the issue of increasing the representation of women in the department when interviewing women and men, and asking how they would approach it. This provides extra tips and also shows the department is serious about the issues.

Application Evaluation at Inria, France

Each hiring and promotion panel at Inria has to follow a charter on Gender Equality and Equal Opportunities.[a] The purpose of this charter is to draw the attention of the panel members to ensure gender equality, and equal opportunities between candidates. It advises the panel chair and its members about best practices and stipulates rules to follow. These best practices include:

- The appointment of two "gender equality and equal opportunities (GEO) leads" who will ensure that best practices are followed/applied.
- The monitoring of statistics to detect bias, in particular, to avoid the 'leaky pipeline' phenomenon (i.e., the fact that women resign at various points in their career increases the low numbers of female talent).
- The advice on how to fairly treat diverse profiles, and avoid double standard-type mechanisms.
- The advice on when taking career breaks into account.
- The detection of potential bias in recommendation letters.
- The reminder for the panel chair to ensure that the panel's discussions give every member the chance to express their opinions.

Before starting the evaluation process all committee members are also provided with a short documentation on unconscious bias and invited to watch the video "Recruitment Bias in Research Institutes".[b]

---

[a] https://www.inria.fr/sites/default/files/2020-01/charter%20GEO.pdf.
[b] https://www.youtube.com/watch?v=g978T58gELo.

10.4 Retaining Female Talent and Expertise

The culture of an organisation or a department, and the views of the manager/director, can have a direct impact on whether women stay with an organisation or leave for something better that answers their needs [9, 20, 23]. To retain female talent, organisations must ensure that female employees have the experience and the resources to learn what they need most. This could include encouraging a proper balance of work and family [9, 20, 23], giving guidance for on-the-job learning, as well as coaching, mentoring, and workshops or programs [16].

- Have *Family Friendly Guidelines* in place for scheduling meetings. For example, only schedule meetings between 09:30 and 16:30, so carers of young children can deal with commuting and childcare.
- Have a Policy for disconnection, for example, honour the right to disconnect.
- Practice Positive Discrimination within the institution
  - for example, overcompensate the imbalance of women in the institute by their overrepresentation at institute colloquia. For instance, if 15% of the department is female, then make sure women give at least 25% of the talks. Invite external female speakers too.
  - for example, upgrade a postdoc position to a tenure track position when there is an excellent female candidate and she meets the criteria specified. Include a mid-term review of progress against the criteria.
- Promote an inclusive working environment
  - for example, organise a course for all senior staff members on unconscious bias. These sessions can cover all diversity issues, not just gender equality issues.
  - for example, allocate resources to initiatives such as promoting/encouraging womens' networks within the Department/Institute, including secretarial support and a budget for holding events such as lunches.
- Acknowledge and credit time spent on gender balance initiatives for example, count the hours colleagues spend on support and network issues in the same way as all other departmental commitments and duties are accounted for and valued (Do not assume that employees can deal with this extra load in their "spare time"!)
- Support parents:
  - fund childcare as part of conference travel expenses for participating faculty and researchers with young children.
  - provide specific rooms for breast-feeding.
  - fund travel expenses for a partner to go to the conference location during the breastfeeding period.
  - promote family friendly measures with regard to travelling to conferences with children. For example, inquire if conference venues have childcare

facilities and personnel, and request organisers to provide attendees with childcare and breastfeeding options, and ensure that conferences organised by your department/institution provide such facilities.
- Other best practises
  - Distribute welcome packages with a booklet that lists childcare options as well as other useful info provided by faculty/institute members.
  - Create an 'Ambassador Program' or a personal development plan for researchers with high potential.
  - Ensure that at least 30% of the people on such a programme are women.
  - Provide visibility and self-promotion training for female researchers in both temporary and permanent employment.
  - Consult with women in the department/institution in order to gather opinions about the organisation, her role and her career ambitions and prospects (for example, organise lunch once a month with a different woman, at a different career level).

SUCCESS @ TU Dublin Computer Science
The SUCCESS (Source, Career, Environment, Support for SuCEsS) program of the Computer Science School at TU Dublin is a four strand approach:
- Source: use networks to increase the number of female academic staff applying for academic positions.
- Career: run female-focussed skills development initiatives such as Performance Management Development Systems (PMDS) that allows female staff to articulate difficulties or aims with the School, fundings of early career researchers (for example, conferences, PhD supervision schemes, seed-funding of research proposals), and encouraging female staff to mentor more junior female staff (for example, co-supervision in PhD students).
- Environment: create an environment of support and encouragement for female staff (for example, offering role models, participating in the Women Leaders in Higher Education (WLHE) network).
- Support: implement practical supports that offer flexibility to female staff in particular after maternity leave

As a result of the SUCCESS programme, in an academic team of approximately 55 full-time equivalents, 36% of the academic staff are female, 50% of our senior academic leadership team (2 of 4) are female and 75% of our School Executive are female (3 of 4), including a female Head of School (May 2019).

> **Caregiver and Childcare Support @ Schloss Dagstuhl**
> Schloss Dagstuhl supports parents who would otherwise not be able to attend the events due to a lack of childcare opportunities at home.[a] Schloss Dagstuhl offers the following childcare alternatives:
>
> - Guests are welcome to bring a caregiver of their choice (spouse, relative). This person receives free room and board and is accommodated in a room together with the child and parent(s).
> - Qualified childcare (for children up to 12 years of age) is provided by the Schloss Dagstuhl nanny.
>
> ---
> [a]https://www.dagstuhl.de/en/guests/childcare.

10.5 Promoting Women

Women continue to face barriers and challenges to move up the career ladder [19]. According to She figures [6], women in grade A positions in ICT comprised 2.7% of women in the 1990s, and stood at 8% in 2020. Over the last thirty years, awareness of gender balance and gender blindness has increased [15, 22]. While there are improvements at PhD level and early-stage research positions, there has been no significant progress in gender balance in research leading positions. This is recognised by European Research Area (ERA), UNESCO, and other world organisations [6, 14]. The ERA commits to the development of inclusive Gender Equality Plans (GEP) across European academia and research institutions [17] but creating a plan might not be enough when what is needed is an organisational change that starts by recognising the gender leadership gap and its effects at an institutional level [5]. This gender leadership gap does not represent the values and current structure of our society and also misses the opportunities for increased creativity, profitability, and performance that diversity could bring [3]. However, these benefits are contingent upon a supportive organisational culture that genuinely values diversity rather than treating it as a buzzword or legal obligation. Achieving organisational change requires commitment from governing boards and a willingness to assess and change the current situation.

The under-representation of female academics in leadership roles is broadly understood in terms of the "leaky pipeline", that is, women resigning at various points in their careers, and the "glass ceiling", that is, structural barriers that prevent access to senior positions. However there are other situations that keep women in the lower echelons of leadership, including the "sticky floor", that is, the existence of discriminatory employment patterns, often subtle and unconscious, that keep women in lower ranked and lower-paid occupations; and the glass cliff, that is, when women are only placed in leadership roles during times of crisis when there is a higher risk of failure and, usually, no man will take the baton. The role of the organisational culture in all these situations has been studied in the literature identifying a number of gendered experiences [24] that create a chilly climate [1] and have a negative impact in women self-esteem [12].

The term "chilly climate" was introduced back in 1982 to refer to "a pervasive and systemic institutional order and references a compounding of everyday practices which block women's full participation in the university" [11]. Whilst in the past gender discrimination was openly exerted, most institutions still have this chilly climate that does not only refer to sexual harassment or unwanted physical attention, which already persists in some cases, but to a plethora of often unconscious practices that undermine women objective and subjective chances to promote [1]. Among these gendered experiences, the report elaborated after 40 semi-structured interviews at the National Institute of Standards and Technology (NIST) in 2020 [24], identified practices such as subtle put-downs, lack of respect, questioning competence, making women feel invisible or isolated, relegating them into the mommy track or burying them into "housekeeping" and non promotable tasks. All of them affect women's confidence, self-esteem as well as their level of achievement. Even when meritocracy is claimed as the leading criteria for promotion that does not always result into a fair and not biased evaluation procedure. There are many objective parameters, like number of citations, co-authorship, number of grants, quality of the recommendation letters, or teaching evaluations, in which women are consistently penalized for their gender [1, 3].

Another issue that has been identified when analysing the barriers women face to promote is that their leadership ability is often questioned under the assumption that some stereotype-based skills for effective leadership do not match "typical" women personalities [13]. In such exclusionary and hostile cultures, where leadership is identified with masculine traits and is dominated by the so-called "boys club", women often opt out as a self-defence strategy. This, in turn, makes inequality more difficult to deal with, since the responsibility of the organisation for the absence of feminine leadership role models is hidden by a fake personal decision. The sense of "not belonging" is further constrained by a lack of self confidence. In fact, there is evidence that women have consistently lower expectations of success than men; whilst women tend to underestimate their achievements, men are more inclined to be overconfident about their capabilities [12]. However, this does not mean there is anything wrong with women nor that we have to change women to solve inequalities. As very graphically explained in [1], the solution does not lie in "the metaphorical distribution of sweaters to women and underrepresented groups, but rather involve a concerted effort to raise the overall temperature so that women are able to participate fully and fairly".

Raising the overall temperature is a joint effort that involves all the institution, not only women, not only those in leadership positions. It has to be a change in the organisational culture permeating all its levels. The first step is to analyse the current situation, identify existing biases and gendered experiences, and then take action to reduce the leadership gap with specific and feasible policies, strategies, and practices. Models like the emerging Equality Maturity Model [5] developed in the EUGAIN network can enable discussion around the institution policies, strategies and practices and how they are perceived and experienced by workers.

There are some strategies that can help to deal with the barriers that women face to advance in their academic career, including:

- Ensure that there is a positive representation of women in Decision Making Positions and in Institutional Committees (for example, above the proportion of women in your department).
- Ensure that female members are not overloaded with these functions or with non promotable tasks.
- Ensure that salaries, promotion opportunities, and endowments are distributed equitably among male and female faculty members [3].
- Propose suitable women for prestigious tasks—i.e. tasks considered valuable for career advancement, such as prizes, representing the department, Ph.D. Committees, etc.
- When organising or supporting conferences, ensure that there is positive female representation across the list of invited speakers and members of program committees (for example, withdraw funding if there is no reasonable gender balance in keynote speakers).
- Run a mentoring program: in universities, mentorship programmes help promote researchers at all levels of academic success, further fueling their growth throughout their career journey. Explicitly recognize the work of good mentors.
- Raise awareness on gender bias in evaluation procedures as well as in letters of recommendation for applicants [3].
- Offer opportunities to take part in leadership courses and networking events for women [3].

In the next paragraphs we describe three examples of policies applied in different European universities.

Promotion at UCL, UK

In order to ensure equal consideration, all non-professorial members of staff are required to submit their CVs for consideration in a yearly meeting of the promotions committee. This goes beyond the standard UCL process which requires individuals to put forward an application to their Head of Department (HoD). Previously the committee would review only those non-professorial academic staff who submitted their CVs, and those considered worthy would be invited to apply for promotion. However, the survey results from 2013 indicated that only 51% of the staff members were satisfied with the process, 51% males and 45% females. The results of the survey prompted the Department to change its promotion procedures to that described above

(continued)

in which all non-professorial staff are required to submit their CVs and feedback is provided whether promotion is recommended or not. This feedback process is being further formalised into an appraisal starting this year. The promotion criteria have remained unchanged recognising excellence in teaching, research, administration, support and outreach work. This larger evaluation group was chosen to ensure that there is no bias created through, for example, differences in propensity for self-promotion. Potential candidates for promotion are identified by this group through a rigorous reviewing process that provides feedback to all staff through their Head of Group (HoG). Those identified are then invited to apply and appropriate letters of support are supplied by the HoD with suitable reference letter writers identified with the help of HoG.

Mentor Scientific Program, IDUN, NTNU, Norway
In Norway, at NTNU's Faculty of Computer Science and Electrical Engineering "IDUN—from PhD to professor[a] " mentorship project aims at increasing the number of female scientists in top positions in the faculty. IDUN Scientific Mentoring Program brings together researchers from different career levels, in similar fields, but still different, and gives them the opportunity to create new knowledge together. The scheme is flexible, confidential and fits mentees availability and preferences. It includes both men and women as a collaborative environment, but with a clear focus on women (70% of the mentees are women). The mentoring activities focus on group work on a specific research topic, networking, proposal writing and career planning activities. In the program, mentees stand to benefit from a range of things, like receiving encouragement and training from the university, interacting with other researchers to learn from their experiences; develop strategies for dealing with both personal and academic issues; gain valuable insight into researchers' next stage of their university journey, to name a few.

Mentors, on the other hand, can develop a range of skills including leadership, communication and personal skills; enhance their CV and develop new research; in addition to benefiting from a sense of fulfilment and personal growth. IDUN works on three different issues to improve gender balance: recruiting more women to all levels from Ph.D. to professor, helping to limit dropout of women and increasing the number of female scientists involved in international research projects.

---
[a]https://www.ntnu.edu/idun.

> **Women Promotion Policies at UC3M, Spain**
> In the last decade, Spanish public universities had to face very restrictive conditions to hire and promote academics imposed by the government. For example, a new full professor position was only created if there was a full professorship retirement, and in a new university like Universidad Carlos III de Madrid the number of retirements per year was marginal. Being aware of the existing gender gap and how a shrinking number of openings could increase this gap, Universidad Carlos III de Madrid put in practice a number of strategies to support women promotion from 2015 to 2022. The university has three faculties, the School of Engineering, the Faculty of Social Sciences and Laws, and the Faculty of Humanities, Documentation and Communication. However, the personnel policy is not delegated to the centres but it is defined by the vice-rectorate and, hence the strategies applied to increase the number of women promoted were not specific for computing or engineering. In particular, four different strategies were applied: force gender diversity in all university commissions; use gender as a tie-breaking criterion, so that in any ranking women always have preference; increase research dedication after maternity periods by decreasing teaching dedication; increase the periods for the evaluation of merits in any processes that involve time periods. Thanks to these strategies, the promotion of women was significantly improved. Thus, whilst the overall growth of permanent teaching staff in the University was a 18.36%, the increase in women professors was a 50.68%, going from a representation of women of 14.19% to 28.7%.

10.6 Conclusion

This chapter offers a road-map of best practices designed to improve gender balance and create equal opportunities for women and other minority groups throughout their academic journey—from PhD to Professor. By addressing the entire career spectrum, we highlight critical areas such as unbiased recruitment, fair application evaluation, and inclusive promotion processes. Additionally, we emphasize the importance of fostering a supportive and family-friendly environment that not only attracts but also retains female talent. We have also showcased real-world examples from various institutions that have successfully implemented these strategies, demonstrating that progress is both achievable and impactful. By raising awareness of the underlying issues and barriers, and by detailing actionable steps to enhance gender balance and diversity, we hope to inspire similar initiatives within your organisation. Implementing these proven strategies can transform our academic landscape into one where everyone, regardless of gender class, race, age, or other background, has the opportunity to thrive. Our commitment to these initiatives will be pivotal in driving change and setting a new standard for inclusivity and equity in academia.

References

1. D. M. Britton. Beyond the chilly climate: The salience of gender in women's academic careers. *Gender & society*, 31(1):5–27, 2017.
2. G. Bujdosó, C. Ghezzi, L. Hardman, J. Hillston, M. L. Jaccheri, H. Kirchner, and C. Pereira. More women in informatics research and education. Informatics Europe, 2016.
3. M. I. Cardel, E. Dhurandhar, C. Yarar-Fisher, M. Foster, B. Hidalgo, L. A. McClure, S. Pagoto, N. Brown, D. Pekmezi, N. Sharafeldin, A. L. Willig, and C. Angelini. Turning chutes into ladders for women faculty: A review and roadmap for equity in academia. *Journal of women's health*, 20(5):721–733, 2020.
4. B. J. Casad, J. E. Franks, C. E. Garasky, M. M. Kittleman, A. C. Roesler, D. Y. Hall, and Z. W. Petzel. Gender inequality in academia: Problems and solutions for women faculty in stem. *Journal of Neuroscience Research*, 99(1):13–23, 2021.
5. P. Díaz, P. A. Silva, and K. Tuma. The equality maturity model: an actionable tool to advance gender balance in leadership and participation roles. In *2024 IEEE Global Engineering Education Conference (EDUCON)*, pages 1–5. IEEE, May 2024. doi:10.1109/EDUCON60312.2024.10578577
6. European Commission and Directorate-General for Research and Innovation. *She figures 2021: gender in research and innovation: statistics and indicators*. Publications Office, 2021.
7. GFZ German Research Centre for GeoSciences. Cascade Model. https://www.gfz-potsdam.de/en/career/the-gfz-as-an-employer/equal-opportunities/cascade-model/, 2022. [Online; accessed 31-March-2022].
8. C. Goldin and C. Rouse. Orchestrating impartiality: The impact of "blind" auditions on female musicians. *American Economic Review*, 90(4):715–741, Sept. 2000.
9. D. Gürer and T. Camp. An ACM-W literature review on women in computing. *SIGCSE Bull.*, 34(2):121–127, June 2002.
10. J. Gvozdanović and K. Maes. Implicit bias in academia: A challenge to the meritocratic principle and to women's careers - and what to do about it. League of European Research Universities (LERU) Advice Paper No 23, 2018.
11. R. M. Hall and B. R. Sandler. The classroom climate: A chilly one for women?, 1984. http://eric.ed.gov/PDFS/ED215628.pdf (accessed June 1st, 2024).
12. T. H. Herbst. Gender differences in self-perception accuracy: The confidence gap and women leaders' underrepresentation in academia. *SA Journal of Industrial Psychology*, 46(0), 2020.
13. C. L. Hoyt and S. E. Murphy. Managing to clear the air: Stereotype threat, women, and leadership. *The leadership quarterly*, 27(3):387–399, 2016.
14. S. Huyer. Is the gender gap narrowing in science and engineering? Technical report, UNESCO, 2022. [Online; accessed 31-March-2022].
15. L. Jaccheri, C. Pereira, and S. Fast. Gender issues in computer science: Lessons learnt and reflections for the future, 2021.
16. M. Klawe, T. Whitney, and C. Simard. Women in computing—take 2. *Commun. ACM*, 52(2):68–76, Feb. 2009.
17. LeTSGEP. Leading towards sustainable gender equality plans in research performing organisations - EU horizon 2020 research and innovation program, grant agreement n. 873072. https://letsgeps.eu, 2020. [Online; accessed 31-March-2022].
18. MDC. Constant dropping wears away a stone, 2014. https://www.mdc-berlin.de/news/news/constant-dropping-wears-away-stone.

19. C. O'Connell and M. McKinnon. Perceptions of barriers to career progression for academic women in STEM. *Societies*, 11(2), 2021.
20. C. M. Sanzari, A. Dennis, and C. A. Moss-Racusin. Should I stay or should I go?: Penalties for briefly de-prioritizing work or childcare. *Journal of Applied Social Psychology*, 51(4):334–349, 2021.
21. P. Sekuła and P. Pustułka. Successful gender equality measures and conditions for improving research environment in the fields linked to physics. Technical report, GENERA project, 2016.
22. M. Sheeran. Improving gender balance in academia a computer scientists suggestion of where to start part 1 (of 2). SIGPLAN Blog PL Perspectives - https://blog.sigplan.org/2022/01/27/improving-gender-balance-in-academia-a-computer-scientists-suggestion-of-where-to-start-part-1-of-2/, 2022. [Online; accessed 31-March-2022].
23. W. Shi, D. D. Silva, D. Xu, T. Abdelzaher, G. Singh, L. Golubchik, and J. Weston. NSF report on 2nd computing systems research PI meeting. Technical report, National Science Foundation, 2018.
24. M. F. Theofanos, S. Spickard Prettyman, J. Evans, and S. Furman. Voices of NIST: A study of gender and inclusivity. findings from in-depth interviews). NIST Technical Note 2143, 2021.
25. F. Trix and C. Psenka. Exploring the color of glass: Letters of recommendation for female and male medical faculty. *Discourse & Society*, 14(2):191–220, 2003.

Open Access This chapter is licensed under the terms of the Creative Commons Attribution 4.0 International License (http://creativecommons.org/licenses/by/4.0/), which permits use, sharing, adaptation, distribution and reproduction in any medium or format, as long as you give appropriate credit to the original author(s) and the source, provide a link to the Creative Commons license and indicate if changes were made.

The images or other third party material in this chapter are included in the chapter's Creative Commons license, unless indicated otherwise in a credit line to the material. If material is not included in the chapter's Creative Commons license and your intended use is not permitted by statutory regulation or exceeds the permitted use, you will need to obtain permission directly from the copyright holder.

Chapter 11
Breaking Barriers: Strategies for Achieving Equity in Academic Careers in ICT/Informatics/STEM

Paula Alexandra Silva, Brenda Murphy, Karima Echihabi, Katja Tuma, Paloma Diaz, Birgy Lorenz, and Marieke Huisman

11.1 Introduction

In recent years, considerable attention has been devoted to understanding the barriers women face in securing their education, pursuing academic careers, and advancing within academic institutions. The challenges encountered not only revolve around diversity but also extend to equality and equity.

This chapter explores these obstacles and proposes potential actions to address them. It is crucial to note that although our primary focus is on improving the position of women in academia, many of the suggested actions can significantly benefit other underrepresented groups as well.

The pursuit of gender equality within academia in general, and specifically in ICT/Informatics/STEM, is not only an issue of moral significance but is also closely

---

P. A. Silva (✉)
University of Coimbra, Coimbra, Portugal
e-mail: paulasilva@dei.uc.pt

B. Murphy
South East Technological University, Waterford, Ireland

K. Echihabi
Mohamed VI Polytechnic University, Ben Guerir, Morocco

K. Tuma
Vrije Universiteit Amsterdam, Amsterdam, Netherlands

P. Diaz
Universidad Carlos III de Madrid, Leganés, Spain

B. Lorenz
Tallinn University of Technology, Tallinn, Estonia

M. Huisman
University of Twente, Enschede, Netherlands

© The Author(s) 2025
B. Penzenstadler et al. (eds.), *Actions for Gender Balance in Informatics Across Europe*, https://doi.org/10.1007/978-3-031-78432-3_11

tied to the obligations set forth by the European Union (EU) and the United Nations, as defined in Goal 5 of the 2030 Agenda Sustainable Development Goals. The EU holds a treaty obligation to promote equality between women and men across all its activities, forming the foundation for gender mainstreaming [4]. This mandate underscores the necessity of tackling the challenges that impede women's progress in this academic space, to ensure their participation, retention, and advancement in this sector.

Neglecting the talents and contributions of women in fields like Informatics not only hinders the progress of the discipline itself but also poses significant repercussions for broader societal development, especially in an era of rapid digital transformation. Indeed, the loss of female talent in Informatics not only hampers the discipline but also undermines societal progress, particularly in an era where the economy is rapidly digitising, and Europe seeks to catch up on key technologies to ensure growth, competitiveness, sustainability, and inclusion [69]. Achieving these goals necessitates harnessing the full potential of all individuals, and cultivating a diverse and inclusive academic environment.

In this chapter, we emphasise the importance of promoting change in academia through targeted career development and mentoring programs. Such initiatives can play a pivotal role in empowering women, fostering an equitable and diverse academic community, and ultimately contributing to the progress of our society as a whole. In the two personas below, we demonstrate how the chapter can be used in the everyday lives of people working in, or planning to work in ICT/Informatics/STEM spaces. In the first, Derya is an early career researcher, and in the second, Kim is a Full Professor in Engineering. The personas demonstrate how the chapter can be 'brought to life' and have a meaningful application for each, despite their very different career stages and degrees of agency.

> ***Derya*** *has just completed an MSc in Informatics and is on the brink of making a big decision in relation to her future. Does she remain in research and education, or does she join industry? She can use this chapter to spotlight, in advance, some of the key issues to help her make that final decision, and navigate a successful career in academia.*
>
> ***Kim*** *is a Professor at a well-established UK university, and her area of research is Engineering. She is aware of the poor representation of women in her field, and in other STEM/STEAM spaces and she wants to support and retain other female colleagues as they enter academia. She is very familiar with the fact that the leaky pipeline means that women leave due to many challenges and barriers they subsequently face. She can use this chapter to establish robust mentoring programmes – which she is already committed to as a strategy – and help 'roll out' to other departments in her Faculty.*

11.2 Towards an Inclusive and Diverse Environment in Academia

In academia, and beyond, it has been thoroughly documented and demonstrated that women persistently face challenges and barriers that subsequently disadvantage them—regardless of the institution they are working within. These barriers have been identified, named, researched and described in great detail. The 'power of naming' is key to addressing those barriers. For example, when barriers block women and other minoritised groups[1] from moving upwards in an organisational hierarchy we now recognise this as the glass ceiling [57]. When women and other minoritised groups find themselves 'stuck' in poorly paid or lower positions, we 'call out' the sticky floor [10]. The glass elevator [76] describes the rapid promotion of men in female-dominated professions or sectors, where they surpass their female counterparts.

Horizontal segregation [15] refers to the gender disparities observed in the types of occupations or fields that men and women tend to pursue, leading to an uneven distribution of the workforce between genders across different sectors or professions. This can result in specific occupations being dominated by one gender, contributing to gender stereotypes and wage disparities. Vertical segregation [15] refers to the hierarchical disparity within organisations or professional fields, where one gender disproportionately dominates the higher-level positions, decision-making roles, or leadership positions. This segregation creates barriers for the underrepresented gender to advance in their careers and can contribute to the persistence of the glass ceiling and gender inequality in the workplace.

Recruitment unconscious bias [54] refers to the unintentional and subtle prejudicial influences on hiring decisions that stem from implicit attitudes and stereotypes, leading to unfair and discriminatory outcomes against certain groups during the recruitment process, and glass cliff [65] describes the phenomenon where women are more likely to be appointed to leadership positions during periods of crisis or downturn, setting them up for potential failure due to the increased risks associated with these roles.

The golden skirt phenomenon [67] refers to a situation where a small group of highly qualified and influential women hold multiple board seats in various companies, often as a result of gender quota systems, potentially leading to a concentration of power and influence among a select few women in corporate governance, and the one woman scenario describes a situation where a single woman is appointed to a leadership position or board seat within an organisation, tokenising her presence and creating a false sense of gender diversity while failing to address underlying systemic biases and inequalities.

Naming and understanding the function of these barriers empowers the act of 'calling out' and highlighting gender inequality and systemic biases within aca-

---

[1] On the use of the term minoritised in this chapter, we quote Wingrove-Haugland and McLeod "Rather than referring to "minorities," "members of minority groups" or "underrepresented minorities," we should refer to such individuals as "minoritized." Using "minoritized" makes it clear that being minoritized is about power and equity not numbers, connects racial oppression to the oppression of women, and gives us an easy way to conceive of intersectionality as being a minoritized member of a minoritized group. The term "minoritized" reveals the fact that white males and other dominant groups minoritize members of subordinated groups rather than obscuring this agency." [77].

demic (and other) organisations, which affords better opportunities to address these challenges. Table 11.1 details these and other barriers that have been documented and researched, and provides references for further reading, as well as definitions and examples for better understanding.

As referenced and mapped above, invisible barriers continue to exist, even though there are no visible or explicit obstacles keeping women (and other minoritised groups) from acquiring advanced job positions, both broadly, in the wider context of employment and careers, and specifically in academia. While the glass ceiling tends to cripple women from securing key decision-making, and higher earning posts in the organisation, they also encounter the *glass elevator/escalator* [76].

Women are also likely to be 'caught in axis' of *horizontal and vertical segregation* [78]. The barriers within organisations remain scrutinised, however, while *ceilings* and *floors* prevent upward mobility, women also face challenges before they ever join the organisation.

Research has shown that unconscious bias is present in recruitment processes [1, 59]. When the gender or appearance of a candidate is known—whether by a human or an algorithm—unconscious bias influences how the candidate is perceived, either positively or negatively, affecting the candidate's chances of success in securing the job. The use of artificial intelligence (AI) in recruitment can amplify existing biases [16], a known example of this concerns the Amazon's AI tool, designed to screen resumes, that while intended to streamline hiring, ended up reinforcing gender bias, systematically downgrading resumes from women. This highlights the risk of AI tools perpetuating existing biases if they are trained on biased data.

Caroline Criado Perez found that "men think of 'a man' 80% of the time they think of 'a person'" [59], and the UN 2020 found that *90% of men/women globally are biased against women* [1]. It has been found that blind recruitment, a process that removes identification details from applications, removes or prevents unconscious bias and might help with hiring more women to the workforce. Implementing blind recruitment processes has been shown to increase the diversity of hires by focusing solely on skills and qualifications, but this is not all to equalise the possibilities. We need to be aware of the systemic challenges women face across different spheres but also highlight the need for ongoing efforts towards achieving gender equality and inclusivity in the workplace.

Finally, the *glass cliff* (coined by [65]) emerges as a more subtle barrier than the others above. It explains the phenomenon whereby women who can break through the glass ceiling are more likely than men to find themselves in positions of risk at the top. For example, if the organisation is in crisis, management often turns to and promotes a woman, placing her in a likely position of failure. Research by Haslam found that, when shown resumes of male and female candidates, 300 interviewees chose the male candidate when the company was successful and the female candidate when the company was failing, suggesting that the '*old boy's network*' persists, and as soon as there is trouble the network won't want to give the job to their 'old boys', so a woman will be appointed/promoted. This section, with its easy-reference table would inform anyone engaged in, and working to address

11 Breaking Barriers

Table 11.1 Challenges faced by women in the workplace: a list of key barriers

Glass ceiling [53]

Definition: Invisible barrier that prevents women from rising to higher positions in an organisation *Example:* Despite equal qualifications, a woman may be overlooked for a promotion that is instead given to a male colleague

Sticky floor [5]

Definition: Discriminatory employment patterns keep women in lower-ranked and lower-paid occupations *Example:* Women get minimal chance for advancement roles, e.g. administrative positions, while male counterparts are fast-tracked into management

Glass elevator/escalator [76]

Definition: The phenomenon of men being rapidly promoted over women into leadership positions, especially in female-dominated fields *Example:* In fields like education or healthcare, male are more quickly promoted to senior positions than their female colleagues with similar or even superior credentials

Horizontal and vertical segregation [15]

Definition: Horizontal segregation concentrates one gender in specific professions, while vertical segregation restricts advancement based on gender *Example:* Women may be prevalent in nursing (horizontal segregation) but rarely advance to hospital administration roles (vertical segregation)

Recruitment unconscious bias [54]

Definition: Biases affect hiring decisions when the candidate's gender is known *Example:* Men are envisioned as the default 'person' in professional settings, leading to a preference for male candidates in hiring

Glass cliff [65]

Definition: Women are more likely to be placed in leadership roles during times of crisis, with a higher risk of failure. *Example:* Women are often chosen for leadership roles with higher risk, potentially reinforcing stereotypes of female leadership inadequacy

Gender bias [2]

Definition: Widespread bias against women, affecting perceptions and opportunities. *Example:* People worldwide hold biases against women, impacting their professional and personal lives

Golden skirt [67]

Definition: Practice of appointing a single woman to prominent roles to symbolise gender diversity without genuinely addressing systemic inequality. *Example:* A corporation includes one woman on its executive team to showcase diversity but fails to implement broader inclusive policies or practices

The 'one woman' scenario [39]

Definition: Repeatedly choosing the same women to represent gender diversity across projects/committees, limiting the visibility and opportunities for other qualified women. *Example:* A company repeatedly features the same female executive in all diversity promotions and panels, sidelining other capable women and reducing the impact of diversity efforts

Second-generation discrimination [36]

Definition: Prejudice that results from earlier systemic gender biases, e.g. organisational practices, cultural norms, or societal expectations, often subtly manifest. *Example:* Being (self)excluded from promotion for not being part of the informal working networks (old boy's club)

Gendered experience [31]

Definition: Different perceptions of the same situation due to gender identity. *Example:* Microaggressions or expectations about lack of leadership skills are typically engendered gender inequality in their discipline. Both Derya and Kim (the persona's above) would find this section useful.

11.2.1 Change the Culture Not the Women

While we have documented the key issues that women face when they access institutions, the rhetoric that women often hear is that 'they should work hard', 'do their best', 'strive to excel' etc., and they will succeed. However, we know that despite the best efforts of women everywhere, the barriers persist (see also [66]). The onus should *not* be placed on women to succeed when we know that the barriers and challenges exist within the organisation, and are systemic. It is the culture and the environment that we need to change and the onus needs to be on the organisations and institutions to do just that [43, 45].

Thus, we need to change the culture of the academic organisation or institution and as a result, change everybody's perspective on the position of women in that organisation. For this, two things are important: (1) both management, and everybody involved in decision-making in the organisation should acknowledge that change is needed and that this will be beneficial for the organisation as a whole, and (2) at the same time the managers and senior leaders should provide support for women in the organisation to secure and improve their position. This document will discuss what can be done to realise this culture change, and it will interrogate and develop two lines of action to improve the situation for women in academia: *career development* and *mentoring*.

11.2.2 Career Development

According to *the Encyclopedia of Career Development* [26], career development is a multifaceted topic that can be explored from personal, organisational, social or legal perspectives. From a personal perspective, career development is a process of exploration and action that an individual undertakes to fulfil professional aspirations. The strategies and decision-making styles vary according to the individual's abilities, personality, and values system. In contrast, organisations consider career development as a series of programs and practices that help participants achieve success in their careers. Such programs include academic advice, career counselling, mentoring, and health/well-being initiatives.

The legal and social contexts also have a direct impact on how individuals and organisations approach career development. For example, labour laws on employment security and unjust termination and social class, culture and ethnicity can have a strong influence on career decision-making at both the individual and organisational levels [26].

There is a consensus that women are not well-represented in academia [12, 47], either because they do not consider it as an option at all or because they leave it prematurely due to the leaky pipeline and barriers that they face across all disciplines but especially ICT/Informatics/STEM [22, 23]. Providing women active career development support is key, as it has been demonstrated to increase motivation, empowerment, and resilience [49].

In this chapter, we focus primarily on career development from personal and organisational viewpoints. We highlight the different career possibilities and paths that exist in the academic world and emphasise the main actions that individuals and institutions can undertake to support career development in academia.

11.2.3 Mentoring

A recent report by the [17] concluded that women are still underrepresented in Science, Technology, Engineering and Mathematics (STEM), especially in the more senior ranks of academic careers, in which only 17.9% of the positions are occupied by women. The same report found that the field of Engineering & Technology is the one with the lowest proportion of women among grade A academic staff, except for five countries: Cyprus, Luxembourg, Malta, Slovenia, and Israel. Mentoring has been recognised as an important instrument for fostering academic women's careers and reducing the underrepresentation of women. However, mentoring is a very broad term, which leads to a lack of agreement on what mentoring is and how the term can be defined [51].

Table 11.2 outlines several definitions of the term, though mentoring can be broadly conceptualised as a single, formalised, dyadic, hierarchical relationship between a senior and junior faculty member [81]. In this form, mentoring closely follows the definition of Kathy Kram (1985), an early mentoring researcher, who defined mentoring as:

> "a relationship between an older, more experienced mentor and a younger, less experienced protégée for the purpose of helping and developing the protégée's career" [62].

This breadth of the definition can be problematic [55] and, hence, the word mentoring is often used interchangeably with such terms as advising and supervising, coaching, and sponsoring (for definitions see Table 11.3). While there are different nuances to each of these roles, all strive to promote career advancement.

11.3 First Steps into Action

In this section, we detail significant approaches and strategies in order to achieve culture change within academic organisations. While acknowledging the need for transformation is the first step, implementing concrete actions to facilitate this

Table 11.2 Different definitions and views of mentoring

"mentoring implies an exclusive relationship in which a more experienced person provides strategic advice to facilitate the professional and personal development of another, less experienced one". [51]
"off-line help by one person to another in making significant transitions in knowledge, work or thinking". [50]
"a voluntary and reciprocal learning relationship that offers professional and career development for the mentee, and opportunities for the mentor to grow through sharing their knowledge. It is typically mentee-driven". [72]
"a form of voluntary help, which is not necessarily gratis, which favors development and learning, based on an interpersonal relationship of assistance and of exchanges in which an experienced person invests their acquired wisdom and their expertise, in order to favor the development of another person, who has to attain some competences and professional objectives". [27]
"mentoring should help the mentee to better understand the organizational context and career opportunities, avoid isolation, and access relevant networks". [51]

Table 11.3 Differences between mentoring sponsoring and coaching

Mentoring involves the provision of guidance, feedback, and psycho-social support on an ongoing basis. [35]
Sponsoring relates to providing specific strategic opportunities to an individual at a particular time. [35]
Coaching tends to be short-term, self-reflective, goal- and skills-specific, and performance-driven and is useful when someone needs help to define what one needs/wants to improve and to achieve that goal or to acquire that. [52]

change remains a significant challenge. This section explores key considerations and steps to organise culture change, set up career development programs, and establish effective mentoring initiatives.

To initiate culture change, what follows describes the steps needed to effect that change: Raising awareness of the issues and the need for transformation among employees and leaders is crucial as a first step. This is followed by guidance for career development programs that would benefit women at all stages of their academic careers, and by dividing academic careers into three stages—training, early-career, and mid-to-late career—we address specific needs and provide tailored recommendations. Finally, we provide a detailed map for setting up mentoring programmes as these play a pivotal role in promoting personal and professional growth. We provide guidelines for setting up effective mentoring initiatives, defining clear goals, creating a pool of experienced mentors, and ensuring optimal mentor-mentee matches.

11.3.1 Organising the Culture Change

Many academic organisations and institutions know that a culture change is needed, but they find it hard to take concrete steps to achieve this. Acknowledging the need for change is the first step, but putting it into practice is a bigger challenge. For this, an intrinsic motivation for change is needed from senior leaders [19, 20].

11.3.1.1 Considerations to Realise a Culture Change

If the need for a culture change is not felt intrinsically, then activities to improve the position and opportunities for women might lead to negative reactions. A change in how things are organised can disturb the existing members of a department (or other organisational units), and they may begin to work against change covertly or openly.

Every change goes through five stages of grief [41]: denial, anger, bargaining, depression, and then acceptance. Change will not be properly implemented until the organisation has completed these stages. So, when pushing for a culture change, it is important to take this into account and to manage the stress that members of the organisation might feel—they have existing ideas of how one should get the degree and position, and how one should be trained or supported. These existing ideas and unconscious biases might be conflicting with what one wants to achieve with the culture change, and need to be addressed. In the end, everyone needs to change their values, attitudes, and behaviours.

It should also be noted that the size and composition of a group or department can play a role in this process. Members of heterogeneous group might have different backgrounds and expectations, and cultural differences can make the culture change even more difficult.

To realise a culture change, lessons can be drawn from the Concerns Based Adoption Model (CBAM)[2] that showcases the need for learning using concerns [30]. According to this model, there are seven stages of concern: from not being concerned at all—"I think I heard something about it, but I'm too busy right now with other priorities to be concerned about it."—to refocusing—"I have some ideas about something that would work even better.", and all the other stages in between. The stage of concern an organisation and its members are in influences the attitude and behaviour of group members towards change. It is also important to consider the incentive for the organisation to act and create a culture change. For example, we learn that only if the members agree that (1) the current situation is a serious issue for the organisation which should be addressed, and (2) the organisation is able to realise the necessary change, and it will lead to visible benefits, then a culture change can then be realised [63].

---

[2] See https://sedl.org/cbam/.

There can be various reasons for an organisation to realise that a change is necessary. This may be external factors, such as the university losing grants due to a lack of women participating in the projects, the realisation that scientific results are valid only for the male population, or the high demands from industry for more trained computer scientists, which cannot be filled by men only.

The realisation could also come from organisational changes or developments, such as: two institutes or groups being merged; having a new leadership or management body; the presence of social pressure (root out sexism, ageism, racism, or intolerance); new practices from human resources; technological changes (where woman are equivalent or more suitable to do some tasks), or simply a change of generations.

Finally, it must be understood that culture as such is a feeling and cannot be changed directly. However, you can change your values, which leads to a necessity to change habits and behaviour. It is necessary to point out and praise small steps, take time for changes to take root, and be ready for setbacks. To encourage people to accept the changes, management should explicitly support the need for a change in culture.

11.3.1.2 Concrete Actions to Implement a Culture Change

The first step to working towards a culture change is to raise awareness of the problems and the need for a culture change among current employees and leaders. This can be achieved by organising training or open table sessions to talk about unconscious biases, and the challenges that women face, such as glass ceilings, sticky floors, etc., but also about sexism, ageism, racism, or intolerance. These sessions should be aimed at everybody in the department and participation should be mandatory. The main goal of such sessions initially should be to create awareness and solutions do not have to be found immediately. There should be an open and safe atmosphere, where all participants feel they can share their personal experiences. Ideally, such sessions are led by somebody from outside the organisation, who can handle negative reactions and ensure that an open and safe atmosphere is maintained.

Additionally, the members of the department should learn about the literature that shows the value of diversity, not only on the benefits of leadership diversity but also the evidence that diverse teams perform better, etc. Given that we are working in academic organisations, this information should be given with a sound scientific basis.

Once the majority of (or all) the members of your organisation have become aware of why a culture change is necessary, the next step is to develop concrete actions that can be taken to improve the situation. First of all, this requires a more concrete understanding of what are the organisational issues that hinder women (and other minoritised employees) in their development. This should be an organisation-wide action, where all the different stakeholders are involved (management, the human resources department, female/and minoritised employees, and others). All stakeholders can mention possible problems they have encountered and an open discussion about this should be held. If the issues are clear, an action plan can be developed to address the concrete problems. This can be a change in policies, redefining evaluation criteria, changes in the organisational structure, etc.

One action can be to improve the communication, both internally and publicly, about the internal organisation, and to make sure that this communication explicitly demonstrates the inclusive values of the organisation. Concrete suggestions on how this can be carried out include:

- Set a standard that the organisation's newsletters and websites show for example a 50% female presence;
- Identify female role models (with a diverse background), and showcase the importance of their (scientific) contributions (see e.g., https://www.aliceandeve.nl/ and [34] for an example of how the contributions of women in computer science can be celebrated).
- Have management explicitly make a statement about the importance of diversity and inclusion, which is communicated both internally and externally (e.g., on the organisation's website);
- Have the organisation explicitly contribute to celebration days, such as International Women's Day.

Another field of action is to offer *training* to make all employees aware of challenges related to diversity and inclusion, such as *active bystander training*,[3] diversity proof selection,[4] unconscious bias training, etc. [48]. Participation in these training programs should be mandatory, and the managers should also take part in those training themselves. New employees should also have an opportunity to take part in such training, i.e., this should be a continuous process, not a single moment of action.

The organisation should also promote the empowerment of women by explicitly acknowledging their contributions, and providing support wherever needed. A concrete way to provide support is to establish an ambassador's program, whose members can be ambassadors for the women in the organisation. Women in the organisation should also be encouraged to get together and exchange experiences, for example, by creating a women's leadership club where they can share best practices. The organisation of such activities must be actively supported, e.g., by providing secretarial support, explicitly counting it as an organisational task, and encouraging new female staff to join such meetings. Finally, it is important to pay attention to how women are treated in the organisation and to ensure that they are not overloaded with administrative tasks. This is always a challenge: if the organisation has small numbers of women, then they are invited to sit on many/every

---

[3] *Active bystander training*: a training that helps to challenge antisocial behaviour at work.

[4] *Diversity proof selection*: a training that helps to make interactions and decision-making at the workplace occur in a neutral and objective manner (gender, question formulations, power relations, examples from practice, soft skills).

committee to ensure the diversity of the committee. This results in women carrying a disproportionate burden, leaving them with less time to attend to their research. It is important to pay attention to this and ensure that somebody supports the women to identify which organisational tasks are beneficial to them so that they can make a choice about which tasks to take on while also keeping time for activities such as research and education. Finally, setting up a mentoring program, as described above, is one of the actions that can be developed as part of the culture change.

Another point where concrete actions can be taken is in recruitment and promotion procedures [11, 33]. First of all, it is important to ensure that enough women apply. This can be done by explicitly encouraging women—or other minorities—to apply. A concrete measure is to ask every member of the hiring committee to suggest some names of suitable female candidates, and then ask them to contact them. Identifying potential female candidates is best handled as a long-term process, so it is also important to scout potential candidates for the years to come (identify the pipeline). Further, the conditions for the application can be made such that women feel encouraged to apply. Allow e.g., a minimum of three months for applications to be submitted, as reaching potential women for the position takes more time. In the vacancy text, avoid a long list of specific requirements, but rather describe openly and globally what you are looking for, to avoid that women do not apply because they do not fulfil all requirements listed. During the hiring process, the hiring committees should be trained to avoid biases. Hiring committees should always have a balanced representation of women and men and should avoid scenarios where women are a small minority within the committee.

Similar advice applies to the promotion process [33]. The goals for promotion should be clear and transparent: all members of staff should be aware of them, and the organisation should facilitate discussions about career ambitions regularly. If a committee decides about a promotion, this committee again should be trained about their biases. Moreover, within the organisation, there should be an open discussion about the recognition and rewards policies: traditionally, academics get promotions based on publications, citations, and projects. However, organisations should also value other achievements such as collaborations, team science, and industrial or societal impact. Educational achievements should be explicitly considered, as should service, namely for mentoring students and/or peers. In the end, the decision on whether to promote somebody should be a balanced decision based on all these factors. Career gaps should be taken into account: whether somebody has been working for a while in an industry, or took a care leave for a certain period, career gaps should be taken into account when evaluating the person and should never be used against them.

Culture change also requires that the *daily practices* of the organisation become inclusive. The organisation should provide possibilities for flexible working hours and acknowledge that, in particular for working parents with small children, as sometimes last-minute flexibility is needed. The working environment should be adapted to the needs of diverse people (for example, a female member of staff might need a quiet place for breastfeeding/pumping, childcare facilities, parental and care leave). Working and meeting hours should be aligned with, for example, school hours, and people should never be expected to work during evenings or weekends.

11.3.2 Setting up a Career Development Program

Women can benefit from career development programs at all stages of their careers. For the sake of structure, we divide an academic career into three stages: (1) a training stage (graduate students and postdoctoral fellows); (2) an early-career stage (assistant professors, lecturers, etc.); and (3) a mid-to-late career stage which starts after getting the first promotion in academia. We provide recommendations that are relevant for all three career stages and those specific to key career junctures.

11.3.2.1 To Be or Not To Be an Academic

Over two decades ago, the [64] stated that fewer than 1% of PhD students become professors, and while that 1% has increased, studies (e.g., [40]) found that women PhDs have lower chances of securing academic positions than men in every field.

While some of these students may have never had the intention to pursue an academic career, this statistic is still very alarming. In informatics, academic institutions are in fierce competition to recruit and retain the best and brightest due to the abundance of less competitive and more lucrative alternative career opportunities in industry. Below are some initiatives that academic institutions can adopt to inspire female PhD students to pursue a career in academia:

- *Organise events to encourage female PhD students to become professors.* This may include seminars that showcase faculty members who chose academia over industry and/or informational interviews and job shadowing opportunities. These events should highlight the unique opportunities available in academia such as sabbaticals, industry collaborations, startups, intellectual freedom, flexible schedules, work-life balance, meaning, long-term stability particularly after tenure, and staying at the forefront of a field.
- *Plan regular informal get-together meetings with successful female academics* to help dissipate some of the concerns about academic careers, in particular the additional responsibility, uncertainty and risk of attracting grants, running a lab, getting tenure, etc. Promote a transparent communication that highlights that academic success does not come as a series of constant successes, but that the road may have setbacks and failures too, e.g. CV of failure [71].
- *Support students to seek varied opportunities* such as serving as a teaching assistant, participating in conference organisation and embarking on internships in industrial research labs. This will help them get, early on, a glimpse of the different possibilities after the Ph.D. and start building their network for future collaborations.

- *Organise hands-on training sessions* to help students learn how to write and publish academic papers, communicate articulately, navigate the relationship with supervisors, and teach effectively, etc.

11.3.2.2 A Foot in the Door

Entry jobs in academia are diverse and can vary depending on the geography, the institution, the economic outlook, and the individual's interest [56]. For example, some Ph.D. holders land their first assistant professor position right after graduation, while others need to first hold one or more postdoctoral positions. Some choose to embark on a teaching-only or research-only career while others prefer a combination of both. The first position is typically on a fixed-term contract, but it can also be on a permanent contract. Compared to senior faculty, early-career faculty are at a higher risk of leaving the pipeline [32]. Below, is a list of recommendations [70] that can help academic institutions retain and nurture early-career faculty.

- *Increase support for research and teaching* through internal grants/funds to purchase equipment, books, pay for travel and hire research/teaching assistants and lab technicians, pedagogical support from the institution's teaching centre or senior faculty, and a reduction of the teaching/service workload for junior faculty.
- *Establish early-career grant development programs* that match junior faculty with senior faculty who have similar research interests, from different institutions. The Excellence in Africa (EXAF) initiative is a great example [21].
- *Put a fair and transparent promotion process* in place that clarifies the promotion criteria, measures of success, and timeline while maintaining enough flexibility to evaluate faculty work from different disciplines. Additionally, regular feedback should be provided to early-stage faculty to help them identify strengths and potential opportunities for improvement. While *strategic ambiguity* [13] remains a common flaw in promotion processes within academia, particularly when promotion concerns tenure, minorities, including women, tend to be more affected by this because they do not have access to the 'hidden rules' located in informal social networks.

11.3.2.3 Success Comes in Different Forms

Although some women choose to follow the conventional lock-step career track, moving from continuous full-time education to continuous full-time work, many find this progression to be incompatible with their personal choices [9], and opt instead for career trajectories that are protean [28, 29], i.e. they are governed by individual rather than organisational choices, and boundaryless [37], i.e. going beyond the boundaries of a single organisation.

However, most academic institutions still adopt the lock-step career model as a yardstick for advancement and promotion [79] which contributes heavily to the leaky pipeline. To limit this leakage, higher education institutions need to support women in advancing according to their chosen career trajectory while adopting a more holistic approach to the measurement of success which can be a continuum in the professorship, taking on leadership positions in the institution and/or engaging in an entrepreneurship endeavour. In the following, we outline some specific actions that organisations and/or scholars can undertake to support mid-level career development.

- *Help women overcome the even more ambiguous and hidden rules*, as they strive to progress to professorship [38], by supporting them in increasing their international visibility and impact, championing their applications to leadership positions within professional associations and inviting them to speak at high-profile conferences.
- *Encourage women who choose to become senior academic leaders* such as dean, provost or president, to build/hone the key competencies for effective academic leadership, while being careful to do so when outlooks are positive and not only during shaky organisational situations [60]. These can be grouped into social skills (e.g., communicate effectively, be a team player, accept criticism), personal capabilities (e.g. show empathy and patience, be decisive and fair, accept change, be well-organised, have a vision, know how to negotiate) and knowledge of academia (e.g. be a successful scholar, know the institution and how to navigate its politics) [25]. These competencies can be obtained with formal (e.g. mentoring and training) or informal activities (e.g. learning-by doing, networking, advice from experienced colleagues).
- *Assist women who are interested in becoming academic entrepreneurs*, i.e. create a spin-off out of their research results or launch a consulting business in their areas of expertise by providing the opportunities and activities that increase their self-efficacy, motivation, access to financing, mentoring and networking [58]. For instance, encourage women to participate in academic-industry research centres and partnerships, support them in expanding heterophilous social networks, and provide them with entrepreneurship education and mastery experiences (experiences where an individual accomplishes a goal [6]) that can help them acquire key entrepreneurship competencies in a safe environment, and match them with senior academic entrepreneurs that can provide positive persuasion and encouragement.

11.3.2.4 Career-Development Recommendations Relevant at Any Career Stage

Students, faculty and institutions alike benefit when the work environment is conducive to creativity and knowledge creation. We have summarised below some key recommendations that can support and sustain women at every stage of their careers in academia.

- *Create a safe and fair environment in academia*, which includes establishing an Ombuds Office.[5] This Office helps mediate work-related conflicts in confidentiality and may implement implicit bias training programs targeted towards individuals involved in hiring and promotion committees, to help them assess their own biases, and provide them with research-based evidence, going beyond the ethical and moral grounds, that can help them dismantle common-held stereotypes [46].
- *Establish policies and programs that support work-life balance* to allow flexible work arrangements (e.g., part-time work, flexible work hours), paid and unpaid leaves of absence for personal or family reasons, stop-the-clock options [8], and quality childcare/elderly care options. It is critical that these programs support women at all stages in their careers as women continue to play a major role in caregiving. Be aware that the nature of the responsibilities can change from caring for young children to caring for instance for elderly parents or adult children with special needs [61]. It is also of paramount importance to ensure fairness and alleviate the fear factor [73] that both faculty and institutions can experience about effectively applying these policies, in particular with regards to losing academic credibility.
- *Support women to engage career development opportunities* such as networking events (e.g. the Grace Hopper Conference [24], mentoring/sponsoring activities, membership in professional associations, and training programs that help acquire critical non-technical skills such as time management, project management, grant writing and negotiation.

11.3.3 Setting Up a Mentoring Program

This section provides an overview of steps that may be taken when setting up a mentoring program,[6] providing insight on how to address different mentoring needs, create a pool of mentors, match mentors and mentees, and on the format and frequency of the meetings. The section then moves on to identify ways to sustain and monitor progress.

---

[5] The Ombuds Office idea was proposed originally in the Scandinavian countries to protect citizens against arbitrary and wrongful governmental actions. It has the authority to file complaints, undertake judicial action and propose reforms [42].

[6] For a literature review on aspects to keep in mind when creating mentoring programs for supporting women, please refer to the chapter titled "Mentoring as a Tool for Better Gender Diversity in Informatics" by Szlavi et al. in this handbook.

11.3.3.1 Getting Started

The first step in defining the goals of the program is to establish the purpose of the mentoring, whether it be retaining, career progression, or supporting the transition to another field or career. Setting up a mentoring program can be a rewarding and impactful initiative. Here are some steps to help you get started:

1. Define your objectives: Determine the purpose and goals of your mentoring program. Clarify the intended outcomes, such as skill development, career advancement, retaining talent, or professional or personal growth.

> *"During the Ph.D., interviewees looked to their supervisors for guidance in academic writing and thinking, networking, and general 'socialization in the discipline'."* [68]
>
> *"Scholarly independence, educational skills, and the development of constructive professional relationships within the institution and beyond are crucial for career development of junior faculty."* [14, 81]
>
> *"Skill development is crucial when moving from PhD to Professor, and to become "fully functioning members of the scientific community" will require one to "able to prepare grant applications, review manuscripts, speak at conferences and engage with scientific administrators in a constructive manner (...), giving them all the skills necessary to carve out their own niches in the academic world."* [44]

2. Identify the participants: Decide who will be involved in the program. You can do this by surveying your colleagues to see (a) who is interested; and (b) what they need (support in publishing, applying for funding, promotion, etc.). Remember to consider the specific needs and preferences of both the mentors and mentees.
3. Recruit mentors: Reach out to potential mentors who possess the skills, knowledge, and experience relevant to the program's objectives. Consider creating an application process to evaluate their qualifications and commitment. Engage colleagues within or outside the University (current or emeritus) based on their experience and skills (promotion, networking, publishing etc.). Consider how to make mentoring attractive to your colleagues, especially to mentors—formal recognition of the work, award of a small amount of money, access to a research fund, or time *in lieu* (buy out) of other duties e.g. reduced load of admin or teaching etc. Mentors can benefit also from a training process aimed at helping them to interact productively with the mentees, setting clear goals and expectations on both sides, managing emotions properly, practising active

listening, etc. This kind of training is usually offered by coaching experts and contributes to lessening the initial fears of mentors who might perceive mentoring as a stressful process.

> *"When establishing a mentoring network, 'networking diversity' – i.e. mentors from diverse backgrounds – and 'networking range'– i.e. the extent to which mentors, 'originate from different contexts or social origins' – should be ensured."*
>
> [18]

4. Recruit mentees: Attract mentees who are interested in receiving guidance and support. Promote the program through internal communications. Clearly communicate the benefits, obligations and expectations of being a mentee.
5. Pair mentors and mentees: Match mentors and mentees based on their goals, interests, and compatibility. Consider their personalities, areas of expertise and the desired duration of the mentoring relationship. Decisions such as 'should the mentor come from the same discipline as the mentee'; 'should the mentor be the same gender as the mentee'; 'should the mentor be internal or external to the university' should be decided on a 'case by case' basis, and on the needs of the mentee. Provide an opportunity for mentors and mentees to meet and establish rapport before committing to the partnership. Be creative—the mentor:mentee can be individuals or a group, depending on the needs and preferences of all. A mechanism must be in place to ensure that all participants are safe, and all parties have an opt-out option, with a safe pathway to exit if the relationship does not work.

> *"The matching process is based on a set of common characteristics or similar interests and relevant experience."*
>
> [81]
>
> *"It is worth considering matching female mentees with female mentors, as studies have noted that the male style of mentoring may "not fit the socialization and styles of most women and their orientation to integration rather than separation, interdependence rather than either dependence or independence and collaborative rather than competitive task engagement."*
>
> [74]
>
> *"In matching mentors and mentees, mentor profiles can also be made available to be viewed by prospective mentees, who may indicate their preferences and they are then matched to one accordingly."*
>
> [7]

6. Establish guidelines: Develop a framework for the mentoring program, including guidelines, expectations, and timelines. Define the frequency and duration of meetings, communication methods, and confidentiality agreements. Ensure that both mentors and mentees are aware of their roles and responsibilities.

> *"Mentees consider frequent regularly scheduled, one-on-one, confidential time with their mentors important to establish a positive and fruitful collaboration, with a study showing that the mentees prefer in-person meetings once a month."*
>
> [7]
>
> *"Online mentoring can facilitate finding more suitable mentors. However, on-site mentoring should be given priority considering the importance of establishing local mentors from the home institution as they can provide "critical input into sharing heuristic knowledge needed for successfully navigating a particular place or work environment."*
>
> [75, 80]
>
> *"It is advisable to have a Code of Ethics such as the one developed by The European Mentoring & Coaching Council."*
>
> [3]

11.3.3.2 Sustaining the Program and Managing Progress

Once the groundwork for your mentoring program is laid out and the initial setup is complete, the focus shifts towards maintaining its momentum and ensuring its effectiveness. This phase involves establishing clear guidelines, providing ongoing support and resources, monitoring the progress of mentoring relationships, and making necessary adjustments to optimise outcomes. The following outline some activities that could be considered in this scope:

1. Provide training and resources: Offer training sessions or workshops for mentors to enhance their mentoring skills. Provide resources such as templates, toolkits, or recommended reading materials. Encourage mentors to share their expertise and knowledge effectively.
2. Monitor progress and provide support: It is crucial to maintain a regular 'check-in' with mentors and mentees to assess the progress of their mentoring relationships. Address any challenges or concerns that may arise. Offer ongoing support, guidance and resources to ensure the success of the program.

3. Evaluate and adjust: Periodically evaluate the effectiveness of the mentoring program. Gather feedback from mentors and mentees through surveys or interviews. Use this information to make necessary adjustments, improve the program, and align it with the evolving needs of participants.
4. Recognise and celebrate achievements: Acknowledge the efforts and accomplishments of both mentors and mentees. Celebrate milestones, success stories and positive outcomes to motivate and inspire others to participate in the program.

Setting up a mentoring program requires careful planning, effective communication, and ongoing commitment. It is crucial to have sufficient resources (human, financial, etc.) if you are planning a program.

11.4 Conclusion

This chapter highlights the multiple challenges and barriers, many of the invisible, that are still being faced by women who are trying to develop their careers in academia. It also offers actionable strategies that can be useful for young and senior academics, especially those in managerial positions who can lead a culture change. Women are not wrong, and they do not need to be fixed. It is the culture of the institution that has to be transformed to promote inclusivity and diversity, in keeping with formal obligations outlined in EU treaties and UN recommendations, and also for the benefits that they bring to research, innovation, and education. It is essential to achieve a managerial acknowledgement of the need for change and active support for women's career development.

Strategies for fostering this cultural shift include initiatives focused on career development and mentoring. Career development programs tailored to women in academia are essential to support and guide transitions across different career stages. By implementing concrete actions, academic institutions can create a more inclusive environment conducive to the success and advancement of women in academia. Additionally, setting up mentoring programs is a valuable tool for supporting women's professional and personal development. This chapter outlines steps to establish and sustain effective mentoring programs.

However, the first step in achieving this culture change is to raise awareness of an existing problem that permeates the whole organisation to avoid negative perceptions about the potential strategies to apply. Diversity has to be perceived by the whole organisation or institution neither as an imposition nor as a trend but as a question of social justice and a valuable asset for all. Overall, achieving a culture change within academic organisations requires a multifaceted approach and sustained commitment and investment from all stakeholders.

In this polarised society, the necessary debate on diversity, inclusion and equity is often disregarded by some members of our institutions as being aligned with certain political currents and not corresponding to a social need. To deal with misinformation and unfounded negative attitudes, it is necessary to integrate diversity into the computer science and engineering curriculum. The value of diversity in order to be fairer, more effective, efficient, or productive in our work has to be perceived as soon as possible. Our students will be the best ambassadors for diversity and are the ones who will be putting it into practice and demanding it very shortly.

References

1. (UNDP), United Nations Development Programme (2020a). *2020 Gender Social Norms Index (GSNI)*. New York.
2. (UNDP) (2020b). *Tackling Social Norms: A Game Changer for Gender Inequalities*. Gender Social Norms Index (GSNI).
3. Association for Coaching and EMCC (2021). *Global Code of Ethics*. URL: https://www.associationforcoaching.com/page/AboutCodeEthics.
4. Auditors, European Court Of (2021). *Special Report 10/2021: Gender mainstreaming in the EU budget: time to turn words into action*. URL: https://www.eca.europa.eu/en/Pages/DocItem.aspx?did=58678.
5. Babcock, Linda and Sara Laschever (2009). *Women Don't Ask: The High Cost of Avoiding Negotiation–and Positive Strategies for Change*. Princeton University Press.
6. Bandura, Albert, William H. Freeman, and Richard Lightsey (1999). *Self-efficacy: The exercise of control*.
7. Bean, Nadine M., Lisa Lucas, and Lauri L. Hyers (2014). "Mentoring in higher education should be the norm to assure success: Lessons learned from the faculty mentoring program, West Chester University, 2008–2011". In: *Mentoring & Tutoring: Partnership in Learning* 22.1, pp. 56–73. DOI: https://doi.org/10.1080/13611267.2014.882606.
8. Berg, Maggie and Barbara K. Seeber (2018). *The Slow Professor: Challenging the Culture of Speed in the Academy*. University of Toronto Press.
9. Bian, Xinyi and Jia Wang (July 2019). "Women's career interruptions: an integrative review". In: *European Journal of Training and Development* ahead-of-print. DOI: https://doi.org/10.1108/EJTD-03-2019-0040.
10. Brown, Jennifer V. E. et al. (2020). "From the sticky floor to the glass ceiling and everything in between: protocol for a systematic review of barriers and facilitators to clinical academic careers and interventions to address these, with a focus on gender inequality". In: *Systematic reviews* 9, pp. 1–7. DOI: https://doi.org/10.1186/s13643-020-1286-z.
11. Cardel, Michelle et al. (2020). "Turning chutes into ladders for women faculty: A review and roadmap for equity in academia". In: *Journal of Women's Health* 29 (5), pp. 721–733. DOI: https://doi.org/10.1089/jwh.2019.8027.
12. Casad, Betsy J. et al. (2021). "Gender inequality in academia: Problems and solutions for women faculty in STEM". In: *Journal of Neuroscience Research* 99, pp. 13–23. DOI: https://doi.org/10.1002/jnr.24631.
13. Cate, Leandra, La Wanda W. M. Ward, and Karly S. Ford (Oct. 2022). "Strategic Ambiguity: How Pre-Tenure Faculty Negotiate the Hidden Rules of Academia". English (US). In: *Innovative Higher Education* 47.5, pp. 795–812. ISSN: 0742-5627. DOI: https://doi.org/10.1007/s10755-022-09604-x.
14. Chao, Georgia T., Patm Walz, and Philip D. Gardner (1992). "Formal and informal mentorships: A comparison of mentoring functions and contrast with nonmentored counterparts". In: *Personnel psychology* 45.3, pp. 619–636. DOI: https://doi.org/10.1111/j.1744-6570.1992.tb00863.x.
15. Charles, Maria and David B. Grusky (2004). *Occupational Ghettos: The Worldwide Segregation of Women and Men*. Stanford University Press.

16. Chen, Z. (2023). "Ethics and discrimination in artificial intelligence-enabled recruitment practices". In: *Humanities and Social Sciences Communications* 10, p. 567. DOI: https://doi.org/10.1057/s41599-023-02079-x.
17. Commission, European (2021). *She Figures 2021: Gender in Research and Innovation: Statistics and Indicators*. Publications Office of the European Union, p. 190.
18. Dobrow, Shoshana R. and Monica C. Higgins (2005). "Developmental networks and professional identity: A longitudinal study". In: *Career Development International* 10.6/7, pp. 567–583. DOI: https://doi.org/10.1108/13620430510620629.
19. Draude, Claude (2023). "Working with Diversity in Informatics". In: *Hochschuldidaktik Informatik HDI 2021 (Commentarii informaticae didacticae)* 13, pp. 13–33. DOI: https://doi.org/10.25932/publishup-61378.
20. Ely, Robin J. and David A. Thomas (2020). "Getting Serious About Diversity: Enough Already with the Business Case". In: *Harvard Business Review* 98 (6), pp. 114–122.
21. *EPFL Excellence in Africa Annual Report* (2021).
22. Gasser, Courtney E. and Katharine S. Shaffer (2014). "Career Development of Women in Academia: Traversing the Leaky Pipeline". In: 4, pp. 332–352. DOI: https://doi.org/10.15241/ceg.4.4.332.
23. Goulden, Marc, Mary Ann Mason, and Karie Frasch (2011). "Keeping Women in the Science Pipeline". In: *The ANNALS of the American Academy of Political and Social Science* 638.1, pp. 141–162. DOI: https://doi.org/10.1177/0002716211416925.
24. *Grace Hopper Celebration* (2023). https://ghc.anitab.org/.
25. Grajfoner, Dasha, Ce´line Rojon, and Farjam Eshraghian (2022). "Academic leaders: In-role perceptions and developmental approaches". In: *Educational Management Administration & Leadership*, p. 17411432221095957. DOI: https://doi.org/10.1177/17411432221095957.
26. Greenhaus, Jeffrey H. and Gerard A. Callanan (2006). *Encyclopedia of Career Development*. Vol. 1. Sage.
27. Guerrier, Christine (2004). "Le mentorat appliqué au monde du travail: analyse québécoise et canadienne". In: *Carriérologie* 9.3-4, pp. 519–530.
28. Hall, Douglas T (1996). "Protean Careers of the 21st Century". In: *The Academy of Management Executive (1993-2005)* 10.4, pp. 8–16.
29. – (2004). "The protean career: A quarter-century journey". In: *Journal of Vocational Behavior* 65.1, pp. 1–13. ISSN: 0001-8791. DOI: https://doi.org/10.1016/j.jvb.2003.10.006. URL: https://www.sciencedirect.com/science/article/pii/S0001879103001647.
30. Hall, Gene E. and Shirley M. Hord (2015). *Implementing Change: Patterns, Principles and Potholes*. 4th. Pearson.
31. Hardey, Michael (2019). "Women's Leadership and Gendered Experiences in Tech Cities". In: *Gender in Management: An International Journal* 34.3, pp. 188–199. DOI: https://doi.org/10.1108/GM-05-2018-0048.
32. Hollywood, Amelia et al. (2020). "'Overwhelmed at first': the experience of career development in early career academics". In: *Journal of Further and Higher Education* 44.7, pp. 998–1012. DOI: https://doi.org/10.1080/0309877X.2019.1636213.
33. Huisman, Marieke and Alexander Serebrenik (2021). *Women in Dutch Computer Science: Best Practices for Recruitment, Onboarding and Promotion*.
34. Huizen, Johannes Cornelis van et al. (2020). "Alice and Eve: a celebration of women in computer science". In: *Engaging, Engineering, Education: Book of Abstracts, SEFI 48th Annual Conference*.
35. Ibarra, Herminia, Nancy M Carter, and Christine Silva (2010). "Why Men Still Get More Promotions Than Women". In: *Harvard Business Review* 88.9, pp. 80–126.
36. Ibarra, Herminia, Robin Ely, and Deborah Kolb (2013). "Women Rising: The Unseen Barriers". In: *Harvard Business Review* 91.9, pp. 60–66.
37. Inkson, Kerr et al. (2012). "Boundaryless Careers: Bringing Back Boundaries". In: *Organization studies* 33.3, pp. 323–340. DOI: https://doi.org/10.1177/0170840611435600.

38. June, Audrey Williams (2016). "The uncertain path to full professor". In: *The Chronicle of Higher Education*.
39. Kanter, Rosabeth Moss (1977). *Men and Women of the Corporation*. Basic Books.
40. Kim, Lauren et al. (2022). "Gendered knowledge in fields and academic careers". In: *Research Policy* 51.1, p. 104411. DOI: https://doi.org/10.1016/j.respol.2021.104411.
41. Kübler-Ross, Elisabeth (1969). *On Death and Dying*. Routledge.
42. Kutner, Luis (1968). "Habeas Scholastica: An Ombudsman for Academic Due Process-A Proposal". In: *U. Miami L. Rev.* 23, p. 107. URL: https://repository.law.miami.edu/umlr/vol23/iss1/6.
43. Laursen, Sandra and Ann E. Austin (2020). *Building gender equity in the academy: Institutional strategies for change*. Johns Hopkins University Press.
44. Lee, Adrian, Carina Dennis, and Philip Campbell (2007). "Nature's guide for mentors". In: *Nature* 447.7146, pp. 791–797. DOI: https://doi.org/10.1038/447791a.
45. Liff, Sonia and Ivy Cameron (1997). "Changing Equality Cultures to Move Beyond 'Women's Problems'". In: *Gender, Work & Organization* 4 (1), pp. 35–46. DOI: https://doi.org/10.1111/1468-0432.00022.
46. Liu, Sin-Ning C., Stephanie E. V. Brown, and Isaac E. Sabat (2019). "Patching the "Leaky Pipeline": Interventions for Women of Color Faculty in STEM Academia". In: *Archives of Scientific Psychology* 7.1, pp. 32–39. DOI: https://doi.org/10.1037/arc0000062.
47. Llorens, Ana et al. (2021). "Gender bias in academia: A lifetime problem that needs solutions". In: *Neuron* 109.13, pp. 2047–2074.
48. Llorens, Anaïs et al. (2021). "Gender bias in academia: A lifetime problem that needs solutions". In: *Neuron* 109.13, pp. 2047–2074. ISSN: 0896-6273. DOI: https://doi.org/10.1016/j.neuron.2021.06.002.
49. London, Manuel (1993). "Relationships between career motivation, empowerment and support for career development". In: *Journal of Occupational and Organizational Psychology* 66.1, pp. 55–69. DOI: https://doi.org/10.1111/j.2044-8325.1993.tb00516.x.
50. Megginson, David, David Clutterbuck, and Bob Garvey (2006). *Mentoring in action: A practical guide for managers*. Kogan Page Publishers.
51. Meschitti, Viviana and Helen Lawton Smith (2017). "Does Mentoring Make a Difference for Women Academics? Evidence from the Literature and a Guide for Future Research". In: *Journal of Research in Gender Studies* 7.1, pp. 166–199. DOI: https://doi.org/10.22381/JRGS7120176.
52. Moorcroft, Melanie and Mary Ann Crick (2014). *A Guide to Mentoring*. The University of Auckland.
53. Morrison, Ann M., Randall P. White, and Ellen Van Velsor (1987). *Breaking the Glass Ceiling: Can Women Reach the Top of America's Largest Corporations?* Addison-Wesley.
54. Moss-Racusin, Corinne A. et al. (2012). "Science faculty's subtle gender biases favor male students". In: *Proceedings of the National Academy of Sciences* 109.41, pp. 16474–16479. DOI: https://doi.org/10.1073/pnas.1211286109.
55. Mullen, Carol A (2009). "Re-Imagining the Human Dimension of Mentoring: A Framework for Research Administration and the Academy". In: *Journal of research administration* 40.1, pp. 10–31.
56. Musselin, Christine (2009). *The market for academics*. Routledge.
57. O'Connell, Christine and Merryn McKinnon (2021). "Perceptions of barriers to career progression for academic women in STEM". In: *Societies* 11.2, p. 27. DOI: https://doi.org/10.3390/soc11020027.
58. Parker, Marla et al. (2017). "Barriers to academic entrepreneurship among women: a review of the constituent literatures". In: Edward Elgar Publishing. ISBN: 9781785364730. DOI: https://doi.org/10.4337/9781785364747.00010.
59. Perez, Caroline Criado (2022). *Invisible Women: Exposing Data Bias in a World Designed for Men*.

60. Peterson, Helen (2016). "Is managing academics "women's work"? Exploring the glass cliff in higher education management". In: *Educational Management Administration & Leadership* 44.1, pp. 112–127. DOI: https://doi.org/10.1177/1741143214563897.
61. Philipsen, Maike et al. (2017). "Academic womanhood across career stages: a work-in-life perspective on what was, is, and could be". In: *Community, Work & Family* 20.5, pp. 623–644. DOI: https://doi.org/10.1080/13668803.2017.1378619.
62. Ragins, Belle Rose and Kathy E Kram (2007). *The handbook of mentoring at work: Theory, research, and practice*. Sage Publications.
63. Rogers, Ronald W. (1975). "Protection motivation theory of fear appeals and attitude change". In: *The Journal of Psychology* 91 (1), pp. 93–114. DOI: https://doi.org/10.1080/00223980.1975.9915803.
64. Royal Society Great Britain (2010). *The scientific century: securing our future prosperity*.
65. Ryan, Michelle K. and S. Alexander Haslam (2005). "The Glass Cliff: Evidence that Women are Over-Represented in Precarious Leadership Positions". In: *British Journal of Management* 16.2, pp. 81–90. DOI: https://doi.org/10.1111/j.1467-8551.2005.00433.x.
66. Schiebinger, L. (1999). *Has Feminism Changed Science?* Harvard University Press.
67. Seierstad, Cathrine and Tore Opsahl (2011). "For the few not the many? The effects of affirmative action on presence, prominence, and social capital of women directors in Norway". In: *Scandinavian Journal of Management* 27.1, pp. 44–54. DOI: https://doi.org/10.1016/j.scaman.2010.10.002.
68. Shaik, Farah Jeelani, Hele'ne Adams, and Caroline Vincke (2016). "Gender sensitive mentoring programme in Academia: a design process". In: *Garcia working papers*.
69. Smit, Sven et al. (2022). *Securing Europe's Competitiveness: Addressing Its Technology Gap*. URL: https://www.mckinsey.com/capabilities/strategy-and-corporate-finance/our-insights/securing-europes-competitiveness-addressing-its-technology-gap.
70. Sorcinelli, Mary Deane and Deborah A. Billings (1992). "The Career Development of Pretenure Faculty: An Institutional Study." In.
71. Stefan, Melanie (2010). "A CV of failures". In: *Nature* 468.7322, pp. 467–467. DOI: https://doi.org/10.1038/nj7322-467a.
72. Victoria University of Wellington (2023). *Alumni as Mentors Programme, Careers and Employment*. https://www.wgtn.ac.nz/careers/employment/alumni-as-mentors. Accessed: 2023-05-29.
73. Ward, Kelly and Lisa Wolf-Wendel (2004). "Fear Factor: How Safe Is It to Make Time for Family?" In: *Academe* 90.6, pp. 28–31. DOI: https://doi.org/10.2307/40252703.
74. Whittaker, Joseph A. and Beronda L. Montgomery (2012). "Cultivating diversity and competency in STEM: Challenges and remedies for removing virtual barriers to constructing diverse higher education communities of success". In: *Journal of Undergraduate Neuroscience Education* 11.1, A44–A51.
75. Whittaker, Joseph A., Beronda L. Montgomery, and Veronica G. Martinez-Acosta (2015). "Retention of underrepresented minority faculty: strategic initiatives for institutional value proposition based on perspectives from a range of academic institutions". In: *Journal of Undergraduate Neuroscience Education* 13.3, A136.
76. Williams, Christine L (1992). "The glass escalator: Hidden advantages for men in the "female" professions". In: *Social problems* 39.3, pp. 253–267. DOI: https://doi.org/10.2307/3096961.
77. Wingrove-Haugland, Erik and Jillian McLeod (2021). "Not "Minority" but "Minoritized"". In: *Teaching Ethics* 21.1, p. 1. ISSN: 1544-4031. DOI: https://doi.org/10.5840/tej20221799.
78. Woodhams, Carol, Grzegorz Trojanowski, and Krystal Wilkinson (2022). "Merit sticks to men: gender pay gaps and (In) equality at UK Russell Group Universities". In: *Sex Roles* 86.9-10, pp. 544–558. DOI: https://doi.org/10.1007/s11199-022-01277-2.
79. Yassinskaya, Natalya et al. (2010). "Mind the Gap: Women in STEM Career Breaks". In: *Journal of Technology Management & Innovation* 5.1, pp. 140–151. DOI: https://doi.org/10.4067/S0718-27242010000100011.

80. Zambrana, Ruth Enid et al. (2015). ""Don't leave us behind" The importance of mentoring for underrepresented minority faculty". In: *American Educational Research Journal* 52.1, pp. 40–72. DOI: https://doi.org/10.3102/0002831214563063.
81. Zellers, Darlene F, Valerie M Howard, and Maureen A Barcic (2008). "Faculty mentoring programs: Reenvisioning rather than reinventing the wheel". In: *Review of educational research* 78.3, pp. 552–588. DOI: https://doi.org/10.3102/0034654308320966.

Open Access This chapter is licensed under the terms of the Creative Commons Attribution 4.0 International License (http://creativecommons.org/licenses/by/4.0/), which permits use, sharing, adaptation, distribution and reproduction in any medium or format, as long as you give appropriate credit to the original author(s) and the source, provide a link to the Creative Commons license and indicate if changes were made.

The images or other third party material in this chapter are included in the chapter's Creative Commons license, unless indicated otherwise in a credit line to the material. If material is not included in the chapter's Creative Commons license and your intended use is not permitted by statutory regulation or exceeds the permitted use, you will need to obtain permission directly from the copyright holder.

Part V
Cooperation with Industry and Society

Chapter 12
Best Practices and Lessons from Academia-Industry Collaboration Initiatives

Alicia Julia Wilson Takaoka ⓘ, Lenuta Alboaie ⓘ, Claudia Maria Cutrupi ⓘ, Andrea D'Angelo ⓘ, Antinisca Di Marco ⓘ, and Jane Hillston ⓘ

> **Bo, Industry Manager.** Based on the resources in this chapter, Bo sees ways in which he can improve the support for female team leaders to enhance their careers and create greater gender equity in his department. He has a better understanding that the problems that he has been facing are common across industry, but that there are well-understood mechanisms for creating an inclusive work environment. He initiates a partnership with a local university to highlight the opportunities available to female undergraduates and create a talent pipeline for his company.

A. J. W. Takaoka (✉)
Erasmus University Rotterdam, Rotterdam, The Netherlands
e-mail: takaoka@rsm.nl

L. Alboaie
Alexandru Ioan Cuza University of Iasi, Iasi, Romania
e-mail: adria@info.uaic.ro

C. M. Cutrupi
Norwegian University of Science and Technology (NTNU), Trondheim, Norway
e-mail: claudia.m.cutrupi@ntnu.no

A. D'Angelo · A. Di Marco
University of L'Aquila, L'Aquila, Italy
e-mail: andrea.dangelo6@graduate.univaq.it; antinisca.dimarco@univaq.it

J. Hillston
University of Edinburgh, Edinburgh, Scotland, UK
e-mail: Jane.Hillston@ed.ac.uk

© The Author(s) 2025
B. Penzenstadler et al. (eds.), *Actions for Gender Balance in Informatics Across Europe*, https://doi.org/10.1007/978-3-031-78432-3_12

> **Nicole, Activist.** The content of the chapter and the further reading that it suggests become a rich source of material for Nicole for her work creating flyers, brochures, and presentations for schools and companies. Based on some of the data discussed in the chapter and associated references, she initiates a targeted campaign for local elected representatives to raise their awareness of the potential benefits, both societal and economic, of getting more women involved in the IT industry.

12.1 Introduction

The importance of the IT industry in Europe is clear as the digital revolution now touches all aspects of our lives, a trend that was only accelerated by the pandemic. This revolution has the potential to bring huge benefits and prosperity, but also threatens to sharpen divides. One way to guard against sections of society being disenfranchised by the change is to ensure that inclusiveness and diversity are key elements of the revolution. However, it has long been recognised that the representation of women within the relevant industries is low, and those that do find themselves working in the sector often feel isolated and unsupported. For example, in a large scale study, 30% of women working in SET jobs in the private sector expressed feelings of isolation within their work environment [29]. In a study of 2008 based in the US Science, Engineering and Technology sector, 40% of women reported that they did not have role models, and nearly half, that they did not have a mentor [28]. As reported by Ashcraft et al. in 2016 [2], lack of support and informal networks has a profound impact on the sense of belonging for women in technical roles, leading to feelings of isolation. Moreover, the women identified the lack of mentorship or sponsorship as a key barrier to retention and advancement.

Sadly, although these problems have been highlighted for over a decade, progress has been slow and women are often faced with a difficult working environment even though it is now more important than ever that they are included in the workforce that is shaping the future of our society. In the paper "The Gender Digital Divide in Europe" [39], the authors discuss the impact of a digital divide across all aspects of women's lives. Urgent action is needed.

On the positive side, the European Commission has set out a five year strategy for gender equality, 2020–2025, which could have far reaching consequences if fully implemented [13]. A range of stakeholders are identified as having a responsibility to change the current situation, and the need for following through on previous proposals. For example, there was a proposal in 2012 relating to gender balance on boards and as non-executive members of company boards. But this was not made into a Directive. In the 2020 strategy, the Commission calls on the European Parliament and the Council of Europe to adopt the proposal for a Directive on this proposal and to adopt measures to improve gender balance at all levels of their own management and leadership positions. The strategy also recognises that there must be a responsibility on member states to implement such a Directive, and to increase their own gender equality in decision-making positions.

In this chapter, we report on previous initiatives, programs, policies, and projects that have been developed in cooperation with industry. The benefits of these can be delivered across the whole pipeline, from encouraging girls in schools to take up the discipline, to career advancement for experienced female professionals. We also consider how governments can support the objectives to improve gender balance in the IT industry, through general initiatives for gender equality in society.

12.1.1 Goal of the Chapter

The goal of this chapter is to highlight some of the initiatives, programs, policies, and projects that create or advance gender balance in informatics across Europe. These include legislation like gender quotas. They also include creating networks, designing family-centered leave policies, and other strategic interventions implemented in the workplace that prioritize the needs of women.

To give greater visibility to such actions, we sought to investigate the landscape of initiatives, programs, policies, and projects in the EUGAIN and adjacent networks to gather examples from university, primary and secondary school, non-governmental organizations, industry, and government.

Specifically we conducted a survey to gather initiatives, programs, policies, and projects that increase gender balance in informatics and ICT fields. The team shared a Google Form through channels that we had access to through organizational connections and the EUGAIN network. They are: Informatics Europe, ACM womENcourage 2023, listservs, direct contact emails. Members of the community were asked to use the survey to share activities from their own context (university, company, region or country), its objectives, actions and outcomes.

12.1.2 Chapter Roadmap

The rest of this chapter presents the survey questions and demographic breakdown of responses. We then present the landscape of policies and best practices for recruiting, promoting, and retaining women in the informatics industry. These include the intersections of university-industry partnerships as well as legislation that impacts women. We then outline best practices for shaping the role of women in informatics in society. These include increased visibility and de-stigmatizing women in tech. Finally, we provide our own commentary and insights from the work we did to support this initiative. We also present ideal next steps for advancing gender balance in informatics.

12.2 Background

12.2.1 The Gender Gap

The gender gap, defined as disparities between men and women in areas such as economic participation, political empowerment, education, and health [24], remains a significant challenge in the informatics industry. Gender quotas, adopted by many countries to correct gender imbalance in legislative and professional domains, have been effective in increasing women's participation across various sectors [23]. However, these quotas alone cannot dismantle the deep-rooted cultural practices, values, and stereotypes that sustain gender discrimination, and serve to highlight the complexity of the issue [11].

Notably, women elected through quotas are often more qualified than the men they displace [4], which demonstrates the potential effectiveness of such measures in promoting capable leadership. However, the persistence of gendered practices continues to impede the full effectiveness of quotas in integrating women into legislative roles and overcoming the barriers posed by the glass ceiling [23].

The gender gap is particularly pronounced in the ICT sector [11, 32]. In the EU, only 16.7% of ICT students are women, reflecting a close relationship and strong association between masculinity and computing studies [36]. Socioeconomic variables such as unemployment, GDP per capita, and the Gender Equality Index do not significantly explain the scant presence of women in ICT fields [11], suggesting more intricate societal forces at play. However, the growth of GDP in the ICT sector has the greatest impact on increasing the number of employed women in ICT [32]. In corporate environments, the lack of female representation on boards underscores the broader issue of under-representation in senior management roles [9, 26].

Addressing these issues requires a multifaceted approach. University-industry partnerships can play a crucial role in bridging the gender gap by providing targeted education and career opportunities for women. Such partnerships can create pathways for women to enter and advance in the informatics field, leveraging academic and industry resources to support women's careers [14].

Research shows that greater alignment between organizational social consciousness and formal institutions, like gender quotas, advances gender representation on corporate boards in Europe. Policymakers are urged to go beyond mere codification of rules and work towards raising social consciousness on gender equality issues. This involves promoting awareness and education about gender biases and implementing policies that encourage inclusive practices.

To further support these initiatives, establishing forums that serve as platforms for dialogue among women stakeholders, including policymakers, can be highly effective. Working groups within these forums could develop policy papers on gender gaps in Science, Technology, Engineering, and Mathematics (STEM), analyzing current situations and providing recommendations for the future. These papers would be discussed in the forums and presented to authorities, with lobbying efforts to ensure the implementation of recommendations.

Additionally, creating educational workshops that introduce young girls to coding in a creative and engaging environment can help break down stereotypes and encourage more girls to consider careers in technology. An active example of this effort is the Creative Coding project [16]. These workshops can combine coding with elements of music and art, providing a unique and supportive community that fosters interest in STEM fields from an early age.

12.2.2 The Importance of an Inclusive Work Environment in IT

Historically, women have been underrepresented in scientific and technical fields and remain under-represented in technological professions in the labor market [20]. Although the proportion of the population with higher education is gender-balanced in the EU, women are less likely to be employed as scientists and engineers. Specifically, a 2021 study shows that women made up less than a quarter of freelance professionals in the fields of Science & Engineering (S&E) and ICT [20]. A 2006 report from the European Commission [31],[21] indicates low participation of women in the ICT sector, especially in decision-making roles. A similar study from 2023 reiterates this observation, showing that only 17% of ICT specialists in the EU are women [12].

Another area of the labor market where women are significantly under-represented is in entrepreneurial activities in technology-oriented fields. A study conducted in Canada [31] shows that the start-up culture is perceived as being dominated by men ("bro culture of alpha males"), which can discourage women from becoming entrepreneurs.

In [15] and [48] the importance of creating an inclusive work environment in IT is emphasized, especially to counter the obstacles women face. These obstacles include gender stereotypes, a lack of female role models, and a work environment perceived as hostile.

Beyond the EU's commitment to gender equality in all areas, the strategic importance of the technology industry to the EU's economy means that gender diversity within this industry is crucial to ensure full participation of women in society. As the EU economy shifts to increased digitalization, greater efforts are necessary to encourage women's participation in the digital economy. Creating an inclusive work environment in IT requires a conscious and sustained effort from companies. The hope of EUGAIN and other gender balance interventions is to contribute to creating a more equitable and conducive work environment for women, leading to a more diverse and innovative IT industry.

12.3 Related Work: Shaping the Landscape of Best Practices in Cooperation with Industry

12.3.1 Networks for Women

As women make their way into the tech field, a sense of community and belonging arises as a necessity for a functioning working environment. In this sense, the role of networks built to (and from) women is growing. Networking and mentoring are crucial for women's career progress, often leading to job offers, project collaborations, and industry conference invitations. In the tech industry, where women are often underrepresented, these connections offer a platform to share experiences, gain mentorship, and receive guidance from those who have faced similar challenges [10]. This support system can be invaluable, offering both emotional encouragement and practical advice. Many companies are adopting this strategy to create a chain of support for their employees. Universities have developed programs to support and advance women undergraduates, graduate students, postdoctoral researchers, and faculty [33]. Government or research associations also play a pivotal role in creating large extended communities across different countries to increase collaboration and support on a large scale [22]. In other cases, instead, women's networks are promoted by the women themselves, usually as a response to perceived advantages that men are thought to derive from the existing implicit networks in the field [10].

Networking activities are also a way for women to gain more visibility. As mentioned by Kovaleva et al., women often do not explore entrepreneurship because of a lack of social support, role models, and success stories [31]. The exchange of experiences and ideas boosts women's contributions in the field, making them great candidates as guest speakers for talks, meetings, or tech events. Moreover, networking activities provide a relatable environment in which to meet peers and professionals to join a collaboration.[1] Facilitating inter- or intra-company networking events for women has been shown to be an effective way for women to gain confidence and knowledge to boost their career growth [1].

One example of a company which is seeking to put these principles into practice is Rubrik,[2] which has won awards in 2024 in both India and the USA as a "Great Place to Work". This cybersecurity company invests in building a community among women and their allies within company, through its employee resource group, Women@Rubrick. This group seeks to create a sense of belonging, advance professional growth for women and their allies within the company, and connect women across the tech industry. It does this through actions such as workshops, speaker events, mentoring and showcasing.

---

[1] https://www.forbes.com/sites/forbesbusinesscouncil/2022/02/15/women-in-tech-why-and-how-to-gain-visibility/?sh=3aea2aa72940.

[2] https://www.rubrik.com/company/careers.

12.3.2 Leadership Training

Leadership training for women in IT is growing in popularity around the globe. These include training and programs to pursue leadership in careers in specific fields like cellular and mobile technologies [47], and cybersecurity [25, 40]. There are also training, and programs for women in informatics focused broadly on entrepreneurship [18] and leadership [35].

Leadership and mentorship programs have a positive impact on the career paths of women in IT, helping them develop leadership skills, build professional networks, and advance into leadership positions [15, 17, 21, 37, 42]. Below are some examples of successful programs and case studies that highlight this impact:

- Telia Sonera, a Swedish multinational telecommunications company, has developed a managerial program that emphasizes equal opportunities and gender balance. Through participation in this program, women discover their leadership potential and are encouraged to apply for managerial positions [15]. The program helps define professional goals and gain the confidence necessary to achieve them [21].
- Fraunhofer Gesellschaft, a German research organization, has developed an initiative that achieved 30% female researchers (compared to an average of 17% in other German institutes) by offering flexible work programs and childcare services in the workplace [15].
- IT for She, a Polish program, supports women who want to start a career in IT through annual technology camps, programming workshops for students, "Kids in IT" initiatives where volunteers teach programming to children, and mentorship programs offered by top companies [12].
- AAFCS Leadership Academy, an American Association, combines leadership training, mentorship, and networking opportunities. Participants have improved their self-confidence and leadership skills, and developed a professional network [42].
- Women TechEU [17] is a European initiative that provides coaching and mentorship for start-ups in the advanced technology sector led by women.
- Women2Invest (EIT) [17] is a European initiative that helps women take their first steps as entrepreneurs by providing training in the investment field and facilitating connections with investors.
- "You in IT" (Aj Ty v IT) [20] is a non-profit organization in Slovakia that offers training courses for women in IT, including software testing academies and data analysis.
- Female Entrepreneurs of the Future [20] is a public-private initiative in Germany that provides coaching for female entrepreneurs.
- 3-month re-skilling programs for women called Digital Academies (with over 1000 graduates), which embed mentorship by experts from industry as the backbone of the programs. These programs are run by Czechitas (based in Czech Republic) non-profit organization [6].

We thus identify the benefits of leadership and mentorship programs:

- Development of leadership skills, as through specific training women learn how to lead, manage, and motivate a team.
- Building professional networks since participants come into contact with other professionals in the field, creating a valuable network of contacts.
- Improving access to opportunities which can help counteract gender stereotypes and encourage women's participation in the IT field.

12.3.3 University-Industry Partnerships and Initiatives in IT and Gender Equality

The collaboration between universities and industry, especially in the IT sector, can take various forms to stimulate innovation and economic development. As shown in [46], Internship and Mentorship Programs provide students with opportunities for practical learning and valuable industry connections. Additionally, joint research projects benefit from the mutual expertise and resources of both sectors. Furthermore, as indicated in [8, 44, 46], universities can transfer technologies and knowledge to the industry through licensing, spin-offs, and other mechanisms. In most European countries, including Netherlands, Finland, Denmark and Italy, industry participation in university research is a common practice, with technology transfer offices at all universities [46]. These types of collaborations occur worldwide, and as mentioned in [3], many companies have been aiming for decades to transform education by focusing on the skills needed for a global, knowledge-based economy.

Studies presenting these types of initiatives emphasize the extreme importance of adapting collaboration initiatives to the specific context of each country or region, taking into account factors such as governmental policies, economic development level, organizational culture, and promoting gender balance, which is the subject of this section. In this context, university-industry collaboration initiatives must actively include and promote the participation of women and other underrepresented genders in STEM.

There are multiple mentoring programs for female students at various universities and institutes [21], all aimed at supporting students in their career development and facilitating their integration into STEM fields. Typically, individual or group mentoring is provided by industry professionals or experienced academic faculty. Main activities include personalized guidance, training, workshops, networking sessions, and examples of best practices [8]. Those discussed above are just a few examples of programs that promote gender equality in partnerships between universities and industry. Such initiatives are important to combat the underrepresentation of women in scientific and technical fields, to create a more diverse and qualified workforce, and to stimulate innovation and economic growth.

12.3.4 Social Initiatives

Social initiatives to improve gender balance have begun to take shape, partially motivated by the United Nations Sustainability Goal 5: Achieve gender equality and empower all women and girls.[3] To help address this objective, the Organisation for Economic Co-operation and Development (OECD) developed the "OECD Toolkit for Mainstreaming and Implementing Gender Equality Implementing the 2015 OECD Recommendation on Gender Equality in Public Life".[4]

The specialized literature contains multiple references (e.g., [19, 30, 41, 43]) highlighting the importance of governmental actions in boosting female participation in various fields, including STEM. For example, in [19], governmental programs are mentioned that encourage women to take leadership positions in local government (Germany) or promote women's access to education and technology (Botswana, Nigeria, Rwanda) [43]. Another important aspect is the role of public funding programs in supporting women's participation in research and innovation, including in fields such as ICT [20, 45].

The European Commission Directorate-General for the Information Society and Media [21] reports that in Finland there is a law that mandates companies to implement a gender equality action plan. This plan must include an analysis of the current situation, specific goals, measures to achieve them, allocated resources, training for employees, and monitoring. Also in [21], a German government initiative called "Girls' Day" is described, during which research institutes like Fraunhofer open their doors to showcase IT career opportunities to girls. A noteworthy situation is in Malta where the Maltese government's efforts are substantial in the process of providing childcare services to support working women, including in the IT field [21].

In She Figures [20], a correlation is drawn between investments in research and development and the gender distribution among researchers. Countries with higher spending on research and development tend to have a lower representation of women in research. This horizontal segregation also manifests in research and development (R&D) fields. In most countries and economic sectors, men are more likely to work as researchers in natural sciences, engineering, and technology. Increasing women's participation at all levels of research and innovation (R&I) holds strategic importance for the European Union. This importance is highlighted by Priority 4 of the European Research Area (ERA) [20], which aims for gender equality and the integration of the gender perspective in research.

One of the first countries to create a national gender quota policy was Norway. Casey et al. write, "The Minister of Trade and Industry steered a quota law through Parliament in 2003 that amended the Companies Act to require companies to appoint 40 per cent of the under-represented gender to their boards" [7].

---

[3] https://sdgs.un.org/goals/goal5.

[4] https://www.oecd.org/gov/toolkit-for-mainstreaming-and-implementing-gender-equality.pdf.

This policy took effect in 2004. As an indirect result, women are thriving in boardrooms, representing 45% of board composition in 2022.[5] The effects in pursuing informatics careers has also been seen with women representing 20% of the informatics workforce in 2018. In addition, 36% women could be seen in docent and professor positions in STEM fields.[6]

All these examples show that governmental policies play an important role in promoting gender balance in IT and other fields, and there is a need for government involvement in creating a conducive environment for women's participation in IT. Implementing effective governmental policies and concrete measures, such as mentorship programs, support for work-life balance, and proactive measures to increase the number of women in leadership positions, is essential for creating a more equitable and inclusive tech sector.

12.4 Methods

EUGAIN is a cost action project aiming at improving gender balance in Informatics at all levels through the creation of a European network of colleagues working at the forefront of the efforts for gender balance in Informatics in their countries and research communities (please refer to the first chapter of this book for more details on EUGAIN project). One of the objectives of EUGAIN was to gather a collection of initiatives, programs, policies, and projects that aim to include more girls and women in informatics in European countries. A small team of researchers from Working Groups 4 and 5 were assembled to accomplish this task. The overall design of the work undertaken represents a grounded approach to data collection and analysis to be as informal and accommodating to submitted responses as possible. A survey was conducted using targeted and snowball sampling to achieve this goal, aligned with a grounded approach. This section describes the population we selected, the design of the survey, and the data analysis methods used.

12.4.1 Population

This study had three distinct target groups. The initial target population for this project was the membership of EUGAIN. A link for collecting projects and initiatives was distributed to all members attending the 2023 annual meeting held June 12–13 in Rome, Italy. The second target group was presenters and attendees of ACM womENcourage 2023 in Trondheim, Norway, 20–22 September 2023. The

---

[5] https://www.spencerstuart.com/research-and-insight/nordic-board-index/diversity.

[6] https://kifinfo.no/en/content/statistics.

final target was selected presenters at the European Informatics Leadership Summit, hosted by Informatics Europe, held 23–25 October 2023 in Edinburgh, Scotland.

Recipients of the targeted emails were encouraged to complete and share the survey with colleagues or complete the survey with one of the Working group team members. As a result of the low submissions, completed projects found on the Informatics Europe Minerva Award repository were also included with applicant consent.

12.4.2 Data Collection

The survey was intended to be simple and short. Modeled after the Hawai'i Government Employee's Association (HGEA)[7] form for designing public policy initiatives and the Open Territories Toolkit,[8] the survey was initially designed to collect policy interventions but expanded to include initiatives, programs, and projects that were intended to improve gender balance in informatics fields across a number of different contexts. The questions were semi-structured and open-ended, allowing for a range of responses that are hard to capture for multi-disciplinary, international, multi-stakeholder collaboration. Each question included a description and example to assist in completing the form with ease. The questions can be seen in the appendix.

12.4.3 Analysis

Because of the unique circumstances and target population of this study, these results are not generalizable. However, best practices and themes can still be identified in the dataset. We accounted for this in our analysis methods. We employed descriptive statistics to present the submitted initiatives, programs, policies, and projects as well as thematic analysis using a structured coding schema. Testimonies and lessons learned are presented as cases, selected for their overall sentiments and experiences that may be examined using other lenses and theories.

12.4.4 Data Privacy

Because all information about the projects are public record and identifiable online, no data management plan for privacy was required.

---

[7] https://www.hgea.org/.
[8] https://toolkit.territoriaperti.univaq.it/.

12.5 Results

In total, 39 responses were submitted between May 2023 and April 2024. Given that the interventions are the unit of interest, respondent demographics are not presented here.

12.5.1 Demographics

Interventions elicited had durations from as little as 6 months to over 27 years. The total direct participants across all interventions reported are 126,226 with 135+ cumulative years of intervention. At least 325 partners are impacted across 25 initiatives, programs, policies, and projects. While 18 projects are completed, 21 are ongoing at the time of writing. Of those, 5 are newly proposed or have not yet started running.

12.5.2 Costs

Costs of interventions range from 0 to €1,000,000 per year, with an average of €75,700 over 18 projects. This figure excludes projects with an unstated annual budget for staff. A cost per year breakdown can be seen in Table 12.1.

Of these programs, some are offered in companies, others in universities, and some in partnership with other domains. By examining the beneficiaries, it is possible to identify the overlaps in populations served across domains.

Table 12.1 Total number of projects by reported costs

Cost per year	# of projects
NA	16
blank	8
0.00	2
Under 10,000	3
10,000–99,999	3
100,000–199,999	2
200,000–299,999	0
300,000–399,999	2
400,000+	3
TOTAL	39

12.5.3 Beneficiaries

Thirty target groups were identified across 39 interventions. The majority of interventions, 52.63%, served a single target group while 36.84% served two target groups. Interventions serving three distinct target groups represented 2.64% while 7.89% of interventions identified five or more target groups as beneficiaries. Table 12.2 highlights the total number of interventions by beneficiary in their domain of work. The column "Exclusively Female" indicates the total number of interventions that target only women and girls. In the first row, for example, thirteen interventions targeted high school students as at least one of their beneficiaries. Of those, two interventions exclusively benefited girls (Figs. 12.1 and 12.2).

Over 126,000 beneficiaries were impacted by these initiatives to date. Some of the target groups can be seen in Fig. 12.3 and Table 12.2 (Figs. 12.4, 12.5, and 12.6).

Table 12.2 Beneficiaries by domain and number of interventions that target that group

Domain	Beneficiary	# Intervention	Exclusively female
Education	High school students	13	2
Education	Middle school students	5	5
Education	Primary school students	2	1
Education	Recent HS graduates	1	
Education	Teachers	2	
Education	Vocational school students	1	
Government	Public administration	2	
Industry	Companies	1	
Industry	Staff of location	3	
Society	Media	1	
Society	Pregnant women	1	1
Society	Underrepresented populations	4	3
Society	Whole population of a region	2	
Society	Women (general)	3	3
Society	Women and under-represented groups	1	1
Society	Women in specific domains	5	
Society	Young adult up to 20 yo	2	
University	Researchers	2	1
University	University departments	1	
University	University faculty and Staff	6	2
University	University students	11	3
University	University-Industry partnerships	1	
Unique	Crosses domains with groups	3	

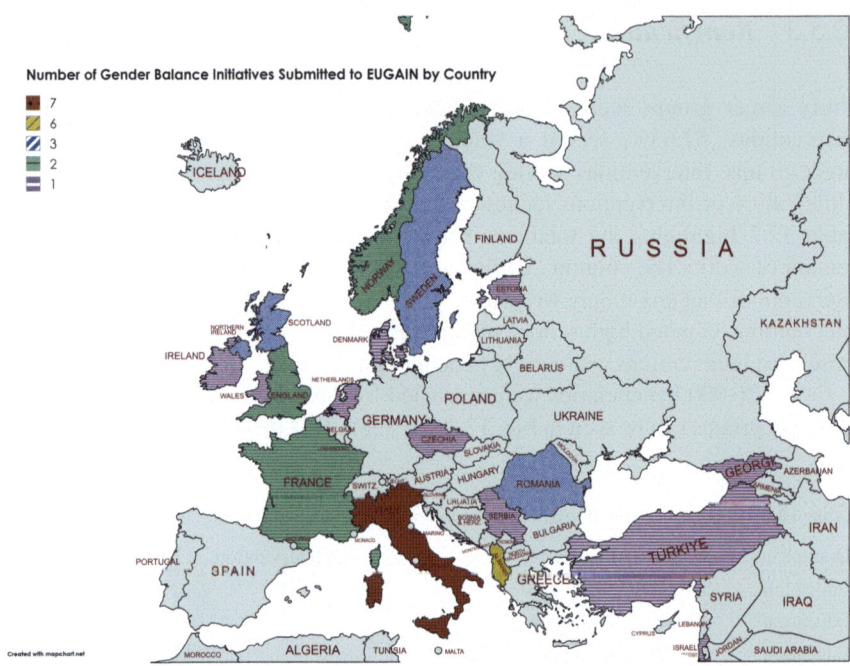

Fig. 12.1 Map depicting the number of initiatives, programs, policies, and projects by country (from Fig. 1, licensed under CC-BY-SA 4.0). Created with mapchart.net (https://www.mapchart.net/)

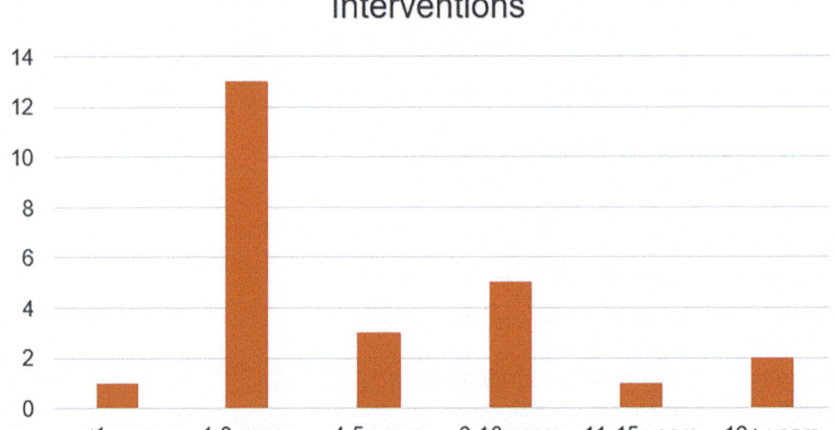

Fig. 12.2 Number of completed and ongoing interventions by years running

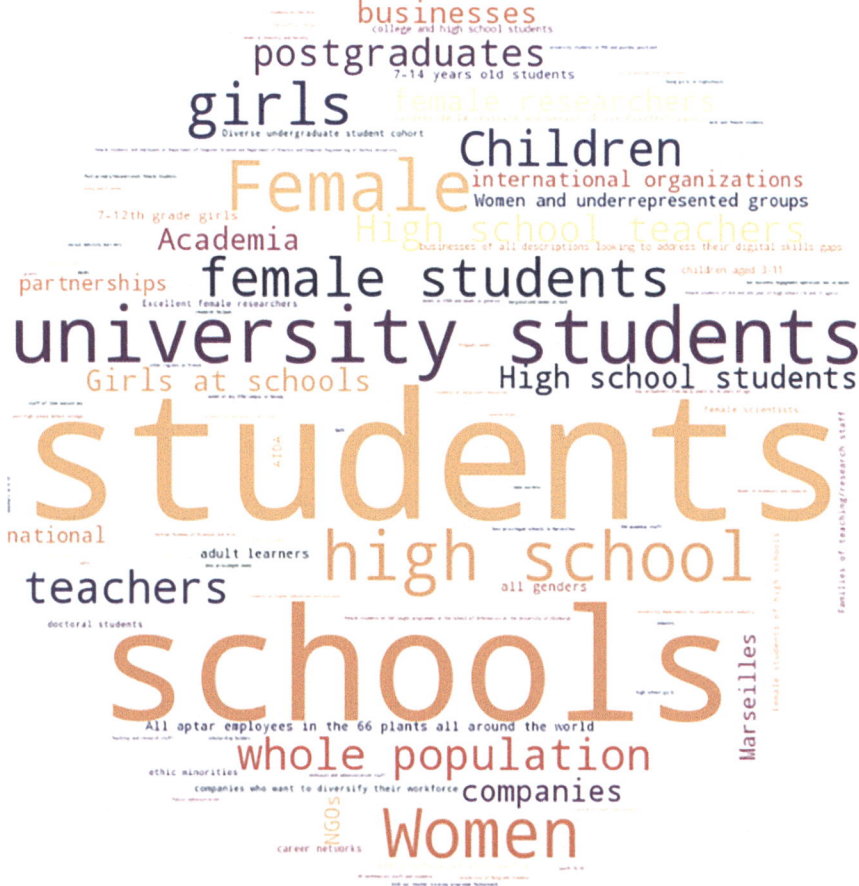

Fig. 12.3 Beneficiaries of the 39 identified initiatives, programs, policies, and projects

12.5.4 Case Examples: Initiatives, Programs, Policies, and Projects

Analyzing the results from our open survey conducted within EUGAIN and additional studies, we present and discuss a series of successful programs that promote gender equality in partnerships between universities and industry:

The Diversity Program by Motorola Poland aims to stimulate high school students' interest, paying particular attention to girls, in the IT field. The competition was launched in 2000, initially limited to four high schools and 120 participating students. Later, the program expanded nationwide [15].

The Roberta Program at Humboldt University in collaboration with Fraunhofer Gesellschaft, aims to increase the number of women in the field of

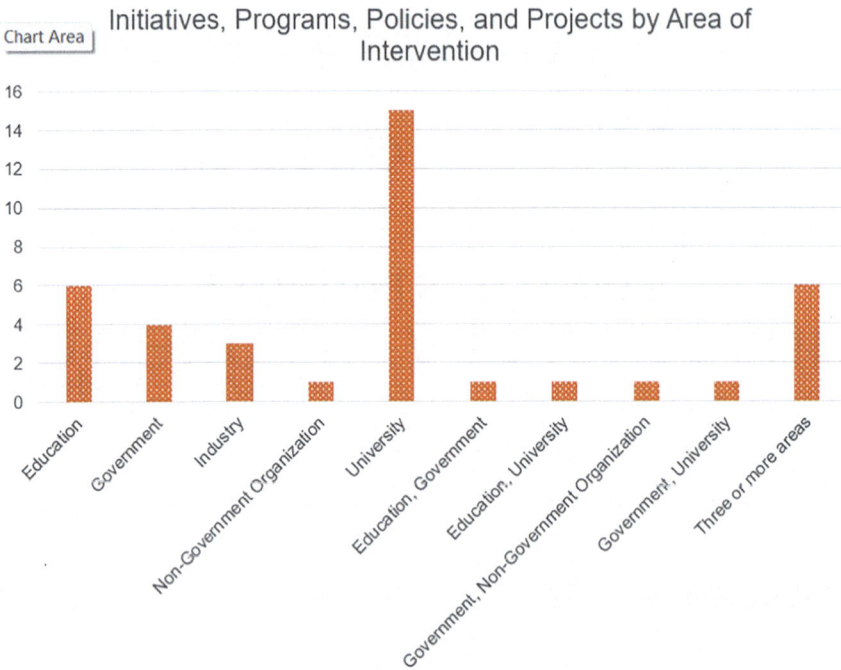

Fig. 12.4 This figure depicts the initiatives, programs, policies, and projects by area or domain of intervention. Single areas of intervention include primary and secondary education (named Education), Government, Industry, Non-Government Organization, and University. This is followed by two areas of intervention and three or more areas of intervention

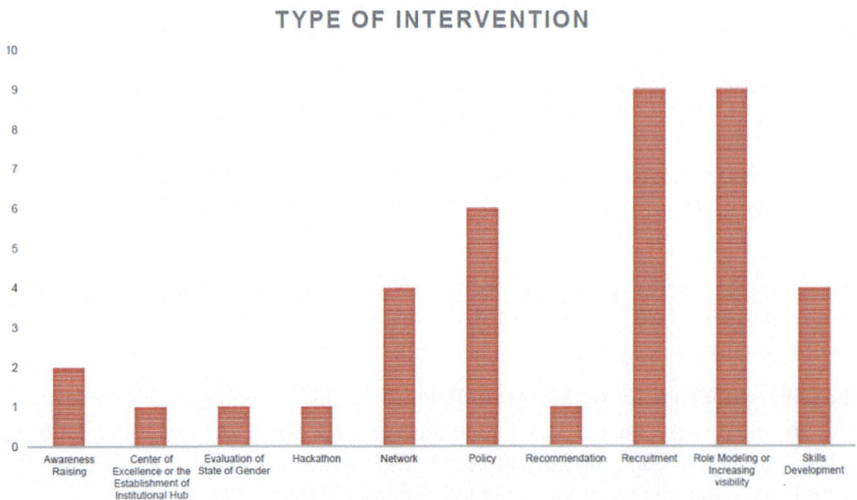

Fig. 12.5 Initiatives, programs, policies, and projects by type of intervention

12 Lessons from Industry and Academic Collaboration 287

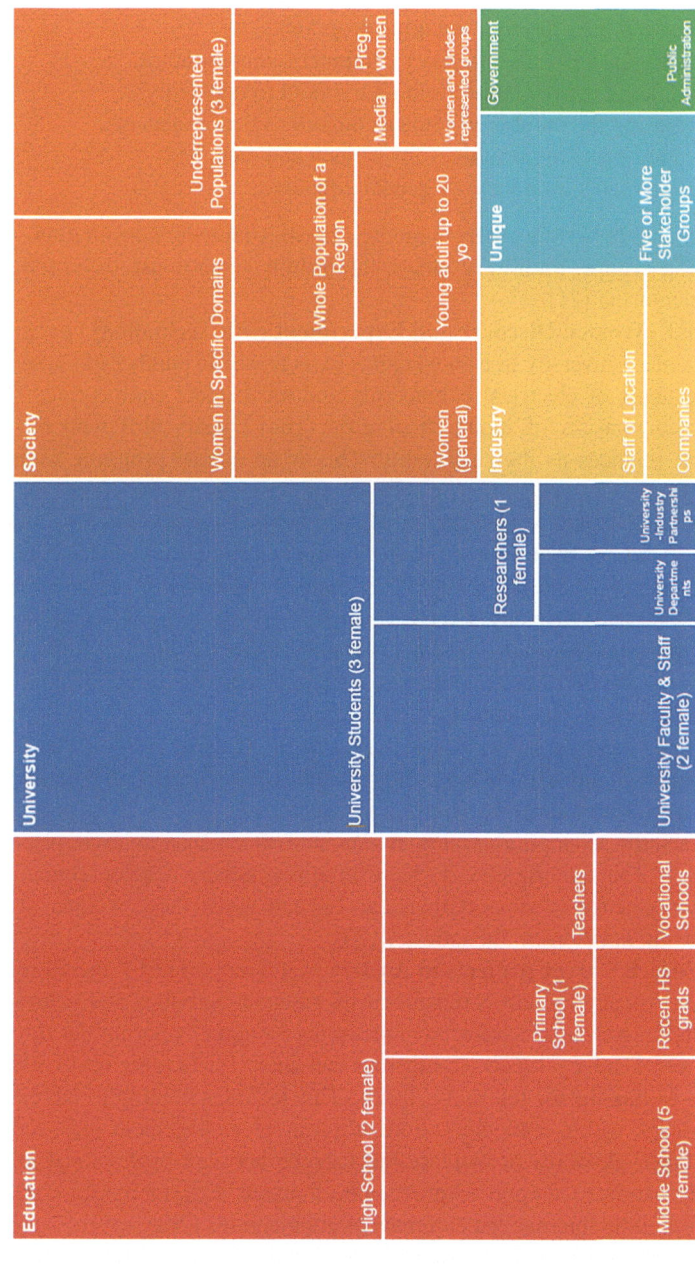

Fig. 12.6 Beneficiary types by area or domain of intervention

computer science. The target audience includes high school girls. The main objectives of the program are:

- Early cultivation of computer and robotics knowledge,
- attracting girls through engaging programs,
- familiarization with university computer science studies,
- facilitating the transition from high school to university,
- increasing the number of female computer science students,
- creating equal opportunities for women and men, and
- raising men's awareness of gender equality.

To achieve these objectives, ongoing activities include: consultation, guidance, working groups, training, courses, internships, open house days, school visits, and mentoring [21].

The FEET (Women Discover and Experiment with Technology) program at Leibnanch University in Hanover aims to increase the number of female students in the fields of electrical engineering and mechanical engineering. The target audience consists of high school girls (16–17 years old) who have chosen natural sciences as their speciality. This is an annual program, running from January to December, offering a variety of activities for the 10 girl participants: presentations and workshops at high schools to spark interest in technical fields, visits to the university, participation in selected university courses (real-life simulation, one day), key skills seminars (one day), company visits, and interesting trips (one day) [21].

The GE Women Network promotes presentations by women in the IT field in schools and universities, working to change perceptions about IT jobs and combat stereotypes. The working mode includes visits to schools and universities, presentations about careers at GE, with a focus on successful female role models.

The Academia-Industry Scholarship for the Advancement of Women in Science and Technology in Israel was introduced in 2001. This program offers scholarships to support young researchers to engage in joint research with industry. The funding aims to help these researchers develop connections and gain experience to support their careers and assist these women in reaching leadership positions in the industry [20].

The FEMtech Career projects in Austria are supported by the Research Promotion Agency to help companies with research activities and extra-university research organizations implement measures for equal opportunities through their FEMtech Career projects. Companies can apply for funding up to 50,000 EUR for 6–24 months for relevant projects. This includes training to increase gender knowledge within companies, human resources management (e.g., recruitment, branding), measures to increase the balance between professional and private life, measures to support employee development (e.g., mentoring), and support for improving internal and external communications [20].

The w-fFORTE program in Austria supports female researchers in science and technology through free training, workshops promoting interdisciplinary work, and networking events for women. Between 2008 and 2018, the program provided 15 million EUR for funding the Laura Bassi Centre of Expertise programs. This funding supported research based on the potential and current achievements of the selected researchers, focusing on supporting excellent female researchers and promoting a culture of collaboration and equal opportunities [20].

We also identified programs from our own members. They include:

Women in Cybersecurity—Role models for girls (Estonia) The main goal of this program is to combine relatable educational material, engaging activities, and inspiring stories from diverse female experts in the field, empowering girls to envision themselves as successful IT and cybersecurity professionals. This program was targeted to 7–12th graders and included tests like "Is IT for me?", reading materials, where you acquire expertise and skill sets, exercises, discussion materials. As artifacts to inspire more girls and women to pursue informatics careers, they collected personal stories from 59 role models and video stories of 6 to showcase top women in cybersecurity in Estonia [34].

Hack GRRRL (The Netherlands and Brazil) The main goal of the program was to increase the number of women in hackathons and give them the confidence to join hackathons in the future. Hack GRRRL helped overcome the confidence-competence gap, which is when you feel afraid of not having sufficient skills to complete a task you can do. This program was implemented by a Masters, now PhD, student. A next edition is being planned. The goal for the next iteration is to attract more participants and retain them in STEM fields. The cost to run the event in Brazil was approximately 2000 euros, but running the event online is free [38].

Gender Equality Plan (GEP) (Italy) In 2021, the Italian government implemented the indications of the European Parliament and enacted the National Strategy for Gender Equality.[9] The main goal of this strategy is to contribute to the promotion of gender equality and the achievement of equality, participation, and non-discrimination objectives. GEP 2021 has 26 goals and objectives grouped into 6 areas:

- Work/life balance and organizational culture;
- Gender balance in top management positions and decision-making bodies;
- Gender equality in recruitment and career progression;
- Integration of the gender dimension in research, teaching programs and training;
- Measures to combat gender violence, including sexual harassment;
- Communication and networking initiatives—internal and external networking measures.

---

[9] https://www.pariopportunita.gov.it/it/politiche-e-attivita/parita-di-genere-ed-empowerment-femminile/strategia-nazionale-per-la-parita-di-genere-2021-2026/.

This national strategy was adopted at universities like University of L'Aquila to benefit diverse genders in informatics education from high school through academic career. The budget for the GEP in 2022 was 127.000€.

These initiatives, programs, policies, and projects represent a collection of experiences that share lessons learned, best practices, and future perspectives about the landscape of gender balance in informatics across Europe.

12.6 Discussion

It was challenging to get people to submit their initiatives, programs, policies, and projects or best practices. This can be for a variety of reasons. Mostly, people did not feel their work was a good fit. In these cases, we asked for the link, and one of our team members completed the information for the program if we felt it was appropriate. This aligns with the idea that work to advance the standing of women and gender balance in tech is undervalued [5].

12.6.1 Lessons Learned

Lessons learned represent room for future growth. First, there is the need to emphasise that gender is a spectrum. By acknowledging there is more than just a gender binary, we can create room for trans, gender-queer, and non-binary individuals in informatics as well. This is an important lesson that we prioritize using a gender-forward intersectional approach to examine workplace dynamics and culture, training and mentorship. and other recruitment, retention, and promotion plans in informatics.

From the IPSIS program in Albania, the main lessons were ownership and to promote better involvement of high decision-making people. In order to have a successful system, everyone must feel a connection to it, and the system has to have the support of those who not only fund it, but those who embed its use into policies, practices, and habituation.

One survey respondent noted that helping people break out of the user role is challenging. They note, "Even though people like ICT, they don't think it's for people like them." This sentiment expresses the challenges and limitations from social narratives that some people place on themselves, illustrating the obstacles we must overcome in recruiting the next generation of informatics and ICT professionals.

Finally, many stakeholders and decision-makers are in areas where gender stereotyping is seen as the norm. In these countries, the presentation of data may help to make decisions for gender balance. One participant noted, "There is still a big gap... between men and women in engineering and ICT fields. In some areas of a country, persistent gender stereotypes are existing in the education system..." This is an urgent hurdle to overcome. It is a societal issue that we can hope to incrementally impact over time. Presenting best practices and examples can help to create change, making informatics and ICT professions more inclusive for women and other marginalized genders.

12.6.2 Best Practices

Analyzing successful programs, as they have been presented both in the studies conducted and by respondents of our survey, has helped us identify good practices in collaboration between academia and industry:

- Early Industry Involvement is important to define the industry's needs and set common goals from the beginning of the collaboration, ensuring that the needs and perspectives of all groups, including underrepresented ones, are considered. Some examples include partnership activities like creating a bridge program for students and industry teams or creating working groups of faculty and leaders to identify points of stress.
- Effective Communication relies upon establishing clear and regular communication channels between partners, including measures to ensure equal participation of all genders and diversity in communication teams. This can be reinforced through clear and transparent policies about harassment, open communication, and work responsibilities. Some of these can be created collaboratively.
- Mutual Trust means building a relationship based on trust and transparency, promoting an inclusive environment where all individuals, regardless of gender, are treated with respect and fairness. This can be reinforced through policies and trainings.
- Institutional Support involves creating structures and mechanisms to facilitate collaboration, such as technology transfer offices, technology parks, and dedicated funding programs, taking care to include specific initiatives and resources to support gender balance and equal participation in all stages of collaboration.

These principles will not only stimulate innovation and competitiveness but will also contribute to creating a more equitable and inclusive collaborative environment.

We outline a series of strategies for creating a more inclusive work environment that values diversity and offers women equal opportunities for professional development:

- Mentorship programs, especially those led by women in the STEM field, can be beneficial for women in IT [48]. They can provide support, advice, and role models. However, it is important for mentorship programs to address structural inequalities and not just focus on the perceived deficiencies of women [27]. A feminist approach to mentorship, which focuses on transforming the workplace and promoting the rights and needs of all employees, can be more effective [27].

- Developing recruitment policies that promote equal opportunities. Job advertisements should be gender-neutral and should not discourage women from applying. Companies should also consider using recruitment methods that reduce the risk of discrimination, such as structured interviews and objective competence tests.
- Training and career development programs should be equally accessible to women and men. It is also important for women to have access to equitable promotion opportunities and not be excluded from informal power networks within companies [15, 21].
- Balancing professional and personal life through offering flexible work options, such as remote work, flexible schedules, and paid parental leave, can contribute to creating a more inclusive work environment for women. These policies can help women balance their professional responsibilities with family duties.
- Combating gender stereotypes and discrimination at work is essential. This can be achieved through awareness campaigns, employee training, and clear policies against harassment [5, 15, 48].
- A greater representation of women in leadership positions can help create a more inclusive organizational culture. Companies should set concrete goals for increasing the number of women in leadership positions and implement programs that support women in their careers.

Diversity is not simply a goal in its own right. It has been demonstrated to have significant benefits for organisations as well as individuals.

12.7 Conclusion

The present work aimed at presenting the landscape of policies and best practices currently interesting women in informatics. The chapter delves into the current initiatives involving industry and academia collaboration. The analysis presented 39 initiatives involving several beneficiaries and stakeholders across multiple countries. The findings of this study are constrained by several factors that may limit their generalizability. While best practices and recurring themes have been identified, they may not fully capture the complexity of gender balance initiatives across different settings. Additionally, the responses and lessons learned were presented based on cases. While these offer valuable insights, they reflect subjective perspectives of the stakeholders involved that may vary when examined through different theoretical lenses. Nevertheless, the study is the first attempt to map the different collaboration initiatives aimed at improving gender balance, and provides valuable insights to practitioners and researchers that aim to investigate further the effectiveness of these interventions.

While we want to remain optimistic, we must critically reflect on how some nations view gender as a social construct. These limiting beliefs will have lasting ramifications, especially as we further embed technology into our society through digitalization. As one EUGAIN respondent writes, "...I have a big concern regarding the concentration of women and girls in traditionally female-dominated fields of study and their under-representation in science, technology, engineering and mathematics and information and communications technology, which reduces their employment prospects. Therefore, I think it is very important to develop concrete recommendations and support projects based on it, in order to reduce this difference to a minimum." Women and Girls in Tech (Georgia). We share this sentiment.

The under representation of women in STEM, particularly in fields like informatics and ICT, continues to pose significant barriers to achieving gender balance. This issue contains deeply ingrained societal perceptions about who "belongs" in these fields, perceptions that discourage women and other marginalized groups from pursuing careers in technology. A crucial takeaway from our study is the importance of creating inclusive frameworks that address these societal narratives and promote gender diversity not only through policy but also through cultural changes. We promote collaboration across sectors, with universities, government, and industry working together to create lasting change. Mentorship and leadership programs tailored to the needs of diverse gender identities, as well as polices promoting flexible work environment will be keys to retaining talent and fostering diversity in the workplace.

12.8 CRediT Taxonomy

Conceptualization, Formal Analysis, Investigation, Methodology, Project Administration, Writing- original draft, Writing—review and editing: Lenuta, Antinisca, Alicia, Jane.

Visualization: Alicia.

Writing—original draft, Writing—review and editing: Claudia, Andrea.

Appendix: Survey Questions

The survey questions were:

- Name (What is your name?)
- Country (What is the main country of the initiative?)
- Email (What is the best email to contact you if we have questions or would like to follow up with you?)
- Your area of specialization (What type of organization do you currently work in?) [multiple options, structured responses: Education K-12, Government, Industry Non-Government, Organization, University, Other- to be added in notes]
- Area of intervention (What is the area where the intervention or recommendation was applied?) [multiple options, structured responses: Education K-12, Govern-

ment, Industry Non-Government, Organization, University, Other- to be added in notes]
- Intervention Type (What is the intervention?) [multiple options, structured responses: Hackathon, Policy, Recommendation, Project, Evaluation of the State of Gender, Role Modeling or Increasing Visibility (no direct connection), Mentoring (direct contact between mentors and mentees), Skills Development, Training or Workshop, Networking or Sense of Belonging, Awareness- Raising or Educational Campaign, Center of Excellence or the Establishment of Institutional Hub, Recruitment, Other- to be added in notes]
- Title of Recommendation or Intervention (The title is the name of the project.)
- Goal of Recommendation or Intervention (The goal is what the project is designed to accomplish.)
- Link and/or Description of Recommendation or Intervention (Provide a URL and/or brief overview of the project, recommendation, or intervention.)
- Beneficiaries of the Recommendation or Intervention (Who was the target population in the recommendation or intervention?)
- Your Testimonial for the Recommendation or Intervention (Your short personal opinion about the recommendation or intervention.)
- If this recommendation is part of a completed action or program, how long was the program or intervention? What was the total number of beneficiaries or participants?
- If this recommendation is part of a completed action or program, what were the program costs and lessons learned?

References

1. Women on boards: Building the female talent pipeline. Technical report, International Labor Organization, 2015.
2. C. Ashcraft, B. McLain, and E. Eger. *Women in tech: The facts*. National Center for Women & Technology (NCWIT) Colorado, CO, USA, 2016.
3. H. Belfield. Making industry-university partnerships work, lesson from successful collaborations. *Science/Business Innovation Board AISBL*, 2012.
4. T. Besley, O. Folke, T. Persson, and J. Rickne. Gender quotas and the crisis of the mediocre man: Theory and evidence from sweden. *American Economic Review*, 107(8):2204–42, August 2017.
5. P. Bjørn, M. Menendez-Blanco, and V. Borsotti. *Diversity in Computer Science: Design Artefacts for Equity and Inclusion*. Cham: Springer International Publishing, 2022.
6. B. Buhnova, L. Jurystova, and D. Prikrylova. Assisting women in career change towards software engineering: experience from czechitas ngo. In *In Proceedings of the 13th European Conference on Software Architecture*, volume 2, pages 88–93, 2019.
7. C. Casey, R. Skibnes, and J. K. Pringle. Gender equality and corporate governance: Policy strategies in norway and new zealand. *Gender, Work & Organization*, 18(6):613–630, 2011.
8. C. Chais, P. Ganzer, and P. Munhoz Olea. Technology transfer between universities and companies: Two cases of brazilian universities. *Innovation & Management Review*, 15(1):20–40, 2018.

9. C. E. Clark, P. Arora, and P. Gabaldon. Female representation on corporate boards in europe: The interplay of organizational social consciousness and institutions. *Journal of business ethics*, 180(1):165–186, 2022.
10. M. Coleman. Women-only (homophilous) networks supporting women leaders in education. *Journal of Educational Administration*, 48(6):769–781, 2010.
11. R. Colomo-Palacios and C. Casado-Lumbreras. National cultures and gender balance in ict: A preliminary study. In *Proceedings of the 13th European Conference on Software Architecture-Volume 2*, pages 76–81, 2019.
12. E. Commission. Women in digital. Technical report, European Union, 2019. https://digital-strategy.ec.europa.eu/en/library/women-digital.
13. E. Commission. The gender equality strategy 2020–2025. Technical report, European Commission, 2020. https://ec.europa.eu/newsroom/just/items/682425/en.
14. M. Company. Diversity wins: How inclusion matters. *McKinsey Reports*, 2020.
15. S. Da Silva Reis and E. Schulze. Gender equality, women in ICT. Technical report, Policy Department C - Citizens' Rights and Constitutional Affairs, European Parliament, 2012.
16. Department of Computer Science and Engineering, Chalmers University of Technology. Creative coding, 2024. Accessed: 2024-06-27.
17. EIT. EIT girls go circular. women and girls in STEM forum 2022: Policy brief. Technical report, EIT, 2022. https://eit-girlsgocircular.eu/wp-content/uploads/2022/12/WGSF-2022-Policy-Brief-1-1.pdf.
18. C. Elliott, C. Mavriplis, and H. Anis. An entrepreneurship education and peer mentoring program for women in stem: mentors' experiences and perceptions of entrepreneurial self-efficacy and intent. *International Entrepreneurship and Management Journal*, 16(1):43–67, 2020.
19. D.-G. f. J. European Commission and Consumers. 2023 report on gender equality in the EU. Technical report, Publications Office of the European Union, 2023. https://data.europa.eu/doi/10.2838/4966.
20. D.-G. f. R. European Commission and Innovation. She figures 2021 – gender in research and innovation – statistics and indicators. Technical report, Publications Office of the European Union, 2021. https://data.europa.eu/doi/10.2777/06090.
21. D.-G. f. t. I. S. European Commission and Media. Best practices for even gender distribution in the 25 member states in the domain of information society. Technical report, European Commission, 2006. https://data.europa.eu/doi/10.2759/11343.
22. M. Feeney and M. Bernal. Women in stem networks: who seeks advice and support from women scientists? *Scientometrics*, 85(3):767–790, 2010.
23. J. M. Fernandes, M. Lopes da Fonseca, and M. Won. Closing the gender gap in legislative debates: The role of gender quotas. *Political Behavior*, 45(3):897–921, 2023.
24. W. E. Forum. *Global Gender Gap Report 2023*. World Economic Forum, 2023.
25. M. D. Gonzalez. Building a cybersecurity pipeline to attract, train, and retain women. *Business Journal for Entrepreneurs*, 2015(3), 2015.
26. E. Hamplová, V. Janeček, and F. Lefley. Board gender diversity and women in leadership positions–are quotas the solution? *Corporate Communications: An International Journal*, 27(4):742–759, 2022.
27. D. A. Harris. Women, work, and opportunities: From neoliberal to feminist mentoring. *Sociology Compass*, 16.3, 2022. https://doi.org/10.1111/soc4.12966.
28. S. Hewlett, C. Buck Luce, L. Servon, L. Sherbin, P. Shiller, E. Sosnovich, and K. Sumberg. *The Athena factor: Reversing the brain drain in science, engineering, and technology*. New York: Center for Work-life Policy, 2008.
29. S. Hewlett, L. Sherbin, F. Dieudonné, C. Fargnoli, and C. Fredman. *Athena Factor 2.0: Accelerating female talent in science, engineering, & technology*. New York: Center for Work-life Policy, 2014. http:/www.talentinnovation.org/publication.cfm?publication=1420.
30. J. Iszkowska, K. Kawecka, J. Lázár, M. Matécsa, P. Pawe l Nawrocki, J. Novak, D. Róna, and I. Štverková. Win-win: How empowering women can benefit central and eastern europe, 2021.

31. Y. Kovaleva, S. Hyrynsalmi, A. Saltan, A. Happonen, and J. Kasurinen. Becoming an entrepreneur: A study of factors with women from the tech sector. *Information and Software Technology*, 155:107110, 2023.
32. H. Krchová and K. Š. Höesová. Selected determinants of digital transformation and their influence on the number of women in the ICT sector. *Entrepreneurship and Sustainability Issues*, 8(4):524, 2021.
33. V. A. Lagesen, I. Pettersen, and L. Berg. Inclusion of women to ICT engineering – lessons learned. *European Journal of Engineering Education*, 47(3):467–482, 2022.
34. B. Lorenz. Women in tech–role models for girls. Estonian case. *Educational Media International*, 60(3–4):292–305, 2023.
35. K. S. Lyness and A. R. Grotto. Women and leadership in the united states: Are we closing the gender gap? *Annual Review of Organizational Psychology and Organizational Behavior*, 5:227–265, 2018.
36. K. M. Miltner. Girls who coded: Gender in twentieth century u.k. and u.s. computing. *Science, Technology, & Human Values*, 44(1):161–176, 2019.
37. S. Montoya. UNESCO, new UIS data show that the share of women in STEM graduates stagnant for 10 years. https://world-education-blog.org/2024/04/25/new-uis-data-show-that-the-share-of-women-in-stem-graduates-stagnant-for-10-years/, 2024.
38. L. Paganini and K. Gama. Female participation in hackathons: A case study about gender issues in application development marathons. *IEEE Revista Iberoamericana de Tecnologias del Aprendizaje*, 15(4):326–335, 2020.
39. M. Perifanou and A. A. Economides. Gender digital divide in Europe, 2020.
40. T. C. Plato. Women c-suite executives in cybersecurity: Transformational experiences and gender barriers on their leadership journeys. 2021.
41. N. Pop. Transilvania business, impulsionarea antreprenoriatului feminin: Rolul conferinței the woman în modelarea viitorului afacerilor conduse de femei, 2024. last modified March 14 2024.
42. M. Russell, B. Stewart, and L. Brooks. Advancing gender equality and women's leadership capacity: Mentoring, networking, training. *Advancing Women in Leadership Journal*, 42:88–97, 2023.
43. G. E. M. R. UNESCO. Gender report – technology on her terms. Technical report, United Nations Educational, Scientific and Cultural Organization 7, 2024. https://doi.org/10.54676/WVCF2762.
44. *Experimental development in public-private partnership for local cloud platforms with advanced data protection features - PrivateSky Project*, 2016.
45. V. Valentina Tartari and A. Salter. The engagement gap:: Exploring gender differences in university – industry collaboration activities. *Research Policy*, 44:1176–119, 2015. https://doi.org/10.1016/j.respol.2015.01.014.
46. S. Vicol, N. Sedlețchi, and A. Șușu-Țurcan. Practica internațională a relațiilor de cercetare în colaborare între universități și industrie. *Analele Științifice ale Universității de Studii Europene din Moldova*, 2014.
47. S. Vossenberg et al. Women entrepreneurship promotion in developing countries: What explains the gender gap in entrepreneurship and how to close it. *Maastricht School of Management Working Paper Series*, 8(1):1–27, 2013.
48. W. Warsito, N. Choiro Siregar, and R. Rosli. STEM education and the gender gap: Strategies for encouraging girls to pursue STEM careers. *Prima: Jurnal Pendidikan Matematika*, 7.2:191–205, 2023. https://jurnal.umt.ac.id/index.php/prima/article/view/8411/4331.

Open Access This chapter is licensed under the terms of the Creative Commons Attribution 4.0 International License (http://creativecommons.org/licenses/by/4.0/), which permits use, sharing, adaptation, distribution and reproduction in any medium or format, as long as you give appropriate credit to the original author(s) and the source, provide a link to the Creative Commons license and indicate if changes were made.

The images or other third party material in this chapter are included in the chapter's Creative Commons license, unless indicated otherwise in a credit line to the material. If material is not included in the chapter's Creative Commons license and your intended use is not permitted by statutory regulation or exceeds the permitted use, you will need to obtain permission directly from the copyright holder.

Chapter 13
Innovative Ways of Cooperating with Public Administration for Gender Equity in Informatics

Sonay Caner-Yıldırım ⓘ, Miranda Harizaj ⓘ, and Salome Shakarishvili

13.1 Introduction

Gender inequity in informatics remains a persistent global challenge. Despite numerous initiatives aimed to promote inclusivity, women continue to be significantly underrepresented in both educational and professional domains within the field. For instance, in 2022, women made up only 19.1% of ICT specialists across the European Union, and comprised just 32.8% of the workforce in high-technology sectors [1]. This underrepresentation not only stifles diversity and innovation but also impedes the achievement of global development goals, including the United Nations Sustainable Development Goal 5 (SDG 5), which seeks to achieve gender equity and empower all women and girls [2]. Addressing this inequity is crucial for fostering innovation, enhancing problem solving capabilities, and ensuring that technological advancements meet the needs of a diverse population. Public administration plays a pivotal role in this effort. As both a major employer and policymaker, it has the power to drive systemic change by implementing inclusive policies, promoting equal opportunities, and setting an example for other sectors to follow. However, women face multiple barriers in informatics, including stereotypes, limited access to resources, digital literacy disparities, and underrepresentation in decision-making roles and entrepreneurial positions. Cultural biases often reinforce

---

S. Caner-Yıldırım (✉)
Erzincan Binali Yıldırım University, Erzincan, Turkey

M. Harizaj
Polytechnic University of Tirana, Tirane, Albania
e-mail: miranda.harizaj@fti.edu.al

S. Shakarishvili
Ministry of Education and Science, Tbilisi, Georgia
e-mail: sshakarishvili@mes.gov.ge

the notion of informatics as a male-dominated field, further discouraging women's participation.

The purpose of this chapter is to explore innovative ways of cooperating with public administration to promote gender equity in informatics. We aim to analyze the current challenges, develop a transformative vision for creating a supportive ecosystem, and propose concrete actions and innovative instruments to empower women in the field.

Our approach entails a comprehensive analysis of the barriers women face in informatics and the vital role that public administration can play in overcoming these challenges. We focus on key areas such as policy leadership, role modeling, education and training, strategic partnerships, and accountability measures to develop strategies that foster systemic change.

The chapter is organized as follows: Sect. 13.2 outlines the methods used to analyze the current challenges and shape our transformative vision. Section 13.3 presents the findings, detailing the concrete actions and innovative instruments proposed to support women's empowerment in informatics. Section 13.4 explores the implications of these findings, incorporating case studies and best practices to highlight successful implementations. Section 13.5 provides recommendations and future directions for policymakers, public administration leaders, educational institutions, and private sector partners. Finally, Sect. 13.6 concludes the chapter by summarizing the key points and emphasizing the importance of public administration's role in advancing gender equity in informatics.

13.2 Methods

To understand the scope and depth of the gender inequity in informatics, we conducted an extensive review of current statistics, reports, and scholarly articles. This included analyzing data from the [1, 3, 4], and [5]. These sources provided valuable insights into the underrepresentation of women in both educational and professional domains within the informatics sector.

We identified multiple barriers that contribute to this underrepresentation, including stereotypes, lack of confidence, limited access to resources, digital literacy disparities, underrepresentation in decision-making roles and entrepreneurial positions and directly public administration related challenges. Societal and cultural biases often reinforce the notion that informatics is a male-dominated field, further discouraging women's participation. By systematically analyzing these challenges, we aimed to identify the root causes of gender inequity in informatics and understand how public administration can play a role in addressing them.

13.2.1 Current Reality and Challenges in Promoting Gender Equity

13.2.1.1 Gendered Nature of Informatics

In 2022, high-technology sectors in the EU employed 9.8 million people, with men comprising over two-thirds (67.2%) of this workforce. These sectors, vital for economic growth and productivity, include high-technology manufacturing (e.g., pharmaceuticals, computer, electronic, and optical products) and knowledge-intensive high-technology services (e.g., IT, telecommunications, scientific research). Despite the potential for well-paid employment opportunities, significant gender inequities persist. A notable gender disparity is observed across various regions. For instance, 23 regions, mostly in capital/urban areas, employed at least 100,000 people in high-technology sectors, collectively accounting for 39.3% of the EU's high-technology employment. Regions like Ile-de-France, Comunidad de Madrid, Oberbayern, Lombardia, and Cataluña reported the highest employment numbers. Women represented only 32.8% of those employed in these sectors, with the female share varying significantly across regions. Nyugat-Dunántúl in Hungary was the only region where women outnumbered men in high-technology employment (50.2%). Other regions with higher female participation included Marche in Italy (48.6%) and Észak-Magyarország in Hungary (48.1%), whereas regions like Thessalia in Greece had as low as 8.3% female employment. These statistics highlight the ongoing gender inequities in the high-tech industries across Europe, underscoring the need for targeted efforts to improve gender equity in these critical sectors [6].

13.2.1.2 Digital Literacy Disparities

Digital literacy disparities significantly impact gender equity in informatics. Women face multiple challenges in accessing digital technology and acquiring relevant skills. According to the International Telecommunication Union (ITU), women and girls are generally at a disadvantage compared to men regarding access to digital technology such as mobile phones and smartphones with Internet connectivity. Although the situation has improved over time, significant gaps remain. For instance, in 21 countries, women lag behind men in mobile phone ownership, and the gender gap in smartphone ownership is still notable, particularly in low- and middle-income countries [7].

Data from LinkedIn indicates that while the concentration of female AI talent has more than doubled since 2016, it remains significantly lower than that of male AI talent. In 2016, only 0.09% of LinkedIn's female members had AI engineering skills, compared to 0.18% of male members. By 2023, these figures had increased to 0.2% for women and 0.41% for men, respectively [5].

Despite the overall growth in female AI talent, women still have a smaller industry presence compared to men, particularly in sectors like Education, Technology,

Information, and Media. The sectors with the most significant increases in female concentration over time are Technology, Information, and Media, followed by Professional Services and Financial Services. This gradual increase in gender parity in AI engineering talent is a positive sign, yet targeted interventions are necessary to bridge the gender gap and ensure equitable access to emerging technological competencies [5].

Moreover, disparities are becoming more pronounced within the sphere of online-skilling in AI and digital skills, which are increasingly shaping the overall skills and job landscape. Despite a notable uptick in enrolment in these courses across genders between 2015 and 2023, certain technical proficiencies—notably in AI and big data, programming, and networks and cybersecurity—lag in achieving gender parity [5]. These findings underscore the need for targeted interventions to bridge this gap and ensure equitable access to emerging technological competencies, particularly since generative AI is a fast-growing technology with the potential to enable tailored learning experiences fitting the needs of diverse learner populations.

Addressing these digital literacy disparities is crucial for promoting gender equity in informatics. Policies and initiatives that focus on increasing women's access to digital technology, providing targeted digital skills training, and creating supportive networks can help bridge these gaps. Ensuring that women fully benefit from the opportunities offered by the digital economy will contribute to a more inclusive and equitable informatics sector.

13.2.1.3 Underrepresentation in Decision-Making Roles

Women have less access to networks, knowledge-sharing platforms, and decision-making roles in the ICT field. This limited access hampers their leadership opportunities and perpetuates gender disparities in informatics. Despite the overall progress in female representation in some areas, significant challenges remain in achieving gender parity in decision-making positions.

According to the Global Gender Gap Report 2024, women make up 42% of the global workforce, yet only 31.7% hold senior leadership roles. The underrepresentation is more pronounced in STEM fields, where women constitute only 28.2% of the workforce, highlighting significant leadership gaps and ongoing challenges in achieving gender parity [5]. In the high-technology sectors of the EU, men comprise over two-thirds of the workforce, and women are significantly underrepresented in decision-making roles [1].

13.2.1.4 Start-Up Founder Positions

In the digital sector, women occupy only 14.8% of start-up founder positions and earn almost 20% less than men in ICT roles. Despite representing a small proportion of entrepreneurs, digital start-ups led by women are more likely to achieve success compared to those led by men. Additionally, investments in start-ups founded by women outperform those founded exclusively by men by 63% [5]. These statistics highlight the potential for women-led start-ups to drive innovation and economic growth, yet underline the persistent gender disparities in entrepreneurial opportunities and earnings.

Addressing these disparities requires targeted interventions to support women in accessing networks, funding, and leadership training. By creating a more inclusive entrepreneurial ecosystem, we can leverage the unique perspectives and skills that women bring to the table, fostering a more diverse and dynamic digital economy.

13.2.1.5 Public Administration Related Challenges

In the 1940s, Woodring stated, "Women might be conductors on a tram, but only men could be drivers" [8] p. 152, as cited in [9], highlighting gender biases that persist to this day. Despite significant improvements in the proportion of women in the public sector workforce since the 2000s, the cultural, social, and institutional barriers identified by Woodring in the 1940s, which were also prevalent in the 1970s and 1980s, remain significant obstacles today.

There are two major areas of silence in public administration concerning gender. The first is the underrepresentation of women and the lack of gender equity within public service workforces [9]. The second is the limited application of feminist theories in addressing contemporary public management challenges. Feminist theories can provide valuable insights into topics such as collaboration, boundary-spanning, and the skill requirements for future public sector workers [9].

Women in public administration often face significant challenges related to career progression and representation in leadership roles. Research indicates that women in public service programs tend to take on a disproportionate amount of advising and mentoring responsibilities. Despite these contributions, they are less likely to be in leadership positions at universities and other public institutions. This inequity can impact job satisfaction, advancement, and promotion prospects for female faculty members [10].

Moreover, women in STEM fields, including informatics, continue to be underrepresented. Academic departments' commitment to gender diversity strategies often depends on the administrative power of department chairs and the current gender diversity status. However, simply having more women in a department does not necessarily lead to the adoption of effective gender diversity strategies, suggesting that these strategies may be compensatory in nature [11].

Addressing these disparities requires targeted interventions to support women in accessing networks, funding, and leadership training. By creating a more inclusive public administration ecosystem, we can leverage the unique perspectives and skills that women bring to the table, fostering a more diverse and dynamic public sector.

13.2.2 Creating a Transformative Vision for Supportive Ecosystem

A transformative vision of public administration for a supportive ecosystem aims to redefine the role of government and its agencies in fostering an environment where all sectors of society can thrive. This vision emphasizes cooperation, innovation, and sustainability as cornerstones of governance. By integrating inclusive policies, promoting resource sharing, and encouraging continuous improvement, public administration can create a framework that supports individuals, businesses, and communities.

13.2.2.1 Policy Leadership

Policy leadership is crucial in advancing gender equity in informatics, both within and outside public administration. Internally, policy leaders establish the vision and commitment to gender equity, influencing workplace culture, recruitment, retention, and professional development. Externally, policy leadership sets national agendas, enforces legislation, and promotes educational reforms, creating a broader supportive ecosystem [12].

Internally, policy leaders in public administration play a pivotal role in promoting gender equity by setting a vision and demonstrating commitment to gender equity. Their leadership drives the development of strategies and policies such as anti-discrimination laws and gender-sensitive hiring practices. Leaders foster a culture of inclusivity, ensuring women feel valued and supported in their careers in informatics [13] and [14]. Recruitment and retention strategies, including targeted outreach and unbiased recruitment processes, increase female representation in informatics roles [15].

Professional development and training programs tailored to women in informatics, along with mentorship and networking opportunities, are crucial [16]. Policy leaders address gender biases through training and revising evaluation criteria, ensuring fair treatment for all employees. Policies supporting work-life balance, such as flexible working hours and parental leave, are essential for retaining women in informatics roles. Accountability mechanisms and resource allocation ensure continuous progress towards gender equity in informatics.

Externally, policy leaders set national agendas, establish comprehensive policies, and enforce legislation to promote gender equity in the workplace. Educational reforms and initiatives encourage women to pursue careers in informatics through STEM programs, scholarships, and gender-inclusive curriculums [17]. Public awareness campaigns challenge stereotypes and showcase successful women in informatics.

Incentives for private sector companies to promote gender equity include tax breaks, grants, and recognition programs [18]. Partnerships between public administration and the private sector facilitate mentorship, internships, and networking opportunities. Monitoring and reporting gender diversity data ensures transparency and accountability.

Internationally, policy leaders engage in cooperative endeavors to share best practices and establish global standards for gender equity in informatics, enhancing local initiatives and promoting a unified approach to gender inclusivity [19]. Resource allocation is strategically directed towards initiatives that empower women in informatics through targeted training, research funding, and community support networks.

Ultimately, policy leadership outside public administration not only shapes legislative and regulatory landscapes but also cultivates societal attitudes and practices that uphold gender equity in informatics. By advocating for comprehensive policies, fostering partnerships, promoting education, and advocating for systemic change, policy leaders contribute significantly to creating a supportive ecosystem that empowers women and promotes diversity in the informatics sector.

13.2.2.2 Role Modeling

Role models are concrete examples of positive characteristics or behaviors across diverse fields, serving as potent motivators, striving to achieve ambitious goals [20]. In public administration, the entire organization can serve as a role model by exemplifying inclusiveness and leadership in addressing gender equity, especially within the IT sector. This can be done by focusing on promoting the position of various individuals or groups within the organization as internal role models and also by positioning the organization as a whole successfully as a role model [21].

As highlighted above, internal role models refer to individuals or groups which directly or indirectly promote and/or positively influence the status quo of gender equity in the organization's IT. Some examples of internal role modeling are women in leading positions who serve as an example to aspirants, stakeholders who actively pursue a more gender-inclusive workspace by actively taking measures to promote gender equity within the organization, and more. To this end, it would be beneficial to identify the relevant stakeholders [22].

Externally, public administration's role modeling extends beyond its own workforce. It acts as a visible advocate for gender equity in IT, showcasing its commitment through leadership examples and inclusive policies. This external visibility not only sets benchmarks for other sectors but also encourages them to adopt similar practices, promoting a broader societal shift towards gender-inclusive workplaces. Role modeling supports the transformative vision by demonstrating the tangible benefits of gender diversity and reinforcing the organizational commitment to inclusivity [21].

13.2.2.3 Education and Training

Education and training initiatives are fundamental mechanisms for advancing gender equity within informatics, addressing both internal workforce development and external community engagement. Internally, these initiatives encompass certifications, workshops, and tailored programs that enhance technical skills while promoting awareness of gender disparities and fostering inclusive practices. They empower employees to advocate for gender equity within their organizations, driving cultural change from within, and enabling the transformative vision for a more supportive ecosystem [12, 23].

Additionally, internal education efforts also encompass mentorship programs and leadership development courses designed to support women in advancing their careers in informatics. These programs provide targeted support and guidance, equipping women with the skills and confidence needed to excel in traditionally male-dominated fields. Moreover, education efforts can be extended to the entire workforce irrespective of gender, to promote a shared understanding of the current internal situation and desired behavior. Gender-responsive training methods can serve to specifically target the skill sets of each gender profile, and provide a complementary measure to gender-neutral training efforts [24].

Externally, education and training extend through outreach programs that engage diverse communities and organizations. These initiatives aim to educate stakeholders about the importance of gender diversity in IT and provide them with practical tools to implement inclusive policies and practices. By promoting collaboration between public administration and educational institutions, these efforts amplify the impact of gender equity initiatives, nurturing a pipeline of diverse talent entering the informatics field.

Through strategic education and training, public administration not only strengthens its internal workforce but also cultivates a supportive external environment that fosters gender equity and drives innovation in informatics.

13.2.2.4 Partnerships and Collaborations

Partnerships and cooperation play a crucial role in advancing gender equity within informatics, leveraging both internal and external collaborations. Internally, partnerships with various departments and agencies within public administration facilitate a unified approach to gender equity initiatives. These collaborations foster a cohesive organizational culture that prioritizes diversity and inclusion in IT roles, ensuring that gender equity remains a cornerstone of organizational values.

Intra-organizational partnerships and cooperation support knowledge sharing in organizations. Moreover, gender-inclusive cooperation between actors in public administration benefits the work culture, by showcasing the benefits of gender inclusion in various internal projects and initiatives. These partnerships allow for the exchange of expertise and resources, enhancing the effectiveness of gender equity efforts across public administration.

Externally, public-private partnerships broaden the impact of gender equity initiatives beyond internal policies. Collaborations with industry leaders, NGOs, and educational institutions facilitate mentorship programs, internship opportunities, and networking events that promote gender diversity in informatics. Moreover, partnerships with advocacy groups and international organizations drive global standards for gender inclusivity in technology sectors, influencing systemic change on a broader scale. Through strategic partnerships and cooperation, public administration enhances its role as a catalyst for gender equity in informatics, fostering a transformative vision for a supportive ecosystem [12, 25].

13.2.2.5 Accountability Measures

Accountability measures are essential tools for promoting active responsibility and transparency in achieving gender equity within informatics. Internally, within public administration, accountability measures include tracking diversity metrics, conducting regular audits, and establishing clear goals for gender representation in IT roles. These measures ensure that gender equity remains a priority across all organizational levels, from recruitment to leadership positions. Furthermore, internal accountability mechanisms hold decision-makers accountable for implementing inclusive policies and fostering a supportive work environment for all employees [12, 26].

Externally, accountability extends to reporting practices and public disclosures that showcase progress and challenges in achieving gender equity. By publicly committing to measurable goals and benchmarks, public administration enhances its credibility and encourages other sectors to adopt similar accountability frameworks. Moreover, accountability measures facilitate stakeholder engagement and feedback, allowing for continuous refinement of gender equity strategies based on data-driven insights.

Through robust accountability measures, public administration reinforces its commitment to creating a supportive ecosystem where gender diversity in informatics is not only encouraged but actively promoted.

13.2.3 Objectives and Situational Analyses

The core objective is to develop and enact comprehensive policies and legislation that uphold and promote gender equity, demonstrating leadership in policy-making. The intention is to establish a model of gender equity in government positions, serving as role models in administration to inspire societal transformation. Through educational outreach and awareness campaigns, public initiatives and educational programs initiate to challenge biases and underscore the significance of gender equity in the workforce. A plan is envisioned to forge partnerships with educational institutions to cultivate an interest in computer science among students, thus building a talent pipeline for Informatics roles in public administration. Furthermore, specific instruments are devoted to accountability through monitoring, establishing a framework to track and evaluate the progress and impact of our gender equity initiatives. This commitment to transparency and ongoing enhancement is essential for assessing and refining our governmental strategies to achieve our mission [27].

Nowadays, growing facts and data prove that gender equity and the UN Sustainable Development Goals cannot be successfully achieved without the economic empowerment of women. Therefore, in order to ensure sustainable change and create an environment conducive to women's economic empowerment, effective cooperation with different parties, including government structures, private sector companies, UN agencies, development support partners, professional unions, civil society and local public organizations is crucial for the sector' development [19].

This assistance includes the development of gender-oriented policies necessary for establishing women's economic empowerment as a priority, integrating gender into national and sectoral strategies and action plans. This process focuses on strengthening the capacity of government institutions to use international standards to develop and implement gender-sensitive laws, strategies and programs that actively focus on women and impact their lives [15, 18].

Certain activities have to be implemented to empower women in technology. One of these means is the organization of employment forums. In order to participate in the employment forum, local and international technology companies should be interested, which will provide women with extensive career development opportunities. On the forum, companies may present vacancies that involve employment both in the local and international employment market, both as a freelancer and with the prospect of on-the-spot employment [28, 29].

In order to ensure more involvement of women in the field of technology, it has to be welcomed from the side of state administrations to organize large-scale training projects for women, such as: "Women in Informatics", preparation of joint mentor programs for sharing the experience of role models, etc. Implementation of "Women's Mentorship" is an important step to strengthen human resources and women's involvement in the digital sphere [30].

The promotion of such projects by state administrations is generally the basis of the economic empowerment of states, since such schemes emphasize the importance of developing various skills for women, which will enable them to become competitive in the local and international labor markets. The initiatives will contribute to the convergence of the United Nations Sustainable Development Goals (SDGs), especially in the areas of quality education, gender equity, decent working conditions and economic growth, through specific courses offered within such projects [3]. Women's economic empowerment is one of the important prerequisites for more efficient use of economic opportunities and rapid economic development of the country.

At the legislative level, the state administrations rely mainly on the principle of essential equity guaranteed by the constitution, however, in some cases, it is necessary to add packages of legislative changes to establish the vision of women's empowerment and define the main policy. Such concepts should justify the need and targeting of measures at both the macro- and micro-level and should be aimed at empowering women in informatics, which, in turn, will contribute to the increase of the country's well-being and economic power [31]. The need for such legislative changes may be caused by the creation of a quota system. In particular, to increase the participation of women in the field of informatics, the preparation and support of a number of financial support projects by public administrations, if the necessary participation of women is determined in advance among the project team and participants [12, 32].

A number of important steps have been already taken throughout the Informatics' sector in the direction of equal participation of women in informatics and their empowerment, however, there are still challenges that require the introduction of systematic approaches and the implementation of effective measures. Among the mentioned challenges, despite the characteristic differences of the states, approximately the same problems are observed: the inequity of access to resources, barriers to the recognition, reduction and distribution of unpaid and care work, the need to improve social policy, stereotypical attitudes related to professions, gender wage gap, including as a result of structural discrimination, and the individual financial inequalities caused by this difference, as well as other structural barriers. The existing barriers especially affect the socio-economic welfare of women who are underrepresented in the economy.

13.3 Results: Concrete Actions and Innovative Instruments to Promote Inclusion

In this section, we present the concrete actions and innovative instruments identified through our analysis to promote gender equity in informatics. Building upon the challenges outlined earlier, these actions aim to address systemic barriers and create a supportive ecosystem through public administration's active involvement.

13.3.1 Specific Actions and Innovative Instruments

To achieve the main goal of fostering a fair and transforming work environment in the public administration sector, we propose the following specific actions and innovative instruments. These are designed to strengthen collaboration among academia, the private sector, and other key stakeholders, with a focus on empowering women and girls in informatics.

13.3.1.1 Integrate Gender into Legislation

Integrating gender perspectives into legislation is fundamental to achieving systemic change. A key practice is the adoption of the Gender Impact Assessment (GIA) methodology [33], which evaluates the gender-specific effects of policies, programs, and services. As an evidence-based tool, it aims to improve governance and efficiency by incorporating a gender perspective. The methodology offers practical guidelines for officials, policymakers, and others involved in policy planning, implementation, and evaluation.

13.3.1.2 Strategic Planning Focused on Public Administration Initiatives

Strategic planning within public administration ensures that gender equity goals are prioritized and systematically addressed. Future goals should be strategically planned with a comprehensive approach, emphasizing public administration's role.

13.3.1.3 Invest in Women-Led Startups

Supporting women entrepreneurs is crucial for fostering innovation and economic empowerment. Strengthen connections with women-led startups to help them access funding and improve their technological skills. This will empower women and girls to develop independent sources of income based on their acquired knowledge.

13.3.1.4 Develop Training Programs Through Public-Private Partnerships

Collaborative training initiatives can enhance women's participation in the technology sector. Implement training programs focusing on skills development, internships, and employment opportunities through public-private partnerships.

13.3.1.5 Create Inclusive Learning Environments

Inclusive educational settings are essential for equipping women with the necessary digital skills. Establish safe, gender-responsive learning environments and implement targeted programs to boost interest in STEM fields.

13.3.1.6 Promote Innovative, Gender-Focused Learning Methods

Innovative learning approaches can reach wider audiences and overcome accessibility barriers. Utilize distance and blended learning methods to engage populations with limited access to the Internet and digital devices.

13.3.1.7 Launch Campaigns to Encourage Women in STEM and ICT

Awareness campaigns play a significant role in challenging stereotypes and encouraging participation. Organize campaigns to increase the participation of women and girls in STEM and ICT fields.

13.3.1.8 Address Gender Biases in Education and Training

Eliminating biases in educational systems is critical for achieving gender parity. Reduce gender biases that contribute to inequity in professional and higher education.

13.3.1.9 Promote Inclusive Science Education

Integrating scientific thinking into diverse fields like the arts and humanities can broaden interest in STEM careers. Encourage inclusive science education to reduce gender, socio-economic, and regional disparities and support women innovators and entrepreneurs.

13.3.1.10 Connect Women with Role Models and Mentors

Mentorship and role models are instrumental in breaking stereotypes and fostering an innovative culture.Facilitate connections between girls, women, and mentors in the field.

13.3.1.11 Establish Data Monitoring Mechanisms

Monitoring progress is essential for accountability and continuous improvement. Develop data sets and indicators to track the representation of women in technology and innovation.

13.3.2 *Effective Instruments to Promote Inclusion and Career Paths*

To support the implementation of the specific actions outlined above, we identify effective instruments that public administration can leverage to promote inclusion and create career pathways for women in informatics. These initiatives not only contribute to a more equitable workplace but also enhance innovation and productivity within the informatics sector.

13.3.2.1 Digital Skills and Future Technology Trends

Ensuring universal access to inclusive and high-quality digital education and training, and addressing the digital divide, can be achieved by creating a coherent framework encompassing investment, governance, and mentor training for effective and inclusive digital education. In 2023, EU member states launched new initiatives as part of the European Year of Skills to tackle two main challenges: the lack of a whole-of-government approach to digital education and training, and difficulties in equipping people with necessary digital skills. The aim is to reach a target of at least 80% of all adults possessing basic digital skills and to have 20 million employed ICT specialists, including a significantly higher number of women, by 2030 [3].

Firstly, targeted training programs, early education initiatives, and professional development are crucial. Coding bootcamps, data science workshops, and cybersecurity training sessions tailored for women can provide the foundational skills needed to enter the informatics field. Integrating STEM education early in the school curriculum and establishing coding clubs and competitions for young girls foster interest in informatics. Additionally, continuous learning opportunities and certification programs in key digital areas enhance the employability and credibility of women already in the workforce [12, 34].

Future technology trends like artificial intelligence (AI), machine learning, remote work, digital collaboration tools, blockchain, and the Internet of Things (IoT) hold significant potential for promoting gender equity. Encouraging women's participation in AI development helps create algorithms free from gender bias, and AI-driven mentorship programs offer personalized career guidance. Digital collaboration tools support flexible work arrangements, while virtual networking events facilitate professional connections. Technology-focused projects and hackathons targeting female participants stimulate interest and innovation, and smart work environments enable flexible working conditions, making the tech industry more inclusive and supportive for women [12, 35].

13.3.2.2 Representative Quotas

Representative quotas are a powerful tool for promoting gender equity in informatics within and outside public administration. Internally, quotas ensure women are well-represented in decision-making and technical roles, addressing gender inequity and enhancing the development of inclusive policies and projects. This contributes to greater workplace diversity, which improves organizational performance and innovation. Effective implementation of quotas requires clear guidelines, regular monitoring, and support structures such as mentorship programs and unbiased recruitment processes. National levels and inclusive workplace policies can increase women's participation in the STEM workforce like support governments in introducing gender quotas in incubator or accelerator programs, with the perspectives of women as employers and users being taken during the design process of products/services [12].

In the private sector, representative quotas mandate significant representation of women in leadership and technical positions, encouraging companies to address gender disparities. This fosters more equitable workplaces and drives innovation through diverse viewpoints [31]. Educational institutions can also adopt quotas to encourage more women to pursue studies in informatics, supported by scholarships, internships, and outreach programs [36]. Public administration can lead by example, setting industry standards and demonstrating the benefits of gender-inclusive teams.

The benefits of representative quotas include increased innovation, improved performance, and the creation of role models for future generations of women in informatics. However, implementation may face resistance, necessitating effective communication of the advantages of diversity and equal representation. Overall, adopting quotas can significantly advance gender equity in informatics, fostering a more equitable and dynamic sector that develops technologies benefiting all members of society [12, 31].

13.3.2.3 Promotion of Workforce Jobs

Visible promotion of workforce jobs is a powerful tool for supporting gender equity in informatics, both within and outside public administration. By making job opportunities and career advancements transparent and widely known, organizations ensure that women are aware of and can access these opportunities, fostering an inclusive work environment. This mechanism involves advertising job openings through various channels, implementing clear promotion processes, and highlighting successful women in the field to inspire others and demonstrate that gender equity is achievable [7, 28].

Inside public administration, increasing awareness through internal newsletters, public job boards, and social media helps women apply for roles they are qualified for, thus balancing gender representation. Transparent promotion processes with explicit criteria, regular feedback, and unbiased evaluations ensure equal opportunities for career advancement. Additionally, promoting role models and establishing mentorship programs where experienced female professionals guide and support other women further enhances their career development and confidence [7, 21].

Outside public administration, corporate transparency in job opportunities and career advancements can be achieved using company intranets, public job listings, and professional networks. Collaborations with industry organizations and professional networks through career fairs, workshops, and networking events focused on women in technology can attract more women to the field. These efforts contribute to enhanced diversity and innovation, build a supportive culture, and address challenges in changing organizational culture and overcoming resistance to transparency [28].

13.3.2.4 Educating Decision-Makers

Educating decision-makers is pivotal for promoting gender equity in informatics, spanning both public administration and the private sector to foster environments that actively support women in informatics careers.

In public administration, targeted educational initiatives are essential for raising awareness among leaders about the advantages of gender diversity. Training programs focused on gender inclusion enable decision-makers to recognize how diverse teams drive innovation and organizational success. Armed with this understanding, they can implement policies that foster gender equity, such as inclusive recruitment practices, specialized mentorship programs for women in technology, and flexible work arrangements that cater to diverse needs [12, 24]. Similarly, in the private sector, educating corporate decision-makers about the benefits of gender equity can lead to transformative shifts in organizational culture. Educational efforts that emphasize the positive impact of diversity on creativity and problem-solving can motivate leaders to implement inclusive practices in hiring, promotions, and workplace policies. Collaborative efforts among informed decision-makers can establish industry benchmarks for gender equity, creating environments where women thrive and make substantial contributions to technological advancements [28].

13.3.2.5 Enhancing Communication

Improving communication plays a crucial role in promoting inclusion and advancing career paths in the field of informatics. Within public administration, effective communication fosters a culture that values diversity and inclusion. By raising awareness of the benefits of inclusivity in informatics, leaders can enact policies such as gender-sensitive recruitment and mentorship programs, which facilitate career advancement. Additionally, open dialogue and feedback mechanisms help ensure that all employees have equitable opportunities, address barriers, and create a supportive workplace environment [37].

Externally, robust communication strategies are essential in the private sector and other sectors to promote inclusive practices in informatics. Organizations can leverage communication channels to underscore the business advantages of diversity, such as heightened innovation and problem-solving capabilities. Transparent communication about inclusive workplace policies, flexible work arrangements, and professional development opportunities encourages women to pursue successful careers in informatics. By nurturing networks and support systems through effective communication, stakeholders can establish collaborative environments that cultivate diverse talent and foster continuous career growth [38].

In summary, enhancing communication plays a pivotal role in creating inclusive environments and supporting diverse career paths in informatics. It empowers organizations across public administration and beyond to foster understanding, implement inclusive policies, facilitate open dialogue, and empower individuals through knowledge sharing and supportive networks. These efforts collectively contribute to a more equitable informatics sector where diversity not only thrives but also drives sustained innovation and success.

13.3.2.6 Removing Cultural Barriers

Removing cultural barriers within public administration and beyond is crucial for maintaining gender equity in the informatics sector. By fostering inclusive workplace cultures, public administration can create environments where all individuals, regardless of gender, feel welcomed and valued. This inclusivity encourages women to pursue and continue their careers in informatics, knowing their contributions are recognized and appreciated. Promoting diversity and respect within workplace cultures helps build a foundation for gender equity in the informatics field [18, 19].

Implementing gender-sensitive policies is another key aspect of removing cultural barriers. This involves revising existing policies to address unconscious bias, ensure equal opportunities for career advancement, and support work-life balance. Gender-sensitive policies help create a level playing field, enabling women to compete fairly and progress in their careers within the informatics sector [15]. Encouraging diverse leadership is also essential, as seeing women in leadership roles can inspire others to aspire to similar positions, driving further progress toward gender equity.

Facilitating open communication and feedback mechanisms allows organizations to continuously improve their practices to support gender equity. Addressing cultural barriers through training and awareness programs focused on diversity and inclusion helps build a more inclusive and supportive environment [16].

13.3.2.7 Supporting Career Choices

By offering targeted programs and initiatives, such as scholarships, internships, and career fairs, public administration and private sector organizations can specifically encourage female participation in informatics. These opportunities provide women with the necessary skills, experiences, and exposure to various career paths in informatics, creating a level playing field and empowering them to pursue and excel in these roles [17, 36].

Establishing mentorship programs and showcasing successful women in informatics significantly influence career choices and development for women. Mentors and role models offer guidance, support, and valuable insights into navigating the field, helping women build confidence, set career goals, and overcome barriers. Seeing themselves represented in leadership roles inspires and motivates women to pursue similar positions, increasing their likelihood of remaining in and advancing within the informatics sector [7, 21, 22].

Implementing flexible work policies, including remote work options, flexible hours, and parental leave, enables women to balance their career aspirations with personal and family responsibilities. By reducing the conflict between work and life commitments, these arrangements help retain women in the workforce and support their career progression. Flexibility in the workplace ensures that women do not have to choose between their professional and personal lives, promoting sustained career growth. These strategies collectively foster a more inclusive and equitable environment that allows women to thrive and succeed in their careers [12, 13].

13.4 Discussion and Analysis of Best Practices

In this section, we discuss the implications of our findings by analyzing case studies and best practices from diverse organizations and countries. These examples demonstrate how similar initiatives have been successfully implemented, providing valuable insights and lessons learned.

13.4.1 Case Studies and Best Practices

13.4.1.1 EUGAIN Booklets: Advancing Gender Equity in Informatics

EUGAIN has produced a series of booklets that compile best practices and recommendations targeting different stages of the educational and professional pipeline in informatics. These booklets serve as valuable resources for educators, policymakers, and industry leaders seeking to implement effective strategies to promote gender equity. The key booklets include:

- From School to University: This booklet focuses on encouraging girls to pursue studies in informatics by providing insights into outreach programs, workshops, and initiatives that spark interest in computing among young women.

- Future Informatics Students: Aimed at potential informatics students, this resource highlights compelling reasons to consider a career in informatics, featuring role models and showcasing the diverse opportunities available in the field.
- From Bachelor/Master Studies to Ph.D.: This booklet offers guidance on supporting women transitioning from undergraduate and master's programs to doctoral studies in informatics. It emphasizes the importance of mentorship, networking, and creating supportive academic environments.
- From Ph.D. to Professor: Addressing the advancement of women's careers in academia, this resource provides best practices for career planning, overcoming challenges, and leveraging opportunities to progress from doctoral research to professorships in informatics.
- Career Planning and Mentoring: This booklet underscores the significance of mentorship programs and career development initiatives in fostering women's professional growth in informatics, both in academia and industry.
- Policy Recommendations for Gender Balance in Informatics: EUGAIN offers strategic policy recommendations for institutions and governments to implement measures that promote gender equity in informatics education and careers.

13.4.1.2 European Union Initiatives

- The European Union has launched several initiatives to promote gender equity in the digital sector, such as the European Network of Women in Digital (EWiD) and the Women in IT Day. These initiatives aim to increase the number of women in ICT jobs and leadership positions [29].

13.4.1.3 UNDP's GEPA Initiative

- The Gender Equity in Public Administration (GEPA) initiative by UNDP has produced 13 case studies and a global report to establish a baseline for gender equity in public administration. This initiative supports women's leadership and participation in public institutions, providing valuable insights and recommendations to spur change [12].

13.4.1.4 Gender Responsive Policy

- Countries such as Iceland, Finland, and Norway have implemented robust policies promoting gender equity in public administration. These countries have consistently ranked high, achieving over 80% closure of their gender gaps, and serve as models for integrating gender-responsive policies and practices (p. 5) [5].

13.4.1.5 Girls Who Code

- Since its founding in 2012, Girls Who Code has built the largest pipeline of women and nonbinary computer scientists in the world. As of 2022, the organization has served 580,000 students, including 185,000 college-aged alumni. Girls Who Code is on track to close the gender gap in entry-level tech jobs by 2030 and has set an ambitious goal to reach 1 million students in the coming decade [30].

13.4.1.6 Harvey Mudd College

- Harvey Mudd College revamped its introductory computer science course to be more inclusive and engaging for women. The percentage of women computer science majors increased from 10% to 40% over five years, demonstrating the positive impact of redesigning curricula with diversity in mind [39].

13.4.1.7 Czechitas Programme

- This initiative in the Czech Republic aims to improve gender equity in tech across the country, focusing on young adult women. Activities include upskilling/reskilling programs and partnerships with various stakeholders [40].

13.4.1.8 Les Cigales: The Cicadas

- This program in France organizes events for high-school girls to develop their interest in mathematics and informatics, aiming to achieve better gender equity in technical and scientific professions [41].

13.4.1.9 Welsh Technocamps Programme

- Based in Welsh universities, this program provides support for digital upskilling, particularly in isolated regions, engaging with schools, teachers, students, businesses, and adult learners to promote digital education and training [42].

These case studies and best practices highlight the importance of targeted initiatives, inclusive policies, and strategic partnerships in promoting gender equity in informatics. By adopting similar approaches, other regions and institutions can foster an equitable environment that supports the advancement of women in the digital sector.

13.4.2 Lessons Learned

From these case studies, several key lessons emerge that inform our recommendations.

- **Importance of Targeted Initiatives:** Tailored programs effectively address specific barriers faced by women.
- **Role of Inclusive Policies:** Policies promoting gender equity create enabling environments.
- **Impact of Strategic Partnerships:** Collaborations amplify efforts and resources.
- **Value of Early Intervention:** Engaging girls at a young age fosters sustained interest in informatics.
- **Need for Continuous Monitoring:** Tracking progress ensures accountability and guides adjustments.

These best practices highlight the effectiveness of comprehensive strategies that combine policy interventions, educational programs, and collaborative efforts. They reinforce the feasibility and potential impact of the actions and instruments we propose, demonstrating that public administration can play a transformative role in achieving gender equity in informatics.

13.5 Recommendations and Future Directions

The Global Gender Gap Report 2024 underscores the necessity of a multi-faceted approach to closing gender gaps [5]. Based on our findings, the following key recommendations are proposed to advance gender parity in public administration and informatics:

Fostering Professional Networks
Establish and support networks for women in informatics to provide mentorship, support, and opportunities for collaboration. These networks can facilitate knowledge sharing and create a sense of community among women professionals.

Implementing Equitable Care Systems
Develop policies that offer flexible working arrangements, parental leave, and other support systems to help women balance professional and personal responsibilities. Equitable care systems are essential for retaining women in the workforce.

Ensuring Equal Opportunities for Skills Development
Provide access to continuous learning opportunities, such as advanced courses and workshops, to help women acquire the necessary skills to excel in informatics and AI-related roles. Investing in skills development is crucial for career advancement.

Increasing Female Representation in AI
Encourage the participation of women in AI through scholarships, mentorship programs, and targeted recruitment efforts. Public policies should aim to bridge the gender gap in AI talent and leadership.

Supporting Women's Professional Development in AI
Governments should provide access to continuous learning opportunities, such as advanced courses and workshops, to help women acquire the necessary skills to excel in AI-related roles. This support is vital for building a robust female workforce in AI.

Promoting Gender-Inclusive AI Research
Ensure that research in AI considers gender perspectives, encouraging diverse teams to work on AI projects and publishing findings in a way that highlights gender impacts. Gender-inclusive research leads to more equitable technological advancements.

Promoting Early Intervention and Education
Engage girls at a young age through STEM programs and early education initiatives to foster sustained interest in informatics. Early intervention is key to building a pipeline of future women leaders in technology.

Facilitating Strategic Partnerships
Collaborate with private sector entities, educational institutions, and civil society organizations to amplify gender equity initiatives. Strategic partnerships enhance resource sharing and collective impact.

Implementing Continuous Monitoring and Accountability Measures
Develop data monitoring mechanisms and accountability frameworks to track progress and ensure transparency in gender equity efforts. Continuous monitoring allows for timely adjustments and sustained progress.

13.6 Conclusion

Throughout this chapter, we have explored the current status and challenges of gender equity in informatics, highlighting significant disparities in digital literacy, representation in decision-making roles, and entrepreneurial opportunities for women. Despite progress in certain areas, women and girls continue to face systemic barriers that hinder their full participation and advancement in the informatics sector.

Key Findings Include:

- Significant gender gaps in AI talent and digital skills.
- Underrepresentation of women in leadership and decision-making positions.
- Persistent cultural and institutional biases that limit women's opportunities.
- Effective policy leadership, role modeling, education, partnerships, and accountability measures are critical to addressing these disparities and fostering a more inclusive and equitable environment.
- Stereotypes and negative perceptions about women's abilities in technology.

Public Administration's Pivotal Role
Public administration plays a critical role in driving systemic change toward gender equity. By implementing gender-responsive policies, it can embed gender equity into organizational culture and practices, setting a benchmark for other sectors and demonstrating the tangible benefits of gender diversity. Collaborating with private sector entities, educational institutions, and civil society organizations amplifies the impact of these initiatives, creating a robust support system for women in informatics.

The analysis highlights several barriers to achieving gender equity in informatics, including stereotypes, gaps in digital literacy, and the underrepresentation of women in decision-making and entrepreneurial roles. To address these challenges, the chapter proposes targeted actions and innovative tools, such as integrating gender into legislation, fostering professional networks, establishing equitable care systems, ensuring equal opportunities for skills development, increasing women's representation in AI, advancing gender-inclusive AI research, and facilitating strategic partnerships.

By embracing these strategies, public administration can promote a more equitable and innovative informatics sector, enhancing diversity, problem-solving capacity, and contributing to broader societal and economic progress.

Final Reflections:
By leveraging the influential position of public administration and fostering collaborative efforts, it is possible to create a more inclusive and equitable informatics sector that benefits individuals and society as a whole.

13.7 How You Can Do This

Here are concrete suggestions for the target audience on what they could do (referring to personas) with the policy recommendations or the social media dissemination.

Kim/Kimmy/Kymi—The university professor. Looking at the resources in this chapter. Kim presents the recommendations to her university steering committee. She aims to enhance student support during their education and encourage girls to become active leaders in informatics. Additionally, she is developing supportive strategies to help girls and women transition smoothly from studying Informatics to starting their careers.

Nicky/Nicole/Nicolas, the activist—Nicky organizes community gatherings to promote the rights of women and girls. She needs support from governmental public agencies and is considering collaboration for effective participatory policy development with public administration. However, she lacks experience in public consultation and coordinate actions with these agencies. Therefore, she is exploring the resources in this chapter to find the easiest ways for future cooperation.

Des/Deniz/Derya, student about to graduate—Des is completing an MSc in Informatics and is trying to decide between a career in academia and industry. She is considering using mobility grants offered by the Public Administration to go abroad for professional development. Des is exploring the recommendations in this chapter to learn how she can apply for these mobility grants, discover supportive tools for a future academic career, and find ways to encourage other girls in her student union, especially those from socially vulnerable families, to become more active in university activities and successful in their careers.

Acknowledgments We would like to extend our heartfelt thanks to Alicia Julia Wilson Takaoka for her invaluable contributions to this chapter. Her ideas and the documents she provided were instrumental in shaping our work. Although she is not listed as an author, her support and insights were crucial, and we are deeply grateful for her assistance.

References

1. European Commission/EACEA/Eurydice. (2022). Informatics education at school in Europe. Luxembourg: Publication Office of the European Union. Retrieved from https://ec.europa.eu/eurostat/web/products-eurostat-news/-/ddm-20221011-1
2. United Nations, "The 17 Goals," 2024. [Online]. Available: https://sdgs.un.org/goals. [Accessed: Oct. 4, 2024].
3. European Commission. (2023). Enabling digital education and providing digital skills. Available at: https://ec.europa.eu/commission/presscorner/detail/en/ip_23_2246 (accessed July 7, 2024).
4. Skillsoft. (2024). Women in tech report (3rd ed.). https://s3.us-east-1.amazonaws.com/skillsoft.com/prod/documents/Skillsoft-Women-In-Tech-Report-24.pdf
5. World Economic Forum. (2024). Global Gender Gap Report 2024. Retrieved from https://www.weforum.org/publications/gender-gap-report-2024
6. Eurostat, "Key figures on Europe—2023 edition," Publications Office of the European Union, Luxembourg, 2023. [Online]. Available: https://ec.europa.eu/eurostat/documents/15234730/17582411/KS-HA-23-001-EN-N.pdf/5d783d9e-9cb3-897c-8360-5122563ae8f3 [Accessed: Oct. 4, 2024].
7. ITU. (2024). National Center for Computing Education. From International Girls in ICT Day 2024: https://www.itu.int/women-and-girls/girls-in-ict/?ref=blog.teachcomputing.org
8. WOODRING, CAPTAIN PD: Some Psychological Aspects of Employee Selection. Australian Journal of Public Administration 5(4), 152–156 (1944)
9. Carey, G., Dickinson, H.: Gender in public administration: Looking back and moving forward. Australian Journal of Public Administration 74(4), 509–515 (2015)
10. Rauhaus, B., & Carr, I. (2020). The invisible challenges: Gender differences among public administration faculty. Journal of Public Affairs Education, 26, 31–50. https://doi.org/10.1080/15236803.2018.1565040
11. Su, X., Johnson, J., Bozeman, B.: Gender diversity strategy in academic departments: Exploring organizational determinants. Higher Education 69, 839–858 (2015)
12. United Nations Development Programme (UNDP). (2021). Gender Equity in Digitalization: Key issues for programming.
13. Scandura, T. A. (1997). Relationships of gender, family responsibility and flexible work hours to organizational commitment and job satisfaction. The International Journal of Industrial, Occupational and Organizational Psychology and Behavior, 377–391.

14. Subramaniam, A. G., Overton, B. J., & Maniam, C. B. (2015). Flexible working arrangements, work life balance and women in Malaysia. International Journal of Social Science and Humanity, 5, 34–38. https://api.semanticscholar.org/CorpusID:54873603
15. Kluber, A. (2023). Recruitment and retention strategies for women in government. GovCIO Media & Research.
16. Russell, M., & S. B. (2023). Advancing Gender Equality and Women's Leadership Capacity: Mentoring, Networking, Training. Advancing Women in Leadership Journal, 88–97.
17. Informatics Europe. (2023). Informatics Europe. From https://www.informatics-europe.org/society/minerva-informatics-equality-award/best-practices-in-supporting-women.html
18. Fatourou, P. P. (2019). Women are needed in STEM: European policies and incentives. Communications of the ACM, 52–57.
19. CGI. (2023). Building a more sustainable and inclusive world. 2023 Environmental, Social and Governance Report.
20. Morgenroth, T., & T.-R. (2015). The Motivational Theory of Role Modeling: How Role Models Influence Role Aspirants' Goals. Review of General Psychology, 19.
21. EU4Digital. (2020). Setting up mentorship programmes to bridge the gender gap in ICT: A guide for the EU Eastern partner countries.
22. EIGE. (2024, July). Gender Equality in Academia and Research - GEAR tool. From European Institute for Gender Equality. Available at: https://eige.europa.eu/gender-mainstreaming/toolkits/gear/which-stakeholders-need-be-engaged-gep?language_content_entity=en (accessed July 7, 2024).
23. UNESCO. (2019). UNESDOC Digital Library. From UNESCO.ORG: https://doi.org/10.54675/IJGQ3826
24. World Bank. (2021). Gender-Responsive Training Methods A Guidance Note. Washington: International Finance Corporation.
25. Kweilin Ellingrud, M. K. (2017). Partnering for parity: Strengthening collaborations for gender equality. McKinsey & Company.
26. United Nations Development Programme (UNDP). (2020). From www.undp.org: https://www.undp.org/sites/g/files/zskgke326/files/migration/sa/Gender-Balance.pdf
27. United Nations Development Programme (UNDP). (2021). Gender equality in public administration: Executive summary. Retrieved from https://www.undp.org/sites/g/files/zskgke326/files/2021-12/UNDP-UPitt-2021-Gender-Equality-in-Public-Administration-Executive-Summary-EN2.pdf
28. RippleMatch. (2023). 11 Companies Doing the Work to Support Women in STEM. From RippleMatch: https://ripplematch.com/career-advice/companies-doing-the-work-to-support-women-in-stem-f2c47cd1
29. UN-Women. (2024). Placing Gender Equality at the Heart of the Global Digital Compact.
30. Girls Who Code. (2022). Girls Who Code - 2022 Annual Report. https://girlswhocode.com/2022report/
31. ILO. (2020). International Labour Organisation. From ilo.org: https://www.ilo.org/media/8891/download
32. Profeta, P. (2020). Gender Equality and Public Policy. *CESifo Forum*, ifo Institute - Leibniz Institute for Economic Research at the University of Munich, 21(04), 37–40.
33. UN Women. (2021). Gender Impact Assessment Methodology. Retrieved from https://georgia.unwomen.org/en/digital-library/publications/2022/11/gender-impact-assessment-methodology
34. PAGANINI, L. F. (2023). Repositorio. From UFPE: Universidade Federal de Pernambuco: https://repositorio.ufpe.br/bitstream/123456789/51372/1/DISSERTA%C3%87%C3%83O%20Lav%C3%ADnia%20Francesca%20Paganini.pdf
35. United Nations. (2021). The Future is Equal: Gender Equality in the Technology Industry. United Nations, Economic and Social Commission for Asia and the Pacific (ESCAP).
36. Kurti, E., & F. M. (2024). Closing the gender gap in ICT higher education: Exploring women's motivations in pursuing ICT education. Frontiers in Education.

37. Afridah, L. (2024). The role of communication and employee engagement in promoting inclusion in the workplace: A case study in the creative industry. In: Feedback International Journal of Communication, 1, 1–15.
38. Mark, T.-R. (2024, February 8). Nexford University Newsletter. From nexford.edu: https://www.nexford.edu/insights/importance-of-communication-in-an-organization
39. Harvey Mudd College. (2021, August 20). Harvey Mudd's computer science program now a Harvard Kennedy case study. https://www.hmc.edu/about/2021/08/20/harvey-mudds-computer-science-program-now-a-harvard-kennedy-case-study/
40. Czechitas. (n.d.). About Czechitas. Retrieved July 7, 2024, from https://www.czechitas.cz/en-2/about-czechitas
41. Centre International de Rencontres Mathématiques. (n.d.). Home - CIRM - Centre International de Rencontres Mathématiques. Retrieved July 7, 2024, from https://www.cirm-math.com/
42. Crick, T., & Moller, F. (2016, January). A national engagement model for developing computer science education in Wales. 9th International Conference on Informatics in Schools: Situation, Evolution, and Perspectives, ISSEP 2016. Retrieved from https://cronfa.swan.ac.uk/Record/cronfa43586/Description

Open Access This chapter is licensed under the terms of the Creative Commons Attribution 4.0 International License (http://creativecommons.org/licenses/by/4.0/), which permits use, sharing, adaptation, distribution and reproduction in any medium or format, as long as you give appropriate credit to the original author(s) and the source, provide a link to the Creative Commons license and indicate if changes were made.

The images or other third party material in this chapter are included in the chapter's Creative Commons license, unless indicated otherwise in a credit line to the material. If material is not included in the chapter's Creative Commons license and your intended use is not permitted by statutory regulation or exceeds the permitted use, you will need to obtain permission directly from the copyright holder.

Part VI
Strategy and Dissemination

Chapter 14
Synergy Events: Design for Strong Impact

Simona Motogna , Karima Boudaoud , and Antinisca Di Marco

> **Kim, the university professor.** The annual conference in AI that Kim has been attending for the last decade will be hosted by her university. As one of the local organizers, she intends to propose a workshop on supporting young female researchers in academic careers in AI. She can find useful information and recommendations in this chapter.

> **Brandy, the industry manager.** Overwhelmed with the requests for gender equity in the company, Brandy decides to organize a workshop addressing the gender gap in IT. He found the information from this chapter useful and formed a task force for the organization of the workshop, using the chapter as the primary source of information.

S. Motogna (✉)
Babeș Bolyai University, Cluj-Napoca, Romania
e-mail: simona.motogna@ubbcluj.ro

K. Boudaoud
Université Côte d'Azur - CNRS - I3S, Sophia Antipolis, France
e-mail: karima.boudaoud@univ-cotedazur.fr

A. Di Marco
University of L'Aquila, L'Aquila, Italy
e-mail: antinisca.dimarco@univaq.it

© The Author(s) 2025
B. Penzenstadler et al. (eds.), *Actions for Gender Balance in Informatics Across Europe*, https://doi.org/10.1007/978-3-031-78432-3_14

> **Nicky, the activist.** She wants to influence regional and national politics regarding gender balance in technology-related domains. She can use the information from this chapter to determine the best event format and to find the necessary resources for planning it.

14.1 EUGAIN Events

Proposing an event or a conference for women in Informatics involves careful planning and consideration of various key aspects to ensure its success and impact in terms of *professional development, networking, and community building*. This section describes stand-alone events or those associated with other events and shares our experience about them.

It is our strong belief that it is important to identify venues where it may be relevant and very positive to include events related to women in informatics, and the format of such events should be designed in order to obtain a high impact. Meticulously planning and executing the event's organization assures its success and inspires the audience while also addressing challenges such as the perception of low standards, exclusion of men, or long-term sustainability.

During our project timeline, several types of events, described below, were organized with the support of the EUGAIN community, which covered a broad spectrum of possible attractive activities, offering suggestive ideas to different similar stakeholders.

General public annual conferences, for example *womENcourage*, are annual conferences aiming to connect women in the computing profession and related technical fields to share knowledge and experiences. Open to all genders, it provides inspiring support for those pursuing an academic or research career in Computing and related domains. The conference offers diverse activities, including keynote speeches, panel discussions, workshops, and networking sessions. Such an example is the *EUGAIN Workshop* at womENcourage 2023 (Trondheim, Norway).

This conference series, with the aim to support, encourage, and celebrate women in computing and technology, has a special focus on young researchers and students. It offers a large number of scholarships to aid participation, especially for less favored regions. The conference program includes various workshops related to career development, and the traditional poster session provides a stressless venue to disseminate early research results.

Another key feature of womEncourage is its connection with industry. Each edition includes a hackathon, where participants work in teams to solve real-life challenges, and a career fair presenting working opportunities in computing and technology.

Network building events create a supportive environment where women can connect, share experiences, and foster relationships that are crucial for career advancement. In a field where women are often underrepresented, these gatherings offer a sense of community and belonging, helping to mitigate feelings of isolation. They serve as platforms for discussing challenges specific to women in the field, promoting good practices in overcoming them. They play a critical role in fostering diversity, inclusion, and equity within the tech community. The community formed around such events can lead to collaborative projects. A successful example of network building events is the *WIRE workshops* at *ECSS* annual summit organized by Informatics Europe, which was the trigger that formed the community for EUGAIN project, further continued as *WIRE EUGAIN workshops* in 2021–2023.

Project internal events serving as crucial milestones in the project's timeline, provided structured opportunities for all project stakeholders to come together, evaluate progress, and plan future activities. They represented the main venue for sharing best practices, research findings, and innovative strategies contributing to the project's goals. *EUGAIN annual workshops* represent meaningful examples, with *EUGAIN Final conference "Opening the doors to the world", Lisbon 2024* representing the flagship event.

Professional inclusion and diversity events. Inclusion of diverse perspectives in specific research domains is known to be beneficial. Several scientific communities have adopted events dedicated to women, such as networking events organized by *Women in AI* at ECAI, or *Women in Formal Methods Workshop (WiFM)*. Such events have the power to support young researchers and to inspire through role models. EUGAIN supported one of such workshops, initiated by the WIRE group of Informatics Europe, namely *GE@ICSE*, with the goal of bringing together software engineering researchers and external experts to discuss the interplay of software engineering with gender diversity and other diversity aspects. It aims to advance gender equality and enhance the principles of inclusion and diversity within the software engineering community.

One of the main achievements of GE@ICSE is the community that has been built and extended each year, with people dedicated to the cause, debating open issues, and proposing solutions. The association of such workshops or satellite events with prestigious conferences in the specific scientific domain of Computing (such as Software Engineering, Artificial Intelligence, or Formal Methods) has the power to raise awareness of the entire research and practitioners' communities about the current status.

Award ceremonies. Awards for women in Informatics and other similar domains have been created to recognize excellence, inspire future leaders, and foster the importance of diversity and inclusion in a male-dominated domain. Such initiatives emerged worldwide, celebrating women's individual achievements, are *Women in AI awards*,[1] *IEEE Women of ENIAC Computer Society Computer Pioneer Award*,[2]

---

[1] https://www.womeninai.co/wai-awards.

[2] https://www.computer.org/volunteering/awards/cs-women-in-computing.

Anita Borg Early Career Award, ACM Rising Star and *ACM Athena Lecturer Award*.[3]

Another category of awards is recognising institutional efforts in promoting and supporting diversity and inclusion, such as *Athena Swan charter* or *Minerva award*[4] supported since 2016 by Informatics Europe and, in the last three years, with the contribution of the EUGAIN network.

Minerva Award recognizes initiatives that have a significant impact on the academic careers of women at various stages. It was created with the goal of offering examples of good practices to the entire European academic community, with the potential of widespread adoption by other departments, research institutions, faculties, and universities. The award acknowledges the support of different career stages: attracting young girls to study Informatics and to continue their education, facilitating transitions from doctoral and postdoctoral researchers to tenure positions in faculties, and advancing their academic careers.

14.2 Design and Planning of Events

Organizing an event is a complex process that requires a competent team and continuous communication. All activities, from setting the objectives to planning and program engineering, require people with experience and dedication. Without providing step by step guide, in the following, we provide some insights and good practices highlighted by people who were actively involved in organizing such events in the EUGAIN framework. In particular, in the following, we focus on selecting the event's objectives, shaping the event's program, and selecting invited speakers. For each step, we report the lesson learned by the answers of the interviewed experts, who have been actively involved in organizing events within EUGAIN framework.

14.2.1 Objectives

Whether it is a standalone event or included in a larger conference, the objectives should clearly focus on diversity and inclusion, with actionable goals, while considering the audience and other stakeholders.

Anna Slavi (organizer of EUGAIN Workshop at womENcourage 2023) highlighted: "Our goal was to bring together the EUGAIN community, reflect on best practices accumulated by the working groups, and connect academia and industry.

---

[3] https://women.acm.org/awards/.

[4] https://www.informatics-europe.org/society/minerva-informatics-equality-award.html.

It was a key aim to take EUGAIN's findings and practices outside of academia into the real world."

Jane Hillston (organizer of WIRE EUGAIN workshop at ECSS 2023) reported: "The participants in the event were leaders (Deans, Heads of Department, etc.) from Universities and research institutions across Europe. The objective of the workshop was to encourage this important group to consider the importance of diversity and inclusion and their role as leaders in promoting these values."

Bara Buhnova (organizer of EUGAIN Final conference "Opening the doors to the world" 2024): "The main objective of the event was to activate the EUGAIN representatives of the individual countries to create plans of activities in their countries that would disseminate EUGAIN results (mainly the booklets) and turn them into an impact in the countries. Besides, the second primary objective of the event was to build relationships with policymakers for mutual learning and exchange on maximizing EUGAIN impact through partnership with policymakers."

Karima Boudaoud (organizer of WIRE EUGAIN workshop at ECSS 2021): "The workshop focused on sustainability in Computer Science and particularly on "How to retain girls and women in computer science" at all the career stages. More specifically, it addressed: *(1)* understanding the reasons that push girls and women in Computer Science to leave (considering whether there are different reasons in different cultures), *(2)* discussing mitigation measures to retain them and *(3)* exchanging views on the best strategies to retain women in Academia. It also encompassed exploring from a perspective of Science how to progress in a more scientific approach when dealing with sustainability in gender balance."

> **Lesson Learned**
> Objectives for a diversity and inclusion event should take into consideration: (1) effective communication—awareness and solutions for closing the diversity gap and for adopting inclusion should be tailored to all participants; (2) engagement—the goal of the event should match the expectations of the audience to assure active participation and a positive experience; (3) external factors—the format and the timeline of the event should be adapted based on the general context where it will take place.

14.2.2 Program Shaping

A comprehensive program should ensure a mix of technical and non-technical topics aligned with the stated objectives and should include opportunities for learning, collaborating, and professional progress in correlation with the audience's interests and needs.

Anna Slavi (organizer of EUGAIN Workshop at womENcourage 2023): "The focus was motivated by a significant amount of members from academia, as well as a lot of knowledge in the field of gender balance in informatics."

Jane Hillston (organizer of WIRE EUGAIN workshop at ECSS 2023): "The program was designed to stimulate the participants to think about the issues. So, as far as possible, we aimed to make the sessions in the event interactive, with only a few based on presentations. Since many of the participants would not have much personal experience of being in the minority in their workplace we wanted to give them the opportunity to listen to the lived experience of others who were from less represented groups. The program also included sessions in which participants were asked to work in groups to discuss topics and potential problems."

Letizia Jaccheri (organizer of Annual EUGAIN workshop at ECSS 2022): " The program was decided in the core group, to satisfy the objectives of the project, namely focusing on digital transformation and informatics from a gender point of view. It included plenary presentations, networking activity and inspirational stories."

Bara Buhnova (organizer of EUGAIN Final conference "Opening the doors to the world" 2024): "A scientific committee for the event has been established, which designed the program of the event via regular joint meetings. It was clear since the start that the first day would be dedicated to a Management Committee meeting for presenting the project results and designing policy influence plan taylored for each participating country; the second day to the final conference with invited guests (e.g., policymakers) to share with them the EUGAIN policies and recommendations drawn during the project itself and to discuss with them how to actuate them."

Karima Boudaoud (organizer of WIRE EUGAIN workshop at ECSS 2021): "The workshop was chaired by two experienced academic staff, assuring different perspectives (one female and one male) and roles (one associate professor and one lecturer). The program was decided in successive iterations for over 6 months to achieve all objectives. However, the structure of the program was defined at the first meeting as it was already clear that we wanted to collect the retention issues and strategies at the three career stages (i.e., from School to University, from Bachelor and Master to Ph.D and from Ph.D. to Professor) but exploring more deeply the 1st stage. Therefore, we decided to dedicate a session for each stage focusing mainly on retention, in addition to a policymakers' session to have the point of view of the European Commission and a panel discussion with external speakers to discuss the best strategies to retain women in Academia."

The opinions of key stakeholders from various EUGAIN workshops provide insight into how these programs are crafted to meet diverse objectives and audience needs, highlighting aspects related to the audience, participants' engagement, and meeting the project's objectives. The analysis of these opinions reveals that effective conference program shaping hinges on aligning content with the expertise and interests of the audience, fostering interactive and experiential learning, and strategically meeting project objectives.

> **Lesson Learned**
> Programs should be designed not only to be informative and relevant but also engaging and impactful for the audience, such that participants will feel inspired and motivated to get involved in promoting gender balance in Informatics once the event is over.

14.2.3 Invited Speakers

The selection of invited speakers usually takes into account their expertise, relevance to the conference objectives, and their ability to engage the audience. In our case, we recommend prioritizing diversity in their background and in the perspectives of their talks. We always put an increased focus on trying to attract people who are inspirational and provide valuable inclusive approaches.

Anna Slavi (organizer of EUGAIN Workshop at womENcourage 2023): "The organizing board was made up of 7 young researchers, and based on the theme of the conference, we made recommendations from our circles, preferably outside of EUGAIN."

Jane Hillston (organizer of WIRE EUGAIN workshop at ECSS 2023): "We had one invited speaker in the classic sense, of giving an invited presentation. We also invited a professional facilitator to lead a stimulating workshop, leading to some lively debates, both within the small groups and then each group shared their decisions with all the participants... We also invited a set of panelists, who represented a number of different minority characteristics. Other sessions were led by the organisers of the workshop."

Letizia Jaccheri (organizer of Annual EUGAIN workshop at ECSS 2022): "We selected past winners of Minerva award, to promote them as role models and also to disseminate to all ECSS participants good practices in supporting women's academic careers"

Bara Buhnova (organizer of EUGAIN Final conference "Opening the doors to the world" 2024): "The second day of the event featured many invited speakers. The candidates for the invited speakers have been gathered from the EUGAIN Core Group, which focused on dissemination and partnership with industry and society."

Karima Boudaoud (organizer of WIRE EUGAIN workshop at ECSS 2021): "We had a considerable number of speakers from EUGAIN network and WIRE group from Informatics Europe. We also invited the winner of the 2016 Minerva Award and a professor from Bangladesh, who offered a totally different perspective on girls in Computer Science and Technology. To select them, we asked each WG leader of EUGAIN to propose and contact different potential speakers. Then, we organized a virtual meeting with each of them (particularly those external to the EUGAIN network) to explain in more detail the goal of the workshop, the session, and their talk."

The opinions from various EUGAIN workshop organizers highlight different strategies and considerations in choosing these speakers, such as attracting young researchers who are enthusiastic to contribute to the cause, promoting diversity of speakers, and considering their influence as role models. The analysis of these opinions demonstrates that the selection of invited speakers for gender balance should consider a balance of innovative perspectives, interactive facilitation, diverse representation, and inspirational role models.

> **Lesson Learned**
> With more than 50 speakers from the community and outside EUGAIN, we reckon the following as the most impactful consideration when inviting speakers to address diversity in Informatics: (1) interactive format fosters participation like debates, collaborative problem solving, and interactive panels; (2) inspiration and guidance through role models; (3) inclusion of young people to bring fresh ideas and trust in future actions.

14.3 Assessment and Impact

After organizing a conference dedicated to women in Informatics, assessing its impact is crucial to understanding its effectiveness and identifying areas for improvement. The assessment should not restrict itself to the conference objectives but also to the broader goal of promoting gender diversity and inclusion in Informatics, with an effective increase of representation and open opportunities for women in Computer Science. We give the feedback and opinions of our colleagues who act as event organizers in an attempt to envisage a strong impact in designing similar events.

14.3.1 Audience

We asked the organizers their perception on the participation: Were you satisfied with the participation? What was the gender proportion (percentage of women and men)?

Anna Slavi (organizer of EUGAIN Workshop at womENcourage 2023): "EUGAIN's community has a large presence of women, which is also true for ACM womENcourage. So we have more women than men, but it was a goal for us to involve men as well since gender balance is not only the interest of women."

Jane Hillston (organizer of WIRE EUGAIN workshop at ECSS 2023): "My impression was that there were about 100 participants and probably about 65:35 male:female. I was quite satisfied with the participation, even though some of the male participants found the topics difficult and uncomfortable. We will only bring about change if it becomes the responsibility of all the community to challenge prevailing behaviours. Many participants did engage very positively with the material, which led to some great discussions."

Letizia Jaccheri (organizer of Annual EUGAIN workshop at ECSS 2022): "Most of the participants were women, but being organized as a satellite event to ECSS, also men participated and contributed to the discussion."

Bara Buhnova (organizer of EUGAIN Final conference "Opening the doors to the world" 2024): "We were very happy about the participation. The gender ratio was 15% male, 83% female, 2% undisclosed."

Karima Boudaoud (organizer of WIRE EUGAIN workshop at ECSS 2021): "The workshop was organized as a hybrid event, given existing restrictions to travel in different countries. We were satisfied with the number of online and onsite participants. Being organized as an event within the Informatics Europe summit, men were well represented (approximately 25%)."

The composition and engagement of the audience at conferences focused on gender balance in Informatics are crucial for fostering meaningful dialogue and driving change. The opinions of our organizers emphasize that gender balance should concern everyone, not just women, and decision-making stakeholders should be attracted.

> **Lesson Learned**
> Enhancing participation in gender balance initiatives can be achieved through inclusive participation ("everyone is welcomed"), strategic integration with other events, and encouraging cross-gender commitment.

14.3.2 Impact

The success of the events is crucial for future opportunities to strengthen and enlarge the community. There might be several quantitative methods to evaluate them, but from the organization's perspective, the opinions of organizers may provide a more meaningful outcome. We asked our colleagues how they evaluated the success and how they felt about it.

Anna Slavi (organizer of EUGAIN Workshop at womENcourage 2023): "We assessed the conference to be a success. We received a lot of positive feedback both from within EUGAIN and from the invited guests. As it was co-located with ACM womENcourage, we have a good reach of people interested in the issue of gender balance but not yet affiliated with EUGAIN. It is still often talked about within EUGAIN, and the organizing committee was specifically empowered by the experience of having to work on it together for several months and witnessing its final success."

Jane Hillston (organizer of WIRE EUGAIN workshop at ECSS 2023): "There was a post-event questionnaire sent to all participants after the workshop by Informatics Europe. The reaction to the workshop had been positive and people had particularly appreciated the interactive nature of the workshop. This was influential within Informatics Europe to make it more interactive and focused on fostering skills and awareness of future events. I did feel that the event was a success and I felt very pleased about that. Raising awareness of issues faced by minorities, especially women, in the University Informatics environment, with people who have a leadership position and the power to change policies and expectations, can only be a good thing, even if it might take some time for the results to be tangible. I liked the fact that the workshop itself was an exemplar of a more diverse and inclusive way of organising a workshop. Instead of focusing on talks from a small number of invited speakers, we created an event in which the attendees were real participants and helped to shape the outcomes themselves."

Letizia Jaccheri (organizer of Annual EUGAIN workshop at ECSS 2022): "We considered it to be a success mostly because of the steps forward in our project work. During the workshop, through collaborative work, we were able to produce the Value Manifesto for EUGAIN."

Bara Buhnova (organizer of EUGAIN Final conference "Opening the doors to the world" 2024): "We have received many individual compliments on the event, both from the EUGAIN members as well as the invited guests. However, we did not organize a systematic evaluation (by survey or similar). One of the signs of success is the attention it received from the invited guests who have dedicated a number of days of their precious time to join the event in person. With many of them, we are now planning follow-up meetings to continue collaborating with them."

Karima Boudaoud (organizer of WIRE EUGAIN workshop at ECSS 2021): "We believe that the most import impact was the ideas formulated that were later expressed as objectives in different research investigations of the five EUGAIN working groups. As immediate success indicators, we looked at onsite and online participants. We considered it a successful event because it was actually the first live event in the EUGAIN project, and the interactive participation generated ideas that were then researched in working groups, and the results are tangible in the different deliverables."

Events focusing on gender balance in Informatics play a crucial role in raising awareness, fostering discussions and also in constructing a network that can lead to future initiatives. The insights provided by the EUGAIN network show that the impact should consider the middle or long-term influence and focus on broadening the community and actions. The analysis of these viewpoints concludes that the event impact includes raising awareness and engagement and enhancing collaboration.

> **Lesson Learned**
> In the case of addressing gender balance in Informatics or, in general, to STEM, the impact of the events should not restrict themselves to immediate indicators such as the number of participants or level of satisfaction but also focus on middle and long-term effects to support the sustainability of such initiatives.

14.4 Challenges

While trying to create and grow a community where women from Informatics, like in several other domains, can feel supported, recognized, and promoted, organized events deal with associated challenges. We will try to address some of the issues we considered while organizing and running such events and suggest ways to avoid or reduce them. The positive impact of the event depends on future inclusiveness in the professional, scientific, and academic communities.

Challenge *Threat of gender segregation*: since the objectives of the event focus on women and their careers, and in consequence, the majority of participants would be women, it might be the case that men might not feel welcomed or, worst, might not be interested in participating to such events. There can be several causes for this perception. The assumption of exclusivity might be suggested by the event call for participation or by the agenda, implying that their presence is not welcomed or needed. Men might feel uncomfortable or out of place in a predominantly female environment, worrying that the discussion will include criticism of their attitude instead of seeing them as supports and collaborators. Some men may not be aware of the importance of gender diversity and inclusion efforts or the role they can play in supporting these initiatives.

It is important to address ways to provide a diverse representation of speakers, panelists, and attendees.

Action Points
- Select speakers and panelists to represent a diverse range of gender and professional backgrounds;
- Consider geographic distribution, including different career stages and areas of expertise;
- Formulate call for participation to assure inclusiveness and design the event program to be attractive from a diversity perspective;
- Distribute the call for participation to various communities and organizations and try to ensure worldwide dissemination.

Such events should not restrict themselves to gender-specific topics, but it is recommended to include topics that are up-to-date and relevant to the entire community and foster a collaborative environment between all participants.

Moreover, the events should also point out that diversity and inclusion are key emergent dimensions to consider in designing future systems since digitalization is pervasive and impacts the whole population. This means the women's desiderata should also be included in the software system design. Otherwise, half of the potential users will be cut out from future services. To devise a multi-gender system, we need more women and gender diversity in informatics and computing teams working together in a pleasant and open environment where all feel comfortable expressing their opinions and suggestions.

Challenge *Perception of low standards*: Women-focused tech events are relatively newer compared to longstanding scientific conferences, leading some to view them as less established or credible. There exists also a misunderstanding of their purpose. Even more, there can be a mistaken belief that the focus on diversity and inclusion comes at the expense of technical rigor or professional relevance.

Action Points
- Cover a broad range of topics, including high-quality scientific content and professional development;
- A boost to visibility and credibility can be given by constructing partnerships with established organizations, universities, or other institutions to host or sponsor the event;
- Use diverse feedback methods to collect participants' opinions and to improve future editions, together with promoting testimonials about the impact and quality of the event.

We promote the idea that events that bring focus on diversity and inclusion are essential to any domain, and addressing this topic does not diminish their quality standards or societal relevance, rather it is a new challenging dimension to keep in all processes related to Informatics.

Challenge *Long-term sustainability*: Events focused on women in Informatics can face sustainability challenges in the long term due to several factors. Funding can be limited due to a small number of sponsors, which do not see a direct return on investment or limited access to funding coming from projects or governmental sources. There is also the risk of repetitive content, together with an abundance of similar events due to current interest, that affects the relevance and impact of such events. The continuity of the organizing committee and the willingness of the community to contribute as a volunteering activity also play an important role in long-term sustainability.

Action Points
- Continuously search for funding opportunities from different sectors, including companies, universities, and national and international grants;
- Understand the importance of the event agenda and activities to be new, relevant, and engaging for all participants;

- Assure a live community that is willing to contribute and carry on the work to ensure continuity;
- Partnerships with well-established conferences can help reduce the organizational burden and also provide access to a large audience.

A good strategy to enhance engagement and relevance and to maintain organizational stability can lead to the long-term sustainability of events for women in Informatics.

14.5 Recommendations

Based on our experience within EUGAIN, summarizing different aspects presented in this chapter, we want to equip our potential readers with step-by-step recommendations for organizing impactful events addressing gender balance in Informatics and engineering domains.

Looking at Fig. 14.1, we identified eight steps in organizing events:

1. **Set the objectives:** Are you targeting to raise awareness, educate, develop actionable strategies, or create communities? Clear goals will guide all subsequent planning. The objectives should include gender topics but also address the professional domain (i.e., Informatics) to assure focus and impact and also to attract all gender participation;
2. **Determine the audience:** Are your objectives targeted towards students, academic staff, decision-making roles, or a broad audience? Clearly identify several categories of participants. For example, if your objectives are related to attracting

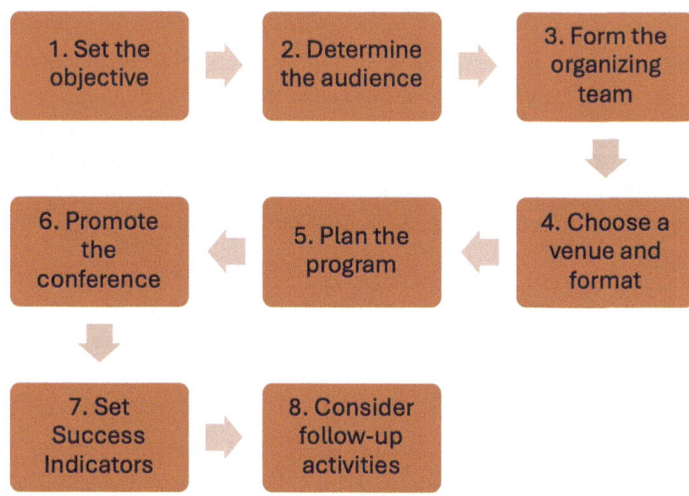

Fig. 14.1 Steps in organizing events

girls to Informatics, the audience should include girls, educators, school principals, but also families.
3. **Form the organizing committee:** Assemble the committee to reflect the diversity you aim to promote. This team should include individuals from different cultural backgrounds, genders, ages, and abilities to bring varied perspectives, but also people who are willing to allocate time and effort to this cause;
4. **Choose a venue and format:** Location, capacity and technical facilities are important parameters in the success of the event, but also in terms of available resources.[5] Assure a format that promotes engagement and inspires participants.
5. **Plan the program:** Decide a theme and key topics, then include a mix of different session formats. Allow time for networking and discussions;
6. **Promote the conference:** Assure inclusion and diversity through all written and visual materials that promote the event. Use different communication channels (digital and traditional); use professional networks and groups to disseminate the call for participation;
7. **Set Success Indicators:** Consider how you will measure the success of the event. Think about the short-term and long-term impacts. This ensures that the event not only achieves its immediate goals but also contributes to sustained progress in promoting diversity and inclusion. These indicators should also take into consideration the professional domain of the participants;
8. **Consider follow-up activities:** For a real impact on addressing gender representation, these events must act as triggers and must be continued through built networks, future events, or collaborative projects. Follow-up activities could include shared conference materials, recordings, and key takeaways of participants.

Considering the personas we identify at the beginning of the chapter, in the following, we define some takeaways specifically tailored to them.

Kim, the university professor In designing the workshop she intends to propose, Kim can find useful information related to the womENourage workshop or GE@ICSE. She can get inspiration on how to design the program and select speakers but also, given the specificity of the event, how to measure its impact. Also, the steps in organizing the event can ease the workload and help manage the organization. She will also know how to better address concerns regarding low standards.

---

[5] We did not address the financial resources and funding since our experience might offer limited recommendations on this matter. All the events were financially supported by EUGAIN, and other organizations, such as Informatics Europe, ACM, or hosting universities.

14 Synergy Events: Design for Strong Impact

Brandy, the industry manager can supervise the task force organizing the workshop on the gender gap in IT based on guidelines and lessons learned from this chapter. He can benefit from experiences from network building and project events and better address calls for participation and targeted audience. He is now more aware of the thread of gender segregation in such an event, and he can find mitigation solutions in advance.

Nicky, the activist can get inspiration from the EUGAIN final conference and better prepare invited speakers, program, and participant lists. She can address the challenge of the long-term sustainability of the event based on the action points presented in this chapter.

Open Access This chapter is licensed under the terms of the Creative Commons Attribution 4.0 International License (http://creativecommons.org/licenses/by/4.0/), which permits use, sharing, adaptation, distribution and reproduction in any medium or format, as long as you give appropriate credit to the original author(s) and the source, provide a link to the Creative Commons license and indicate if changes were made.

The images or other third party material in this chapter are included in the chapter's Creative Commons license, unless indicated otherwise in a credit line to the material. If material is not included in the chapter's Creative Commons license and your intended use is not permitted by statutory regulation or exceeds the permitted use, you will need to obtain permission directly from the copyright holder.

Chapter 15
The EUGAIN Policy Recommendations: Strategic Dissemination Across the Media Jungle

Karima Boudaoud, Birgit Penzenstadler, Sonay Caner-Yıldırım, and Fanni Bobák

15.1 Introduction: Why Policy Recommendations Matter

Equality means each individual or group of people is given the same resources or opportunities. Equity recognizes that each person has different circumstances. Equality is a founding value of the European Union, anchored in the European Treaties.[1] We also have a gender equality strategy in place.[2] Unfortunately, equity is not anchored in EU legislation in the same way—yet. While there are guidelines for the use of gender-inclusive language,[3] we found ample evidence in our network

---

[1] https://www.europarl.europa.eu/factsheets/en/sheet/59/equality-between-men-and-women.

[2] https://commission.europa.eu/strategy-and-policy/policies/justice-and-fundamental-rights/gender-equality/gender-equality-strategy_en.

[3] https://ecas.org/publication/gender-inclusive-language-guidelines/.

K. Boudaoud (✉)
Université Côte d'Azur - CNRS - I3S, Sophia Antipolis, France
e-mail: karima.boudaoud@univ-cotedazur.fr

B. Penzenstadler
Chalmers University of Technology, Göteborg, Sweden

University of Gothenburg, Göteborg, Sweden

Lappeenranta University of Technology, Lappeenranta, Finland
e-mail: birgitp@chalmers.se

S. Caner-Yıldırım
Erzincan Binali Yıldırım University, Erzincan, Turkey

F. Bobák
Ex Ante Consulting Ltd., Budapest, Hungary

that implementing such guidelines is not necessarily common practice and that more guidance is needed for how to put policies into place on a more local level.

Policy influence matters for supporting both equality and equity. It plays a crucial role in shaping the societal, economic, and environmental landscapes that affect the well-being and prosperity of populations. Policies, which are formal and informal rules or guidelines that govern behavior, are instrumental in directing the allocation of resources, guiding economic growth, and addressing social issues. The ability to influence policy ensures that diverse stakeholder perspectives are considered, potentially leading to more equitable and effective outcomes. This introduction explores the importance of policy influence through several key lenses: public health, environmental sustainability, economic development, and social equity. We then describe how our chapter provides the facts and numbers as well as guidelines for implementing effective policies for gender balance.

Firstly, policy influence is vital in public health, which is highly relevant for all gender equity work since most medical studies were carried out with male participants and hence do not hold validity for application to women's bodies. Policymakers determine funding allocations for healthcare services, regulations on pharmaceuticals, and public health initiatives. Influencing these policies can lead to improved health outcomes, more efficient healthcare systems, and enhanced disease prevention measures.

Secondly, environmental sustainability is deeply affected by policy decisions, and caring for the land is traditionally an occupation that is more ascribed to women, which reflects in their engagement in projects from preschool to higher education all the way through their careers. Policies related to energy production, land use, and pollution control can have long-lasting impacts on the environment. Effective policy influence can drive the adoption of sustainable practices, promote conservation efforts, and mitigate the effects of climate change.

Thirdly, economic development is shaped by policies that influence trade, taxation, and innovation. Policymakers who are well-informed and receptive to expert input can create environments that foster economic growth, reduce poverty, and improve living standards. For example, policies that support small businesses and entrepreneurship can stimulate job creation and economic diversification. Economic development is strongly linked to equity, and we wish to highlight feminist entrepreneurship: Entrepreneurial feminists as "change agents who seek to improve women's quality of life and well-being through innovative services, products and processes" [1].

Lastly, social equity and justice are profoundly impacted by policy decisions. Influencing policies related to education, housing, and civil rights can address systemic inequalities and promote inclusive growth. Grassroots movements and advocacy groups play a crucial role in bringing attention to marginalized communities and influencing policies that seek to rectify disparities. One aspect that is present very strongly here is equity. In the case of EUGAIN, we specifically look at gender equity.

In summary, policy influence is a critical mechanism for driving societal progress and addressing complex challenges. It enables stakeholders to contribute to the decision-making processes that shape the policies governing their lives, ensuring that these policies are responsive to the needs of the population and conducive to sustainable development. Understanding the mechanisms of policy influence and actively engaging in the policy-making process are essential for fostering a more just, healthy, and prosperous society.

This chapter is relevant for all 6 personas in this book representing our audience:

- Kim/Kimmy/Kymi, the university professor—"Give me visuals and stories", to help them convince university to install policies;
- Brandy/Bazyli/Bo, the industry manager—"With speed to excellence", to support them establish company policies;
- Nicky/Nicole/Nicolas, the activist—"Same value deserves the same rights", to advocate in public;
- Alex/Andrea/Anh, the school principal—"I raise the future generations", to lay out school policies and voice their concerns in the school district;
- Des/Deniz/Derya, student about to graduate—"Life is an adventure", to advocate for more support from the university; and
- Jem/James/Jamila, school teacher—"Science rocks", to request help for offering more science projects for underrepresented minorities.

In Sec. 15.2, we give an overview of the recommendations, and in Sec. 15.3, we share possible dissemination methods through real examples. In Sec. 15.4 we describe our dissemination efforts with posters, brochures, social media and videos. In Sec. 15.5, we describe for four of the personas how they can exemplarily use the contents of this chapter, and Sec. 15.6 concludes the chapter.

15.2 The EUGAIN Policy Recommendations

One of the aims of EUGAIN was to propose a set of policy recommendations directed to policymakers, at national and European level. In this context, we provided concise and practical measures that policymakers can adopt to support gender equity in Informatics.

Before defining the policy recommendations, we had first to identify the target audiences that would be interested by these recommendations. We have identified four key audiences: Schools, Universities, Public Administration and Private Sector. Then, we have followed a focus group methodology with twenty experts from twelve European countries, having different expertise and working either in an university, a private company or in a public administration/government.

For each of the target audiences, described in the following sub-sections, we have first defined our vision (i.e. the changes that we are looking for) and our mission (i.e. the main goals that need to be reached). Then, we have analyzed the current reality to identify the gaps, barriers and challenges. After, researching the current state of practice and investigating pathways to improve both education and career paths in a number of scientific studies, we have defined the set of policy recommendations. With this section, we hope to inspire policy makers at all levels, from preschool instructor to minister of education, to take action and support more gender equity in Informatics.

15.2.1 Schools: High Level Policy for Stakeholders

15.2.1.1 Vision

Our vision is to establish Informatics as a fundamental and distinct subject within compulsory education across the European Union. We aspire to cultivate a generation of citizens proficient not only in the use of digital technologies but also in their creation and critical evaluation. We envisage a future where students are equipped to navigate, understand, and shape the digital society, free from prejudices and stereotypes that often infiltrate digital tools and systems. In this digitally empowered society, Informatics education is recognized as an autonomous scientific discipline, offering unique perspectives on both natural and artificial phenomena and fostering critical thinking, collaboration, and social responsibility (Fig. 15.1).

15.2.1.2 Mission

Our mission is to integrate Informatics into the school curriculum as an independent subject, emphasizing its scientific and creative aspects beyond mere technological usage. We are committed to developing comprehensive educational resources and gender-responsive pedagogical approaches, ensuring inclusivity and diversity in the classroom. Through these efforts, we aim to provide optimal educational experiences that promote gender equality and equity and prepare all students, especially women but also other minorities, for a future in Informatics. We strive to create a supportive network of students, educators, and community members, all working together to break down barriers and pave the way for inclusive and equitable participation in the field of Informatics.

15.2.1.3 Current Reality

For schools, we have identified the following challenges:

Persistent Gender Disparities

- Despite ongoing efforts, significant progress in reducing gender disparities in Informatics has been limited [2, 6, 7].

15 EUGAIN Policy Recommendations

Fig. 15.1 Illustration of school environment

- The European Commission's report [4] emphasizes the need for early engagement of girls in Informatics to combat stereotypes and increase interest.

Identified Main Causes

- EUGAIN's investigation highlights four key areas: access, stereotypes, confidence, and sense of belonging (see Fig. 15.2).

Access

- Girls often lack exposure to Informatics, with limited access to technology and related extracurricular activities [5, 9, 13]
- Increasing access to early educational programs in Informatics has shown positive impacts on girls' interest in the field.

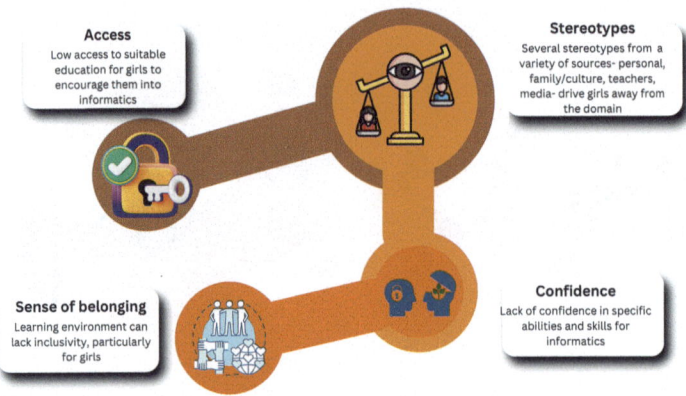

Fig. 15.2 Main causes of persistent gender disparities

Stereotypes

- Informatics is often perceived as difficult or suitable only for "geeks/nerds", influenced by personal, familial, or educational misconceptions [2, 10]
- Promoting relatable women role models is crucial to inspire and encourage girls in this field.

Confidence

- Societal messages and the lack of women role models in Informatics contribute to a lack of confidence among girls regarding their potential in this field [2, 5]
- Creating an inclusive and empowering environment is essential to boost girls' confidence in pursuing Informatics.

Sense of Belonging

- Non-inclusive learning environments contribute to girls feeling isolated and incompetent in Informatics [8, 11]
- Diverse learning experiences and increased representation of women can impact girls' sense of belonging in the field.

See Fig. 15.3 for a visual representation of the 'Towards a Better Future' concept, which summarizes key challenges and solutions for gender balance in school education.

Towards a BETTER FUTURE

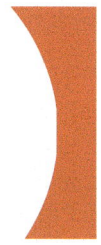

Addressing these challenges requires a holistic approach, involving societal attitude changes, stakeholder engagement, and policy reform. The goal is to create an educational landscape that encourages all students, regardless of gender, to explore and excel in Informatics.

Fig. 15.3 Towards a Better Future: School-level solutions for gender balance through educational reforms

15.2.1.4 Recommendations

For the schools, we have identified four target audiences: ministries of education, regional school administrations, school principals and teachers. Therefore, we have defined the recommendations according to these audiences.

For Ministries of Education

- **Legislation reform for inclusive informatics education acknowledge informatics as a fundamental subject and encourage**: An inclusive approach from the early stages.
- **Nation-wide informatics curriculum**: Establish curricular guidelines for Informatics, balancing technical and social components.
- **Allocate resources for teacher education**: Ensure teachers are well-prepared to teach Informatics in a motivational and inclusive manner.
- **National media campaign**: Promote Informatics in the national media to raise awareness and attract the younger generation to Science, Technology, Engineering, and Mathematics (STEM) activities.

For Regional School Administrations

- **Appoint a top-level official for informatics education**: Oversee the implementation of Informatics as a new subject.
- **Foster public-private partnerships**: Collaborate with regional enterprises for enriching educational experiences.
- **Professional development for teachers**: Provide training for teachers to enhance their confidence and effectiveness.
- **Support Extracurricular Informatics Activities**: Organize workshops, summer schools, and tech camps to engage students.

For School Principals

- **Training Teachers in Inclusivity**: Focus on workshops that create a supportive learning environment and address unconscious biases.
- **Awareness Campaign**: Educate parents on the importance of Informatics and inspire girls through role models.
- **Promote an Inclusive Classroom Culture**: Ensure a positive environment that values diversity and mutual respect
- **Provide a Real-Life Perspective**: Work with local tech companies and nonprofits to provide real world experiences in Informatics.

For Teachers

- **Advocate Early Informatics Exposure**: Introduce Informatics principles early and make them engaging.
- **Inspire with Role Models**: Use personal experiences and stories to motivate students and break stereotypes.
- **Emphasize Social Impact through Projects**: Engage students in interdisciplinary projects that address real world problems.
- **Foster a Gender-Inclusive Environment**: Create a respectful and inclusive atmosphere in the classroom.

15.2.2 Universities: High Level Policy for Stakeholders

15.2.2.1 Vision

Our vision is to transform universities into spaces that actively challenge the reluctance and embarrassment surrounding discussions of inclusiveness and equal opportunities. By breaking down these stereotypes and cultural barriers, universities can foster open dialogue and train individuals to become champions of inclusion and equity, upholding the principles that form the foundation of modern democratic societies. Universities have a crucial role in empowering diverse talent and driving the agenda for gender balance and inclusivity. By celebrating diversity as a catalyst for innovation and societal well-being, universities will contribute to a more just and equitable world. We envision a future where universities not only acknowledge gender diversity but celebrate it, breaking down barriers within academia and beyond (Fig. 15.4).

Fig. 15.4 Illustration of university environment

15.2.2.2 Mission

Our mission is to support universities in delivering actions that aim to recruit and retain women and promote gender balance in Informatics. Universities should become dynamic environments for gender inclusiveness and diversity, encouraging the collaborative creation of educational and scientific settings that value and disseminate gender-related knowledge. We are committed to supporting both rectors and faculty to empower equal opportunities for their students and employees and ensure gender balance across all levels. The success of gender- inclusive practices will encourage the development of a more diverse community where women may thrive and contribute to scientific advancement that adequately represents the world in all its diversity.

15.2.2.3 Current Reality

For universities, we have identified the following challenges:

Women Under-Representation in Informatics

- Workforce Representation: Women held only 15.9% of Informatics roles in the EU in 2021, down from 17.2% in 2020 [41].
- Academic Pipeline: Similar underrepresentation is evident in academia, with women less present in Informatics.

Persistent Gaps in Academic Career

- Women are under-represented in Europe at the highest level of academia—with minor improvements between 2015 and 2018 (from 24.1% to 26.2%) in all fields [14].
- Research Roles: Women constitute 39.7% of researchers in higher education worldwide [40].
- European level data shows that in 2018, women represented more than 40% of academic staff, but women only occupied about 25% of the equivalent full professorship positions.
- Women also remain underrepresented in Europe among the heads of higher education institutions (23.6% in 2019), and as board members (31.1%) and leaders (24.5%) [40].

Academic Leadership Positions

- Global Disparity: Gender parity in university leadership is low globally, with only 15% of rectors being women in Europe [12].
- While women are better represented among full professor positions in the Humanities (35% in 2018), there is a minimal presence of women in the field of Engineering & Technology (17.9% in 2018) for the same positions [42].

Contributing Factors

- Barriers: The gender pay gap, stereotypes, biases, and inflexible conditions are some of the barriers faced by women [15, 40].
- Academic Atmosphere: Challenges include lower social capital, unwelcoming environments, and discrimination [12].

Towards a
BETTER FUTURE

The systemic and cultural difficulties in pursuing the academic career for women have disadvantages not only for their own careers but also for society in general. The Informatics as a scientific discipline and as a profession needs diversity to advance and flourish. To make this happen, the universities have an important role to play.

Fig. 15.5 Towards a Better Future: University-level initiatives for promoting gender diversity

See Fig. 15.5 for a visual representation of the 'Towards a Better Future' concept, which highlights initiatives for promoting gender diversity in universities.

15.2.2.4 Recommendations

For the universities, we have identified the following target audiences: rectors, department heads and university professors. Therefore, we have defined the recommendations according to these audiences.

For Rectors and Department Heads

- **Inclusive recruitment process**: Collaborate with diverse channels to ensure job adverts reach a broad audience. Utilize inclusive language and highlight supportive policies to attract diverse candidates.
- **Equal opportunities in evaluation and promotion**: Form gender-balanced evaluation committees and conduct unconscious bias training. Define clear, inclusive evaluation criteria that account for diverse career paths.
- **Systemic actions to retain women**: Create an inclusive environment through anti-bias training and debates. Offer mentorship and promote visibility for women, alongside introducing family-friendly practices [15].
- **Promotion to tenure and management**: Encourage women's development and awareness of gender issues with a supportive environment and gender equity plans. Fund initiatives for promoting gender balance.

For University Professors

- **Diversification in course syllabus**: Include diverse authors and gender-related materials in the syllabus. Use inclusive language in course communications.
- **Fair division of tasks and responsibilities**: Ensure equitable task assignment in team activities and manage workload fairly in individual settings to prevent gender bias.

- **Gender requirements in evaluation criteria**: Integrate gender considerations into evaluation criteria, encouraging students to reflect on gender impacts in their work.
- **Projects on gender balance**: Propose projects focusing on gender balance and issues to enhance awareness and develop skills considering gender impacts.

15.2.3 Public Administrations: High Level Policy for Stakeholders

15.2.3.1 Vision

Our vision is to establish a transformative and equitable work environment within the public administration sector, particularly in Informatics roles. We aim to create a policy framework that not only addresses gender disparities, but also fosters long-term, sustainable gender-balance. The main pillar of this vision is the promotion of women based on merit (measured in a fair way, which is a challenge in itself), ensuring equal representation in Informatics and leadership roles in public administration. We are committed to driving societal change towards a more gender-balanced Informatics workforce, aligning with broader goals of sustainable development and inclusive governance (Fig. 15.6).

15.2.3.2 Mission

Our mission is to develop and implement comprehensive policies and legislation that support and enforce gender equity, known as policy leadership. We aim to set an exemplary standard for gender balance in government roles, serving as role models in administration to inspire societal change. Through education and awareness, we will launch public awareness campaigns and educational programs to challenge biases and highlight the importance of gender equity in the workforce. We intend to form partnerships with educational institutions to foster an interest in computer science among students, thereby creating a talent pipeline for public administration's Informatics roles. Furthermore, we commit to accountability through monitoring by establishing a system to track and evaluate the progress and effectiveness of our gender equity initiatives. This commitment to transparency and continuous improvement is crucial for assessing and refining our governmental strategies towards achieving our mission.

15 EUGAIN Policy Recommendations

Fig. 15.6 Illustration of public administration

15.2.3.3 Current Reality

For public administrations, we have identified the following challenges:

Lack of Diversity in Informatics

- There is a significant digital divide influenced by factors like race, gender, age, economic status, education level, household type, and geography, moderated by digital literacy support [21]. Due to digital divide women are excluded from actively participating in current life.
- Informatics remains a highly gendered area, contributing to social inequality [16].

- Digitalization impacts the efficiency and effectiveness of women in Informatics [20].

Under-Representation in Leadership

- Women are under-represented in decision-making and leadership roles in Informatics or high-tech companies [17].

Structural Barriers

- Women face barriers such as inadequate public policies, gender discrimination by employers, and insufficient technical skills training [19].
- No equal opportunities in case of parenthood [43].

Gender Employment-Gap

- Gender inequality in public sector employment, including renumeration and gender discrimination [18].

Limited Budget for Gender Balance Initiatives

- Challenges in implementing effective measures due to restricted budget allocations for promoting gender balance in Informatics.

See Fig. 15.7 for a visual representation of the 'Towards a Better Future' concept, which outlines strategies for advancing gender equity in the public sector.

The situation reflects a complex interaction of factors like digital literacy, workforce participation, gender pay gaps, and under- representation in decision-making and leadership roles. A comprehensive approach is required, including digital literacy support, policy interventions to address gender discrimination, and efforts to enhance women's technical skills and representation in Informatics roles.

Fig. 15.7 Towards a Better Future: Public sector strategies for advancing gender equity

15.2.3.4 Recommendations

For Legislation and Policy Changes

- Identify gaps in legislation to support a gender-balanced ecosystem in Informatics.
- Mainstream initiatives in legislation and policy affecting women and gender equity.
- Implement gender-based instruments in Human Resources policies for equal opportunities.
- Elaborate social standardized supportive system for parental care policy.
- Strengthen the Gender Impact Assessment with effective instruments.
- Launch National and European-Wide awareness campaigns for dispelling stereotypes and promoting inclusivity.

For Skill Development and Empowerment

- Equip girls and women for the transition from Informatics learning to earning.
- Raise competencies by boosting skills, particularly in Informatics, through training programs and professional development.
- Emphasize continuous up-skilling in rapidly changing technologies, especially in underrepresented roles.

For Financial Support and Monitoring

- Ensure a gender-balanced state budget to support initiatives for gender equity in Informatics.
- Regularly monitor and evaluate gender balance improvements, through intelligent solutions.
- Guarantee targeted funds and grants to support women-led tech projects, encouraging women initiatives in the tech sector.

For Public-Private Partnerships and Programs

- Develop specialized programs for advancing women's engagement in innovation and technology through public-private partnerships.
- Establish platforms and initiatives that connect women and girls with inspiring role models and mentors in the tech industry.

For Promoting Inclusion and Career Paths

- Implement representatives to refine gender imbalance in leadership and decision-making roles.
- Promote gender-balanced Informatics workforce in the job market.
- Conduct anti-bias training for decision-makers to reduce gender biases and stereotypes.
- Improve communication policies and tools for inclusion and career paths of women in Informatics.
- Overcome institutional cultural barriers hindering the inclusion and advancement of women.

15.2.4 Private Sector: High Level Policy for Stakeholders

15.2.4.1 Vision

Our vision is to achieve a transformative shift towards a balanced Informatics workforce in the private sector. Our vision is to create a work environment that excels in competitiveness and efficiency, while also fostering creativity, well-being, and flexibility. We aim to establish a landscape where diversity in Informatics is not just welcomed but celebrated, leading to a more holistic and inclusive industrial practice in the field (Fig. 15.8).

15.2.4.2 Mission

Our mission revolves around two fundamental pillars: (1) Promotion of Inclusion and Career Paths, and (2) Improving the Work Environment. First of all, we are committed to elevating the visibility of role models in Informatics, celebrating the achievements of women in the field. Our goal is to cultivate a supportive, creative and welcoming work environment that attracts and retains diverse talent. Besides, we strive to implement educational initiatives that address and reduce gender bias, focusing on societal and institutional patriarchy and psychological biases affecting gender perceptions. Additionally, we are dedicated to supporting family-friendly practices, including flexible home office and remote work options, and accommodating primary childcare responsibilities. Through these efforts, we aim to support gender equity, reduce biases, and create a work environment that truly embodies inclusivity and diversity in the private sector of Informatics.

Fig. 15.8 Illustration of private sector

15.2.4.3 Current Reality

For the private sector, we have identified the following challenges:

General Overview

- Gap in Industry: Despite progress in women's rights and workplace equity, the ICT industry still faces a significant gap in actual gender equity.
- Unbalanced context: The ICT workforce is not representative of our general population, and a more diverse workforce can help overcome the shortage of qualified ICT people.

Challenges for Women in ICT

- Barriers to equity: Women are a minority in the ICT industry and face challenges like inequality of opportunities and discrimination. These issues impact both product development and women's professional aspirations in ICT [22, 29, 34].

Efforts for Gender Balance

- Road to success: Various initiatives have been undertaken across different fields to balance gender representation in ICT. However, progress remains slow [30].

The Gender Equity Paradox

- Relevance for changes: ICT industry faces a gender imbalance even in countries known for gender equity.
- Engine of change: Persisting gender stereotypes and norms are identified as major contributing factors [25].

Drop-Out Rates and Job Satisfaction

- Losses in talent: High drop-out rates among women in ICT, with 50% leaving the industry within 12 years, despite high job satisfaction rates [29].

Identifying and Addressing Barriers

- Getting to know the challenges: Recognition of barriers women face in ICT and the absence of specific best practices to eliminate these barriers [33].
- Desire for new solutions: Need for well-founded and effective proposals to address these challenges.

Impact on the ICT Industry

- Importance of women in ICT: The lack of women and the challenges they face in ICT have significant negative impacts on the industry.

See Fig. 15.9 for a visual representation of the 'Towards a Better Future' concept, which emphasizes actions for gender balance and inclusion in the private sector.

Fig. 15.9 Towards a Better Future: Private sector actions for gender balance and inclusion

15.2.4.4 Recommendations

For Promoting Inclusion and Career Paths

- **Role models**
  - **Definition of role models**: Start with the basic understanding. A role model, as defined by the Cambridge Dictionary, is "an individual admired for their behavior, which others aspire to emulate."
  - **Importance of ethical leaders**: Emphasize the value of leadership. "It's crucial to have leaders, particularly ethical ones", as highlighted by [26]. They significantly influence both self-perception and how others view us.
  - **Role of adult role models across lifespan**: Discuss lifelong impact and mentorship. Adult role models play a pivotal role throughout life, including post-retirement. As [36] notes, "fulfillment is attainable at any age, allowing role models to impart wisdom continually".
  - **Celebrating women contributions**: Highlight the need for recognizing achievements. Acknowledging women contributions is vital, especially considering [27] findings that men employees often receive more recognition. Celebrating women as role models is a step towards empowerment.
  - **Digital storytelling as a tool**: Suggest practical methods. Digital storytelling is an effective method to honor role models. This can include general infographics about women contributions in a company or individual stories, either as anonymized personas or identified individuals.
  - **Example of role model promotion**: Provide a concrete example. Consider, for instance, a 'Role Model Flyer' for a working group leader in EUGAIN (see EUGAIN Template Role Model Celebration). This flyer could highlight both career achievements and personal strengths, serving as an inspiration to others. For instance, consider a 'Role Model Flyer' for a working group member in EUGAIN, Prof. Jane Hillston. Figure 15.10 illustrates such a flyer, showcasing both her career achievements and personal strengths, serving as an inspiration to others.

Fig. 15.10 An example of role model flyer

- **Job ads**
  - **Framing position descriptions**: Emphasize inclusive language. We recommend carefully framing and phrasing position descriptions to appeal to women applicants. Highlighting a collaborative and supportive work environment is key in conveying a welcoming atmosphere.
  - **Utilization of gender-inclusive tools**: Introduce practical tools. To assist in this endeavor, for example the GenderMag project offers tools designed

to ensure language inclusivity, helping to avoid stereotypes in user-facing software and other communications.
- **Explicit Welcome to Women Applicants**: State a direct invitation. Including a simple statement like "we strongly welcome women applicants" can be impactful. This explicit encouragement is particularly meaningful in fields where women are underrepresented.
- **Importance of Acknowledgment**: Highlight the significance of recognition. Although it might seem trivial to some, acknowledging the underrepresentation of women in certain fields can make a substantial difference to potential women candidates, offering them the encouragement needed to apply.

- **Explicit targets**
  - Apply explicit targets as a temporary measure in areas like upper management to correct gender imbalances.
  - Carefully communicate the purpose of explicit targets to avoid negative perceptions like imposter syndrome.

- **Maturity Models.**
  - Use maturity models to show clear levels of gender equity achievements and goals.

For Improving the Working Environment

- **Self Development**
  - Courses for women to expand skills and networks.
  - Special emphasis on early skill acquisition.
  - Education on societal and institutional patriarchy and psychological biases affecting gender views [24, 35].

- **Mentoring**
  - Implement active mentoring across all career stages, focusing on women-to-women empowerment and advice [31].
  - Acknowledge different career development phases and provide appropriate support [32].
  - Incorporate failure as a part of personal development and learning [23].

- **Family Support**
  - Support flexible work arrangements, including home office and remote work for family care.
  - Adapt work schedules to accommodate primary childcare responsibilities.
  - Create tools that encourage family management by men.

- **Engagement and Collaboration**
    - Encourage collaborative teams and informal mentoring.
    - Promote collaboration as a leadership style and create awareness on agency [28].

15.3 Creating Impact

From the very beginning, it was important to ensure that the project had a measurable impact. To quote the original purpose, among other outcomes, EUGAIN aimed to provide the academic community, policymakers, industry and other stakeholders with recommendations and guidelines to address the following key challenges:

- How to have more girls choosing Informatics as their higher education studies and profession;
- How to retain girl and women students and assure they finish their studies and start successful careers in the field;
- How to encourage more women Ph.D. and postdoctoral researchers to remain in the academic career and apply for professorships in Informatics departments;
- How to support and inspire young women in their careers and help them to overcome the main hurdles that prevent women to reach senior positions.

The previous section summarises the policy recommendations EUGAIN provided to policymakers at the national and European levels. These are concise and practical measures that can be adopted to support gender equity in Informatics. The main findings are summarised in the booklet called EUGAIN Deliverable 7: Policy recommendation document to reach all the target groups. As a result of the dissemination of the EUGAIN network, plenty of stakeholders from all over Europe have been informed and supported on the road to gender equality and equity in Informatics. However, mainly at the national level much remained to be achieved. To further support the dissemination, a Policy Influence Plan was created (for more details see Chap. 16 'Policy-making as an extension of disseminating research results: The Policy Influence Plan Canvas'). At the final EUGAIN event in Lisbon in April 2024, participants created plans to share the results in their environment. A few months later they were asked about their achievements. Apart from that, EUGAIN participants were asked in a questionnaire about the impact they have created in their near and far environment. All the inputs are summarised in the sections below. These real examples aim to serve as motivation and a crutch for everyone who feels there is room for improvement in one's workplace/company/university/school/country/elsewhere. It is important to stress that the list below is not exhaustive, since the EUGAIN network may have taken or plans to take further activities.

15.3.1 Examples from School

- Anita, a Researcher from Lithuania translated the dedicated policy recommendations and shared them with schools to be distributed to parents through the school's digital diaries.
- Birgy, a Senior Scientist from Estonia contacted an NGO of Informatics teachers to organise a panel and a workshop at their Summer School, therefore promoting the materials.
- The Italian EUGAIN members planned to organise and run a project within the National Operational Project's (PON) framework by involving school networks. It would focus on gender equity, therefore the topic would become part of the Three-Year Plan of the Educational Offer (PTOF—Piano Triennale dell'Offerta Formativa) of each school.
- Eylem, an English Teacher from Turkey presented Deliverable 7 to the Department of Computer Engineering at Yeditepe University. She got positive feedback, and a team was formed to work on including activities in the classroom that would motivate university students. An Erasmus + Project on the subject is also planned.
- Simona, a Professor as a member of the Department of Computer Science at Babes Bolyai University of Cluj-Napoca, Romania has regular annual meetings with teaching staff from highschool at regional level. She presented the booklet "From School to University" (Deliverable 4) to Informatics teachers. As some of them were not even aware of some of the issues, they were pleased to have access to resources and had asked Simona for advice in designing future activities for girls in Informatics.

15.3.2 Examples from University

- Birgit, an Associate Professor from Sweden presented Deliverable 7 to the leadership group of her department at Chalmers Technical University. She got positive feedback and was requested by a few colleagues to help them with individual follow-up actions.
- Several researchers and professors from the EUGAIN network have printed out the EUGAIN posters to hang in their Departments, in the STEAM Center and around the Institute. Thus, they are continuously visible.
- Anita, a Researcher from Lithuania wrote a newsletter about the final EUGAIN event and about the results of the project (linked the website and deliverables). It was shared with the Head of Marketing and Communication at Vilnius University. After sending out the newsletter, she received positive feedback and interest from colleagues and students.
- Sonay, a Research Assistant from Turkey applied and was awarded for the poster session of womENcourage 2024 Responsible Computing for Gender Equality,

ACM Celebration of Women in Computing to share the messages with hundreds of people.
- Olexandra, a Professor from Ukraine planned to organise a Carrier Lunch with students at her faculty based on the guidelines Booklet Career Planning and Mentoring prepared by EUGAIN Working Group 3.
- Gosia, an Assistant Professor from Poland had started to build a network supporting women at her faculty. She asked for the support of some colleagues to discuss and plan the actions and organised a meeting with the target group.
- Birgy, a Senior Scientist from Estonia initiated a team group discussion at her university for the Women-Leaders group and the IT School Board about the topics: "Is the situation similar in your field? What does the uni do visibly to include more women?"
- Antinisca (Associate Professor), Serena (Ph.D. Student) and Daniel (Ph.D. Student) from Italy planned to organise a one-credit course that can be run by each degree course management committee interested in the topic. During the course, the bachelor students would attend (1) a webinar (2 hours) presenting the EUGAIN results and explaining the importance of paying attention to gender equity issues so that students prepare and deliver; (2) a 4-hour online webinar for school teachers recognized for them as professional development; and (3) a short (max 2 min.) dissemination video on gender equity for social network channels.
- Ignatiuc, a Lecturer from the Republic of Moldova analysed the possibility of organising the Girls' Student Senate within the ASEM Information Technologies Faculty with the Dean of the Faculty of Information Technologies. They had discussed the possibility of organising a roundtable on gender equality opportunities in IT and STEM.
- Simona and Lenuta, Professors from Romania organised an event for representatives from Romanian Universities in the field of Computer Science. The objectives of the online meeting, which took place on March 17, 2021, were the following: (1) to present the EUGAIN COST Action and the opportunities within the project (STSM, conferences, training schools); (2) to build a network of connected women in Informatics; (3) to discuss possible collaborations; (4) to present initiatives that exist in different cities.

15.3.3 Examples from Public Administration

- Anita, a Researcher from Lithuania translated the recommendations and the dedicated booklet and shared them with their national education agency.
- Salome, Head of Division from Georgia shared the recommendations and other results with the administration of the educational institutions at all levels of education in her country. On behalf of the Ministry, they could translate and distribute all of the materials developed under Deliverable 7.

- Birgy, a Senior Scientist from Estonia contacted the AI group of the Ministry of Education about initiating a discussion on what dedicated topics and materials raised by EUGAIN to include in the developments.
- Eliot, a Professor Assistant from Kosovo presented the links to Deliverable 7 (policy recommendation, booklets, posters) to the Advisor to the Minister. They had shown interest and welcomed that Kosovo was presented as a case study in one of the booklets.
- Eylem, an English Teacher from Turkey presented Deliverable 7 to the administration of k-12 school, 'Istek Vakfi Okulları. She got positive feedback, and a team was formed to work on including recommendations in the classroom activities which would motivate k-12 students.

15.3.4 Examples from the Private Sector

- Patricio, a Director from Italy planned to organise an ECM course focused on gender equality issues for the Professional Association of Information Engineers.
- Fanni, a Consultant from Hungary contacted the Association of Hungarian Women in Science for a joint brainstorming about disseminating the EUGAIN results.
- Antinisca (Associate Professor) and Enrico (Full Professor) from Italy sent several emails summarising the project outcomes and pointing to online access to Policy Recommendations, Booklets, Posters, and Videos.
- Bara, an Associate Professor and Vice Dean from the Czech Republic presented the EUGAIN results at the 20th European Informatics Leaders Summit (ECSS) 2024.
- Fanni, a Consultant from Hungary shared Deliverable 7 with HUN-REN Hungarian Research Network and asked to hang out some posters and send out a newsletter about the EUGAIN results. She got positive feedback and planned to reach out to the relevant universities.
- Tiziana (Chairwoman), Enrico (Full Professor) and Vittoria (Full Professor) from Italy presented EUGAIN at the annual assembly of GII, GRIN, CINI and Laboratorio Informatica e Scuola.
- Laura (Professor) and Tiziana (Chairwoman) from Italy planned to make private companies involved in PNRR and Repubblica Digitale aware of EUGAIN booklets and policy recommendations. By doing so, they translated the documents into Italian, identified the contacts and reached them via email.

15.3.5 Examples of Cross-Cutting Activities

- Reyyan Ayfer, Letizia Jaccheri, Bara Buhnova, and Valentina Lenarduzzi organised an EUGAIN webinar on International Women's Day 2021.

- Since EUGAIN was launched, it has represented itself at the yearly womENcourage conference. In 2021, there was an EUGAIN roundtable "Path Towards PhD and Successful Academic Career".
- In 2021 and 2022, EUGAIN co-organised, with Informatics Europe, the WIRE-EUGAIN Workshop as part of the annual European Computer Science Summit (ECSS). The Women in Informatics Research and Education (WIRE) workshop had a different focus every year. In 2021 it spotlighted the theme "Sustainability in Gender Balance in Computer Science", with several sessions covering different aspects of engagement, retention, and progression of women students and academics in computer science and related disciplines. In 2022 it was about "Workforce for the Digital Transformation—Attracting and Retaining Female Students from Bachelor and Master to PhD", with several sessions covering different aspects of engagement, retention, and progression of women in computer science and related disciplines.
- EUGAIN was one of the eight European-funded projects that participated in the ACT TOGETHER Workshop, organised by the H2020 project RESET. The Workshop was part of the 4th Summit on Gender Equality in Computing—GEC 2022.
- Sonay, a Research Assistant from Turkey presented EUGAIN at the Management Committee meeting of BEiNG-WISE COST Action (Behavioral Next Generation in Wireless Networks for Cyber Security). She got positive feedback, and the printed and displayed posters and brochures kept the participants' attention.

15.4 Dissemination Across Media Channels

EUGAIN employed a comprehensive approach to disseminate its policy recommendations through various media channels. The creation process for posters, brochures, and social media content involved extensive collaboration among EUGAIN members, ensuring that the materials accurately reflected the network's collective expertise. Stakeholder feedback was instrumental in refining the content and design to effectively address the needs and interests of target audiences.

Design considerations across all media channels focused on visual appeal, clarity of message, and accessibility [37]. For posters and brochures, emphasis was placed on creating eye-catching visuals with concise, impactful text. Social media content was tailored to each platform's unique features and audience preferences [38], leveraging multimedia elements to enhance engagement.

The collaborative process involved iterative rounds of review and revision [39], incorporating insights from diverse perspectives within the EUGAIN network. This approach ensured that the dissemination materials were not only informative but also culturally sensitive and inclusive, aligning with EUGAIN's core mission of promoting gender balance in Informatics.

15.4.1 Posters

Posters serve as a visually striking medium for conveying EUGAIN's key messages quickly and effectively. They play a crucial role in capturing attention at events and in public spaces, making complex policy recommendations more accessible to a broader audience. The eight posters included in this book cover a range of suggestions from different levels which are school level, university level, public administration level and private sector level, each designed to highlight different aspects of EUGAIN's policy recommendations. Some of *these posters are visually represented in Figs. 15.11 and 15.12*.

Example At the ACM WomenEncourage conference, EUGAIN displayed a series of posters highlighting specific policy recommendations for universities. One poster focused on "Inclusive Recruitment Processes," featuring eye-catching graphics and concise bullet points outlining key strategies. This poster garnered significant attention, prompting discussions among conference attendees about implementing these practices in their institutions.

For the full set of EUGAIN posters, click here.

15.4.2 Brochures

Brochures are an essential tool for disseminating EUGAIN's policy recommendations, providing detailed information in a concise and accessible format.

The brochures included in this book cover a wide range of recommendations tailored for different stakeholders, including schools, universities, public administration, and the private sector. Specifically, at the school level, there are four distinct brochures designed to address the needs of different audiences: teachers, principals, regional school administrations, and ministries of education. Each brochure is crafted to highlight specific strategies and actions that can be taken at various levels to support gender balance in Informatics. For instance, the school-level brochures provide actionable recommendations for teachers to foster a gender-inclusive learning environment, for principals to promote an inclusive classroom culture, for regional school administrations to support extracurricular Informatics activities, and for ministries of education to implement legislation reforms for inclusive Informatics education. These brochures aim to create an inclusive and supportive educational framework that encourages all students, especially girls, to pursue Informatics. The university-level brochure offers guidance for rectors and department heads on promoting gender equity in academic settings, while the public administration brochure addresses policy changes and initiatives to enhance gender balance in governmental roles. The private sector brochure emphasizes the importance of creating a balanced workforce, offering practical steps for industries and NGOs to foster an inclusive and supportive work environment.

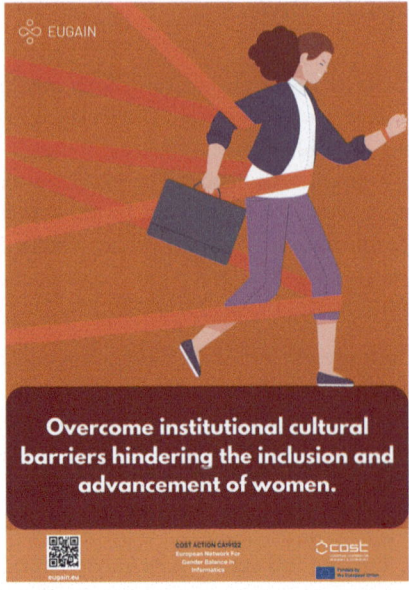

Fig. 15.11 Example posters from EUGAIN

15 EUGAIN Policy Recommendations 371

Fig. 15.12 Example posters from EUGAIN

Figure 15.13 visually represents some of the brochures' key recommendations. These brochures will be distributed at key events and through various digital channels to maximize their reach and impact. By providing detailed and actionable recommendations, the brochures aim to drive meaningful change and support the implementation of EUGAIN's policy recommendations across different sectors.

For the full set of EUGAIN brochures, click here.

15.4.3 Social Media

The objective of leveraging social media platforms is to amplify EUGAIN's policy recommendations and engage with a broad and diverse audience. Through platforms like, LinkedIn, Facebook, and Instagram, EUGAIN can disseminate its policy recommendations swiftly and effectively, ensuring they reach the right stakeholders and spark meaningful discussions. The dynamic nature of social media allows for real-time updates, professional networking, and visually appealing content, making it an indispensable component of EUGAIN's communication strategy. By harnessing the power of these platforms, EUGAIN not only broadens its visibility but also fosters a deeper connection and engagement with its audience, driving home the importance and impact of its initiatives.

Disseminating EUGAIN's materials through social media is advantageous because it ensures that the messages reach a broad and diverse audience across genders [3]. This balanced reach enhances the potential impact of EUGAIN's policy recommendations, promoting gender balance in informatics and related fields. Furthermore, users in Europe, who spend over 1.5 hours daily on social media platforms [3], present a valuable opportunity for high engagement with EUGAIN's content, making social media an indispensable tool for effective dissemination.

By leveraging these platforms, EUGAIN can ensure that its policy recommendations are not only widely disseminated but also actively engaged with by both men and women, supporting the organization's goals of promoting gender equity in the field of informatics.

15.4.3.1 Key Uses of Social Media

The Internet is used for various purposes including seeking information, staying in touch with friends and family, staying updated with news, and consuming video content. According to [3], 38.3% of internet users engage in education and study-related purposes, highlighting the significance of the internet for learning. Additionally, 47.6% of users use the internet for researching how to do things, which often involves finding educational content.

In terms of social media, the report indicates that 47.1% of users stay in touch with friends and family, 36.2% use it to stay updated with news, and 34.2% use it to seek information. Additionally, 30.3% of social media users engage in educational

15 EUGAIN Policy Recommendations

Fig. 15.13 Example brochure from EUGAIN

activities [3]. This blend of personal, informational, and educational use makes social media a powerful tool for disseminating EUGAIN's policy recommendations effectively.

15.4.3.2 Trends and Engagement

Engagement rates on social media are influenced by the quality and relevance of content. Effective posts that resonate with the audience can drive higher engagement and interaction, essential for spreading EUGAIN's messages and recommendations [3].

15.4.3.3 Social Media Networks

The posters were/will also be shared on social media platforms, including X, LinkedIn, Facebook, and Instagram. Each platform has a tailored strategy to maximize engagement:

- **X(Twitter)**: Quick updates and highlights of the posters, encouraging retweets and discussions. According to [3], X's fast-paced environment and real-time nature make it an ideal platform for sparking immediate conversations and spreading information rapidly. By leveraging hashtags and engaging with trending topics, EUGAIN can significantly increase its visibility and reach a diverse audience quickly.
  To follow our X account, click here.
- **LinkedIn**: Professional insights and in-depth discussions on the themes of the posters. LinkedIn's focus on professional networking makes it particularly effective for reaching academics, industry leaders, and policymakers who are likely to be interested in EUGAIN's policy recommendations. The platform's high engagement rates for professional content, as highlighted in [3], ensure that in-depth discussions and detailed posts about EUGAIN's initiatives receive substantial attention and interaction.
  To follow our LinkedIn account, click here.
- **Facebook**: Broad reach posts with engaging visuals and interactive content. According to [3], Facebook's extensive user base and diverse demographics make it an excellent platform for raising awareness and encouraging widespread engagement. The platform's features, such as groups, events, and pages, allow EUGAIN to create communities around its initiatives, facilitating deeper engagement and interaction with the content.
  To follow our Facebook account, click here.
- **Instagram**: Visually appealing posts and stories to reach a younger, visually-driven audience. Use of hashtags and collaborations with influencers to increase visibility. According to [3], Instagram's high engagement rates, particularly among younger demographics, make it a vital platform for spreading EUGAIN's

messages. Stories and reels, which offer quick, engaging snippets of content, are especially effective in maintaining viewer interest and encouraging shares and interactions.

15.4.3.4 Video Platforms

Grouping and Descriptions Videos on the YouTube channel are grouped based on themes such as policy recommendations, success stories, and educational content. Each video has an engaging description tailored to the target audience, making it easier for viewers to find relevant content and understand its significance (See Table 15.1).

Metrics and Impact YouTube remains a critical platform for reaching a broad audience. According to [3], YouTube is the second most visited platform after Google, with over 34.3 billion visits and 1.94 billion unique visitors monthly. Users spend an average of 21 minutes and 32 seconds per visit, indicating a high level of engagement. Metrics to track include the number of views, watch time, likes, shares, and subscriber growth. Successful videos will be highlighted, showcasing their impact on the audience. By leveraging these metrics, EUGAIN can gauge the effectiveness of its video content and continuously improve its strategy to maximize reach and engagement.

15.4.3.5 Social Media Plan

Strategy A social media plan involves a comprehensive strategy for each platform, focusing on maximizing engagement and reach. Specific goals and metrics have to be set for each platform to measure success. It may make sense to focus on a few social media channels and do those well as opposed to creating too many accounts and channels that then do not get used much over time and feel like a burden. We suggest to focus on a favorite two or maximum of three to keep the momentum going.

Create and Involve a Team It can be tough to do this alone—therefore, to keep engagement and momentum going, gather a team of like-minded individuals to share the responsibility and to support each other in content creation and posting. Social media posts have a short lifetime. Hence, regularity in posting and having a team behind to support will help ensure that regular updates, e.g. on a project, actually take place and the channels stay lively. If dissemination of policy recommendations is a goal, posts have to contribute regularly to a conversation in a given online space.

Create Sample Posts and Metrics Creating sample posts for each platform helps your team follow along with a certain envisioned style for the channel and with aligned content creation. In addition, it might be useful to have projected

Table 15.1 Overview of the most important EUGAIN videos

Content and link	Description	Video usage
About EUGAIN	Video presentation of the EUGAIN COST Action project, following the 1st Workshop held in Madrid in October 2021	**For everyone.** Regardless of your background, having a look at this video helps to frame the structure and aims of EUGAIN
Policy recommendations 1st Annual EUGAIN Workshop at ECSS 2021	Recorded material (video) from the EUGAIN Annual Workshop held on October 27, 2021 in Madrid Spain. Mina Stareva (EC) opened the conference, then we introduced the Working Groups, and there were panel discussions about Diversity and Sustainability in Computer Science. The panel discussions were mainly about successful mentoring programs and best practices	**Kim, the university professor.** Searching for best practices in mentoring Kim was inspired by SIGPLAN (Special Interest Group on Programming Languages), BWIT (Bangladesh Women in Technology), and the Dutch National Initiative. Kim, the university professor discusses a potential mentoring program with colleagues and brings the idea to the Dean with the support of the Department
Policy EUGAIN member country videos, MC opening, and panel 8th March 2022	These videos were recorded during the Management Committee meeting of March 2022. The purpose of this playlist is to give an overview of the initiatives about gender balance in Informatics in different countries for the benefit of the stakeholders in the given countries and of the International researchers who wish to compare the different initiatives. Stakeholders include schools, universities, ITC industry, and society	**Alex, the school principal.** Looking for international best practices and current realities, Alex, the school principal collects the most relevant ideas from the EUGAIN member country videos. Since Alex wants to support their students in succeeding, brings the shortlist of best practices to the next board meeting for collecting colleagues' feedback
Education Informatics Europe "Gender Equality in Informatics' webinar series	Launched in June 2022, this Gender Equality in Informatics webinar series aimed to contribute to sharing best practices as well as relevant research about gender equality and diversity in computer science. The series is a way to strengthen both the understanding as well as the action perspective of this topic. EUGAIN, in collaboration with Informatics Europe, organised this webinar series, with a total of 11 webinars, between June 2022 and July 2023	**Brandy, the industry manager.** Being "overwhelmed" with the request of gender equity in his department, Brandy looks for some quickly adaptable but effective actions. Having a look at the webinar series, Brandy, the industry manager not only understands the challenges of gender inclusion but gets useful ideas and best practices. Taking them into the next board meeting, Brandy starts a workshop with the other managers by using the World Cafe Method to discuss the shortlisted six best practices chosen by Brandy from the webinars

Education EUGAIN Webinars	The webinars focus on Academia while introducing exchange (e.g. Scientific Mission, STSM) and other (e.g. Conference Grants) opportunities. Apart from that, Professor Laura Kovacs (ERC grantee three times) gives an inspirational talk about her research and researcher life	**Des, a student about to graduate.** Looking for opportunities for mobility grants to go abroad, Des found the EUGAIN webinars about several possibilities in Academia. Besides, Des, a graduating student can also collect information about the benefits and challenges of being a researcher
Success stories Why Choose IT?—EUGAIN Young Researchers	Motivational and inspirational reels of EUGAIN Young Researchers about why they chose this profession	**Jamila, the school teacher.** Looking at the videos in this chapter, Jamila the high school teacher takes the reels to their next class with the graduating students. After having seen all the short videos, Jamila created small groups from the class and let them discuss what was the most motivational for them in choosing IT as a profession, but also listing its disadvantages. The activity seems to be effective in supporting the student's career search

engagement metrics. For example, "We aim for a 5% engagement rate on X and a 10% click-through rate on the YouTube videos."

Tracking and Analysis Tools and analysis methods are useful to track and evaluate the effectiveness of social media performance, including platform-specific insights like Google Analytics. Reviewing metrics periodically can help adjust strategies and improve engagement over time.

15.5 How You Can Do This

Here are concrete suggestions for the target audience on what they could do (referring to personas) with the policy recommendations or the social media dissemination.

> **Kymi, the university professor.** Kymi is delighted that EUGAIN provides a large set of brochures and visuals—that's exactly what they need. The new semester is about to start, orientation week is next week, and she wants to make sure that all women students feel especially welcome, since the computer science program is currently at only 15% women students. Kymi downloads and prints out the posters from the EUGAIN website in A3 and hangs twenty copies on the various walls of her department, the entrance to the floor, as well as in the rooms where the computer science students will have their orientation days.

> **Bazyli, the industry manager.** Bazyli wants to show upper management how important it is to showcase their successful women employees as role models and positive examples for both good content work and for their dedication to team spirit and inclusion. They decide to use the role model template from EUGAIN Deliverable 7 (p. 36) to create a few posters with the consent of some of the women employees who have been at the company for a while to give more visibility to their successes and to celebrate them for their contributions.

> **Nicky, the activist.** Nicky knows that same value deserves the same rights and is super excited to see a large set of recommendations compiled in EUGAIN Deliverable 7. They decide to print it and deliver copies to the city representative for gender equity as well as the mayor and encourages them to take those recommendations into account when deciding on how to plan for and distribute the city budget for the following year.

> **Anh, the school principal.** Anh sees it as her mission to raise the future generations, and hence wishes to create a school environment where all students feel empowered and supported. Knowing that there are still a lot of societal stereotypes about what are suitable jobs for women versus uncommon jobs, she decides to find pictures of successful women scientists across history and have the end of school year talent show around the theme of "Women in Science". Kids choose to perform little theater scenes, sing songs, write and recite poems, or show a dance to let some historical scenes of women in science come to life.

There is a million ways of how to make use of the material in this chapter as well as in this entire book, and we hope these initial examples give you some motivation to pick up whatever material or thought inspires you most and do something with it.

15.6 What's Next?

In this chapter, we introduced the EUGAIN policy recommendations. Shortly after publishing those, we realized that we needed to educate our fellow project members as well as other stakeholders, like our personas, about how to influence policy making. For that, we point you to the following chapter, which introduces a Policy Influence Plan to map out strategies and timelines.

References

1. B. J. Orser, C. Elliott, and J. Leck. Feminist attributes and entrepreneurial identity. *Gender in Management: An International Journal*, 26(8):561–589, 2011.
2. B. Lorenz, K. Kikkas, and T. Sõmer, "IT as a career choice for girls: breaking the (self-imposed) glass ceiling," in *ECEL 2021 20th European Conference on e-Learning*, Academic Conferences International limited, 2021, pp. 266–274.
3. Social, We Are and Meltwater, "Digital 2023 Global Overview Report. We are Social," 2023. [Online]. Available: https://wearesocial.com/wp-content/uploads/2023/03/Digital-2023-Global-Overview-Report.pdf.
4. J. Monnet, "Informatics education at school in Europe," *Publications Office of the European Union: Luxembourg*, 2022.
5. L. Happe, B. Buhnova, A. Koziolek, and I. Wagner, "Effective measures to foster girls' interest in secondary computer science education: A literature review," *Education and Information Technologies*, vol. 26, pp. 2811–2829, 2021.
6. T. E. S. Charlesworth and M. R. Banaji, "Gender in science, technology, engineering, and mathematics: Issues, causes, solutions," *Journal of Neuroscience*, vol. 39, no. 37, pp. 7228–7243, 2019.
7. A. Master, A. N. Meltzoff, and S. Cheryan, "Gender stereotypes about interests start early and cause gender disparities in computer science and engineering," *Proceedings of the National Academy of Sciences*, vol. 118, no. 48, p. e2100030118, 2021.

8. E. Nardelli and I. Corradini, "Informatics Education in School: A Multi-Year Large-Scale Study on Female Participation and Teachers' Beliefs," in *Informatics in Schools. New Ideas in School Informatics: 12th International Conference on Informatics in Schools: Situation, Evolution, and Perspectives, ISSEP 2019, Larnaca, Cyprus, November 18–20, 2019, Proceedings 12*, Springer, 2019, pp. 53–67.
9. Z. Şahin Timar and Ö. Mısırlı, "Effective Strategies for Encouraging Girls in Informatics," in *International Conference on Human-Computer Interaction*, Springer, 2023, pp. 377–392.
10. S. Torres-Ramos et al., "Mentors as female role models in STEM disciplines and their benefits," *Sustainability*, vol. 13, no. 23, p. 12938, 2021.
11. F. Vainionpää, M. Kinnula, N. Iivari, and T. Molin-Juustila, "Girls' choice: why won't they pick it?," in *Proceedings of the 27th European Conference on Information Systems (ECIS)*, Stockholm & Uppsala, Sweden, June 8-14, 2019, Association for Information Systems.
12. B. J. Casad et al., "Gender inequality in academia: Problems and solutions for women faculty in STEM," *Journal of Neuroscience Research*, vol. 99, no. 1, pp. 13–23, 2021.
13. Girls Who Code, "2019 Advocacy Report—THE STATE OF GIRLS IN K-12 COMPUTER SCIENCE CLASSROOMS: MAKING THE CASE FOR GENDER-SPECIFIC EDUCATION POLICIES," Girls Who Code, 2019. [Online]. Available: https://girlswhocode.com/wp-content/uploads/2019/06/GWC_Advocacy_2019K12Report_PDF-min-1.pdf.
14. J. Gvozdanović and K. Maes, "Implicit Bias in Academia: A Challenge to the Meritocratic Principle and to Women's Careers–and What to Do About It," *League of European Research Universities (LERU) Advice Paper No*, vol. 23, 2018.
15. S. Motogna, L. Alboaie, I. A. Todericiu, and C. Zaharia, "Retaining women in computer science: The good, the bad and the ugly sides," in *Proceedings of the Third Workshop on Gender Equality, Diversity, and Inclusion in Software Engineering*, 2022, pp. 35–42.
16. E. Ferreira and M. J. Silva, "Portuguese research on Gender and ICT: The place of education," in *2016 International Symposium on Computers in Education (SIIE)*, IEEE, 2016, pp. 1–6.
17. C. Figueroa-Domecq et al., "Technology double gender gap in tourism business leadership," *Information Technology & Tourism*, vol. 22, no. 1, pp. 75–106, 2020.
18. K. Johnston, "Women in public policy and public administration?," *Public Money & Management*, vol. 39, no. 3, pp. 155–165, 2019.
19. V. W. A. Mbarika et al., "IT education and workforce participation: A new era for women in Kenya?," *The Information Society*, vol. 23, no. 1, pp. 1–18, 2007.
20. Prof. Samanta, "Impact of Digitalisation on Efficiency and Effectiveness of Women-A Case Study," *International Journal of Finance, Entrepreneurship & Sustainability (IJFES)*, vol. 2, no. 1, 2022.
21. R. Tirado-Morueta et al., "The socio-demographic divide in Internet usage moderated by digital literacy support," *Technology in Society*, vol. 55, pp. 47–55, 2018.
22. K. Albusays et al., "The diversity crisis in software development," *IEEE Software*, vol. 38, no. 2, pp. 19–25, 2021.
23. D. E. Boyd, J. Baudier, and T. Stromie, "Flipping the mindset: Reframing fear and failure to catalyze development," *To Improve the Academy*, vol. 34, no. 1–2, pp. 1–19, 2015.
24. L. Brannon, *Gender: psychological perspectives*, Routledge, 2016.
25. T. Breda et al., "Gender stereotypes can explain the gender-equality paradox," *Proceedings of the National Academy of Sciences*, vol. 117, no. 49, pp. 31063–31069, 2020.
26. M. E. Brown and L. K. Treviño, "Do role models matter? An investigation of role modeling as an antecedent of perceived ethical leadership," *Journal of Business Ethics*, vol. 122, pp. 587–598, 2014.
27. G. F. Dreher and R. A. Ash, "A comparative study of mentoring among men and women in managerial, professional, and technical positions," *Journal of Applied Psychology*, vol. 75, no. 5, p. 539, 1990.
28. M. G. Fine, "Women, collaboration, and social change: An ethics-based model of leadership," *Women and leadership: Transforming visions and diverse voices*, pp. 177–191, 2007.
29. J. L. Glass et al., "What's so special about STEM? A comparison of women's retention in STEM and professional occupations," *Social Forces*, vol. 92, no. 2, pp. 723–756, 2013.

30. L. Jaccheri et al., "Gender issues in computer science: Lessons learnt and reflections for the future," in *2020 22nd International Symposium on Symbolic and Numeric Algorithms for Scientific Computing (SYNASC)*, IEEE, 2020, pp. 9–16.
31. A. L. Mitchell, "Woman-to-woman mentorship: exploring the components of effective mentoring relationships to promote and increase women's representation in top leadership roles," Ph.D. dissertation, University of La Verne, 2018.
32. D. A. O'Neil and D. Bilimoria, "Women's career development phases: Idealism, endurance, and reinvention," *Career Development International*, vol. 10, no. 3, pp. 168–189, 2005.
33. J. D. Patón-Romero et al., "Gender equality in information technology processes: A systematic mapping study," in *Future of Information and Communication Conference*, Springer, 2023, pp. 310–327.
34. R. Singh et al., "Stemming the tide: Predicting women engineers' intentions to leave," *Journal of Vocational Behavior*, vol. 83, no. 3, pp. 281–294, 2013.
35. U. Soman, "Patriarchy: Theoretical postulates and empirical findings," *Sociological Bulletin*, vol. 58, no. 2, pp. 253–272, 2009.
36. S. K. Whitbourne, *The search for fulfillment: revolutionary new research that reveals the secret to long-term happiness*, Ballantine Books, 2010.
37. V. Jahns, "Information visualization: perception for design by Colin Ware," *ACM SIGSOFT Softw. Eng. Notes*, vol. 39, pp. 43–44, 2014.
38. M. Kitsa, "The Peculiarities of Popular Social Networks: Interface, Functionality, Content," *State and Regions. Series: Social Communications*, no. 3 (51), pp. 73–79, 2022.
39. T. Reeves, "Design research from a technology perspective," in *Educational design research*, Routledge, 2006, pp. 64–78.
40. European Commission, Directorate-General for Research and Innovation, *She figures 2021: gender in research and innovation: statistics and indicators*, Publications Office, 2021. doi: https://doi.org/10.2777/06090.
41. Eurostat, "More men with an ICT education employed than women," Eurostat News, October 11, 2022. [Online]. Available: https://ec.europa.eu/eurostat/web/products-eurostat-news/-/ddm-20221011-1.
42. UNESCO International Institute for Higher Education in Latin America and the Caribbean [IESALC] and Times Higher Education, "Gender Equality: How Global Universities are Performing," 2022. [Online]. Available: https://unesdoc.unesco.org/ark:/48223/pf0000380987.
43. C. Thun, "Excellent and gender equal? Academic motherhood and 'gender blindness' in Norwegian academia," *Gender, Work & Organization*, vol. 27, no. 2, pp. 166–180, 2020.

Open Access This chapter is licensed under the terms of the Creative Commons Attribution 4.0 International License (http://creativecommons.org/licenses/by/4.0/), which permits use, sharing, adaptation, distribution and reproduction in any medium or format, as long as you give appropriate credit to the original author(s) and the source, provide a link to the Creative Commons license and indicate if changes were made.

The images or other third party material in this chapter are included in the chapter's Creative Commons license, unless indicated otherwise in a credit line to the material. If material is not included in the chapter's Creative Commons license and your intended use is not permitted by statutory regulation or exceeds the permitted use, you will need to obtain permission directly from the copyright holder.

Chapter 16
Policy Making as Extension of Disseminating Research Results: Policy Influence Plan Canvas

Birgit Penzenstadler, **Simona Motogna**, **Patricia Lago**, and **Cristy Montes**

16.1 Why Policy Influence Plans Are Needed

Meaningful change based on research results requires effective policy influence that bridges public interest, politics, and professionalism. Already in 1968, Lindblom noted that power in contemporary society is passing from those who hold conventional sources of authority, like arms, public office, or wealth, to those who know [5]. 'Those who know', that is to some extent us researchers, and this chapter offers an easy-to-adapt way to get started with policy influence based on research results.

B. Penzenstadler (✉)
Chalmers University of Technology, Göteborg, Sweden

University of Gothenburg, Göteborg, Sweden

Lappeenranta University of Technology, Lappeenranta, Finland
e-mail: birgitp@chalmers.se

S. Motogna
Babeş Bolyai University, Cluj-Napoca, Romania
e-mail: simona.motogna@ubbcluj.ro

P. Lago
Vrije Universiteit Amsterdam, Amsterdam, The Netherlands
e-mail: p.lago@vu.nl

C. Montes
Chalmers University of Technology, Göteborg, Sweden

University of Gothenburg, Göteborg, Sweden
e-mail: montesc@chalmers.se

© The Author(s) 2025
B. Penzenstadler et al. (eds.), *Actions for Gender Balance in Informatics Across Europe*, https://doi.org/10.1007/978-3-031-78432-3_16

Definition: *Policy influence plans (PIPs)* are essential strategic tools employed by organizations, advocacy groups, and researchers to shape public policies and regulatory frameworks.

These plans aim to guide decision-making processes, ensuring that policies are informed by the best available evidence and align with societal needs and values. The significance of policy influence plans extends across various domains, including public health, environmental protection, social justice, and economic development.

One of the primary reasons for the importance of policy influence plans is their role in promoting evidence-based policymaking. Evidence-based policies are developed through rigorous research and data analysis, which provide a solid foundation for effective and efficient solutions to societal challenges. Policy influence plans facilitate the translation of scientific findings into actionable recommendations, bridging the gap between research and policy implementation. This approach ensures that policies are not only theoretically sound but also practically applicable and beneficial to the target populations.

Policy influence plans are instrumental in enhancing public engagement and trust in the policy-making process. By involving stakeholders, including citizens, experts, and interest groups, in the development and advocacy of policies, these plans foster a participatory approach. This inclusivity helps to democratize the policy process, ensuring that diverse perspectives are considered and that the policies reflect the interests and needs of various communities. Consequently, this leads to greater public trust in governmental and institutional actions, as policies are perceived as more transparent and representative [11].

Modern societal challenges, such as climate change, public health crises, and economic inequality, are complex and interconnected [8]. Policy influence plans are vital to address these multifaceted issues through coordinated and comprehensive strategies. These plans enable the integration of multidisciplinary insights and the alignment of efforts across different sectors and levels of governance. By fostering collaboration among various stakeholders, policy influence plans improve the coherence and effectiveness of responses to global and local challenges.

The long-term sustainability of policies is a critical concern in the dynamic and rapidly changing global landscape. Policy influence plans contribute to sustainability by advocating for policies that are forward-looking and resilient. These plans emphasize the importance of considering long-term impacts and potential unintended consequences, and promoting policies that are adaptable and capable of withstanding future uncertainties. This forward-thinking approach is crucial to addressing current and emerging issues in a way that preserves resources and opportunities for future generations.

In summary, policy influence plans are indispensable for the development of effective, equitable, and sustainable policies. They play a crucial role in promoting evidence-based policy-making, enhancing public engagement and trust, addressing complex challenges, and ensuring long-term sustainability. As societies continue to face pressing global and local issues, the strategic implementation of policy influence plans will be essential in shaping policies that improve public welfare and foster a just and prosperous future.

This introduction outlines the critical and multifaceted importance of policy influence plans, highlighting their role in creating effective, equitable, and sustainable policies, and setting the stage for a deeper exploration of their applications and impacts.

The rest of this chapter is structured as follows. We introduce the most relevant background and related work in Sect. 16.2, the canvas in Sect. 16.3, its instantiation in Sect. 16.4, and its usage in Sect. 16.5. We suggest how you can apply it in Sect. 16.6.

16.2 Background and Related Work

In this section, we provide some foundational background as well as related work.

16.2.1 Background

Policy goals and means exist at different levels of abstraction. Defining and thinking about polices and policy-making in this way is very useful because it highlights how policy design is all about the effort to match goals and instruments both within and across categories. Successful policy design requires that policy aims, objectives, and targets to be coherent; that furthermore implementation, tools and calibrations to be consistent; and finally that policy aims and implementation should also to be congruent and convergent. Howlett [4] provides a contextual model for policy instrument choice.

Craft and Howlett [2] describe policy formulation, governance shifts and policy influence with regards to location and content in policy advisory systems.

Cook [1] contributes a book on lobbying for Higher Education in which she describes how colleges and universities influence federal policy making (in the USA).

Tompkins [9] write about philanthrophic influence in education policy and how foundations work in this context.

Rigby et al. [7] work on understanding how structure and agency influence education policy implementation and organizational change.

Trostle et al. [10] investigated how researchers influence decision-makers in a number of case studies on Mexican policies.

16.2.2 Related Work

There are two other important COST actions that also intend to influence policy making for gender equity in informatics.

The EU COST Action ENHANCE represents a new alliance of research-intensive universities with a focus on science and technology, based on longstanding bilateral or network cooperation among two or more of the member institutions in other configurations. The Alliance can thus draw on the experience, tested models and methods of collaboration at different academic levels in the various predecessor arrangements, scale these up to the level of the new confederation and enhance them by developing new structures and processes to make a quantum leap in cooperation.

VOICES is a COST Action that aims to increase the visibility of inequalities faced by Young Researchers and Innovators (YRIs) from a gender perspective, and to promote a sustainable dialogue between YRIs and stakeholders in the research ecosystem at the systemic level (European and national policy-makers) and at the institutional level (senior researchers, academic managers) by creating a community of gender equality practitioners composed of various stakeholders (YRIs, independent researchers, academic managers, organizations) across Europe. Over the last decades, European higher education and research systems have been characterized by deep changes. Those processes tend to exacerbate and create new forms of gendered inequalities for YRIs, first and foremost women. Those inequalities are also reinforced by disparities within academia linked to other social determinants, such as origin, socioeconomic status, sexuality, or ability.

In contrast, one of the main objectives of EUGAIN was to influence policy makers with the research results we create, hence we developed the deliverables discussed in Chaps. 2–15 of this book and the policy influence plan canvas we present in the following section.

16.3 The Policy Influence Plan Canvas

We created a policy influence plan canvas as we only had limited time, to convey the foundations of policy influence to a large set of prominent European stakeholders.

We developed the Policy Influence Canvas (see Fig. 16.1) to provide an easy and illustrative way to collaborate on a policy influence plan. It is inspired by the Business Model Canvas, a tool designed to sketch out business plans in a visual format [6].

Using our accumulated knowledge of policy influence strategies, we created this canvas to encapsulate the most relevant information succinctly and effectively. In the following, we walk through each quadrant of the canvas, and explain the purpose and content of each field: Partners and Alliances, Activities, Resources and Materials, Timeline for Communication and Actions, Relationships and Windows of

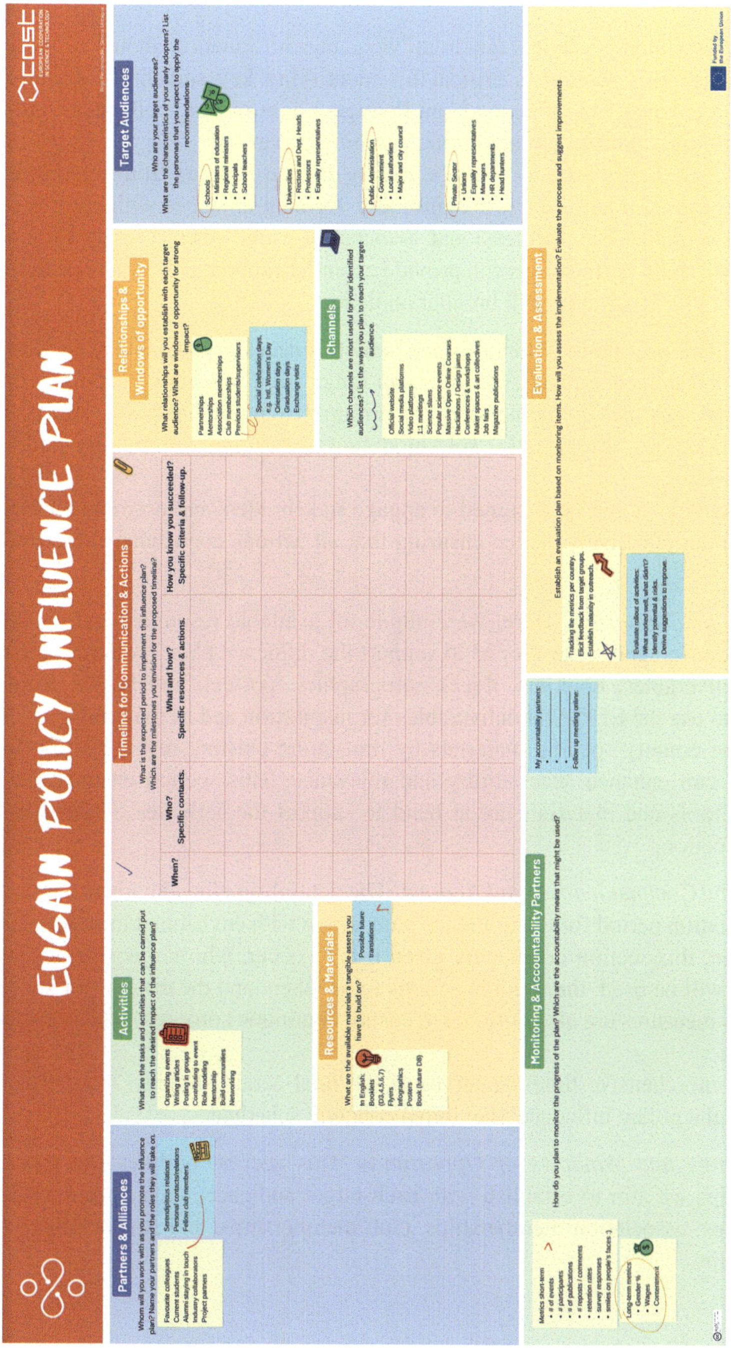

Fig. 16.1 The EUGAIN policy influence plan canvas

Opportunity, Channels, Target Audiences, Monitoring and Accountability Partners, and Evaluation and Assessment.

Partners and Alliances In this quadrant, we gather information about our partners and alliances. This section is critical for identifying key stakeholders who can support and enhance the influence plan. Partners might include colleagues, current students, alumni, industry collaborators, and project partners.

The roles of these partners should be clearly defined, ranging from serendipitous contacts to formal relationships. Additionally, forming alliances with entities such as student organizations, professional associations, and other relevant groups is encouraged. These partnerships can provide essential support and resources, helping to amplify our efforts and reach broader audiences.

Activities This section lists the tasks and activities necessary to achieve the desired impact of the influence plan. Activities can range from organizing events, writing articles, and posting in online network groups to more hands-on efforts like hosting workshops, giving talks, role modeling, mentoring, community building, and networking.

Each activity should be designed to engage stakeholders and promote the policy influence plan effectively, hence ensuring that all actions contribute to the overall goals.

Resources and Materials Here, we compile all available resources and materials that can be leveraged or developed to support the influence plan. Examples include project deliverables, booklets, flyers, infographics, posters, and books. You are welcome to use the EUGAIN deliverables for inspiration and as materials.

Creating country-specific materials by translating existing resources into local languages can enhance accessibility and relevance. This section ensures that all necessary tools and materials are at hand to support the activities outlined in the previous section.

Timeline for Communication and Actions The central timeline details the expected implementation period for the influence plan, along with envisioned milestones. For each action, this section documents when it is to occur, who is responsible, what resources will be used, the specific actions to be taken, and the criteria for success. Follow-up measures are also outlined to ensure continuous progress and adjustment as needed.

This comprehensive timeline serves as the final action strategy, integrating all aspects of the policy influence plan into a coherent schedule.

Relationships and Windows of Opportunity This section outlines the types of relationships we aim to establish with each target audience, such as partnerships, mentorships, association memberships, club memberships, and student/supervisor relationships.

Additionally, it identifies windows of opportunity for making a significant impact, such as International Women's Day, orientation days, graduation days, and exchange visits. By leveraging these opportunities, we can maximize the effectiveness of our influence efforts and engage our audiences at optimal times.

Channels This category encompasses different communication means, with the purpose of finding the most suitable ones regarding the target audience and the message we want to transmit. We grouped traditional communication venues such as conferences, publications, events and 1:1 meetings, but also consider other events that can include diversity and inclusion aspects, such as hackathons, job fairs or science fairs. An important channel that needs to be exploited is represented by the online space, such as websites and social media platforms.

Target Audiences In this quadrant, we define the audiences we aim to reach. This involves identifying early adopters, supporters, advocates, and potential champions. Specific personas are listed to ensure targeted communication and engagement.

For schools, this could include ministers of education, regional ministers, principals, and school teachers. For universities, targets might be rectors, department heads, professors, union representatives, and equality representatives. In public administration, relevant audiences could include government officials, local authorities, and city councils.

The more specific the details, including contact information, the better we can tailor our approach and ensure effective outreach.

Monitoring and Accountability Partners This section describes our plans for monitoring the progress of the influence plan. We outline potential accountability measures and identify metrics to track short- and long-term progress.

Short-term metrics might include the number of events, participants, publications, reposts, comments, retention rates, survey responses, and observable engagement, such as smiles on participants' faces.

Long-term metrics could include percentages of gender representation, wage equity, and overall satisfaction ratings. We also recommend enrolling accountability partners and scheduling follow-up meetings (e.g., monthly, quarterly) to maintain motivation and peer support.

Evaluation and Assessment In the evaluation and assessment section, we establish a comprehensive evaluation plan based on the monitoring metrics. This includes tracking progress across different countries, gathering feedback from target groups, and assessing the maturity of our outreach efforts. We evaluated the implementation of activities to determine what worked well and identify areas for improvement.

After the initial implementation phase, we assess potentials and risks, using these insights to refine and improve future actions. This **continuous feedback loop** ensures that the policy influence plan remains dynamic and effective, adapting to new challenges and opportunities.

In the following section, we provide a couple of examples from instances we developed across EUGAIN.

16.4 Country-Specific Policy Influence Plans (PIPs): Implementation

During the final EUGAIN conference in Lisbon (April 2024), the organizing team decided to facilitate a session dedicated to drawing personalized policy influence plan tailored for each member country. Given the diversity of project members, the particularities of each country, and all the other specifics, the policy influence plan canvas was the template that we designed as we considered that it is capable of accommodating, on one hand, all the principles we wanted to share and follow and, on the other hand, all the specific needs of each country.

The sessions were run as a co-creation collaborative activity, in which members from different countries (grouped by geographic proximity or similar status of gender balance in Informatics) worked together and exchanged ideas to construct their country-specific policy influence strategy. The idea that governed the session was that everyone would go home with a detailed plan that can then be shared, implemented, deployed.

During two sessions, participants debated each component of the Policy Influence Plan Canvas. They were split in:

- **Session 1: What? and Who?** in terms of *Partners, Activities, Resources, Relationships* and *Channels* already established or produced during the 4 years of EUGAIN, and
- **Session 2: How? and When?** which consisted in (1) designing a plan to move to action, and (2) completing the *Timeline for Communication and Action* of the canvas.

In order to envision the potential of the policy influence plan, we present three examples on how participants applied the plan through different actions:

> **Example** Birgit has presented the Deliverable 7 (see https://eugain.eu/results/deliverables/) to the leadership group of her department at Chalmers Technical University, Sweden. She got positive feedback and was requested by a few colleagues to help them with individual follow-up actions.

> **Example** Simona, as member of the Department of Computer Science at Babeş Bolyai University of Cluj-Napoca, Romania has regular annual meetings with teaching staff from highschool at regional level. She presented the booklet *"From School to University"* (Deliverable 4 from https://eugain.eu/results/deliverables/) to Informatics teachers. As some of them were not even aware of some of the issues, they were pleased to have access to resources and had asked Simona for advice in designing future activities for girls in Informatics.

> **Example** Patricia, a full professor in the Netherlands, mentioned open access to the booklet *"From Ph.D. to Professor"* (Deliverable 3 from https://eugain.eu/results/deliverables/) at a weekly meeting of the Software and Sustainability Research Group that she is leading at Vrije Universiteit Amsterdam. Young female researchers felt inspired and encouraged to consider academic career as a future option, and asked Patricia to further discuss the subject.

We aim to provide actionable steps that can be tailored to specific contexts and needs, ensuring a sustainable impact. These recommendations can serve as starting points to raise awareness, implement change, and at the same time promote Informatics as an indispensable science in today's life. Following the principles stated in [3], we outline in the following steps our Policy Influence Plan based on our template:

1. **Collect the available resources, find potential partners and devise the potential activities:** iteratively complete sections *Resources and Materials, Partners and Alliances* and *Activities* to determine all available assets;
2. **Determine connections, establish audience and find ways to reach it:** in successive steps, envision how you want to achieve your goals by filling the quadrants *Relationships and Windows of opportunity, Target Audiences* and *Channels*;
3. **Establish indicators and evaluation procedure:** to track progress and improve the influence plan, complete *Monitoring and Accountability Partners* and *Evaluation and Assessment* sections;
4. **Outline concrete steps:** summarize all available assets and transform them into actionable points with specific details in *Timeline for Communication and Actions*.

The steps are illustrated in Fig. 16.2 and show which elements of the Policy Influence Plan (Fig. 16.1) get affected.

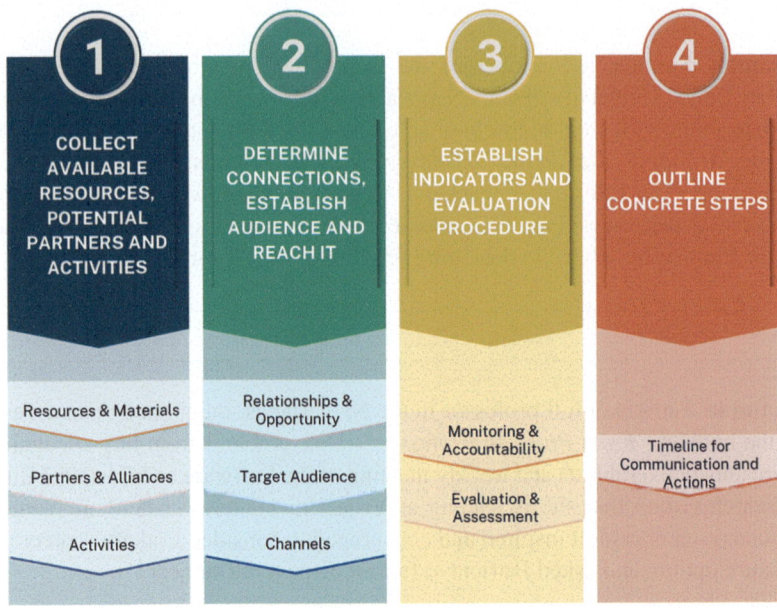

Fig. 16.2 The steps of developing a policy influence plan

16.5 Following Through and Following Up

Following up on the evaluation of policy influence plans involves several key steps to ensure that the desired outcomes are being achieved and to make the necessary adjustments. First, it is crucial to establish a clear monitoring and evaluation framework. This framework should outline specific indicators and metrics that will be used to measure progress and impact. These indicators should align with the goals of the policy influence plan and be both quantitative and qualitative. Regular data collection and analysis are essential to track these indicators over time. This can include surveys, interviews, focus groups, and other methods to gather feedback from stakeholders and target audiences. By systematically monitoring these indicators, organizations can assess whether their strategies are working as intended and identify areas for improvement.

Figure 16.3 shows an example instance after a couple of hours of work at the EUGAIN PIP workshop at the final conference in Lisbon.

16 Policy Influence Plan Canvas

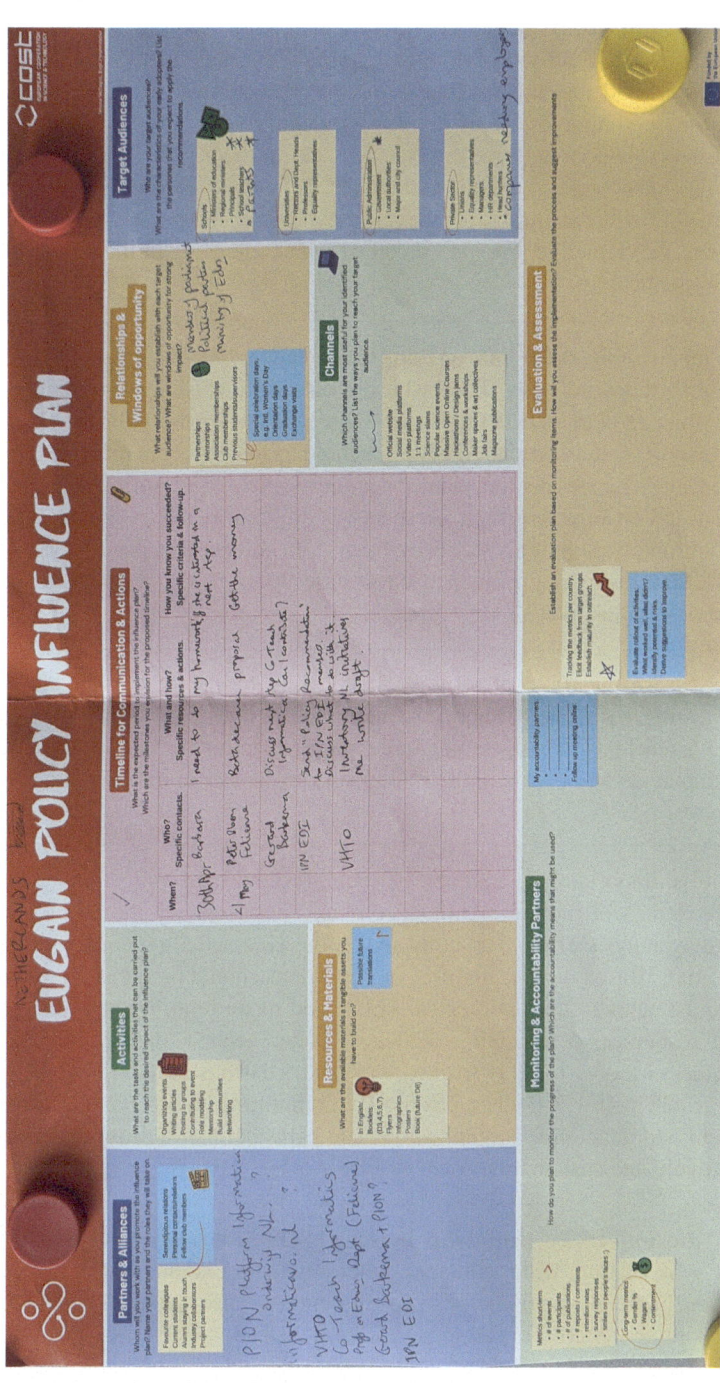

Fig. 16.3 PIP instance for EUGAIN in the Netherlands

> **Patricia, the university professor.** During the brainstorming session, we mainly focused on identifying the most important partners and alliances part of our network and that have influence nation wide. We then discussed the Timeline for Communication and Actions by identifying (1) the key members of the partners to whom we have direct access, (2) what specific actions would resonate the most (e.g., share the policy recommendations, discuss how to implement follow-up actions in the specific context of the partner, etc.), and (3) filled the PIP Timeline. We also sketched which elements in the other PIP fields were applicable.

Second, maintaining open and ongoing communication with all stakeholders is vital. This includes not only those who are directly involved in implementing the policy influence plan but also those who are affected by the policies. Regular updates and reports should be shared with stakeholders to keep them informed about progress and any changes to the plan. Engaging stakeholders in this way helps to build trust and ensures that their perspectives are considered in the evaluation process. Additionally, soliciting feedback from stakeholders can provide valuable insights into how the policy influence efforts are being received and perceived, which can inform adjustments to the strategy.

> **Patricia, the university professor.** We made sure to get on the agenda of regular meeting with our partners, the identified gender balance actions. In addition, we reached out to the target audience organizations in the whole value chain, like parents and pupils in the school system, and IT companies looking for new hires.

Lastly, it is important to conduct periodic reviews and reflections on the overall effectiveness of the policy influence plan. These reviews should involve a comprehensive analysis of the data collected, comparing actual outcomes with the anticipated goals. Based on this analysis, organizations should be prepared to make informed adjustments to their strategies. This could mean refining the messaging, reallocating resources, or changing tactics to better achieve the desired policy changes. Reflecting on what has worked well and what has not can also provide lessons for future policy influence efforts. By committing to an iterative process of assessment and adaptation, organizations can enhance their ability to influence policy effectively and sustainably.

> **Patricia, the university professor.** It is early days, but we have periodic meetings with nation wide alliances where we discuss and evaluate the progress on national target metrics. To this end, we use the metrics of the Women Professors Monitor presented yearly by the Dutch Network of Women Professors (LNVH).

16.6 How You Start Using the Canvas

Here are concrete suggestions for the target audience on what you could do with the policy influence plan and how you can start putting it into practice.

Kim, the university professor. Kim needs to promote females in academic careers in Computer Science and Engineering. They decide, as a department strategy, to promote the department as a safe and pleasant place for women to work. *Actions:* Her assistant will create weekly posts on social media using EUGAIN YouTube shorts and will track numbers of views and likes; the posters from Deliverable 7 will be printed and displayed in the department's hall.

Bazyli, the industry manager. Bazyli needs to address the request of gender equity in the company. They decide, at a board meeting, to run a campaign to attract female students to the domain. *Actions:* Senior women executives are encouraged to dedicate time for the next 12 months to act as mentors for university students, and an assessment report will be produced at the end of the period. EUGAIN Deliverable 8 can be used as a primary resource.

Nicole, the activist. Nicole needs supportive data from research for their campaigns. They decide to make a report on different career stages of educating women in IT. *Actions:* A team of volunteers within the organization will combine the analysis produced in EUGAIN deliverables with the detailed data by Informatics Europe to produce a report on the current situation in the region by the end of the year.

Alex, the school principal. Alex needs to find ways to support their students in succeeding. Alex decides to form a task force of teachers to organize extracurricular STEM activities for the next academic year. *Actions:* He translates the brochure for teachers provided by EUGAIN and discuss Deliverable 4 with the task force. Then establishes a monthly meeting to organize activities

Deniz, student about to graduate. Deniz needs to choose between academia and industry. Denis decides to search for opportunities for an academic career and explores its advantages. *Actions:* She follows the activities of the EUGAIN's Young Researchers and Innovators group and contacts some of the members for advice

> **James, school teacher.** James needs to propose in-class activities to inspire students. James decides to discuss with fellows teaching Informatics in his school. *Actions:* James translates the EUGAIN brochures for schools and during meeting with fellows, they decide to engage parents and older siblings in these activities that will be organized monthly for the whole academic year. Inspired by EUGAIN posters, he also organize a drawing contest for poster with his class.

16.7 Conclusion

In this chapter we introduced the Policy Influence Plan Canvas, a useful tool to get started on policy making, transforming key finding from EUGAIN projects into actionable points that can be implemented by everyone. We also reported from our experiences of using it and make suggestions for how to get started.

We have focused our attention throughout the chapter on the collaborative and iterative nature of the proposed influence plan template. It is our believe and approach that efficient and sustainable change can be achieved only in collaboration with key partners and only by proposing concrete actions that are achievable in a foreseen period of time.

We hope you choose to use it. We encourage stakeholder from education, academics, industry and public administration to adopt and adapt this canvas to their specific needs.

References

1. C. E. Cook. *Lobbying for higher education: How colleges and universities influence federal policy*. Vanderbilt University Press, 1998.
2. J. Craft and M. Howlett. Policy formulation, governance shifts and policy influence: Location and content in policy advisory systems. *Journal of Public Policy*, 32(2):79–98, 2012.
3. Hellen Tilley, Louise Shaxson, John Young, Joanna Rea, and Louise Ball. 10 things to know about how to influence policy with research, Overseas Development Institute. 2017.
4. M. Howlett. Governance modes, policy regimes and operational plans: A multi-level nested model of policy instrument choice and policy design. *Policy Sciences*, 42:73–89, 2009.
5. C. E. Lindblom. *The policy-making*. Citeseer, 1968.
6. A. Osterwalder and Y. Pigneur. *Business model generation: a handbook for visionaries, game changers, and challengers*, volume 1. John Wiley & Sons, 2010.
7. J. G. Rigby, S. L. Woulfin, and V. März. Understanding how structure and agency influence education policy implementation and organizational change. *American Journal of Education*, 122(3):295–302, 2016.

8. D. Stokols. *Social ecology in the digital age: Solving complex problems in a globalized world.* Academic Press, 2018.
9. M. E. Tompkins-Stange. *Policy patrons: Philanthropy, education reform, and the politics of influence.* Harvard Education Press, 2020.
10. J. Trostle, M. Bronfman, and A. Langer. How do researchers influence decision-makers? case studies of mexican policies. *Health policy and planning*, 14(2):103–114, 1999.
11. L. Turnbull and P. Aucoin. *Fostering Canadians' role in public policy: a strategy for institutionalizing public involvement in policy.* Citeseer, 2006.

Open Access This chapter is licensed under the terms of the Creative Commons Attribution 4.0 International License (http://creativecommons.org/licenses/by/4.0/), which permits use, sharing, adaptation, distribution and reproduction in any medium or format, as long as you give appropriate credit to the original author(s) and the source, provide a link to the Creative Commons license and indicate if changes were made.

The images or other third party material in this chapter are included in the chapter's Creative Commons license, unless indicated otherwise in a credit line to the material. If material is not included in the chapter's Creative Commons license and your intended use is not permitted by statutory regulation or exceeds the permitted use, you will need to obtain permission directly from the copyright holder.

The manufacturer's authorised representative in the EU is Springer Nature Customer Service Centre GmbH, Europaplatz 3, 69115 Heidelberg, Germany. If you have any concerns regarding our products, please contact ProductSafety@springernature.com

Printed and bound by CPI Group (UK) Ltd, Croydon, CR0 4YY

26/03/2026

02078979-0003